'This revelatory account of George Mackay Brown's spiritual journey is wonderfully wise and humane, often unsettling, even distressing, but always affirmative. It illuminates the turmoil and yearning within him, and his tortuous relationship with his "ministering angels" and with Orkney. With its rich patterning of extracts from his prose and poetry and from intimate letters, it promises the reader a deeply rewarding experience.'

Stewart Conn, poet, Edinburgh's first Makar

'For those who thought they had the measure of George Mackay Brown, this fascinating and compelling book shows we have not hitherto grasped his full complexity.'

Alec Webster, Professor Emeritus, University of Bristol

'Ron Ferguson has written an extraordinary account of two spiritual journeys, his own and that of the wonderful poet George Mackay Brown, which interweave with the moving pathos of a Beethoven violin sonata, against the haunting background of the magic of Orkney. This is a courageous and honest book which confronts some of the deepest dilemmas of faith and vocation – priestly and poetic. Beautifully written, Ferguson's highly original story reveals the unique impulses of imagination and character that shape an individual's spiritual story. '

John Cornwell, author and commentator

'A brilliant evocation of George Mackay Brown, his spiritual journey, his dark nights of the soul, his art, his relationships. This is a book shot through with remarkable insight, humour and pathos, under-pinned by a deep, life-affirming humanity.'

Alison Miller, novelist and short-story writer

'This is at once a vigorous biography of a great poet and a rich celebration of Orkney life. At its heart is a challenging, gut-gripping account of a controversial religious conversion. It's a sympathetic yet clear-sighted book; Ron Ferguson does not shrink from the occasional need to visit some dark places.'

Dr Harry Reid, author, former Editor of *The Glasgow Herald*

'This is a remarkable, compelling and I think rather profound book, examining George Mackay Brown's life and art through the unifying lens of his spiritual beliefs. This approach makes for a fresh and moving study of a great writer and struggling man. This is as absorbing and inspiring a study of an artist's life and work as I have read. It is for anyone who believes the examined life is worth living.'

Andrew Greig, poet and novelist

'The spiritual journey of any person should be a very intimate account of their journey towards their Maker. I found this book fascinating reading, giving insight into George Mackay Brown's spiritual journey. At times it was as if I was looking into someone else's soul – and making sense of all I have known about them, while not yet fully understanding my own soul! I am sure many will be encouraged to think more about themselves and our present world situation, rather than about George Mackay Brown, after reading this enthralling book.'

Cardinal Keith Patrick O'Brien

'In revealing the inner life of a poet whose work was a form of personal salvation as well as a creative expression of faith, Ron Ferguson has given us a portrait of George Mackay Brown which is not only brave in its candour but profound in its insights.'

Kenneth Roy, Editor, *Scottish Review*

'Here is an enthralling search for the well-springs of George Mackay Brown's genius. Ron Ferguson's enquiries reveal the poet of beauty, pain and loss as unique yet universal. But Ferguson gives us more than simply an insight into a great poet. This book engages profoundly with the place of tradition in contemporary culture, and with the role of religious, and Christian, ceremony in illuminating life's mystery. A book to cherish.'

Very Reverend John Miller

'This is not just a voyage around George Mackay Brown, it is a sincere and honest journey into the inner workings of the writer's heart and mind.'

Kenneth Steven, poet and short story writer

'In this fascinating book Ron Ferguson takes us inside George Mackay Brown's rag and bone shop. Ferguson clearly loves and admires Brown, so there is nothing voyeuristic about his research, no great revelation about a newly discovered weakness. And the known weaknesses are dealt with sympathetically. The alcoholism. The sexual anxiety. The sponging off the goodwill of others. The fussy, puritanical bowdlerising of his own early poetry. The idealisation of the past and hatred of the present. Yet it is from this unpromising material that Brown made his art.'

Richard Holloway, author and broadcaster

'This book is a new Orkney Tapestry. The life and work of GMB are stitched intricately into the islands with deftness and delicacy. It is also crafted with great humility. Despite the personal approach, Ron

Ferguson never gets in the way of the telling but lets the tale and the tellers (especially the main teller) have their say. A line came into my mind, from RLS. "Bright is the ring of words when the right man rings them." I often thought this applied to George more than any other Scottish writer. But it also applies to the author of this revealing and riveting biography. Quite simply, I come out of this book more human than when I went in, more spiritual (dare I say it) and somehow happier!'

Christopher Rush, poet and novelist

George Mackay Brown

George Mackay Brown

The Wound and the Gift

RON FERGUSON

SAINT ANDREW PRESS
Edinburgh

First published in 2011 by
SAINT ANDREW PRESS
121 George Street
Edinburgh EH2 4YN

Hardback edition   ISBN 978 0 7152 0935 6
Paperback edition   ISBN 978 0 7152 0962 2

British Library Cataloguing in Publication Data
A catalogue record for this book is available from the British Library.

It is the publisher's policy to only use papers that are natural and recyclable and that have been manufactured from timber grown in renewable, properly managed forests. All of the manufacturing processes of the papers are expected to conform to the environmental regulations of the country of origin.

Typeset in Palatino by Waverley Typesetters, Warham, Norfolk
Printed and bound in the United Kingdom by MPG Books, Bodmin

IN MEMORIAM
JAMES AND ELIZABETH MAITLAND

Contents

Preface

The poet W. H. Auden hated the idea of anyone writing his biography. He did not relish the idea of people rummaging among the skeletons in his cupboard – but that was not his main objection. Auden made a distinction between artists and their work. He advised us to concentrate on the art and to pay little attention to the life of the one who produced it. He wanted to save us from the danger of losing our appreciation of the art because of our disappointment in the artist. He hinted at this in his great poem on the death of W. B. Yeats, in which he described Yeats as 'silly like us'. And it is to Yeats he goes to justify his warning against making windows into the lives of poets. In one of his late poems, *The Circus Animals' Desertion*, Yeats wrestles with the origins of his own art, thinking his inspiration has deserted him. He had believed it came down a ladder from a celestial domain high above the squalor of his life; but he finally realises that it was from the squalor itself that the poetry emerged. He ends the poem:

> Now that my ladder's gone
> I must lie down where all the ladders start
> In the foul rag and bone shop of the heart.[1]

Unlike Auden, I don't think we should be afraid to enter the maker's heart. When we do so, it will strengthen our wonder at the beauty that is transmuted from the rags and bones of the artist's life.

In this fascinating book, Ron Ferguson takes us inside George Mackay Brown's rag-and-bone shop. Ferguson clearly loves and admires Brown, so there is nothing voyeuristic about his research, no great revelation about a newly discovered weakness. And the known weaknesses are dealt with sympathetically. The alcoholism. The sexual anxiety. The sponging off the goodwill of others. The fussy, puritanical bowdlerising of his own early poetry. The idealisation of the past and hatred of the present. Yet it is from this unpromising material that Brown made his art. Like Larkin, he was a poet who hated the passing of things. Larkin said that the impulse to preserve lies at the bottom of all art; but he was only half right. The impulse to preserve lies at the bottom of *conservative* art, an art that mourns the way time devours everything. I think it was this sorrow at time that lay at the bottom of Brown's conversion to Roman Catholicism, an institution that claims to be not of time but of eternity. It isn't, of course – but, if you can believe it, it will banish a lot of heartache.

Running like a crimson thread through this book is Ron Ferguson's honest bafflement at such certainty and how he can reconcile it with his own more doubting faith. He loves Brown and wants to understand his theology. In the end, however, he realises that it is not Brown's theology that compels him. Like the rest of us, he goes to Brown to feel the ache of loss and to touch the wound of time itself. It is more than enough.

RICHARD HOLLOWAY

Acknowledgements

Where to begin? In so many ways, this book has been a communal effort.

Right at the beginning, I was encouraged by the invitation to give the Maitland Memorial Lecture at Edinburgh University. Since it was Dr James Maitland who introduced me to George Mackay Brown (often referred to as 'GMB'), the subject of GMB's spiritual journey was entirely appropriate. Sadly, Jim Maitland's widow, Elizabeth, died some months before the lecture. They were an inspiring couple, and I am glad to dedicate this book to their memory.

My thanks are due to the Maitland Memorial Lecture trustees, in particular to Mrs Fiona Macintyre (née Maitland). I would also like to thank the Divinity School of Edinburgh University, which hosted the event so generously. Particular thanks are due to Professor David Fergusson, Professor Larry Hurtado, Dr Jolyon Mitchell, Dr Jessie Paterson, Keith Jarrett and Karoline McLean.

My grateful thanks go to Dr Richard Holloway for providing such a fine Preface for the book. In Orkney, my long-standing friends Archie and Elizabeth Bevan have been warmly supportive of this venture. Archie, as GMB's literary executor, kindly gave me permission to quote anything I wanted from George's work. My good friend Brian Murray, joint author, with his daughter Rowena Murray, of *Interrogation of Silence*, an indispensable literary biography of GMB, not only pointed me to a variety of sources but also provided copies of much of the material I sought. As with Archie and Elizabeth Bevan, Brian and Eliza Murray were generous hosts.

I am indebted to the staff of Orkney Library and Archive, particularly Karen Walker, Alison Fraser, Lucy Gibbon and David Mackie. They could not have been more helpful in my researches, as was Frances Sinclair, librarian at Stromness Academy. In Edinburgh, the staffs of the National Library of Scotland and Edinburgh University Library were kindness itself during my study of the GMB–Stella Cartwright letters.

Many people have helped me with the book over the past two-and-a-half years, several giving me hours of their time as I reflected with them at various stages of the project – especially Sandra Leslie, Morag MacInnes, John McGill, Maxwell MacLeod, Alison Miller and Jocelyn Rendall. I was also greatly enriched by extended conversations with other people who knew George or were influenced by him, particularly Dr Timothy Baker, Pamela Beasant, Linden Bicket, Dr John Flett Brown, Joyce Gunn Cairns, Angus Peter Campbell, David Campbell, Christine Clarke, Stewart Conn, Father Jock Dalrymple, Professor Kate Davidson, Sir Peter Maxwell Davies, Professor Tom Devine, Allison and Fraser Dixon, Irene Dunsmuir, Rev. Kathy Galloway, Stanley Roger Green, A. L. Kennedy, Iain Macleod, Michael McGrath, Tam McPhail, Rowena Murray, Surinder Punjya, Joanna Ramsey, George Rosie, Christopher Rush, Dr Donald Smith, Kenneth Steven, William P. L. Thomson and Bunty Wishart.

My panel of manuscript readers included some of the above, but also Tony Fairman and Professor Alec Webster. I also had help and encouragement from May Amar, Graeme and Sibyl Brown, Ron Butlin, David Drever, Yvonne Gray, Jane Harris, Sylvia Hays, Liz Lochhead, Dan Mackay, Caroline Melody, Dr Harry Reid, and Jim and Rosie Wallace. Maggie Fergusson, author of the award-winning biography of George Mackay Brown, was also a great help and support.

ACKNOWLEDGEMENTS

I would like to thank Sandy and William McEwan, who generously gave me the use of Brotchie Cottage on the island of Westray for concentrated spells of writing; they not only encouraged me but also provided their eager spaniel, Charlie, as an enjoyable companion on head-clearing walks at nearby Mae Sands.

Former staff members of the old Saint Andrew Press – Richard Allen, Christine Causer and Jonny Gallant – were very helpful. Ivor Normand was, as ever, a superb copy-editor.

I would like to pay particular tribute to Ann Crawford, publishing manager of Saint Andrew Press. Not only did she commission this book, but she also held her nerve through the turmoil which threatened to end the Press's existence, and she was a source of unfailing encouragement and support. No writer could wish for a finer editor.

My thanks are due to Birlinn Publishers, Edinburgh, for their generous permission to quote several passages from their attractive new editions of GMB short stories and novels; to Continuum International Publishing Group for permission to quote from Sally Magnusson, *Glorious Things: A Treasury of Hymns*; to Random House Group for permission to quote from Edwin Muir's *An Autobiography*, published by Hogarth Press and from Howard Jacobson's novel *Kalooki Nights*; to the Orion Publishing Group, London, for permission to quote from R. S. Thomas, *Collected Poems, 1945–1990*; to SPCK Publishing for permission to quote from Kathy Galloway, *Getting Personal*; to Professor Isobel Murray and Bob Tait for permission to quote from *Scottish Writers Talking 1*; to Yale University Press, New Haven, for permission to quote from Sue Prideaux, *Edvard Munch: Behind the Scream*; to Granta Books for permission to quote from John Gray, *Straw Dogs: Thoughts on Humans and Other Animals*; to Orkney Heritage Society (secretary, Sandy Firth) for permission to quote from Edwin Muir's letters; to Orkney Library and Archive for permission to quote from Ernest Marwick's letters; to Hymns Ancient and Modern for permission to quote from Robert Carroll, *Wolf in the Sheepfold: The Bible as Problematic for Christianity*; to Steve Savage Publishers Ltd for permission to quote GMB's final *Orcadian* column about April; to the *Orkney Herald* for permission to quote excerpts from the newspaper; to the Orkney Media Group for permission to quote material from *The Orcadian*; to Robert Hale Ltd for permission to quote from *As I Remember* (ed. Maurice Lindsay); to Bert Rendall for permission to quote from the poems of Robert Rendall; to the Saltire Society for permission to quote from Stanley Roger Green, *A Clamjamfray of Poets: A Tale of Literary Edinburgh*; to Neil Dickson for permission to quote from *An Island Shore*; to John Murray, Publishers, for permission to quote from *The Collected Poems of George Mackay Brown* (ed. Archie Bevan and Brian Murray); to Faber and Faber Ltd for permission to quote from *Edwin Muir: Collected Poems*, from Karl Miller (ed.), *Memoirs of a Modern Scotland*, from Seamus Heaney, *District and Circle*, and from John McGahern, *Memoir*; to Saint Andrew Press for permission to quote from Harry Reid, *Reformation: The Dangerous Birth of the Modern World*; to Newsquest Ltd for permission to quote from the *Sunday Herald*, 6 September 2009; to Scotsman Publications for permission to quote from the *Scotsman*, 12 October 2010; to Edinburgh University Press (www.euppublishing.com) for permission to quote from Timothy Baker, *George Mackay Brown and the Philosophy of Community*; to Hodder & Stoughton for permission to quote from Humphrey Carpenter, *Robert Runcie*; and to Penguin Ltd for permission to quote from Robert Crawford, *Scotland's Books: The Penguin History of Scottish Literature*. Every effort has been made to clear permissions. If there has been any error or omission, please contact the publisher, who will include a credit in subsequent editions.

On Heidegger matters, I acknowledge my debt to the lucid thinking of Professor James C. Edwards.

Above all, I would like to thank my wife, Cristine, who has lived through several books. She has coped with admirable grace and patience during the researching and writing of this bigger-than-normal book, and has encouraged me right to the last word.

George Mackay Brown: Timeline

1921   17 October: GMB born in Stromness.

1926   Starts at Stromness Academy.

1935   His uncle's body is found in Stromness harbour.

1936   GMB contracts measles.

1937   Stops going to Presbyterian church with family, and goes to local Episcopal church.

1940   His father, John Brown, dies at work.

1941   Call-up medical examination reveals tuberculosis. Sent to Eastbank Sanatorium, Kirkwall.

1944   Francis Scarfe, university lecturer, is billeted with the Brown family.
       GMB is appointed Stromness correspondent for the *Orkney Herald*. Expresses interest in Catholicism.

1946   Visits Rackwick, Hoy, for the first time.

1948   First bar is reopened in Stromness Hotel after 'dry' years. GMB starts drinking. First book, *Let's See the Orkney Islands*, published.

1951   Starts at Newbattle Abbey College, under wardenship of Edwin Muir.

1953   Back in Eastbank Sanatorium. Founding editor of hospital magazine, *Saga*.

1954   *The Storm*, his first poetry collection, published.

1956   Back at Newbattle. Brother Hughie dies, age 43.
        Enrols as student at Edinburgh University. Begins to attend
        Catholic Mass.
1957   Meets Stella Cartwright in Abbotsford Bar, Edinburgh.
1959   New poetry collection, *Loaves and Fishes*, published by Hogarth.
1960   Graduates MA in English language and literature.
        Enrols at teacher-training college. Collapses; sent to Tor-na-Dee
        Sanatorium near Aberdeen.
1961   Gives up teaching. Back to Orkney.
        23 December: received into Roman Catholic Church.
1962   Enrols as postgraduate student at Edinburgh University,
        researching Gerard Manley Hopkins.
1964   Brother Norrie dies, age 45.
1965   New poetry collection, *The Year of the Whale*, published.
        Wins Scottish Arts Council bursary of £750.
1966   *The Five Voyages of Arnor* published.
1967   His first collection of short stories, *A Calendar of Love*, published.
        3 November: his mother dies.
1968   Moves to Mayburn Court, Stromness.
        Twelve Poems published.
1969   *A Time to Keep* and *An Orkney Tapestry* published.
1970   Meets Peter Maxwell Davies on Hoy. Play, *A Spell for Green Corn*,
        published.
1971   *Fishermen with Ploughs, Lifeboat and Other Poems* and *Poems New
        and Selected* published.
1972   First novel, *Greenvoe*, published.
1973   *Magnus* published.
1974   Awarded OBE. Short-story collection, *Hawkfall*, published.
1975   Collection of pieces in *Orcadian* newspaper, *Letters from
        Hamnavoe*, published.
1976   *The Sun's Net* and *Winterfold* published.
1977   Elected fellow of the Royal Society of Literature.
        First St Magnus Festival opens in Kirkwall, Orkney, with *The
        Martyrdom of St Magnus*, words by GMB, music by Peter Maxwell
        Davies.
1979   Another collection of articles, *Under Brinkie's Brae*, published.
1980   *Six Lives of Fankle the Cat* published.

1981   *Portrait of Orkney* published.

1983   *Andrina and Other Stories* and *Voyages* published.

1984   *Time in a Red Coat* published.

1985   *Christmas Stories* and *The Hooded Fisherman* published.
Glasgow University awards GMB an honorary doctorate.
Stella Cartwright dies, aged 48.

1986   *Keepers of the House, Loom of Light* and *The Scottish Bestiary* published.

1987   *Stone, A Celebration for Magnus* and *The Golden Bird* published.

1988   *Songs for St Magnus Day* and *Two Poems for Kenna* published.

1989   Diagnosed with bowel cancer; taken to Foresterhill Hospital, Aberdeen.
The Wreck of the Archangel, The Masked Fisherman and Other Stories and *Tryst on Egilsay* published.

1990   *Letters to Gypsy* published.
3 March: sister Ruby dies.

1991   *The Sea King's Daughter, In the Margins of a Shakespeare* and *Selected Poems 1954–1983* published.

1992   *Rockpools and Daffodils, Brodgar Poems, The Lost Village, Foresterhill* and *Vinland* published. *Vinland* wins Scottish Arts Council prize of £1,000.

1994   *Beside the Ocean of Time* (shortlisted for the Booker Prize; winner of the Scottish Saltire Book of the Year) and *The Sea and the Tower* published.

1996   Dies 13 April in Balfour Hospital, Kirkwall, aged 74. Funeral 16 April (St Magnus' Day).
Books published posthumously include *Following a Lark, Selected Poems 1954–1992, Orkney Pictures and Poems* (text GMB, photographs Gunnie Moberg), *For the Islands I Sing, The Island of the Women and Other Stories, Northern Lights, a Poet's Sources, Travellers, The Son of the Fisherman, The Poor Man in his Castle, Collected Poems, Island Wedding, The First Wash of Spring* and *The Fairground Poet.*

Prologue

It is one of those still, seraphic June evenings that Orkney throws up surprisingly frequently. It has been a benediction of a day. My wife, Cristine, and I have had a meal out here on the decking of our wooden Norwegian house down by the coast. We look out, across a short stretch of water, to the blue hills of Hoy. A few hundred yards farther along the shore stands a ruined manor house, once the home of Orkney's famed Arctic explorer John Rae, creator of a headline-making Victorian scandal.

Orkney is such a beautiful place, especially on calm days like this. It has a different, elemental kind of beauty when the storms rage and the 100-miles-per-hour gales hit full on.

The telephone rings from time to time throughout the evening. We talk on the decking to our three grown-up children, Fiona, Neil and Ally, and to our two little grandchildren, Olly and Dan. They all live in Scotland's central belt.

The cows are lowing in the field next to our house, Bach's Mass in B Minor is on the CD player, and I have in my hand a 12-year-old single malt from Orkney's Highland Park distillery. It is only a couple of days after 21 June, when the sun reaches its northernmost point and we start to head slowly but inexorably towards the long, and sometimes bleak, darkness of a northern winter.

But that's a long way off. Although it is nearly 10pm, and the orange disc of the sun is touching the horizon, the light is still strong enough for me to read, for the third time, an exquisitely written book. *An Orkney Tapestry* first attracted me to these islands nearly a quarter of a century ago. George Mackay Brown's distinctive guide to Orkney is, literally, a fabulous book. It has history, of sorts, but also stories and poems and dramas. The back cover says that the author 'explores the dark mysterious corners, as well as the quiet beautiful fertile places, in his search for the still point of Orkney's history, the true face of the Orkney Fable'. GMB says that, while most writers about Orkney have been practical in their approach, he is doing something different. He writes:

This book takes its stand with the poets. I am interested in the facts only as they tend and gesture, like birds and grass and waves, 'in the gale of life'. I have tried to make a kind of profile of Orkney, which is not a likeness of today only; it has been worked on for many centuries … The facts of our history – what Edwin Muir called The Story – are there to read and study: the Neolithic folk, Picts, Norsemen, Scots, the slow struggle of the people towards independence and prosperity. But it often seems that history is only the forging, out of terrible and kindly fires, of a mask. The mask is undeniably there; it is impressive and reassuring, it flatters us to wear it.

Underneath, the true face dreams on, and The Fable is repeated over and over again.

The true face dreams on: what does he mean by that? What is Orkney's flattering mask all about? What is it that is being covered up?

George Mackay Brown's tale begins with the physical approach to the Orkney Islands from the port of Scrabster on the rugged coast of northern Scotland.

There is the Pentland Firth to cross, first of all. This is looked on as a fearsome experience by some people who are visiting Orkney for the first time. In Scrabster, they sip brandy or swallow anti-seasickness tablets. The crossing can be rough enough – the Atlantic and the North Sea invading each other's domain twice a day, raging back and fore through the narrow channels and sounds, an external wrestle; and the fickle wind can be foe or ally. But as often as not the Firth is calm; the St Ola dips through a gentle swell between Scrabster and Stromness. George Bernard Shaw visited Orkney once in the 1920s. He was impressed by that mighty outpouring of waters. There was power enough in the Pentland Firth, he wrote, to provide all Europe with electrical power. A pair of millstones at the bottom of the Firth grind the salt that makes the sea the way it is; the maelstrom called The Swelkie whirls above the place where the querns forever turn (or so the old people believed).

The cliffs of western Hoy rise up, pillars of flame. This coast has some of the tallest cliff-faces in the world, St John's Head, The Kame, The Berry, Rora Head: magnificent presences. There among them, standing out to sea a little, is the rock-stack called The Old Man of Hoy … An imposing presence; but from some aspects the Old Man looks comical, with his top hat and frock coat, like a Victorian gentleman, the last of the lairds turning his back on Orkney.

I look over to Hoy again. I'd never thought of the familiar Old Man as a Victorian laird. Good writing makes you look at the world differently. Good whisky sometimes does that too. (George Mackay Brown knew all about that.) Another sip.

The author is awed by the sense of history in the islands. The first Orkney peoples, he says, can only be seen darkly, a few figures on a moorland against the sky, between twilight and night. Hardly a thing is known about Orkney's first inhabitants, says GMB, apart from the monuments they left behind them: the huge stones of Maeshowe and Brodgar, and the pastoral village of Skara Brae in the west. These sites are older than the pyramids of Egypt. The Orkney imagination, the writer says, is haunted by time.

History can tell us nothing; not a word or a name comes out of the silence – there are a few ambiguous scratches on a wall at Skara Brae. We wander clueless through immense tracts of time. Imagination stirs about a scattered string of bone beads found in Skara Brae. Did the girl have no time for adornment when a westerly gale choked the doors with sand; or did sea raiders tear them from her neck?

One of George Mackay Brown's great themes – what he sees as the modern worship of progress and technology – soon emerges.

There is a new religion, Progress, in which we all devoutly believe, and it is concerned only with material things in the present and in a vague golden-handed future. It is a rootless utilitarian faith, without beauty or mystery; a kind of blind unquestioning belief that men and their material circumstances will go on improving until some kind of nirvana is reached and everyone will be rich, free, fulfilled, well-informed, masterful. Why should Orcadians not believe in Progress? – everything seems to insist on it. The stone cots of their grandfathers, where men and animals bedded down under the same roof, are strewn all about the parishes and islands, beside the smart modern houses of wood and concrete. The horses are banished, but then tractors and lorries are much less trouble, much more efficient. There is no real poverty any more; tramps and vagrants and tinkers are exiled with the horses. (Only the very backward farmers nowadays don't have a car.) Progress is a goddess who, up to now, has looked after her children well. The sky is scored with television aerials. There is a family-planning centre. There are drifts of books and oil paintings and gramophone records everywhere. And still the shower of good things intensifies.

It is difficult to picture this goddess of plenty other than as some huge computer-figure, that will give our children what they desire easily and endlessly – food, sex, excitement – a synthetic goddess, vast and bland as Buddha, but without love or tenderness or compassion; activated only by a mania to create secondary objects that become increasingly shinier and shoddier and uglier.

I feel that this religion is in great part a delusion, and will peter out in the marsh.

Hmm. I need to think some more about this. Technology has given us this CD player, this music, this whisky and this house, so well insulated against the gales and driving rain. Why is this progress, or even 'Progress', so bad? The lament goes on.

A community like Orkney dare not cut itself off from its roots and sources ... The goddess exacts tribute in subtle ways. For example: there is a kind of shame nowadays in using the old words. And Orkney, only a generation ago, abounded in characters, surrealist folk walked our roads and streets, Dickensian figures with earth and salt in them. Nowadays there is a distinct trimming and levelling-up; a man is ashamed to be different from his neighbour. The old stories have vanished with the horses and the tinkers; instead of the yarn at the pier-head or the pub, you are increasingly troubled with bores who insist on telling you what they think … and you may be sure it isn't their own thought-out opinion at all, but some discussion they have heard on TV the night before, or read in the Daily Express *– and now, having chewed it over, they must regurgitate it for you.*

Word and name are drained of their ancient power. Number, statistic, graph are everything.

We have come a long way in a few years.

Stories and language are this man's passion. His writing is elegant – but is he not mentally and emotionally embedded in a mythical 'golden age'? Or is he a prophet who is naming the losses of a community captivated by the sparkling gew-gaws tumbling from a technological cornucopia?

When he refers to 'a community like Orkney', George Mackay Brown knows what he is talking about. He spent almost all of his life in his native Stromness; he was shaped by Orkney, and was sometimes in conflict with it. Having lived in these islands for two decades, I can testify to the strength of this small community, in which the lines between private and public are blurred. The binoculars that sit on many windowsills are used not only for watching wildlife. In the main, though, they are instruments of curiosity rather than malice. At least, I think so.

Having been brought up in a strong, tight-knit mining community in west Fife, I know from experience that small places can feel claustrophobic; but, when you have children or are more than middle-aged, the strength of townships in which people keep an eye on their neighbours is more reassuring than threatening.

On a recent visit to my home town of Cowdenbeath to watch a football match, I went into a shop to buy some sustenance. The woman behind the counter looked at me, then said quietly: 'You must be a Ferguson'. She studied me further. 'You must be Ronald.' I had not been in that shop for at least three decades. She 'kent my faither' – and I was glad. When I was a teenager, I opted cheerfully for the beckoning anonymity of the big city of Edinburgh; nearly half a century on, I was happy to chat to a knowledgeable and friendly woman about the mine disasters and heroic acts of rescue I had recorded when working as a cub reporter in the town.

Stories passed down the generations constitute the glue that binds communities. GMB is strongly aware of this: *It is a word, blossoming as legend, poem, story, secret, that holds a community together and gives a meaning to its life. If words become functional ciphers merely, as they are in white papers and business letters, they lose their 'ghosts' – the rich aura that has grown about them from the start, and grows infinitesimally richer every time they are spoken. They lose more; they lose their 'kernel', the sheer sensuous relish of utterance. Poetry is a fine interpretation of ghost and kernel. We are in danger of contenting ourselves with husks ... I will attempt to get back to the roots and sources of the community, from which it draws its continuing life, from which it cuts itself off at its peril. With the help of the old stories, the old scrolls, the gathered legends, and the individual earth-rooted imagination, I will try to discover a line or two of the ancient life-giving heraldry.*

George Mackay Brown is an exceptional wordsmith who understands himself as having a spiritual, almost monk-like vocation; but is this type of calling past its philosophically credible sell-by date for people living in the twenty-first century? Is he, as some critics have suggested, a provincial writer with a small-town mentality?

Questions such as these nag at me as I think about this complex, gifted writer who rarely left the archipelago of his birth, yet who has a growing international reputation.

If I want to find answers to at least some of these questions, a disciplined physical and spiritual journey must be undertaken. In order to provide a personal context for this quest – is it a calling, or just the Highland Park speaking? – I must digress in order to talk about a different journey.

It is 9 December 1990. We – my wife, two of our three children, one creaking Labrador, one hamster and I – have left our friends' house in the Scottish Highlands, not much after 6am, in a virtual white-out. Farther up the road, a removal van, packed with our worldly goods from Glasgow, is ploughing through the snows. The drive plays havoc with the nerve-endings – but, after an eternity in a steamed-up Ford Escort, we catch our first sight of the harbour of Scrabster. O blessed Scrabster!

Soon we are crossing the Pentland Firth, notorious for the turbulence of its two colliding tides. Today, though, the sea is calm. About an hour later, we can see the faint outlines of Orkney. When we roll off the ferry at Stromness pier, we are rewarded with a breathtaking sight: the ground is white with sparkling frost, the sky a mixture of blues and pink. In the kitchen of a little house in Stromness, a lantern-jawed man has set aside the lined notebook in which he has been writing neatly with a ballpoint pen.

We turn to the right, towards Orkney's capital, Kirkwall. When we reach the St Magnus Cathedral manse, ready for the unloading of our furniture, a welcoming fire is blazing in the hearth. We are home, even though we have never before lived in Orkney.

At the watchnight service in a packed St Magnus Cathedral, I hardly know anyone. Looking out from the pulpit, I see about a thousand people, many of them standing. Skulls and skeletons along the aisles of the ancient kirk speak of mortality. Having myself survived a serious scare about the state of my lungs, I can do without these spectral whispers.

I welcome people to the cathedral. It seems almost impertinent to do so, because I've only been in Orkney for five minutes, and this is *their* cathedral. The beautiful, yet simple, red-and-yellow sandstone Viking temple belongs not to any one Church but to the people of Orkney. When I think of the long line of bishops and priests and ministers since the cathedral's founding in 1137, I am aware that my time here, however short or long, will be a minuscule part of that historical record.

Believers, semi-detached believers and non-believers have spilled from homes and pubs and parties. Some will have shown up to check out the new St Magnus minister. At least, that's their cover story. Others who hang on to the ledges of faith by their fingernails may be looking for a word of reassurance. There will be those who, under the cover of edgy jocularity, secretly hope that something of the eternal will slip in under their defences. In the safety of the crowd, they will mouth half-remembered Christmas songs. As whisky fumes and yearning fill the air, memories will come flooding back – of more innocent times, of school Nativity plays and carol services, of punches traded with siblings as presents were unwrapped, of family life grievously fractured by divorce or bereavement. Tears will roll down cheeks. At midnight, as the lights of the cathedral are dimmed and the choir sings *Still the Night*, some may unexpectedly experience a striking of the hour of grace, a Word-become-flesh in the mysterious cradle of the heart.

Having been a community minister in the huge Glasgow housing scheme of Easterhouse, and leader of the ecumenical Iona Community, I am nervous about my first attempt at parish ministry. I wonder about the expectations of this big congregation, and whether I will be able to meet them; indeed, whether I should *try* to meet them. Will the hushed congregation want me to believe *for* them? Can I even believe for myself? Probably, yes, with a bit of help from the poets. Maybe even from the bard of Stromness himself. Perhaps with a temporary suspension of doubt, many of us will be captivated this night by the fabulous language of Bethlehem, about a peasant girl, a hidden Madonna, pregnant with hope, in a cattle shed because there is no room at the inn. As the man from Stromness has written in his notebook:

> *From a pub door here and there*
> *A random ribald song*
> *Leaks on the air.*
>
> *The innkeeper over the fire*
> *Counting his haul, hears not*
> *The cry from the byre.*
>
> *But rummaging in the till*
> *Grumbles at the drunken shepherds*
> *Dancing on the hill;*
>
> *And wonders, pale and grudging,*
> *If the strange pair below*
> *Will pay their lodging.*

My first encounter with George Mackay Brown came during a family holiday in Orkney in 1986. A friend of mine, Rev. Dr James Maitland, was in Orkney on holiday with his wife, Elizabeth. When I met them in a street in Stromness, Jim revealed that he was a good friend of the poet, whose work I admired. 'Would you like to meet George?' he asked me. Would I not?

My young family and I spent a pleasant evening with George in his home at Mayburn Court, Stromness. I was surprised to meet a man who was nearly six feet in height. He was thin and angular, with a jutting chin that seemed to have a life of its own. His pale blue eyes and gaunt face gave him a slightly fey look, the more so because his furrowed brow was topped by abundant whitening hair. There was something vaguely troubled about him, though he had a gentle charm. His voice was soft and lilting; I took his accent to be Orcadian, but I was to learn that he sounded exactly like his Sutherland mother, whose first language was Gaelic. I noticed that he said my name a lot, and that he would use my name at the ends of sentences. I hope you've had a nice day, Ron. Have you been in Orkney before, Ron? How do you like Glasgow, Ron?

I tried to engage him in discussion about literature, but what this giant of Scottish letters wanted to talk to me about was football. Oh yes, and also about the island of Iona, where we had lived as a family. He was curious about the history of Columba's isle and the rebuilding of its Benedictine abbey. He signed books for us.

A few weeks later, a letter arrived at our home in Glasgow. The envelope was small, and the script on it was precise. It transpired that Jim Maitland had given GMB a copy of *Grace and Dysentery*, a small book I had written about a visit to India. In his letter, George said some nice things about it. I was impressed – and flattered – that such a highly regarded author had taken the trouble to encourage a rookie writer whom he barely knew. I also noted that he had remembered the unusual, Spanish, spelling of the name of my wife, Cristine. Kindness and attention to detail, I was to learn, were typical of the man. 'I enjoyed our meeting, too, very much,' he wrote, 'and to speak to Cristine and the lovely children. I would love to go to Iona sometime – I feel it's a kind of gap, never having been there. But at a comparatively quiet time, when there aren't too many tourists.' We stayed in touch.

Without those serendipitous meetings with Jim and Elizabeth Maitland and George Mackay Brown, I would not have become minister of St Magnus Cathedral. When the *Orcadian* newspaper announced news of my appointment in November 1990, the first letter I received welcoming me and my family to St Magnus Cathedral and to Orkney was from George Mackay Brown. 'May it be a long and happy ministry for you,' he wrote. 'I'm sure all the family will settle down well in Orkney. It is a good place to live in, weather and all.' And then he added: 'Good for writing too.' From then on, this Roman Catholic writer was a supportive and encouraging friend to this Protestant minister of Kirkwall's cathedral, the prayer-saturated walls of which had resounded down the centuries to the sounds of Norwegian hammers, Catholic chants, Episcopal litanies and Presbyterian sermons.

Over the years, I read more of GMB's work. I went to see him, off and on. When his health worsened, I visited him in the Balfour Hospital in Kirkwall. He came for dinner to the cathedral manse, and spoke calmly to a friend of mine about the prospect of his death.

I wish now that I had asked George more questions about his faith journey. Whether he would have given me any satisfying answers is debatable, though. Even when long-standing friends asked questions which touched on the personal, he employed a repertoire of defences. He would ignore the questions, or lead the discussion in a different direction. More disconcertingly, he would simply start humming as he sat in his rocking chair. Edinburgh's first Makar (poet laureate), Stewart Conn, who produced some of GMB's work for radio, told me: 'Every time I asked him about the meaning of one of his poems, he started either humming the last movement of Beethoven's Ninth, or reciting Hopkins' "Glory be to God for dappled things!" He was incredibly courteous, yet there was this "astronaut in a glass case" – you couldn't get in there! He'd just turn into a statue!'

In his extravagantly outrageous novel, *Kalooki Nights*, Howard Jacobson says of one of his characters, Manny:

He was not a person who responded well to pressure. Demand anything of Manny and he'd hold his breath for half an hour. Try to get his attention and he'd be off down the street, practising his breast-stroke. He knew what he was good at. He understood his own tolerance level. When someone wanted help, he swam away from them.

Substitute 'asked him a personal question' for 'wanted help', and you've got George.

Some of the things I wanted to know are found in four indispensable books – Maggie Fergusson's beautifully understated biography, *George Mackay Brown: The Life*; Rowena Murray and Brian Murray's superb introduction to GMB's work, *Interrogation of Silence*; a collection called *George Mackay Brown: Northern Lights, a poet's sources*, edited by Archie Bevan and Brian Murray; and, of course, GMB's autobiography, *For the Islands I Sing*.

Questions remain. How much of an intellectual struggle did he have to find faith? Did he have times of agnosticism, of dark nights of the soul? Did he observe his religion rigorously at a personal level? Why did he reveal his severe and sometimes suicidal depressions to people who lived far away, yet conceal the depths of his despair from those closest to him in Stromness? Did he, like Orkney, wear a mask?

This book is a personal exploration. Its subject matter is George Mackay Brown's spiritual journey. I am well aware that the concept of 'spirituality' is difficult to pin down. It would be possible – with a great deal of effort – to produce more and more nuanced definitions without ending up much wiser.

Let me offer a rough description that will allow us to get to work. 'Spirituality' encompasses wide-ranging attitudes and practices which focus on the search for meaning in human lives, particularly in terms of relationships, values and the arts. It is concerned with quality of life, especially in areas that have not been closed off by technology and science. Spirituality may, or may not, be open to ideas of transcendence and to the possibility of the divine. 'Religion', on the other hand, is typically associated with the doctrines and practices of institutionalised faith.

I would not go to the stake for this shorthand account; clearly, there is overlap between 'spirituality' and 'religion'. Spirituality may include religion; that is to say, one may express one's spirituality by means of specifically religious commitments and practices. There is a need for a richer, more limpid and more accessible language that will enable humans to talk with greater precision about experiences, feelings and connections which do not fit easily into the categories of scientific discourse or of organised religion.

When I first embarked on this project, my intention was to look mainly at George Mackay Brown's movement from Presbyterianism to Roman Catholicism, and at how he expressed his convictions and feelings in his written work. The original working title was *Transfigured by Ceremony*. However, as the quest developed, I grew to realise more fully the extent of his (sometimes dark) struggles.

When I first got to know George, he struck me as being, for the most part, serene. I was later made aware of the less secure aspects of his faith and life through his own memoir, published after his death, and through Maggie Fergusson's biography. As I looked into existing and new sources and talked to a variety of people, what I was unprepared for was the extent and relentlessness of the inner turmoil despite which – or out of which – his achievements were forged.

The spiritual territory traversed so distinctively by George Mackay Brown is of considerable significance. The examination of a writer's spiritual journey cannot be undertaken by separating the life from the work; therefore, as well as citing some key written passages and letters, I will look at GMB's personal struggles, relationships, change of religious allegiance, sense of vocation and life decisions.

Like many readers, I am curious about the lives of writers whose work I particularly admire; but I am emphatically not arguing that in order to understand a text, one has to know all about the life of the writer. A text is a text is a text. This is not a book of literary criticism – there are others more qualified than I am to undertake such a task – though I will offer personal commentaries on particular pieces of writing.

In this book, attention will be paid to George's relationship with his fiancée, Stella Cartwright, in much more detail than has been possible up until now, incorporating extensive – and so far unpublished – excerpts from their correspondence. This raises troubling questions about intrusion into privacy; I will seek to address these in the book.

The new material includes conversations with an Orcadian woman who shared a flat with Stella Cartwright, and with a Glasgow-based professor who was a self-confessed George Mackay Brown 'groupie' at the age of 17. The latter's area of professional expertise – the relationship between alcohol and depression – makes her contribution all the more significant.

The luminous beauty and craftsmanship of GMB's writing will be set alongside the darker elements of his life; and, in conversations with Scottish writers and artists, the relationship between suffering and creativity will be explored. Hence the title, *George Mackay Brown: The Wound and the Gift.*

This book, then, is part biography, part memoir, part personal quest, part reflection, part conversation. It is about spirituality, institutional religion – particularly Roman Catholicism and Presbyterianism – sex (and no-sex), art, John Knox, poetry, relationships, alcohol, creativity, madness, storytelling and unlived life. It also includes a look at GMB's writing as a spiritual resource for people from different faith traditions and none. I will seek to weave all of the strands together in what is intended as a unique, personal and occasionally idiosyncratic approach to George Mackay Brown's life and work.

The extent of GMB's prolific writings in the fields of journalism, short stories, poetry, drama and novels is so vast that only a small percentage of the total material can be discussed. Since part of my motivation in writing this book is to draw the attention of readers – particularly those who know little of his work – to the quality of GMB's writing, his written material is highlighted on the page by being quoted in italics. Material from interviews and letters appears in quotation marks.

Following on Maggie Fergusson's 2006 biography, new material in the form of letters and other sources is included in this study. I have interviewed a considerable number of people, all of whom have furnished new and sometimes startling insights into the life and work of George Mackay Brown. Almost everybody with whom I spoke said: 'You must talk to so-and-so'. I would have loved to follow their advice in every case. There comes a time, though, when you have to say that enough is enough – even when you know that enough isn't enough – and write the book. I farmed out the developing manuscript to a panel of readers, representing a variety of disciplines and interests; this, in turn, engendered even more dialogues, insights and anecdotes.

I cannot emphasise enough the importance of all these conversations to this project. They have been enlivening, challenging and influential. I regard this book as a form of conversation with GMB and with the reader; like George, I believe that writing is a communal experience. Much of what I have learned from teachers, friends, books, films, radio and television over the years remains embedded in my brain and psyche, long after the names of the contributors have disappeared from the conscious domain. Like all human beings, I am indebted, even though I am not always sure to whom. I am deeply distrustful of all rhetoric by and about 'self-made' people.

While this volume is grounded in detailed research and is intended as a contribution to GMB studies, I want it to have an appeal well beyond the academy. In the interests of accessibility and flow, I have only referenced key written sources; and these references are to be found at the back of the book. The conversations which run through the text are recorded interviews conducted by myself, and are not referenced.

My intention is to do more than lay out descriptive territory. I will raise some existential questions arising out of reflection on the faith, struggles, life and output of this remarkable, complex man.

The fact that the book is intended for a diverse readership, and that it crosses genres, presents particular challenges for the writer. This is highlighted by the question of what to call the subject of the book. If this were simply an academic book, the answer would be straightforward: call him 'Brown'. In several contexts, though, 'Brown' looks cold on the page. The general resolution I have adopted has been to call the subject 'George' in a personal context, and 'GMB' – a commonly used way of referring to George Mackay Brown – when discussing his work as a writer. Despite being a Kierkegaard-loving Protestant with Calvin's pale ghost lurking in my mental attic, I have declined to worry myself sick about consistency of usage.

Because of the personal nature of the exploration, I have used the pronoun 'I' more often than a well-brought-up Presbyterian normally would. The usual convention of saying 'in the view of the author' does not work for a book whose subject is an author.

Before this conversational journey gets under way, I need to disclose two predispositions, so that the reader can deduct points for bias. First, as I have made clear already, I was a friend and admirer of George Mackay Brown, both as an artist and as a person; admiration, though, need not entail the dulling of one's critical faculties. Second, I was reared in the Presbyterian traditions of the Church of Scotland – and, though I am not uncritical of these traditions, my approach to GMB is informed by them, possibly even in ways of which I am not conscious.

The book is in four parts. Part 1, 'The Horizontal Bard', seeks to establish George Mackay Brown in his time and place and to locate the beginnings and early development of his spiritual quest. After that, more attention is paid to issues and themes. Part 2, 'Transfigured by Ceremony', looks at GMB's spirituality largely through his writings. Part 3, 'The Wound and the Gift', turns the spotlight on his personal conflicts and on the relationship between art and suffering. Part 4, 'Finished Fragrance', focuses on George Mackay Brown's ageing, death and remarkable funeral. An outline GMB timeline, to which the reader can refer with ease, is provided.

In his little house in Stromness, like a monk in a cell, George Mackay Brown was refining and refining again words to express the mysteries of life and faith. What drove him as a writer was a mission to purify the sources, to unblock the wells that poison the tribe. He also wanted to demystify the arts, and to repair what he saw as a fatal cleavage between the arts and the trades. *For the past two centuries or so, a kind of snobbery has invested all the arts. The patrons of art and the connoisseurs are more responsible for this unhealthy attitude than the writers and composers and painters themselves ... Why should a painting on the wall be considered superior to the work of joiner or mason? What makes a poem better than a loaf of bread or a jug of ale? Nothing at all.*

The task of the artist, he said, is *to keep in repair the sacred web of creation – that cosmic harmony of God and beast and man and star and planet – in the name of humanity, against those who in the name of humanity are mindlessly and systematically destroying it.* This ambitious vocation, a form of co-creation with God, was exercised by an island writer who described himself as 'a word-voyager who rarely voyages far from his rocking chair'. It is time now to walk around that rocking chair.

On the decking, the June air is still balmy, but it is getting darker now. I must put down my glass and pick up my pen.

PART 1

The
Horizontal Bard

CHAPTER 1

Sweet
Georgie Broon

Wearing pyjamas and dressing gown, Georgie Broon – as he is known in Stromness – lies on top of his bed, looking at the ceiling, wondering what will become of him.

He is a serious man. Before his life changed for the worse, his adolescent self used to mooch around the tombstones of Warbeth cemetery on the edge of Stromness, reading the inscriptions. He wishes he were free to do that now.

Warbeth is one of his favourite haunts. Down near the sea, with its clashing tides and the cliffs of Hoy as dramatic backdrop, it has an elemental feel. He runs yet again in his mind the tape loop of his now-dead father saying to him: 'There are more folk lying dead in this kirkyard than there are living nowadays in the whole of Orkney'.

He pictures his father. He misses him.

In his reverie, the image of one particular tombstone that has held his imagination in thrall since he first stumbled upon it comes again unbidden. It is the memorial of a girl, Ellen Dunne, who died in 1858 at the age of 17. He can see the words, which both draw him and appal him, on the ceiling. He knows them off by heart. He vocalises them silently.

Stop for a moment, youthful passer-by,
On this memento cast a serious eye.
Though now the rose of health may flush your cheek,
And youthful vigour, health and strength bespeak,
Yet think how soon, like me, you may become,
In youth's fair prime, the tenant of the tomb.

At a time when other young men were playing football or seeking to persuade comely Orcadian lassies that they might be more comfortable with their clothes off, George had been worrying about human transience and death. He would write a beautiful poem, 'Kirkyard', on this subject:

A silent conquering army,
The island dead,
Column on column, each with a stone banner
Raised over his head.

A green wave full of fish
Drifted far
In wavering westering ebb-drawn shoals beyond
Sinker or star.

A labyrinth of celled
And waxen pain.
Yet I come to the honeycomb often, to sip the finished
Fragrance of men.

Now he is in a sanatorium in Kirkwall, for the second time, suffering from tuberculosis. His exquisitely painful reverie is interrupted by a familiar, irritating sound: the other patient in this small ward has switched on his radio. George can hardly bear it. He sighs. He wants silence.

He also wants to hit this man. Why can people not tolerate quietness? Why do they have to fill up every bloody minute with loud noise? He must speak to the superintendent to complain.

Some of the patients get on his nerves. Not long ago, a young man had put snow down his back. George had punched him with a ferocity that surprised both the other man and himself.

4

His violent thoughts trouble him. They seem to come out of nowhere.

He picks up a book, and tries to read, but he cannot concentrate. Mercifully, his room-mate switches the radio off and goes out for a walk. He is hardly out of the door when George rolls off his bed, lifts the offending radio and beats it violently against the wall.

Tuberculosis had first been diagnosed in 1941, when George Brown presented himself at Kirkwall's hospital for a medical examination after receiving his call-up papers for military service. The army doctor sent him straight to Eastbank Sanatorium.

There had been hints and shadows. As well as being uncomfortably close to the lit-up sights and sounds of random death – flying shrapnel at a hamlet near Stromness had caused the first civilian death of the Second World War – George had also inhabited a personal war zone. In the aftermath of a debilitating bout of measles, his battle was fought in chest and heart and mind. The weakness in his lungs had been compounded by his cigarette-smoking. He often found himself gasping for breath.

Now, lying on his bed, George had time to reflect on his life so far.

The youngest of five surviving children, he was born on 17 October 1921 in Stromness, with the sea lapping against a pier outside the door of the family house. The town, with its twisting, narrow main street and its tiered closes – made even more romantic by names like Khyber Pass and Franklin Place – grew up, as the writer known as George Mackay Brown was to say, 'like a salt-sea ballad in stone'.

Stromness's prosperity had grown during the expansion of trade in the eighteenth century. The town's rise to prominence as the principal recruiting ground for the Hudson's Bay Company in Canada in the nineteenth century increased its importance. The residents of Stromness had become used to the sight of visiting mariners and – during the First World War – soldiers in uniform making their noisy and unsteady way through the town. By the 1920s, however, Stromness was less prosperous and certainly less boisterous, especially after all

5

its thirty-eight taverns were closed by a public vote. Describing the Stromness of his birth as 'old and gray and full of sleep', George would later observe: 'It was a very depressed local community that I was born into'.

Young Georgie grew up in a world of stories. He heard tales about the notorious Stromness-born pirate John Gow, and about the doings of Orcadian midshipman George Stewart, who sailed on the *Bounty* and joined the mutineers. He also learned about the adventures of John Rae, who was blacklisted by the London naval establishment when he came back from Canada with strange stories about the fate of the expedition to find the Northwest Passage, led by Sir John Franklin. Well-founded reports by the highly regarded Orcadian explorer, suggesting that the starving Franklin crew had engaged in cannibalism, caused outrage in London. Lady Franklin and novelist Charles Dickens made sure that Rae would receive none of the awards that his pioneering work merited.

Tales about press-gangs, shipwreck and smuggling were part of a communal folklore which was a wonderful resource for a would-be poet and novelist.

As a boy, Georgie had what he remembered as a secure childhood in Stromness. As a child between the ages of five and eight, he would say, Stromness seemed to be like Bethlehem, where a child might not be surprised to meet angels, shepherds or kings on a winter night. He would later mythologise Stromness, using its Norse name of Hamnavoe – 'haven inside the bay' – to situate it as a fabulous place in a fabled time.

Contemporaries said that he had inherited the sweetness of his naturally cheerful Gaelic-speaking mother, Mhairi Sheena Mackay. Brought up in the strict Calvinist ethos of the Free Presbyterian Church, Mary Jane – as she was known in Stromness – had moved to Orkney from Strathy in Sutherland at the age of 16 to take up work in the Stromness Hotel.

George was a confident and aggressive footballer; but there were shadows over his childhood. At the age of four or five, he woke up one night and discovered that his mother wasn't there. He later described his fear: *Probably she was out visiting a neighbour, or at a concert or kirk soiree. I was overwhelmed by a feeling of desolation and bereavement: she was gone, she would never never come back again ... I made the night hideous with my keening.* On another occasion, he was sitting on the doorstep at home when a tinker woman came to the door selling pens and haberdashery. He fainted. For years thereafter, he had nightmares about being abducted by tinkers.

Another vivid memory was of the crew of an Aberdeen trawler staggering drunk in the street. The image of those out-of-control strangers on a quiet street filled young George with dread. One New Year's Day, he saw two local fishermen making their way unsteadily and rowdily along the street. He knew them both as peaceable men, and the sight of them behaving in this troubling way sent him hurrying home, white in the face.

When he was 14 years old, he was more seriously destabilised. His depressive uncle, Jimmy Brown, who believed there were fairies in his garden and who often reported seeing apparitions of ships' masts leaving Stromness, went missing; a few days later, his body was fished out of Stromness harbour.

George's imagination was haunted by Jimmy Brown. While there was a sweetness and shy charm about the boy, it was accompanied by fearfulness and by a taste of grey depression in the mouth.

School was not a happy place for him. He described Stromness Academy as an immense, forbidding building, more like a prison. There was no room, he said, for delight or wonderment – even in the teaching of English. The boy who would become one of the finest poets and prose stylists of his generation hated the instruction in grammar. Even late in life, he maintained that he could not parse a sentence.

He remembered writing his first poem, at the age of about 10, on a scrap of paper. It was in praise of Stromness; his parents were very pleased. Sombre and morbid poems came in a spate during an adolescence which, he said, was full of shame and fears and miseries. *One symptom was that whenever my mother left the house to go shopping, I was convinced every time that she would never come home again. I would shadow her along the street, and dodged into doorways if she chanced to look back. I can't remember how long this state of affairs went on, but it's certain that a part of my mind was unhinged.*

His anxieties were not helped by the bout with measles, which affected both hearing and sight, at the age of 15.

To learn more, I drove out to Quoyloo in rural Orkney to talk to Morag MacInnes, Orcadian poet and writer of short stories, whose father was George's best friend at school. Ian MacInnes, who would grow up to be a gifted artist – and a passionate atheist and socialist – would play a continuously significant part in George Mackay Brown's journey.

'When George got ill, it happened fairly quickly that he couldn't kick a ball any more,' Morag told me. 'When he discovered that he did like literature, gates and doors opened for him, but it was a very solitary pursuit. My dad didn't discover literature, and George wasn't particularly close to anybody else in the class. There wasn't anybody else who was finding the beauty of Keats and Shelley and Wordsworth the way George was. Increasingly, as he got depressed, he had that whole adolescent thing where he had a terrible distaste for physical contact, and he was ashamed of his sexuality – whereas by that stage my dad was having innocent tumbles in the heather, and the other boys were too. From about the age of 15, George was really untouchable and untouched.'

George's fragile state worsened on the morning of 11 July 1940, when he was awakened by a sound he had never heard before. His brother, Hughie, was weeping downstairs. The police had called on Hughie at his place of work and told him that his father had died suddenly of a heart attack earlier that morning.

John Brown, who was 64 years old, had retired from his job as a postman in 1936, crippled with arthritis. He had managed to find work as a 'hut-tender' on the island of Hoy. His cheerful demeanour masked a depressive tendency. Young George had been much troubled by hearing his father pace backwards and forwards in his room – 'the man inside was a stranger to me' – speaking to himself about his troubles. After his retirement as a postman, when he had no pension and felt himself to be a burden on his family, he had largely lost his desire to live. 'My next suit will be a wooden one,' he had said when he bought a new outfit. Now he lay in his coffin in the little bedroom downstairs, 'more remote than a star'. George Mackay Brown would later write: *'Touch the forehead,' said someone. There was a belief that you must touch a dead brow, otherwise pictures of the person would linger and disturb you in some way or other. I have never felt a coldness so intense as that touch. He had travelled such a far way from the wells and fires of the blood.*

His father's sympathy for people on the fringes of society – tinkers, tramps, fairground people, eccentrics – made a big impression on George, who would write: *A quintessence of dust, he lies in a field above Hoy Sound among all the rich storied dust of Stromness. The postman had left the last door, he had quenched the flame in his lantern. The tailor had folded the finished coat and laid it aside. He was at rest with fishermen, farmers, merchants, sailors and their women-folk – many generations. I wish there was a Thomas Hardy in Orkney to report the conversations of those salt and loam tongues in the kirkyard, immortally.*

Orkney's own Thomas Hardy felt that his father had never been given his due. George would put that right in 1959 with the publication of his elegaic tribute to John Brown in his collection of poems, *Loaves and Fishes*. The poem, 'Hamnavoe', which George had started writing in 1947, celebrates not just his father but also the town in which he was known to everybody as a cheerful and conscientious postie.

> *My father passed with his penny letters*
> *Through closes opening and shutting like legends*
>   *When barbarous with gulls*
>   *Hamnavoe's morning broke*
>
> *On the salt and tar steps. Herring boats,*
> *Puffing red sails, the tillers*
>   *Of cold horizons, leaned*
>   *Down the gull-gaunt tide*

And threw dark nets on sudden silver harvest.
A stallion at the sweet fountain
      Dredged water, and touched
      Fire from steel-kissed cobbles.

Hard on noon four bearded merchants
Past the pipe-spitting pier-head strolled,
      Holy with greed, chanting
      Their slow grave jargon.

A tinker keened like a tartan gull
At cuithe-hung doors. A crofter lass
      Trudged through the lavish dung
      In a dream of corn-stalks and milk.

Blessings and soup plates circled. Euclidian light
Ruled the town in segments blue and gray.
      The school bell yawned and lisped
      Down ignorant closes.

In the Arctic Whaler three blue elbows fell,
Regular as waves, from beards spumy with porter,
      Till the amber day ebbed out
      To its black dregs.

The boats drove furrows homeward, like ploughmen
In blizzards of gulls. Gaelic fisher-girls
      Flashed knife and dirge
      Over drifts of herring.

And boys with penny wands lured gleams
From tangled veins of the flood. Houses went blind
      Up one steep close, for a
      Grief by the shrouded nets.

The kirk, in a gale of psalms, went heaving through
A tumult of roofs, freighted for heaven. And lovers
      Unblessed by steeples, lay under
      The buttered bannock of the moon.

He quenched his lantern, leaving the last door.
Because of his gay poverty that kept

My seapink innocence
From the worm and black wind;

And because, under equality's sun,
All things wear now to a common soiling,
   In the fire of images
   Gladly I put my hand
   To save that day for him.

John Brown often worried about how his unrobust youngest son would make his way in the world. He would surely have been proud of the skill with which George evoked Stromness, and would have been touched by his boy's devotion – *In the fire of images / Gladly I put my hand / To save that day for him.* Beautifully memorialised in GMB's most-anthologised poem, the postman of Stromness has passed into legend in a fabulously constructed Hamnavoe.

To 18-year-old George Brown, struggling with physical weakness and feelings of anxiety – in a blacked-out Stromness, its cold northern seas filled with the ghosts of young drowning servicemen – life felt like a precarious experiment in which random catastrophe was never far from the surface. The consultant's verdict on the state of his health, eight months after his father's death, was both frightening and strangely comforting.

The records reveal that between 1927 and 1936, tuberculosis was the given cause of death for 41,705 people in Scotland. The most common cause of death in young Scots, TB was something people spoke about in whispers. When he was given the diagnosis, George recognised that the tubercle bacillus must have been burning with a slow smoulder for some time. Going up the steep brae to school, he often had to stop to get his breath, and he would cough up thick phlegm. *When the medical officer confirmed that I had pulmonary tuberculosis, 'an open lesion at the apex of the left lung', I was horrified. In 1941 there was no cure. One simply lay in a sanatorium bed and hoped for the best, with the help of fresh air and wholesome food.*

A poor soul worthy of pity? Yes, but the situation was more complex than that. As much as the prognosis horrified him, George Brown was also grateful for the illness. *It saved me from the world of 'getting and spending' that I had dreaded so much. If there was to be much of a future at all, it would be passed in a kind of limbo where little or nothing was expected of me.*

That first spell in Eastbank Sanatorium reinforced George's turn inward and helped him to develop resources of mind and spirit that would shape the direction of his life.

The illness gave him lots of time for reading. The wound which was sapping his strength – he convinced himself, not without reason, that he would not survive beyond the age of 23 – also gave him opportunities to develop the gift that would eventually transform him from a private nobody in a small island town into a writer with a substantial public reputation. In a telling aside, he wrote: *In some strange way I even exulted that I had been branded with the same illness as Keats, Stevenson, Emily Brontë, Francis Thompson, D. H. Lawrence.*

George had already written a few not very good poems. Now, with a severely shortened life expectancy, he turned to the Romantic poets. He might, like some of them, die young; might he also, like them, produce a few great poems? The heady mixture of morbidity, reading, introspection and dreaming within the walls of a sanatorium provided the psychological and spiritual matrix out of which a vocation as a poet would grow.

After six months in Eastbank, George was told he could go home, even though he was far from being cured. *I knew that the slow smouldering was going on and on in my lungs. The danger was that the smouldering might break into a flame, in which case there was little hope; it would be 'early dark'. I think, at the time, I had little fear of death; I may even have been half in love with it, like Keats.*

Half in love with easeful death? He was the very image of the tubercular poet – pale, coughing, melancholic, and approaching an early grave with more than a hint of a death wish.

Back home, he was looked after by his solicitous mother. Despite her strict upbringing in the Free Presbyterian Church, Mary Jane Mackay did not appear to think, speak or make judgements in recognisably Calvinist ways. She gained a good reputation for reading tea-leaves, something which was not a normal part of the Calvinist curriculum.

George Mackay Brown's writings in *Northern Lights: a poet's sources* are generally freer than his more formal reminiscences in his autobiography, perhaps because they were not initially intended for publication. He talks, for instance, of tensions in the Brown household, particularly over money. *There were never any 'scenes', or rows, that I ever witnessed. Still, a child is very sensitive to the tensions in the cloistered atmosphere of a small house. There were turnings-away, seethings, stony silences. I was all the more frightened because the tuneless song in my mother's mouth withered, maybe for a whole morning. The crisis never lasted. By the afternoon she was back among the flowers again … Brightness flowed through the house! (But I was always aware that sooner or later the shadow and chill would fall again.)*

He had dreams that disgusted him and nightmares that made him cry out with fear.

'There was anger in him,' said Morag MacInnes. 'In that very physical community, everybody who was fit and able was involved in the war effort. There were no Orcadians from his schooldays around; the girls were having a great time with the influx of "talent", which might also have been a problem for George. He was out of things. He wasn't interested in the politics of the war, so he withdrew, and his mother looked after him.

'The whole dynamic between mother and son is interesting, because it was a real love/hate thing. She would allow him to stay in bed, and she would bring him up his egg every day. Sometimes he would chuck it back at her. The treatment for TB and the illness itself gave him highs and lows. Inside him, there was a great burning anger about the injustice of it all and the feeling that nobody understood. There was a terrible lethargy about him that flipped into anger.'

George might as well have carried a bell around with him, like a leper. People avoided TB-sufferers for fear of ending up with the same condition. What added to the pain was the fact that some people – including doctors – believed that TB was caused by moral or spiritual weakness.

Retired headmaster and kirk elder, Iain Macleod, who was brought up next door to the Brown family, told me that George was regarded in those years as a waster. Iain speculated on what might have happened to George had he not been laid low by illness. 'He had lots of time, when he was ill, to be introspective, thinking about things in a way that he would probably never have done if his life hadn't taken that particular turn. If he had been fit and called up into the forces, it would have been very different. If he had gone into the army, would he ever have been a poet? If he had been yanked out of his own life, posted somewhere quite different, it could have changed his life entirely.'

Another person who grew up near the Brown household, and who became close to George in later years, was Irene Dunsmuir.

'When George had the TB diagnosis,' she told me, 'it must have been a very frightening time for him. People would whisper the word "tuberculosis", because it was like a death sentence. People feared it. It affected lots of families at that time. George must have wondered whether he would survive or not. He must also have wondered what would happen if he did survive. How would he earn a living? When he came out of hospital, he got some welfare benefit, some poor relief. The welfare officer gave out money grudgingly.'

George Brown was a frustrated man, and his mother sometimes bore the brunt of his rage. Morag MacInnes told me: 'My mum says George's mother had this beautiful laugh, and she sang wherever she went. In fact, it drove George nuts a lot of the time because he found it so intrusive when he was angry and upset. My mum used to go every Sunday for afternoon tea with Mrs Brown. According to mum, it was always beautifully laid out, with home-bakes and everything. "Nothing's too good for my Georgie" was what she used to say. Mum says that George was spoiled rotten, his mother did everything for him. But he was the youngest, the delicate one, and he stuck around, so she had to. I think there was a sense that – it wasn't competition exactly – all the boys had to do well. It's a very Scottish thing. You had to better yourself – and there was poor Georgie not doing that. She did shout at him a lot, but she also did the opposite thing. She said: "Right, I've got him here, and obviously he's special, so I'll just look after him". It wasn't easy. He was just like an adolescent, according to my mum – temper tantrums and all kinds of things.'

When not throwing strops, and eggs, George Brown was dreaming of becoming John Keats. All he had to do to live up to the image was to produce great poetry.

Living on public subsistence, George started to write poems seriously. Just when he needed a guide, an angel turned up on his doorstep, in the shape of a captain in the Education Corps and a published poet. A lecturer at Glasgow University, Francis Scarfe was billeted with the Brown household. In the evenings, Scarfe, who was in his thirties, and George would sit solemnly at the table writing poetry, and they would comment on each other's work. Scarfe's enthusiasm for T. S. Eliot, D. H. Lawrence and Dylan Thomas fired his eager pupil. Scarfe also introduced George to classical music. He brought from the army base on Hoy a small wind-up gramophone and album containing records of music by Mendelssohn, Mozart, Schubert and Beethoven. George was thrilled. He exulted in Beethoven's Ninth Symphony. *The great outpouring of joy in the choral movement bewildered and excited me – such an affirmation, it may be, strengthened my spirit to opt for life, at a time when 'easeful death' seemed the more likely way.*

I must say I like this Mr Scarfe. What a wonderful thing to do: not only to encourage a shy, rather vulnerable young man to develop his talent, but also to nudge him into opting for life itself. I was touched when I learned that the two men corresponded every Christmas for forty years until Francis Scarfe's death in 1988. I am pleased for Scarfe that he lived to see his protégé develop into a writer of national significance.

The presence of the gramophone, combined with George's liking for T. S. Eliot – whose experimental poetry and strange, dazzling language intrigued and excited George – had one amusing side-effect. Having managed to buy a record of T. S. Eliot reading some of his own work, George regularly played it at full volume. His sister Ruby had returned home after the death at El Alamein of her husband, Ted Ogilvie; and, when she and her mother did the housework, they heard *The Waste Land* so often that they would chant the words along with Eliot. (I have Eliot reciting his lines through the speakers in my study as I write this. There is something quite touching about Mary Jane and Ruby chanting about April being the cruellest month, and getting their tongues around words like 'Starnbergersee' and 'echt deutsch'.)

Irene Dunsmuir told me that, at one stage, George got work as a roadman on the island of Rousay. 'He had to take the work,' she told me, 'or his benefit would have been stopped. He told me how he enjoyed the view, looking over to Eynhallow.'

I love it! I treasure the image of the frail but thrawn poet, dressed in workman's gear, leaning on his shovel and looking wistfully out to the holy island of Eynhallow, the place of the monks. George Brown's career as a labourer was a short one.

In 1944, George got a break that changed his life. Short of staff, James Twatt, owner of the *Orkney Herald*, asked him to be the paper's Stromness correspondent. His ostensible task was to gather bits and pieces of information about events in Stromness, but before long he was also writing essays, columns, short stories and leader comment, all under different pen names. His news articles often contained more opinions than facts. He later reflected: *There may have been less accurate correspondents in the history of journalism, but there can't be many. To tell the truth, I cared for the 'flavour' of a bit of news more than for the stark facts, and so I frequently got into trouble. When writing a man's obituary, for example, I liked to evoke the faint aroma of his personality, and this often led to a neglect of vital facts of his life and career ... I exulted in this novel kind of reporting, which flatly contradicted the full commandments of the god-like Scott of the Manchester Guardian: 'Facts are sacred, comment is free.' With me, as one Stromnessian said, it was just the other way round. As I say, I often got into trouble. But, on the other hand, I walked through frequent showers of roses too. Some people liked to have their shady, or, more often, unimportant deeds justified in fluent and fulsome prose. I got occasional presents of cigars and books.*

The low-paid part-time job gave him a reason to get up in the morning. More than that, the freedom granted to him by the hard-pressed *Orkney Herald* editor allowed him to let his imagination run free in print. As he developed his own writer's voice, he enraged some of his readership, but no-one liked to miss his entertaining and provocative words.

The job also provided him with an outlet for his anger. The received notion that George Mackay Brown was always in love with Orkney is false. He railed against the tendency of parents to give their children fashionable, rather than Orcadian, names. He complained about 'the ridiculous pampering of women' and the tendency of Orkney girls to plaster their faces with cosmetics. In personal life he was shy and retiring; in print he felt freer to be combative and rude. *I have a peculiar and diverse gift of being able to sneer at people in print: a gift which I am quite innocent of in normal conversation.* Well, not totally innocent. His gift of mimicry was sometimes employed to cruel intent. He was someone to be wary of.

The Stromness hack was becoming a writer. In addition to his embellished news articles and provocative opinion pieces, he gained confidence through his short fictions, book reviews, leader articles, diaries and reflections on history. Rowena Murray and Brian Murray reckon that his journalistic output is the equivalent of several novels. GMB saw his journalism primarily as a way of earning a living, allowing him to write poetry; there is no doubt, though, that journalism also allowed him to work at his craft. And, in his spare time, he was writing poetry, as well as plays for the local drama group.

The burst of creativity had been sparked by the discovery of Orcadian writers, such as Eric Linklater and Edwin Muir. Muir's autobiography, *The Story and the Fable,* made a deep impression on George. Most influential of all was a book he borrowed from the Stromness library. Called *The Orkneyinga Saga,* it presented a series of Icelandic tales about the Viking earls of Orkney from the ninth to the twelfth centuries.

George was impressed by the simple, direct and dramatic style of the Sagas. He loved the rollicking stories about the characters in the book. Earl Thorfinn, first Viking ruler of all Orkney, did not get his nickname, 'Thorfinn the Skullsplitter', because he was a gentle and retiring soul. Another man worth avoiding was 'Eirik Blood-axe'. Eirik's daughter, Ragnhild, was no better. She married Earl Thorfinn's son. Yes, a Blood-axe married a Skullsplitter. It was not a pacifist dynasty. Ragnhild murdered three husbands before they realised that something untoward was going on. Frakokk, wife of Ljot the Renegade, made a poisoned shirt with which to kill her sister Helga's son, as part of another game of happy royal families. Unfortunately, another man put it on by mistake and went straight to the happy hunting ground.

As well as enjoying the Viking soap opera, George was inspired by the examples of heroism, courage and honour he found in the book he described as a 'realm of gold'. The *Orkneyinga Saga* was also a spiritual resource for him, in its pagan, moral and Christian aspects. *The desert was actually becoming interesting: the oases lay thicker around than I had imagined, and nearer home. If, in my late teens, I had had a death wish – and so intensely that it destroyed a part of my lungs, I think – now life might be worth living after all. The smoulder inside me was almost quenched.*

Above all, he was captivated by the story of Saint Magnus, who was, he wrote, 'at once a solid, convincing, flesh-and-blood man, from whom pure spirit flashed from time to time'. Magnus Erlendson, joint earl of Orkney with his cousin Hakon Paulson, was executed by Hakon after a power struggle in the islands. The *Orkneyinga Saga* models the death of Magnus on the death of Christ. The story of the saint's life and death was a theme to which George Mackay Brown would return repeatedly.

In his commentary on an old book of essays called *The Orkney Book*, which was first published in 1909, George was savage. He criticised what he saw as the complacency of one of the authors in a chapter dealing with the history of Orkney in the eighteenth and nineteenth centuries. He went on: *True, he knows and deplores the fact of Orcadian degeneracy which has been rotting our native vitality ever since the death of Rognvald, but he speaks smugly about the mechanical, agricultural and transport improvements which had come to our islands in the last two centuries, as if the full development of these facilities would restore the ancient power we have lost. But this complacency was typical of the half dozen generations which preceded the First World War. We who exist today have had most of the self-satisfaction knocked out of us. We say it without pride. The high summer of Orcadian culture was a thousand years ago, and we are the poor remnants of a once mighty race. It is as well to recognise this unpleasant fact, of which most of us, to tell the truth, seem to be unaware.*

Note the tone and the assumptions. Orkney has been in spiritual/ moral decline since the death of St Rognvald, who founded St Magnus Cathedral in 1137; technological advances in farming and transport have been a mixed blessing; Orcadian culture was at its highest 1,000 years ago; and not many people recognise these facts. George Brown is setting out a particular stall, one which will become very familiar.

He continues aggressively: *Now there are one or two selections by eminent writers which I am going to have the audacity to attack. Hugh Miller was a geologist, and as a man of science he has attained a well-deserved fame. J. Storer Clouston was, I think, primarily a historian – I am prepared to bet that his* History of Orkney *will long survive the mass of his romances. They were both then, men of 'facts' rather than men of fancies. Yet we find Miller's two sketches on the Dwarfie Stone and the Standing Stones tainted with what I will call a false 'poeticism', and Storer Clouston's account of the Cathedral of St Magnus riddled through and through with it. If ever this book is reprinted, certainly the last-named article on our fine cathedral will have to be rewritten. As it stands at present it is false, silly and certainly anything but a proud addition to our island literature.*

GMB also savages some of the poetry in the book. *The poems are mostly atrocious – enough, unless he knew better, to make a patriotic*

Orcadian despair. John Malcolm is a very fifth-rate romantic poet. John Stuart Blackie's hideous jingle 'The Old Man of Hoy' deserves to be burnt by the public hangman ... The Orkney Book *is studded throughout with atrociously bad photographs, which would make any intending visitors think twice before packing his bags.*

By the standards of normal local journalism, which tends to provide soft, complimentary reviews of local books, recitals, plays and pantomimes, this is vicious. He is certainly not afraid to attack an Orkney icon like the historian J. Storer Clouston; and the named and shamed poets must have felt more than a little bruised.

George regarded most Orcadians as Philistines, and he was not afraid to say so. *I still believe that the Orkney people lack the creative vision without which no community can be really alive, and I will keep on believing it until it is proved to the contrary.*

There were mutterings in Orkney about an arrogant young man who could not hold down a 'proper' job. Who did Georgie Broon think he was?

More than a decade later, George Mackay Brown would repent of his brash campaign on culture. *One day near the end of the war, I decided that we were all a bunch of clods and that what we needed was more CULTURE. I have since had very strong reason to see the error of my ways, and to recognise that the more people talk about culture and the arts, the less sensitive and responsive they generally are to the good and the true and the beautiful things of life. But in those days I was pretty keen on culture, and I advocated it in every corner of The Orkney Herald to which I could lay claim ... I would certainly blush now to re-read some of these naive effusions which, generally speaking, looked forward to a day not too far remote when Orkney would be crazy about Picasso and Bach and Ezra Pound. It was a hideous mirage and I was a false prophet ... But mostly I enjoyed those rough-houses, for I had the gift (nowadays considerably damped down) of cutting people to the quick; and one man lurked about Kirkwall a whole day with a walking stick, with which he proposed to chastise me.*

Back in the late 1940s, though, the normally reticent George was enjoying his new platform. Although he lived in the heart of Orkney, he saw himself as an outsider, and he revelled in the role of a lonely prophet. He gave voice to this in a poem, simply called 'Orkney':

There are no forests in Orkney;
Only, blossoming in storms,
the dark swaying boughs of the sea.

There are no trains in Orkney;
Only great winds roaring through the land
From the beginning to the end of eternity.

There is no respectability in Orkney;
Only what the blood dictates
Is done. Spirit and mind are free.

And there are no poets in Orkney;
Stirred by breeze and blood and ocean
I set the trumpet to my lips. I only.

This astonishing, unpublished poem was written in August 1944. It carries intimations of the stylistic gifts that would mark the poet's mature writing. At the age of 22, this weakened, defiant, sometimes depressed man-child was making the bold claim that he was the only poet in Orkney. 'I only.' In case you didn't know. He may have been 'trenched with wounds', as he would later describe his physical and mental sufferings, but he knows deep down that he possesses a gift. Not only that, he knows that he has a vocation. *The talent that will not let one rest.* Although he is not known outside Orkney, he is already convinced that his calling – from life? from God? – is both his burden and his glory. Nursed by a doting mother, and believing that he is not long for this earth, he takes his stand with the Romantic, tubercular poets of legend. The trumpet is set to his lips. It shall make no uncertain sound. He is special. He is called.

Despite his apparent confidence, he is no happy prophet, no Dr Pangloss. Quoting Gerard Manley Hopkins, he writes: *I am gall, I am heartburn.* He then goes on to say: *I look on the lean earth, and loathe it; on the dirty sky, and loathe it; on the ill-natured sea, and loathe it. I hate reading, writing, but sitting with my own unquiet thoughts is worst of all. I hate humanity and the things that the spiteful gods make them do. But above and beyond everything I hate myself; everything about me revolts me beyond belief.*

It is worth pausing here to read these sentences again, preferably aloud, to get the full impact of what George is saying. In these searing words, the pain of this 27-year-old awkward, self-hating man is shrieking. He is uncharacteristically exposing his wounds to his own community.

What is he looking for? Understanding? Pity? Acceptance? I don't know. I don't know if he knows. The image which comes to my mind is that of Edvard Munch's celebrated painting, *The Scream*. Munch provides a background to the painting in these terms:

> I was walking down the road with two friends when the sun set; suddenly, the sky turned as red as blood. I stopped and leaned against the fence, feeling unspeakably tired. Tongues of fire and blood stretched over the bluish black fjord. My friends went on walking, while I lagged behind, shivering with fear. Then I heard the enormous, infinite scream of nature.

He was to write later: 'For several years I was almost mad ... I was stretched to the limit – as if nature was screaming in my blood ... After that, I gave up hope ever of being able to love again.'

George Brown certainly knew what it was to have days of unspeakable tiredness. He had his own tongues of fire and blood, when he painfully coughed up poisonous phlegm. He could read the red runes, and the message was not good. He had made it past the age of 23, but he did not expect to see his 30th birthday. All this at a heady time when he was learning, in weekly instalments, to release a gift for writing which had the potential to justify his existence – not only to what he regarded as his culturally dysfunctional community, but also to the lurking Jehovah of the Warbeth tombs. And, just as important, to his inwardly hating self.

No wonder he felt frustrated rage, as he considered the probability that the trumpet which he alone in Orkney had picked up solemnly and ceremonially would be snatched from his lips before he had found his own grace notes.

CHAPTER 2

The View
from the Magic
Mountain

It is the year 1943. More than 600 Italian prisoners-of-war, captured during the North Africa campaign, are trudging along the skyline on the island of Lamb Holm, about seven miles south of Kirkwall. Having finished work for the day, they are heading for home – a group of thirteen huts called Camp 60.

The men have been sent to Orkney to work on a massive series of concrete causeways linking the southern isles of South Ronaldsay, Burray, Glims Holm and Lamb Holm to Orkney's Mainland. It is a defensive measure, even though the Geneva Convention forbids the use of prisoners-of-war in war work. After the disaster in October 1939, when a German U-boat penetrated the Scapa Flow defences and sank HMS *Royal Oak* with the loss of more than 800 lives, prime minister Winston Churchill was determined that the eastern approaches to the Flow would be sealed. The project was presented as one which would be of benefit to the Orkney Islands after the war.

In the time they have been at Camp 60, the prisoners have planted flowers and made concrete paths. In their spare time, they have built a theatre and a recreation hut. One thing is missing, though: a chapel. When they arrive back at the camp, they learn the good news: permission to build a chapel has been granted by the enlightened commandant.

Two Nissen huts are soon joined together, and the work begins. A sanctuary is built at the far end. The altar, altar rail and holy-water stoop are moulded in concrete. The men work with a passion – Bruttapasta, a cement worker; Palumbo, a blacksmith; Primavera and Micheloni, electricians; Barcagolini, Fornasier, Pennisi, Sforza and the rest are willing hands. They scavenge for tin cans. Wood for the tabernacle comes from a wrecked ship. Two candelabra and a beautiful rood-screen are made by Palumbo, who had been a wrought-iron worker in America. For the entrances on either side of the sanctuary, gold curtains are paid for out of the prisoners' welfare fund. This is a labour of love.

The man whose vision it is, Domenico Chiocchetti, paints a beautiful picture above the altar – *The Madonna of Peace*. It is based on a holy picture he has carried on his person all through the war. The lovely sanctuary makes the rest of the Nissen huts look shabby; the camp commandant, who has got completely caught up in the project, manages to procure enough plasterboard to line the whole building. Chiocchetti transforms the interior by his artistry. A façade is erected at the front. In the archway, Pennisi moulds in red clay a head of Christ with a crown of thorns. When the chapel is practically finished, a special service is held, incorporating – by means of gramophone records played in the vestry – the bells and choir of St Peter's, Rome.

In the midst of the war, the building of the chapel has hardly been noticed. In the spring of 1945, the prisoners leave Camp 60 and Orkney. One man stays on – Domenico Chiocchetti. He is determined to finish the baptismal font before he leaves for home. When the font is finished, he turns his back on his creation and returns to the bosom of a loving family in Italy.

The chapel stands on Lamb Holm, a silent witness to the transcendent in the midst of sometimes despairing human life. These rough, skilled men have created out of tin cans and wreckage from the sea, in a time of war, something beautiful for God. Orkney,

Protestant and Catholic, will take the Italian Chapel to its heart and will look after it.

It is sacred space, holy ground. In Philip Larkin's words, it is 'a serious house on serious earth'. It speaks to every soul, whether conventionally religious or not.

Whenever I look at that vulnerable little chapel against the background of the wide Orcadian skies, I am reminded in my heart, as well as in my mind, that there are precious gifts of spirit that no coinage on earth can buy.

George Brown was entranced and inspired by the story of the Italian Chapel. He referred to it often. He wrote about it in the *Orkney Herald* in 1945: *We who are brought up in the Calvinistic faith, a faith as austere, bracing and cold as the winds that trouble Lamb Holm from year's end to year's end, can hardly grasp the fierce nostalgic endeavour that raised this piece of Italy, of Catholicism, out of the clay and the stones* ...

This, I believe, is a statement of great significance for the tracking of George Mackay Brown's spiritual journey. He writes it at the age of 23, the year by which he expected to be dead. It tells his own community that he is emotionally and spiritually estranged from the faith of his fathers. It also gives the merest hint of a turning towards Roman Catholicism.

In order to grasp the controversial nature of such a nuanced move in the direction of a misunderstood and sometimes feared minority religion in a small community, it is necessary to turn a spotlight on the influence of John Brown's thinking and behaviour upon his son's religious development.

George remembered his father as religious, 'in a kind of un-questioning way that brooked no argument'. John Brown's religious faith was egalitarian and informal. He had been to London and Glasgow – and, like the Orcadian poet Edwin Muir, he was profoundly saddened by the wretchedness of the slums. His religious hero was William Booth, founder of the Salvation Army. He had heard Booth preaching to big crowds in Glasgow, and he was impressed not only by his thrilling oratory but also by the Salvation Army's work with, and championing of, the poor. The playing of emotional evangelical hymns by the Salvation Army's brass band pleased him. 'Peedie Georgie' – 'peedie' is an affectionate Orcadian word for 'small' – shared his father's love of the Salvation Army band, and he was often to be seen marching down the street behind the musicians.

John Brown led his family to Sunday-morning worship in the Victoria Street Church, one of three Presbyterian churches in Stromness. In its beginning, it represented the United Presbyterian tradition, and then, after a merger, the United Free Church tradition. The congregation of the established Church of Scotland – often referred to as 'the Auld Kirk' – worshipped in St Peter's Church. The Free Kirk congregation worshipped in the North Church.

How could three forms of Scottish Presbyterianism be on offer in a town of fewer than 3,000 people?

A story is told about a Scotsman who was shipwrecked on a remote island. After some years, he was rescued by the crew of a passing ship. The sailors noticed that there were two church buildings on the island. Puzzled by this, they asked the Scotsman why there were two churches. 'One is for me to attend,' he replied gravely. 'The other is for me to stay away from on principle.' This apocryphal tale is too close to reality for Presbyterian comfort.

The time has come to fill out shorthand terms such as 'Catholic', 'Reformation', 'Protestant', 'Calvinist' and 'Presbyterian', all of which will feature in George Mackay Brown's spiritual journey. This version of the story – which will assume little knowledge on the part of the reader – begins with conflict in the eleventh century and ends with different brands of coffee in the twenty-first century.

The Great Schism of 1054 divided the Christian Church into Eastern and Western branches, which later became known as the Eastern Orthodox Church and the (Roman) Catholic Church.

In the sixteenth century, a protest movement within the Catholic Church, led by Martin Luther, a German Catholic priest and theologian, gained momentum.

In identifying what he saw as abuses, Luther compared the practices of the Catholic Church with the text of the Bible. He found the Church wanting. He and his fellow protesters (hence 'Protestants') sought to reform (hence 'Reformers') the Catholic Church, rather than to break away from it.

Professor Luther made a close study of the letters of St Paul in the New Testament. He concluded that, according to the Scriptures, salvation was a free gift from a loving God. He argued that some of the practices of the Catholic Church obscured this freedom by strictly controlling access to God.

Luther's pamphlets, published widely throughout Europe thanks to the new printing presses, proved popular among reform-minded priests and lay people. Less high-minded princes backed the rebels because they saw opportunities for land-grabbing.

At a time when the Catholic Church was slow to appreciate the implications of the demand for change, the Reform movement became a popular crusade that promised personal and political liberation.

The leading Reformer of the second generation of Protestants was a brilliant French lawyer and university lecturer, John Calvin. His *Institutes of the Christian Religion* became the most influential Protestant text in Europe.

Calvin's theology emphasised the power and the grace of God. His controversial doctrine of Predestination affirmed that while salvation was a gift from God, only those chosen by God would be saved from an eternity in hell.

Calvin organised church life in the city of Geneva in Switzerland on very rigorous lines. It became a model for the Scottish Reformed tradition, which was enshrined in law as the national religion of Scotland in 1560.

The Church of Scotland – the Kirk, as it became known – was Calvinist in its theology. It soon became Presbyterian in government: that is to say, local congregations answered to Protestant assemblies called presbyteries, rather than to bishops.

The Kirk's ministers were not priests offering the sacrifice of the Mass, but black-gowned Bible teachers. The leading Reformer, the fiery John Knox – an ordained Catholic priest – believed that the Catholic Church in which he had been reared had become corrupt.

Knox wanted everyone to be able to hear or read the Scriptures in their own tongue, rather than in Latin. His vision of a church and a school in every parish was egalitarian.

He wanted every ploughboy in the land to understand the Scriptures. He insisted that funds should be set apart so that every boy who was bright enough could, no matter his background, go to university. (Knox was a fearless mould-breaker in so many ways, but he was a man of his time in that his vision did not extend to the education of girls.)

Each congregation in the Kirk was governed by its minister and kirk session (a group of men, 'elders', chosen for their piety, virtue and knowledge of the Bible). The minister and elders had oversight of the Christian education and behaviour of the congregation – and of the parish in which they were set. The Scottish Reform movement represented an ambitious national programme of religious education.

The Reformation was greeted by many people as liberating. There was a critical flaw in the new system, however. In giving power to the people, and placing the Bible in the vernacular in their hands, it was hard to control interpretation of the Scriptures. How could a movement which originated in protest against a Church hierarchy deny legitimacy to rebellion against *their* rule?

The Scottish Reformation undoubtedly injected a new energy and dynamism into the life of the Christian people of Scotland, but it came at a price. That price was increasing division.

Fortified by their individual interpretations of the Bible, people with a grievance left the main body of the Kirk and set up conclaves of their own. Several of these conclaves grew into separate branches of Presbyterianism. The differences in theology were barely visible to the naked eye.

Over many decades, Scotland remained to a large degree sympathetic to Presbyterianism. Nevertheless, the tendency for splits to develop over comparatively minor matters made talk of the unity of the Church sound very hollow.

The most significant of the Scottish secessions came in 1843, when more than a third of the Kirk's ministers and elders walked out to form the Free Church of Scotland. The defining issue at stake was the right of congregations – rather than the local laird – to choose their own minister.

The above is a severely abridged version of a long theological back story. While perhaps less than riveting, it provides important clues for understanding the religious culture in which George Mackay Brown was brought up.

To get an even simpler flavour of Calvinism and Presbyterianism in recent times, try this. Think Presbyterianism, think coffee. The Church of Scotland represents the decaffeinated version of Presbyterianism. It is a bit bland, worthy and generally kindly: a broad church, with all the strengths and weaknesses that the term implies.

The Calvinism of the Free Kirk and its various breakaway movements is more like full-on, 100 per cent proof coffee, in which the granules are positively nuclear. Not only will it set your pulse racing, it might give you a panic attack or a cardio-vascular incident. There is nothing bland about this particular theological brew. The flames are licking about you, and you are either in or out, saved or damned – and you have no choice about your fate; it is predestined by an all-powerful, all-knowing God.

There is no chance of this being confused with sentimental, carey-sharey, ecumenical happy talk about all things being well, and all manner of things being well. It is wild-eyed Jehovah-on-the-rampage terrain. Some of the more zealous drinkers of this industrial-strength Calvinistic brew were always keen to volunteer to do an avenging deity's work for him. The Free Presbyterian Church of Mhairi Sheena Mackay was grounded in this tradition.

Even by the nineteenth century, much of the fire of mainstream Presbyterianism in Orkney had gone out. Looking through the minutes of the local congregations, I was struck by how douce they were. Here was no fierce Calvinism. The day of dragging sinners into church to be rebuked in the face of the congregation was long over.

The minutes of the Victoria Street Church reveal that, in 1822, the beadle (church officer) – who was paid a guinea a year, plus three pence for every baptism – was rebuked before the congregation for 'Sabbath profanation in going out with others on the Lord's Day in a boat after whales'. Fifteen members petitioned the kirk session, disapproving of 'hymn tunes of a quick, giddy and light manner'.

The Free Kirk's minister from 1897 to 1939, Rev. James Christie, was let down badly by a new servant lass. She apparently took an empty whisky bottle from the manse to get milk at the dairy shop. Big mistake.

In the minutes of 1914–18, war was not even mentioned. There was some spluttering about the 'phenomenal rise' of football pool betting, but that was about it.

In 1925, Rev. John Mair Hutcheon from Glasgow was appointed to the 'Auld Kirk' (Church of Scotland). The Stromness Parish Church history says: 'He had a beautiful preaching voice, and also sang well; he and his daughter sang duets on occasion. He was good with the bairns; the Sunday school was flourishing. But what emptied the Kirk in the 1930s was the minister's affair with Mrs Fairclough (draper's shop, John Street)!'

One thing that does come through is the rivalry between the three Presbyterian churches. This was confirmed to me by Iain Macleod. 'Churchgoing was more of a habit than it is now,' he told me. 'The three Presbyterian churches differed very little in doctrine, but there was great enmity between them.' This was borne out in 1933 when Rev. J. L. Terris from Dunfermline was invited to be the minister of Victoria Street Church. His reply to the call stated: 'After much consideration I came to the conclusion that my ministry in Stromness would be rather fruitless owing to the fact that there is much unnecessary rivalry in the Church life of that town, and to me a union of churches was clearly indicated.'

The Episcopal congregation in Stromness was very small. The Salvation Army had lots of supporters, but its membership was dwarfed by the Presbyterians. The two Christian Brethren groups had a handful of adherents. There were only two Roman Catholics in the town.

John Brown was often disdainful of the ministers. He contrived not to be at home when the minister came round on his pastoral visitations, and he railed against Presbyterian humbug. He would often shake his head over the minister's sermon.

Young Georgie was embarrassed by his father's behaviour in the kirk, especially because he *sang the hymns and psalms, full-throated, from the very back seat of the gallery where we always sat, one foot on the seat and with the trouser leg hitched up so that a length of his drawers showed – a thing that caused me deep embarrassment. And, three or four times during the long sermon, my mother passed along the row a paper bag of sweets. I loved the 'sweeties', but the rustling of the bag sounded like a small electric storm in the pauses of the minister's discourse – and that embarrassed me too, for I was sure that all the congregation must be listening to that paper bag and disapproving.*

It is not difficult to understand George Brown's disenchantment with Presbyterianism – he would have agreed with H. L. Mencken's observation that the chief contribution of Protestantism to human thought was its proof that God was a bore – but how did the turn towards Roman Catholicism happen? As a boy, he loved reading – and also writing, in a little magazine he created – about football. Quite arbitrarily, he chose to support Glasgow Celtic. Was that the beginning? George would later observe that it was interesting, in the light of what happened in the years which followed, that Celtic was then the team of 'the powerful Catholic faction in the West of Scotland'.

The earliest driver which pushed him, slowly, along the road to Roman Catholicism was his quest for meaning. The presumed suicide of his uncle, his father's depressive episodes, and the debilitating after-effects of measles, all raised questions for the introverted young man. What was life about? What was *his* life about? Did his life fit into a bigger picture? He would have understood Søren Kierkegaard's cry: 'The thing is to understand myself, to see what God really wishes me to do; the thing is to find a truth which is true *for me*, to find the idea for which I can live and die'.

The first line of Shakespeare that George experienced – the opening of *The Merchant of Venice* – intrigued him: 'In sooth, I know not why I am so sad: / It wearies me'. In later life, he was to reflect: *Those words should be carved over the lintel of my door: in a way they express perfectly my life and my way of looking at things – a tremulous melancholy, a mystery through which are glimpsed and guessed from time to time forms of beauty and delight.*

Stromness Academy's primary 'religion' was all about pupils getting on in life. This message was reinforced in the Brown household. John Brown placed his faith in education as the means whereby his offspring could better themselves, and Mary also encouraged the children to work hard in order, as she put it, to 'get out of the rut'. Another assumption George picked up in school concerned social hierarchy. *It was never openly said in class-room or assembly hall, that I remember; but still it was implicitly conveyed to us that a crofter or a fisherman was much lower in the scale of human worth than, for example, a shopkeeper or a man who wrote in ledgers in an office; and those humble food-gatherers were not to be compared in any way with lawyers, doctors, teachers, ministers, master mariners. (Beyond these, of course, in cities and places of importance, existed a vast hierarchy of wealth and privilege that the likes of us could wonder at, but never touch.)*

George did, though, love the Bible stories he heard at school. He thrilled to the tales of Joseph and his brothers, Noah's Ark, and the wanderings of Abraham, Jacob and Esau. He would say later that though he was a boy of eight or nine when he heard these stories, he was absorbing, unconsciously, form and rhythm and texture. (The form and rhythm and texture that George was absorbing came from that most Protestant of documents, the King James Version of the Bible.)

The first real tug towards Roman Catholicism came at school, when the English master read to the class Francis Thompson's poem, 'The Hound of Heaven'. An opium addict, Thompson wrote the poem in 1888, after a year in which he had been given shelter by a kind-hearted prostitute. The 182-line poem tells of a man being pursued by the divine love:

> I fled Him, down the nights and down the days;
> I fled Him, down the arches of the years;
> I fled Him, down the labyrinthine ways
> Of my own mind; and in the midst of tears
> I hid from Him, and under running laughter.

The poem had an immediate impact. George Mackay Brown was to write much later: *I think, looking back after forty-five years, that the poem has many flaws in its pure, gem-like flame; but I could not have enough of that wonderful discovery. I read it over and over, until I had it by heart. And I knew that the man reeling from delight to vain earthly delight was a Catholic – a very sad and weak and fallible one – and that the Hound in relentless pursuit of him was Christ, or the Church. And for some reason these facts gave to the poem an extra relish.* To what extent the teenage George Brown actually thought in these specific terms, and how much of it is George Mackay Brown's more mature interpretation, is hard to know.

George concluded that Presbyterianism was not going to be the environment in which his quest for answers would be pursued. At the age of 16, he made an independent decision: he quit going to the Victoria Street Church with his family, and started attending the local Episcopal church. He soon became the lighter of the candles for the Eucharist.

Episcopal churches, which were part of the Anglican communion, saw themselves as holding to the best of both Catholic and Protestant churches. George warmed to a form of religion with liturgy and ceremony at its heart. Compared to the word-based Presbyterian service, with its often arid preaching, Episcopalian worship was less cerebral and more aesthetically pleasing to him. Candles, robes, incense, beautiful language, a sense of mystery, open displays of devotion and, above all, weekly celebration of communion appealed to the searching young man.

In 1941, at the age of 20, George made his way from Eastbank Sanatorium to St Magnus Cathedral in Kirkwall for his first-ever visit. The red-and-yellow sandstone cathedral is loved by Orcadians, whether religiously inclined or not.

Alison Miller is a writer whose work I admire. Her debut novel, *Demo*, was shortlisted for a Saltire Society Award (for excellence in the arts and sciences), which Maggie Fergusson's biography of GMB won. Brought up in Kirkwall, Alison now lives in Glasgow. I first met her when I was asked to conduct her father's funeral in 1993. We hadn't had much contact since then, but she got in touch when she heard I was writing this book, and a lively and interesting correspondence developed. When I was in Glasgow, I had lunch with Alison and her husband, Liam. I asked her how she felt about the cathedral, as she grew up not far away from it.

'I love the cathedral,' she told me. 'I visit it every time I'm home, and it often appears in my dreams. If you grow up in Kirkwall, the cathedral is a huge presence in your life, even if, as with my family, you're not religious. At least once every summer holidays when we were young, a troop of us would make a pilgrimage to that bit of the town. After we'd done the two palaces – climbed the Moosie Tooer in the Bishop's, danced in the big roofless hall of the Earl's – we would descend on the cathedral, sit in the straw seats, point up at the loose stone in the pillar with Magnus's skull behind it, and the other with Rognvald's bones, pass the altar and pulpit to run our hands along the recumbent statue of John Rae asleep in the Arctic beside his rifle, like an Orcadian Davy Crockett. Then we would climb the narrow spiral of red sandstone to the upper levels, run shrieking past the hangman's ladder in the loft, tumble out onto the platform at the base of the green copper spire and survey Kirkwall spread below us. We would gaze over the roof of the Town Hall to the Peedie Sea, the pier and the boats, and beyond that towards the North Isles in a haze of blue. Only once do I remember being chased by an attendant.'

The cathedral's story goes back to 1129, when the King of Norway granted one half of the earldom of Orkney to St Magnus's nephew, Kali Kolson. Kali took the name Rognvald, in honour of an earlier earl of Orkney. But first he had to defeat Earl Paul, son of Hakon, who had no intention of giving up his share of the earldom. According to the *Orkneyinga Saga*, after one failed attempt, Rognvald's father, Kol, advised him to enlist divine assistance. He should, said Kol, make a vow to God that if he should gain victory, he would build a stone minster at Kirkwall 'more magnificent than any on Orkney'. He should promise to have it dedicated to Magnus and provide it with all the necessary funds.

The Saga presents the victorious Rognvald as warrior, pirate, poet, sportsman, romancer, pilgrim and man of action. He was also a man of his word. In 1137, two years after the canonisation of Magnus, work began on the building of Kirkwall's cathedral, under the direction of Kol.

Here is how George later described that first visit to the cathedral. *Except that the experience was intense, I can't remember the details, apart from the one thought, 'I would like to be buried in this place.' (No one will ever be buried there again.) The Cathedral and the reason for its building, and the building of it, and all that happened in it, have quickened my imagination again and again. Of late years, in the south-east corner of the Cathedral, there has grown a cluster of plaques to Orkney's writers and scholars. I would be glad, I suppose, to have my name and years there, after my death.*

His wish would be granted.

Whether staring at the ceiling of Eastbank Sanatorium or his room at Well Park in Stromness, George struggled to make sense of his condition. One book which helped him was *The Magic Mountain*, by Thomas Mann. Here is how he describes his serendipitous encounter with the German novelist: *One afternoon, in the Stromness bookshop, I took from the shelf the Everyman edition of Selected Stories by Thomas Mann. I think I must have bought it because there was nothing else to read, on that particular day. The Ancient Mariner's hand fell on my shoulder. I sent for The Magic Mountain; it gave me days of intense delight. There is no doubt that writers whom one enjoys so much are taken into the creative imagination and influence one's writing; though one should never be so foolish as to imitate them.*

At first sight, Thomas Mann would seem to be an unusual choice. As a modernist European writer, his concerns and style might have been thought to be outside of George Brown's interests. But George was immediately enchanted, and that enchantment would last for the rest of his life.

The Magic Mountain is set in a sanatorium, just before the First World War. It tells the story of Hans Castorp, a 22-year-old German who travels to a sanatorium in Davos in the Swiss Alps to visit his cousin, Joachim Ziemssen, who is laid low by tuberculosis. When Castorp himself displays some symptoms of bronchial trouble, the sanatorium's director diagnoses TB. His stay at the sanatorium lasts not the anticipated three weeks, but seven years.

I must admit that, early into the reading of the slow-moving 854-page tome, I began, like the central character, to lose the will to live. The more I got into it, though, the more absorbed I became, and I understood just why it was so important to George. Thomas Mann, who based some of his observations on his own visits to see his wife in a sanatorium, subtly evokes the boredom, monotony, rituals and morbidity of the clinic. He slowly, artfully, builds a picture of the gradual institutionalisation of those who are chronically ill. The passage of time itself is an important 'character' in the book. As the weeks move into years, Hans has to learn to relinquish control over what had once seemed secure aspects of his life, including his career. The patient has to learn to be patient.

Mann spurred the Orkney man's interest in the nature of time. George's own recurring bouts of debilitating illness heightened his awareness of differing perceptions of time's passage. It is interesting that chapter 7 of *The Magic Mountain* is titled 'By the Ocean of Time'. GMB's novel *Beside the Ocean of Time*, for which he was shortlisted for the Booker prize, is a meditation on this theme, as is his novel *Time in a Red Coat*.

Thomas Mann's novel did not solve any problems for George Brown; but, by entering into the imaginative world of *The Magic Mountain*, he developed new conceptual tools that helped him reflect in diverse ways on his experience of recurrent illness. He was drawn to Mann's use of the language of symbolism and allegory, and was much taken by the description of the tubercular patients as 'the horizontals'. Indeed, it appealed to him so much that, during another spell in Eastbank Hospital, he used the pseudonym 'The Horizontal Bard' for a poem titled 'Eastbank Blues', which was published in the sanatorium's magazine.

Writing with verve, the Horizontal Bard of Stromness was starting to show what he was made of. In the depths of his being, he knew he was capable of bigger things than Stromness could dream of. If only he could stop himself from dying.

CHAPTER 3

Scarecrow
in the
Community

Feeling himself to be under a death sentence, physically un-confident, cripplingly shy, knowing that he was regarded in his own community as a bit of a waster, afflicted by nightmarish dreams, aware of a singular talent, and seeking a spiritual meaning for his life, George Brown turned to drink.

Stromness had been 'dry' since votes by the community in 1923 and 1926. Drunkenness in the streets had increased since the war, and the successful Temperance movement had highlighted the damage that abuse of alcohol had inflicted on families.

In 1945, George had used his column in the *Orkney Herald* to campaign for the reopening of public houses in the town. In November 1947, Stromness voted to reverse the earlier decisions. When, six months later, the bar of the Stromness Hotel reopened for business, one of the first customers through the door was George Brown. Let the man tell us how it was – or at least how he remembered it in comparative tranquillity.

The first few glasses of beer were a revelation; they flushed my veins with happiness; they washed away all cares and shyness and worries. I remember thinking to myself, 'If I could have two pints of beer every afternoon, life would be a great happiness ...'. It was a comical bizarre slightly surrealistic world to which I had found the key.

I'm reminded of novelist J. G. Ballard's observation that, when he discovered alcohol, the whisky bottle produced a friendly microclimate which encouraged his imagination to emerge from its burrow. In the early stage of his love affair with alcohol, George also found that alcohol opened doors in his imagination. There were other advantages, too.

Apart from the anodyne of the drink, I found myself among a company of 'characters', as they are called in Scotland, a kind of chorus of men, whose comments on the passing scene and reminiscences were an abiding joy. Sober, waiting for the bar to open, they were apt to be stolid and silent. Drink unlocked their tongues and made poets of them (though the only real verse they knew were the ballads of Robert Service and fragments of Burns). I delighted in their company. I learned, over the months that followed, that two pints of draught in the afternoon weren't enough to ensure permanent felicity. The favourite working-class drink in Scotland then, and perhaps now, was 'a half and a half' – that is, a small measure of whisky (a 'nip') and a half-pint of beer. I soon discovered that whisky was a quicker way than beer to the realms of fantasy. Fortunately whisky was expensive, and I could afford it only occasionally. But if you have a sufficient quantity of 'halfs and halfs' under your belt, you can soon become drunk. I was frequently drunk; I earned a certain gray reputation in the town for over-indulgence.

Indeed. The sight of an inebriated George Brown, wending his way uncertainly through the streets of Stromness, was far from unusual. When he was incapacitated, friends took care of him and carried Orkney's fragile Horizontal Bard home. Sometimes the chief barman of the Stromness Hotel, a giant of a man, would lift George up, put him over his shoulder like a fireman would, and take him home. The poet would be left on the doorstep or, in his own words, 'dumped inside like a sack of potatoes'.

He did not escape the notice of Orkney's finest.

On one occasion the police van picked me up, but either the one local cell was full or the officers were kindly disposed, because they drove me home. Next morning the neighbours whispered, 'George Brown was taken home last night in the "Black Maria" ...'. This whisper, when it reached my mother's ear, incensed her (in so far as a woman of her serene nature could be incensed): 'They'll say anything but their prayers. It wasn't the "Black Maria" – I saw it myself – it was a gray van ...' Her attitude to my over-drinking was a mild disapproval or silent anger. Many an afternoon my dinner spoiled in the oven while I caroused and chanted in 'the chorus of the Hamnavoe men'.

When he had no money or was hung over, he would stay in bed and write. The changes in behaviour in people while under the influence of drink, which he observed in the hotel bar, became raw material for his poems or stories.

It gave me a kind of insight into the workings of the mind: how under the drab surface complexities, there exists a ritualistically simple world of joy and anger. It is well known that people who live in northern latitudes are much more given to drunkenness than the Spaniards, or the Italians, where wine has always been an accepted part of life, and a blessing among other blessings. In the north it is considered shameful to show one's feelings and emotions. The stoical mask must always be worn, whatever befalls. But in alcohol – especially the fiery waters of whisky, aquavit, vodka – under the mask they give vent to their feelings, and because their emotions have been so closely pent up, tipsiness tends to have a carnival extravagance.

The writer in me seized eagerly on this Jekyll-and-Hyde aspect of the northern psyche. Literature delights in contrast. There are no drunks in Jane Austen; a good writer can detect subtle shades and contrasts by the turn of the head, the movement of a hand, or a few casual words. My coarser art has to make do with a man or a woman sober or in various states of drunkenness. The complexity of an 'ordinary person' is amazing – in northern lands, drink is the key – inside are treasures and rags-and-bones all jumbled together.

Alcohol also helped anaesthetise the pain of his depressions; however, it made some of his problems much worse.

At least once, about the dangerous time of New Year, I have been on the verge of delirium tremens. It was a foul experience. There is a state of drunkenness where even sleep leaves the wreck of the body. All one night I lay in bed open-eyed. I had to force myself to keep my eyes open, for whenever I closed them a sequence of evil depraved faces filed slowly through my brain; each paused as if to note my wretchedness, and passed on; and another hellish face took its place. It was like a sequence of photographs thrown on a screen: all portraits of the utmost frightfulness, hundreds of them. My only relief was to force open my eyes. But my body was so weary that when I lost concentration the eyelids fell, and another file of dreadful faces came in strict order.

For a man already troubled by nightmares, this was not what George needed. With awareness of his mortality rarely far from his consciousness, the drink-fuelled imaginings were like an Orcadian version of Dante's Inferno.

Nor was he a happy drunk. When the 'stoical mask' which he put on before leaving his house slipped from his face in the bar of the Stromness Hotel, what was revealed was not pretty. It could be downright ugly. The whisky that flushed his veins with happiness and loosened his inhibitions also made him act recklessly and sometimes viciously.

Another New Year's night, I seized the books from the little bookcase at the stair-head and hurled them down, till they lay like shot birds in the lobby below. Finally I fell over my feet and tumbled helter-skelter down the fourteen stairs to join the books. My mother picked me up and put me to bed. She must have been hurt and worried, but there was something so bizarre in the discovery of her writing son in a dishevelled nest of books that she laughed wonderingly, telling me about it next morning. (There must be some deep psychological reason for this casting-down of the books.)

Freeze-frame this portrait of the artist as a young man. He is watched by his tense but devoted mother. 'Poor Georgie' – as Mary often referred to her son – lies drunkenly at the bottom of the stair, surrounded by books. His mother, reared in a Free Presbyterian tradition that is hostile to alcohol, looks upon a scene which is not unfamiliar to her. Yet, when she talks to him next morning about the incident, she laughs.

What is going on here? To make sense of it, I seek help from Orcadian poet Morag MacInnes. 'George's mother's Calvinism was related to things that George couldn't do, like physical work,' Morag said. 'She couldn't be tired out, she was up at dawn and she cleaned and scrubbed and cooked and baked. She was very ambitious for all her kids, and they all did well. By the time she had George, she was probably glad to have somebody still at home, because she was a mothering kind of person. You could only do two things with George: you could shout at him all the time or you could just laugh, and I think, because she loved him, she laughed most of the time. Of course, she was annoyed about the drinking, particularly when he spent all his National Assistance money on booze; but she was weak where he was concerned. When he started writing things, I think she was quite proud. And, of all the kids, he was the one who was most like her in the sense that he loved a story, loved a slightly malicious story.'

Iain Macleod, whose family lived next door, said that Mrs Brown was a very warm, caring person. 'She was quite young when she came to work in the Stromness Hotel, and, although she was from a Free Presbyterian background, Stromness probably had more influence on her life and her outlook. She was very open and welcoming, and I certainly would not have regarded her as narrow-minded at all. She didn't like George's drinking, but I suspect her attitude was not so much Free Presbyterian as the fact that he was her son and was not doing what she would have liked.'

The implication of what Iain Macleod is saying is that Stromness was a gentler and less judgemental place than the Highland Calvinist community that Mary Brown had come from. George Brown, sensitive to the point of paranoia, felt that the Stromness town gossips noticed with relish how he was conducting himself. In one of his early poems, 'The Old Women', he hit back at what he saw as an acerbic Greek chorus:

> Go sad or sweet or riotous with beer
> Past the old women gossiping by the hour,
> They'll fix on you from every close and pier
> An acid look to make your veins run sour.

'No help,' they say, 'his grandfather that's dead
Was troubled with the same dry-throated curse,
And many a night he made the ditch his bed.
This blood comes welling from the same cracked source.'

On every kind of merriment they frown.
But I have known a gray-eyed sober boy
Sail to the lobsters in a storm, and drown.
Over his body dripping on the stones
Those same old hags would weave into their moans
An undersong of terrible holy joy.

That is truly savage. The temptation to confuse the narrator with the writer should most times be resisted; in this instance, it is hard not to see the gossips' talk about the grandfather as being other than a personal reference. (George hinted that his grandfather had a drink problem, though this claim is disputed within the Brown family.) Rightly or wrongly, he associated the old women's judgementalism with the Presbyterianism that he had disavowed and seemed to hate more and more.

The Presbyterian culture of Stromness was often a subject for passionate discussion at the home of Ian and Jean MacInnes, where George was a regular guest. Under the influence of Ian MacInnes – and his own father – he considered himself a socialist. In February 1945, with the war moving closer to a conclusion, he mounted an attack on the Tory Party in an article in the *Orkney Herald*. Entitled 'Toryism in the dock', the article commented on the voting record of the local Conservative MP, Major Neven-Spence, and urged the electorate to throw out the Tories at the post-war general election. George said that only the obtuse and the mentally defective would give their votes again to Major Neven-Spence. He went on: *It is characteristic of the Tory that any proposal to improve the lot of his fellow-man meets with his stern and unbending opposition. It has been so throughout history, as we took the trouble to prove in a previous article; it will be so as long as the Tory Party exists, though fortunately its days are numbered ... The watchword is 'Down with Toryism'. We cannot afford to allow our national life to stagnate for ever, even if it means hoisting the Red Flag over Westminster and Kirkwall Town Hall ...*

I wonder how the notion of the Red Flag fluttering in the Orkney breezes went down with *Orkney Herald* readers. But George was not really a political animal; nor was he much of a prophet – the Tory Party continues to flourish in the twenty-first century.

George's primary interest was in Orkney's spiritual life. In the discussions at the MacInneses' home, the Presbyterian churches in the town were routinely dismissed as being a negative force, and George did not dissent. This was confirmed to me by Allison Dixon, George's niece. I talked with her and her husband Fraser, who is a biology teacher at Stromness Academy, at their home outside Stromness. A warm and wise woman with a good sense of humour, Allison told me that George loved gossip about churchgoing women. 'Some of them were not very Christian ladies,' Allison told me. 'George used to love stories about what was going on in the churches. "Guess what one of the pillars of the church in Stromness said to so-and-so? Guess what she did?" That was all grist to the mill to George.'

A letter to Orcadian scholar Ernest Marwick in the summer of 1947 – which has never been published until now, and was passed to me by researcher Brian Murray – is very revealing. Enclosing some of his poems, which he asked Marwick to comment on, George went on: 'Some disturbing thoughts visited me last month. I grow more and more sick of the Church of Scotland. By nature I am interested in religion (if not strictly speaking a religious person) and the pale watery Calvinism of present-day Orkney frankly disgusts me ... I could live cheerfully in a Catholic country or in pre-Reformation Orkney if that were possible. The present-day organised religious life here is shocking; much worse than atheism. I could write pages and pages, but will stop in the hope – the very pleasant hope – of seeing you both on Thursday.'

I regard this letter as representing a key transition marker in George's journey from Presbyterianism to Roman Catholicism. It shows not just disregard for, but outright hostility to, Presbyterianism. It now sickens and disgusts him.

It is interesting that he objects to 'the pale watery Calvinism of present-day Orkney'. He would later write for the *Orkney Herald* a story about Earl Patrick of Orkney, in prison awaiting execution for treason.

In his tale, Protestant ministers were sent in to the doomed man. GMB goes on: *Those that stamped grimly in to Earl Patrick came reeking hot from the bowels of Calvin and their words smouldered with fire and brimstone.*

And it was not to comfort the man marked for death that they came, but to terrify him with visions of hell and the burning pit.

It should not be assumed that the Earl of Orkney received them gladly for he was an artist, and artists have never looked with favour on the excesses of Calvinism with its hatred of loveliness and sweet proportion. Besides, it is likely that Patrick had been brought up a Catholic and had no regard for these crows croaking so hideously in his ear ... Be that as it may, those arrogant men who had kissed the hem of John Knox's garment asked him if he knew the Lord's Prayer, and when Patrick gravely began to intone: 'Pater noster, qui es in coelis ...', they shrieked and clapped their hands to their ears, crying out at the same time that they did not want true holiness, as practised at Geneva and Edinburgh, profaned by the accents of the Scarlet Woman.

One would not know from this story that Earl Patrick was the most hated man in Orkney's history. An earl with a reputation for brutal despotism, he was a Protestant. Though he and his retinue would sometimes make a short procession from the Earl's Palace to St Magnus Cathedral for Protestant services, he was hardly Gospel-greedy. He initiated the first recorded prosecution for witchcraft in Orkney. Tradition has it that his execution was delayed for a few days so that he could learn the Lord's Prayer.

In his tale, GMB's contempt for 'fire-and-brimstone' Calvinism is clear. Yet, in the letter to Marwick, it was a diluted version of Calvinism which disgusted him. He does not like Calvinism in any of its forms. In fact, he hates it. He has not read a word of John Calvin; but that is beside the point. George Brown is dealing with the Calvinism of his experience – and of his highly developed imagination. While I knew that George had become disenchanted with Presbyterianism, I had not reckoned with the depth of his rage.

In his Island Diary in the *Orkney Herald*, he presents another short story, titled 'Kirkwall's Black Sabbath'. The fictional tale is set in 1888, when the Channel fleet has anchored in Kirkwall bay.

The next day was Sunday, and Sunday in the eighties of last century was a day of frightful boredom and awesome sanctity. To keep that particular day holy, you had to rid your mind of worldly things and behave, as far as you could, like an angel with clipped wings, or like an emasculated saint. And it must be said that, generally speaking, every Orcadian tried to conform to this doleful regime.

We learn that some of the local boatmen had ferried between 400 and 500 seamen over to Kirkwall and that the local publicans, realising that there was money to be made, opened their doors. *But in those Kirkwall pubs of the eighties the English sailors found no pianos and pots of ferns and buxom ladies to cheer them in their mild potations – nothing but the bleak grim austerity of Knox, the furtive pint slid across the counter, the appalling sense of sin everywhere. The black venom of Calvinism was mixed with their beer; and as every Scotsman can tell you, the chemical change wrought by such a mixture is a very diabolical one. To unsuspecting Englishmen it must have been particularly upsetting. There followed that day in Kirkwall, scenes worthy of the San Francisco dockland or of Hogarth's Gin Lane. The streets of the little town were strewn with scores of drunk sailors. The air was ripped with cursing and swearing and ribald song. In the pubs the devil rampaged ever more wildly as the day advanced. Packs of cards were produced and large-scale gambling began. The billiard rooms and the skittle alleys were well patronised; and the Kirkwall lassies, all forgetful of their upbringing, went for long country walks with the boys in blue.*

Altogether, this was probably the most shocking day in the long ministerial career of Rev. Charles Webster. As he passed along King Street that afternoon to visit a dying friend, he had to pick his way carefully between the legs of sprawling drunkards; bottles were flourished in front of him; and maudlin voices tried to persuade him to drink.

Everywhere, as the afternoon drew on, there was shouting and fighting and sickness and singing. Let Rev. Charles Webster describe it in his own inimitable way: 'Bacchanalian songs were sung and chorused to the echo, till the noise of the revelry was heard afar.'

Mr Webster, the dour minister of the Paterson Church in Kirkwall, decided that the townspeople would have to pay for allowing such evil in Kirkwall. Their punishment was a sermon preached by Mr Webster the following Sunday.

He lashed them with a tongue that was sharper than scorpions. He made them writhe and whimper, and today after nearly 70 years, I feel sorry for the young ladies in the congregation who walked up East Road with a Jack tar, and the young men who took a mouthful from a proffered beer bottle. The ship's officers and the magistrates of Kirkwall were also sharply rebuked.

For the publicans was reserved the most flaming denunciation of all. 'Had they kept their doors closed,' cried the Rev. Webster, smashing down his fist on the pulpit rail, 'we would have been saved this public disgrace and scandal. As it is, we have learned what value they set upon the moral elevation and well-being of our people. For the sake of a paltry few pounds of money diverted into their coffers, they have shown themselves ready to turn the town into a scene of brawling and debauchery.'

You simply don't hear such sermons nowadays – such wild, passionate flaming sermons which must have seemed, to those listening, like roaring brimstone or like the vengeful beating of angels' wings.

George's rejection of Presbyterianism was primarily due to a visceral dislike of a Presbyterian culture that, to his mind, undergirded the judgementalism of the town gossips. The accusatory chorus of the external critics reinforced the critical voices inside his own head. He knew that his drinking and his erratic behaviour upset his doting mother and fed into a wider disapproval in the community. This knowledge increased his self-loathing. He judged himself as harshly as any Stromness critic could; but he bitterly resented the accusations of laziness and wantonness made by actual and imagined critics who had no idea of what it was like to suffer from an incapacitating and possibly terminal illness. This goes a long way to explaining the depth of his fury against what he saw as a complacent, moralistic Presbyterian establishment.

Fuelled by frustration and anger, he took the part of the drinkers with whom he felt at home, over against the fulminations of the preachers and the judgements of the elders. He also took the side of the outcasts and the misfits, the people who felt that those who went to church, Bible in hand, every Sunday morning, had life worked out in rather smug or controlling ways, or lived lives that represented – in Iain Crichton Smith's phrase – 'survival without error'.

We are at a significant emotional and psychological staging post on George's spiritual journey. He is raging and howling with misery. Much of his wrath is projected on to his community and its Presbyterian churches.

If this stricken and gifted young man has reached a decisive point of departure from the faith of his fathers, where will he look for – what shall we call it? – salvation?

The importance of George's unpublished letter to Ernest Marwick becomes even clearer. Not only is he averse to any form of Calvinism, he is looking positively towards Roman Catholicism. He says that he could live cheerfully in a Catholic country or in pre-Reformation Orkney if that were possible. This is his unambiguous, though private, position in the summer of 1947.

The following year, in his Island Diary in the *Orkney Herald* of 12 October, he writes about walking with another two people on a river bank during a visit to Aberdeen. The three lay down in the autumn sunlight. *We did then what we always do. We fell to arguing vigorously and with a friendly bitterness on the nature and purpose of life. We mentioned Stalin and the Pope, and God and Orkney and evil and the church and nature and goodness, truth and beauty. We argued savagely and intensely for half an hour. When we walked up the woodland road to catch the bus home, the birds were still at their endless lyrics in the tree-tops, and the happy dogs were barking in the hidden gardens of elysian houses.*

Then, on 26 October 1948, he writes in the *Orkney Herald* of an experience that confirms the direction he is taking. He reflects on a visit to a Roman Catholic church near the end of his visit to Aberdeen.

It was to another kind of drama I went one Sunday morning; a drama full of tremendous gravity and significance.

The great church was full of people of all ages. The last reverberation of the hour had hardly died away in the cupola when the priest, preceded by two boy servers, appeared before the altar with the chalice in his hands. The whole congregation knelt.

One of the boys struck a silver gong and the priest began to recite the holy office in Latin. Inside the altar rails the mystery intensified as the drama proceeded. One could sense the devout eager expectancy in all the hundreds of kneeling figures outside. God was about to be made flesh among them.

And now the miracle happened, as the young priest spoke the words of the supreme mystery and the boy server struck the gong three times. At that moment of ineffable mystery, every good Catholic believes that the bread and wine in the chalice are transformed into the actual body and blood of Christ, which was butchered and shed for all men, so that when they taste of it, they never hunger or thirst again but have life everlasting.

'Vitam aeternitatem,' muttered the priest who was hardly more than a boy, as he placed the thin wafer, now God's holy body, between the lips of the long line of communicants kneeling before the altar rails. There were old blind men and beautiful young women, youths in Air Force uniform and schoolgirls.

The atmosphere of devotion was genuine and very moving. I have never experienced anything approaching it in any Protestant church. The Catholics have a beautiful faith and they enter into it with all their hearts and souls.

This is the language of heart and mind. Presbyterianism has lost George Brown. Now, he is positively inclining towards Catholicism. He sends away for literature about the Roman Catholic faith, and he arranges for the pamphlets to be posted to the house of a friend.

The 27-year-old man is afraid of causing his Free Presbyterian mother even more pain. Although he is making faltering steps in the direction of Catholicism, he is far from ready to make the critical step of joining the Roman Catholic Church.

George's wounds continued to hurt him. Although he learned to mask his depressions when in company, grey despair seeped into him when he was on his own. His days were marked by listlessness. He tells the *Orkney Herald* readers how his day begins.

He wakens about 9 a.m., after a long, dreamless sleep of nine hours. His breakfast is brought up to bed. He eyes it with distaste – he is never hungry at this time of the morning.

He casts a bleary eye through the bedroom window. It is a rainy morning, and swabs of wind rattle the pane. He pulls the bed-clothes up to his chin, turns over on his other side, and drowses deliciously.

When he wakes the next time, he finds that the breakfast tea is grey and cold. He pours it into a suitable receptacle that he keeps under his bed, and begins to chew, with infinite languor, on the toast and egg, which have already grown cold. From downstairs float the last few tunes of 'Housewife's Choice'.

He is now almost fully awake, and begins to read, his head plentifully propped up with pillows. He reads steadily till half-an-hour after noon; at which time he heaves himself out of bed, fingers his bristly chin, and wonders if he will need a shave today. His ablutions are over before dinner, for he hates to have dinner unwashed.

Visits to the pub were the social highlight of his day; but, while they raised his spirits, the aftermath inevitably depressed him. He knew his chances of getting a 'proper' job were negligible. Despite the fact that he had publicly rejected Presbyterianism, he still found it hard to turn down the volume of the Calvinist voices in his head. He seemed to lack the psychological resources to face his internal chaos. He needed spiritual balm for his physical wounds, but where on this earth was he to find it?

The answer was to be found just across the water from Stromness. George was invited to join a picnic party to the island of Hoy. He could see the hills of Hoy from the council house in Well Park, but, despite the fact that it was only a fifteen-minute sail from Stromness, he had never set foot on 'the high island'. At the end of the journey through the hills – 'dark as the valley of the shadow' – the road opened on a green valley that sloped down to the sea, enclosed on both sides by enormous red sea cliffs. The valley was called Rackwick.

George Brown was stunned by the experience. He would write later: *That Sunday, the beauty of Rackwick struck me like a blow. Once it had been a populous valley, but already it was drained of most of its people. Many of the little croft houses were derelict; decay was beginning to eat into others – the roof flags were slipping, doors hung on rusty hinges. Slow fires of rust were devouring the pots inside and the iron ploughs at the gable-ends. It seemed a melancholy place, threatened with imminent utter desolation.*

The poet in George went immediately to work. The reading he had done in his bed on languid mornings did not let him down. He thought of Goldsmith's poem, 'The Deserted Village', with its nostalgic yearnings. The most powerful literary image which came to him was the island valley of Avalon (sometimes written as 'Avilion'), which featured in the Arthurian legends.

The stories of King Arthur and his fabled knights in shining armour, the Knights of the Round Table, had universal appeal, and it is no surprise that they lodged in George's fertile imagination. The man who loved the Viking sagas, with their tales of heroic adventure, was never likely to pass up the folk stories of a mythic king whose magic sword was pulled out of a stone.

According to legend, Avalon was where King Arthur was taken to recover from battle wounds. The island valley was reputed to be inhabited by seven sisters with healing powers. Alfred, Lord Tennyson's version of the Arthurian legends was hugely popular in the Victorian era. In his *Idylls of the King*, the man who would become Britain's poet laureate tells, in verse, the story of Arthur, from his rise to the throne of Britain to his fall and final journey to Avalon. Here are some lines from 'The Passing of Arthur'. The Once and Future King is in the barge, ready for a transition to wholeness or death:

And slowly answered Arthur from the barge:
But now farewell. I am going a long way
With these thou seëst – if indeed I go
(For all my mind is clouded with a doubt) –
To the island-valley of Avilion;
Where falls not hail, or rain, or any snow,
Nor ever wind blows loudly; but it lies
Deep-meadowed, happy, fair with orchard lawns
And bowery hollows crowned with summer sea,
Where I will heal me of my grievous wound.

So smitten was George that he even entertained the notion that Rackwick actually *was* Avalon, since no-one knew the whereabouts of the valley of legend. Why not in this remote, wild, fertile, beautiful place? Could Rackwick heal *him* of his grievous wound?

Soon after I got home, with magic in my eyes, I wrote a prose-poem about a king who was carried to Rackwick for the cure of his battle-wounds. I thought it a good piece of writing at the time, but it is long dust and silence. A lasting spell was cast on me that Sunday, as we sat on the grass with our sandwiches and tea, and heard the slow boom of sea on stones and sand, and saw the two immense sea cliffs that guarded the valley.

George Brown's infatuation with Rackwick was to last for the rest of his life. That first glimpse of the valley was, for him, an epiphany, a conversion – though not yet to institutional religion. It was an overwhelming confirmation of his inclination towards a spirituality of Nature, community and tradition.

Some of the poems George had written were hymns to Nature, sung by a lonely and troubled man. The influence of the Viking sagas and the Nature poems of the Romantics had given some of his own early poems more than a hint of paganism.

If he had a theology around this time, it was one which technical theologians might have labelled 'Pantheism' (God is identified with the world) or, with a greater degree of accuracy, the more nuanced 'Panentheism' (everything exists in God). George did not think in these philosophical terms at any time in his life; he would have been dumbfounded if someone had stopped him as he wended his way home from the Stromness Hotel and asked him if he was a Panentheist.

The visit to Rackwick gave him a symbol of a spirituality that eschewed Calvinism and embraced an enchanted world. The raw material was forming for what would eventually become a more achieved spirituality of the presence of the divine, not only in the beauty of the world but also in the ordinariness of everyday life. It is little wonder that he turned to Tennyson – at school, he had to commit chunks of Tennyson to memory – for whom the natural world was both divine and dangerous. George wrote: *We must always be on our guard not to romanticise: life in a place like Rackwick must always have been stark and dangerous and uncomfortable (imagine three generations crammed into two small rooms, with little privacy, and the men with the salt dampness never out of their clothes, so that the torments of rheumatism and bronchitis came often with age). Yet I believe that their closeness to the elements, their pursuit of whale and herring and their anxious tending of the corn all summer, the winter flame on the hearth that their own hands had dug from the moor, while – if the harvest of sea and land had yielded an adequate bounty – the cupboard was well stocked till spring; that kind of life is more meaningful by far than the lives of people who set out each morning for an office by train with The Times to read; a holiday in Spain with wine and sun the only oasis in their desert.*

George wrote about Rackwick many times. Did he, despite his own caveat, romanticise the fertile valley? Undoubtedly, yes. The importance of Rackwick, though, lies in the place it holds in the poet's imagination. He wants to re-enchant his world; and from now on his envisaged, populated Rackwick will be a key metaphor for that re-enchantment. He will return many times to the physical Rackwick on Hoy; the Rackwick of his spiritual imagination will inhabit him and nourish a clearer sense of vocational direction as a poet. *The symbol is lodged in many of my best stories and poems, and gives them any radiance and power they have. It may be that art, looking before and after, exists to celebrate a good way of life that has vanished, and may be again.*

The newly discovered Rackwick might not have seven sisters with healing powers, but it would soon have a community of friends that would sustain the poet, physically and spiritually, over the years. The haunting valley would become a place of regular retreat and quiet refreshment, but also of companionship, stories and conviviality. Rackwick was also, significantly, not Stromness – it was much emptier, freer and kinder than his native town. It would host his first meeting with composer Peter Maxwell Davies, and would one day be the location for a whisky-fuelled, startling first announcement of his conversion to Roman Catholicism. It would also inspire, very soon, one of his finest published poems, revealing a poet who was beginning to show mastery of his craft. Simply titled 'Rackwick', it was dedicated to his friend Ian MacInnes:

Let no tongue idly whisper here.
Between those strong red cliffs,
Under that great mild sky
Lies Orkney's last enchantment,
The hidden valley of light.
Sweetness from the clouds pouring,
Songs from the surging sea.
Fenceless fields, fishermen with ploughs
And old heroes, endlessly sleeping
In Rackwick's compassionate hills.

Orkney's last enchantment. Orkney's Avalon. Balm for wounds may be found in sacred places, but also deep in the realms of human imagination.

George Brown was in transition. As he approached the age of 30, his physical weakness was still evident, and his dependence on alcohol was a growing problem – but, despite his earlier fears, he seemed likely to survive into his fourth decade.

One of his teachers at Stromness Academy had predicted that he would be a famous writer by the time he was 40. This still seemed fanciful to GMB, but he recognised that if he was to develop as a writer, he needed to break through the constraints of provincial journalism.

Something had to give, and it did. Reflecting in later years on this sometimes desperate, sometimes promising phase of his life, he would write: 'Without literature I would have been a scarecrow in the community'.

With the shackles of his Presbyterian inheritance decisively broken, resourced by a more expansive spirituality, and encouraged by the responses to his *Orkney Herald* articles, he was ready for the next critical stage, both as a writer and as a pilgrim.

But what form should this new step take? What sacrifices might be demanded of him? And would he be up to the task? He might require a little help from his friends.

CHAPTER 4

Ministering Angels

When things have got tough so far for George Brown, some-one has turned up to give him what he needed. During the war, it was Francis Scarfe, who coached him in literature and inspired him to choose life. When he was legless, the barman at the Stromness Hotel carried him home. At a critical time in his life, an unnamed friend invited him to come on the transformational trip to Rackwick.

The question of whether this can be put down to serendipity will be addressed later in the book. I simply put down a marker in the form of words spoken on a popular gramophone record of the 1920s by a music-hall comedian, the self-styled Vicar of Mirth: 'We are here on earth to serve others; but what the others are here for, the Lord only knows'.

Meanwhile, attention will be paid to several men who came into George's life at the right time and who played significant roles in both his development as a writer and the direction of his spiritual journey. First, Ernest Marwick, the scholarly man to whom George wrote about his disaffection with Presbyterianism. Marwick not only befriended and encouraged the younger man, but also opened wide a door of opportunity for him.

Serious spinal problems from the age of 10 meant that, instead of being in school, Ernest spent hours each day, over several years, lying flat on his back on a hard board. Rather than give way to despair, he regarded his plight as an opportunity to read classical texts.

It is not surprising that a deep friendship developed between the two men. Both had experienced disabling illness. Both had had many solitary hours, which they filled by reading. Both were prone to depression. Horizontal bards must stick together.

Although Marwick was only six years older than GMB, the earlier struggle with serious illness, and the sheer range of his reading and scholarship, made him seem much the senior man. As a reader of the *Orkney Herald*, Marwick had recognised the Stromness writer's singular talent. He soon became a mentor to George. One early poem that GMB asked Marwick to comment on was called 'The Storm'. It would become the title poem of his first published collection. It is another significant signpost on his spiritual path.

The poem describes a raging storm. It begins:

> What blinding storm there was! How it
> Flashed with a leap and lance of nails,
> > Lurching, O suddenly
> > Over the lambing hills,
>
> Hounding me there! With sobbing lungs
> I reeled past kirk and ale-house
> > And the thousand candles
> > Of gorse round my mother's yard,
>
> And down the sand shot out my skiff
> Into the long green jaws, while deep
> > In summer's sultry throat
> > Dry thunder stammered.

The life-threatening storm casts man and skiff on to a rock; the adventurer ends up in Brother Colm's cell in the monastery of the island of Eynhallow. The poem ends thus:

Next morning in tranced sunshine
The corn lay squashed on every hill;
 Tang and tern were strewn
 Among highest pastures.

I tell you this, my son: after
That Godsent storm, I find peace here
 These many years with
 The Gray Monks of Eynhallow.

Echoes of Francis Thompson and Gerard Manley Hopkins can be detected in this poem. As well as showing the development of the poet's craft, 'The Storm' is further evidence of his spiritual turmoil and a sense of at least partial resolution. The tumult is followed by many years of peace with the monks of Eynhallow.

In the same unpublished letter to Marwick in August 1947, GMB wrote: 'I like "The Storm" and I'm glad to have written it. The sources of the allegory may be obscure but the purpose of it is not, I think … The whole story might be taken to represent the soul's flight from evil into the peace of God.'

The role of the monk intrigues the man who, dressed as a labourer in Rousay, had looked wistfully over to Eynhallow. George's spirituality is slowly taking a more overtly religious shape. I believe that the story signifies not only 'the soul's flight from evil into the peace of God' but also a stage in the poet's turning towards a more institutionally religious view of life.

Enter another Orcadian Renaissance man. Through Marwick, GMB met an extraordinary man of letters, Robert Rendall. While he does not have the same standing as the big three Orkney writers – Edwin Muir, Eric Linklater and George Mackay Brown – Rendall is a poet of substance. Very deaf and somewhat eccentric, Rendall worked in a draper's shop in Kirkwall. A member of the (evangelical Protestant) Christian Brethren, he was a marine biologist, conchologist, artist and theologian. GMB's generous judgement was that a dozen of Rendall's perfect lyrics would outlast all that the other Orcadian writers had done.

Robert's health as a child was poor. When he was seven years old, three different doctors told his mother that the boy would not live for a year. Young Robert went through a religious conversion experience at the age of seven, and he remained a devoted member of the Brethren. His depressive father tried to commit suicide by cutting his throat; it was 13-year-old Robert who found him. The traumatic incident haunted him all his days. His father died in a mental hospital three years after his suicide bid, at the age of 47.

The Brethren congregation in Kirkwall was part of the 'Open' Brethren tradition rather than that of the exclusive or 'Closed' Brethren. Although its theology was conservative, several of its leaders were open to Biblical scholarship and to the arts and sciences.

Robert Rendall viewed Nature as shot through with the glory of God. He saw no contradiction between God's creation and the findings of science. One of his religious poems, 'Without God', which was based upon a German original, expresses his faith well:

> Without God, I am a raindrop in the fire,
> Without God, a fish upon the strand,
> Without God, a sparrow whose wings tire,
> And a blade of grass within the sand.
> But when God calls me by my name,
> I am air, water, earth and flame.

Rendall made several trips to Germany in the 1930s to meet with Brethren groups, and he saw at first hand the rise of Adolf Hitler. Because of his religious faith, and his admiration for St Magnus, he became a pacifist. This evangelical Protestant also made several trips to Italy in order to pursue his love of Catholic Italian Renaissance art.

His first book of poems, *Country Sonnets*, was published in 1946. It was well received, and it sold out within two weeks. Rendall's poetry is of uneven quality – his best poems are in the Orcadian dialect – but, as well as appreciating the dialect gems, GMB was impressed by the range of the older man's learning. The two men – Rendall was twenty-three years older than GMB – became firm friends.

George Brown tells of a memorable visit he and Rendall made to St Magnus Cathedral. *One day in a Kirkwall street I met Robert Rendall. Together we went into the roseate gloom of St Magnus Cathedral, and climbed the stone stair into the triforium. The hangman's ladder from three centuries earlier was lying there, and also fragments of a very old pulpit. The ladder was constructed with three verticals so that two men could climb it at the same time. 'Only one climbed down again,' said Robert. The worms and the centuries had been at the pulpit.*

Rendall made a poem about it, 'I' the Kirk Laft', in Orcadian dialect:

Here i' the sooth laft's neuks sae dim,
Twa aald-time relics – Haad thee wits!
A hangman's ladder twa could clim',
A widden pulpit, geen tae bits.

Whaur ither should they than in kirk
O' guid and evil mind us a'.
Time plays, hooever, mony a quirk:
Prelate and tief are baith awa.

In the space of two short verses, Rendall manages to pen a lovely reflection on mortality and the passage of time. Two people of contrasting reputations and destinies, the churchman and the thief, are now dust. The hangman's ladder, with its adjoining sets of thirteen wooden steps, still lies in the triforium of St Magnus Cathedral.

While the two men shared a view of the presence of the divine in Nature, they would have disagreed about Calvin's legacy. As Neil Dickson put it in his book about Rendall:

Rendall's faith, though secure, was not complacent and so he had investigated the challenges to it. He felt that to depict Scottish religious life as being all gloom, an image that was popular with contemporary writers (and which Rendall called 'the Calvin myth') was to ignore its other aspects.

I suspect that Rendall and GMB had an unspoken understanding that they would not traverse that particular terrain. Rendall did present GMB with a copy of one of his theological books. GMB was less than impressed. *I struggled through five pages of the alien stuff, then gave up. I always feared he might ask me, next time we met, what I thought of it. But he was a man of tact; he knew that in these matters we were very far apart; and so a delicate silence was observed.*

On 8 April 1948, Rendall wrote to GMB concerning a poem GMB had written about Magnus and Hakon, and which had been published in the *New Shetlander*:

> You have projected yourself imaginatively into your subject, so that as a poem it doesn't matter tuppence whether Hakon felt that way or not. I really think you've got off with it this time! You will appreciate this all the more when I say that I do not share your leanings to a Catholic approach to religious experience … You have a mind that takes imaginative flights, and when these, as in this poem, have *an actual historical incident to flutter about in*, they heighten that incident into poetic truth. But I find that to take such flights in fantasies out of one's own mind often results in indeterminate wanderings … It is a paradox that if we would soar to the clouds we must (to mix the metaphor) keep one foot firmly on the earth.

In other words, both facts and imagination are important.

GMB's writings give the impression of an uncomplicated, warm and respectful friendship with Robert Rendall. But was it as straight-forward as that?

I often go to the Stromness swimming pool, and in the sauna I have conversations with Dr John Flett Brown, who, with Brian Murray, is writing a book about Robert Rendall. Dr Brown, a geologist, is also George Mackay Brown's nephew. He told me that, as well as being friends, GMB and Rendall were also competitors.

'It's wrong to think of Robert Rendall coming to poetry late,' he said. 'Robert was writing poetry during the war. He had a big body of work by the time he published his first book, which pre-dated George's first published book by eight or nine years. There definitely was a bit of competition. In Robert's archive, there are letters from George conceding some points. They were religious opposites – the Brethren versus George with his new Catholicism. George had this hatred of the Wee Free thing. He thought the Scottish Presbyterian Kirk held man back and suppressed freedom of thought, whereas the Catholic Church was handmaiden to all the advances in the world.' (After one of the Stromness sauna seminars, I read an article that George had written in the *Orkney Herald* on 8 May 1945 about a campaign to build a swimming pool in Stromness. *Do I want to see Stromness with a swimming-pool? To be quite frank, I don't. Swimming-pools are primarily intended for inland towns, the inhabitants of which have little opportunity for sea-bathing. In Orkney we have the great Atlantic Ocean foaming at our very doors. Nature has provided us with a bathing-pool that stretches all the way to America.* Intrigued, I asked John Brown whether George ever went swimming in the freezing Atlantic waters foaming at his very door. 'No,' he laughed. 'Never.')

In the late 1940s, George Brown drew a great deal of artistic and spiritual nourishment from these new friendships. With their open-hearted passion for history and literature, Marwick and Rendall gave GMB the writer not only encouragement but also much-needed critical appraisal. There was another dimension, though: Marwick the Episcopalian and Rendall the Christian Brother expressed Christian sensibilities which, even at the points at which he might disagree with them, informed GMB's own life. George had a particular affection and regard for Ernest Marwick's wife, Janette, who had been a nurse in Palestine. She was a devout Anglican, but there was no solemnity in her religion. Through the Marwicks, GMB made other friendships that brought a measure of sober stability to his life. *In strict contrast to my Stromness chorus of drinking friends, those Kirkwall scholars and poets and their acquaintances were Temperance folk. They knew for sure of my splurges and sprees, but our friendship remained true.*

Just as significant was the return to Orkney in 1949 of George's old school-friend Ian MacInnes and his wife Jean. Their hospitality became central to George's life. MacInnes, an art teacher at Stromness Academy, was a ferocious debater. The MacInneses' home in Stromness was a hotbed of fierce discussion about the political, social and religious issues of the day. George Brown spent increasing amounts of time there, to the point at which he became like a member of the family. He preferred to observe, rather than to participate in, the heated discussions, but the homebrew sometimes loosened his tongue.

As he looked at his life and his prospects at the end of the 1940s, George recognised that the decisions he had to make were not just professional but also personal. Living on National Assistance did not boost his sense of self. Walking down to the pub every day and staggering back, or being carried home, was no way to live.

In his own self-disgust, he ached for spiritual fulfilment. He longed for an overarching sense of meaning in his life, one that would give him both stability and a sense of purpose. He wanted to explore more fully the Catholic dimension that he felt, at a gut level, might provide him with the richer frame of reference he yearned for; Stromness, where people could hear you thinking, was not the best place for the open exploration he now needed. Having to get religious pamphlets sent to the house of a friend, for fear of upsetting his mother, was less than satisfactory.

Approaching the end of his third decade, George Brown was not only still breathing, but also he was finding his own distinctive writer's voice. Could that voice be amplified and heard with appreciation outside of the Northern Isles?

It was becoming clear to him: he must leave Orkney. He would later write of his life in Stromness at this time: *The tide of the spirit was shrunken, ebbed out. The great clouds of 'morbus Orcadensis' hung overhead, threatening engulfment. In short, it was time to make a break.* He told Ernest Marwick that he had to get out, or he would have gone mad.

George's thinking about these matters was taking place against a background of wider movements for change. The Labour government, under Clement Attlee, promised to provide national healthcare. In the newspapers and on radio, there was a ferment of debate about nationality, Scottishness and the creation of a society marked by justice. Some people returned to Orkney determined to make political waves locally. A number of pressure groups and societies – such as the lively Stromness Debating Society – grew up. Returnees from the war demanded opportunities for further education.

George had been aware of his need to leave the security of Stromness for a while, but there was still something indecisive, something passive, about him. Chronic illness was leaching away his strength; heavy drinking and its consequent depressions were sapping his vitality; and life was just too comfortable at home.

The problem of what he would actually do away from Orkney also exercised him. How would he earn a living? Who would look after him? How could he make the break?

Enter two more ministering angels, in the form of Alex Doloughan and John Shearer. Bored, and afflicted by winter depression – the 'morbus Orcadensis' he talked of – George was taking part in an evening class. Doloughan, Orkney's director of adult education, asked him if he was interested in attending Newbattle Abbey College. Located not far from Edinburgh, the adult education centre provided study opportunities for those – particularly returnees from the war – who had few qualifications. George was interested; but how could the move be funded? Director of Education, John Shearer, who was determined that Orkney should provide financial support for those interested in further education, made sure that George Brown got the money to enable him to go to college.

Without the intervention of these two kindly 'fixers', George might never have left Orkney.

Out of all the serendipitous appearances in his life around this time, the next one was the most influential. It was life-changing. Edwin Muir, the warden of Newbattle Abbey College, was, at that time, Orkney's finest poet. George had read a few poems by Muir and had found them difficult. What had made a big impression on him, though, was Muir's autobiography, first published as *The Story and the Fable* and later, in a new version, as *An Autobiography*.

Muir's parents were not strict Calvinists, but they regarded the Bible as the inspired word of God. They were caught up in the prevalent feverish speculation about which contemporary events would trigger the return of Christ and the end of the world. Discussion about the apocalyptic themes of books such as Daniel in the Hebrew Scriptures and Revelation in the New Testament – usually involving numbers and secret codes – caused great excitement in the world of evangelical Protestantism in the late nineteenth and early twentieth centuries. The young Edwin Muir was much affected by these matters.

It was not all religious bliss for Muir. There were intimations of more frightening realities. The death of a neighbouring farmer disturbed him and put a question mark against the child's image of the harmony of all things. The family had to move from Wyre to mainland Orkney – and it was in Kirkwall, when a visiting evangelist came to town, that the rather fearful and guilt-ridden boy underwent a conversion to Christianity at the age of 14. Muir wrote:

> To pretend that it was a genuine religious conversion would be ridiculous. I did not know what I was doing; I had no clear knowledge of sin or of the need for salvation; at most I wished to be rescued from the companions among whom I had fallen and to be with the good, with my father and my mother and my sister. Yet the change itself was so undeniable that it astonished me. I was not trying to be changed; I was changed quite beyond my expectation; but the change did not last long.

Poverty finally drove the Muirs out of Orkney. Edwin's father decided to take the family to Glasgow. The poverty and squalor depressed Edwin's spirit. He turned again to religion and underwent another conversion experience, this time at a Baptist chapel. He carried a pocket New Testament with him at all times. If he thought God would protect him from any more of life's troubles, he was mistaken: within the space of two years, his father, two of his brothers and his mother were dead. In his melancholy solitude, he devoured books.

Muir looked back to his childhood in Orkney with great longing, as did George Brown, who disputed later accusations that his romanticising of the Orkney of his childhood led him to turn

Orkney into a Garden of Eden. He defended Muir against the same charge: *Edwin Muir was too intelligent to confuse Orkney with Eden; Eden is a part of the heritage of every child. But he believed that an agricultural community lies closer to 'the fields of Paradise'. The life of an industrial city is subject to an uncontrollable cycle of booms and slumps, while a farming community exists within a clear pattern of labour and fulfilment – seed-time, reaping, the coupling of beasts, the harvest home, the gravestone.*

In the winter of 1918 in Glasgow, Muir, who had suffered from nervous illnesses that necessitated Jungian psychoanalysis, met and fell in love with Willa Anderson. It was, he said, the best thing that ever happened to him. It was in London that Muir's literary gifts flourished. As essayist, critic, novelist and translator, this son of Orkney was a rising star. Throughout the 1920s and 1930s, the Muirs travelled extensively throughout Europe.

Having seen the socialist dream collapse in Russia, and having witnessed the destruction wrought by Fascism in Europe, Muir had become more despondent and pessimistic. Tired of literary fashions and intellectual cleverness, he was a man searching for a spiritual vision. The conventional Calvinism of his upbringing had long since failed to satisfy him. He was disillusioned with politics, and he was disillusioned with himself. He began to keep a diary, and he made entries such as:

> After a certain age all of us, good and bad, are guilt-stricken because of powers within us which have never been realised; because, in other words, we are not what we should be ... I am astonished by the contrast between the powers I am aware of in me and the triteness of my life. As I grow older I feel more and more the need to make that barren astonishment effectual, to wrest some palpable prize from it; for I cannot see that the astonishment itself is of any use to me ... We all come out of a hole and go back into a hole. Leave hiding and go back into hiding. The distance between is disguise.

Guilt and disguise: the George Brown of the masks would have known what he was talking about.

In St Andrews, not long before the outbreak of the Second World War, Muir had a profound religious experience. Willa was ill, in hospital. He wrote in his diary:

> Last night, going to bed alone, I suddenly found myself (I was taking off my waistcoat) reciting the Lord's Prayer in a loud, emphatic voice – a thing I had not done for many years – with deep urgency and profound disturbed emotion. While I went on I grew more composed; as if it had been empty and craving and were being replenished, my soul grew still; every word had a strange fullness of meaning which astonished and delighted me. It was late; I had sat up reading; I was sleepy; but as I stood in the middle of the floor half-undressed, saying the prayer over and over, meaning after meaning sprang from it, overcoming me again with joyful surprise; and I realised that this simple petition was always universal and always inexhaustible, and day by day sanctified human life.
>
> I had believed for many years in God and the immortality of the soul; I had clung to the belief even when, in horrifying glimpses, I saw animals peeping through human eyes. My belief receded then, it is true, to an unimaginable distance, but it still stood there, not in any territory of mine, it seemed, but in a place of its own. Now I realised that, quite without knowing it, I was a Christian, no matter how bad a one.

It is not difficult to see why George Brown was drawn to Muir's life story. The Wyre man's secure yet fearful childhood, his feelings of guilt, his terrors, his spiritual yearnings, his depressions, and the nightmarish animal pictures which flooded Muir's imagination would all have made sense to the sensitive young man who had experienced panic attacks when his mother had gone out to the shops. He admired Muir as a writer, both in terms of his style and his themes, and he would certainly have understood the older man's spiritual search.

A spell in Rome took Muir's quest on to a new level. The presence of what he saw as signs of divinity made a big impact on him.

> The grass in the courtyard of the Temple of the Vestals seemed to be drenched in peace down to the very root, and it was easy to imagine gods and men still in friendly talk together there.
>
> But it was the evidences of another Incarnation that met one everywhere and gradually exerted its influence. During the time when

as a boy I attended the United Presbyterian Church in Orkney, I was aware of religion chiefly as the sacred Word, and the church itself, severe and decent, with its touching bareness and austerity, seemed to cut off religion from the rest of life and from all the week-day world, as if it were a quite specific thing shut within itself, almost jealously, by its white-washed walls, furnished with its bare brown varnished benches unlike any others in the whole world, and filled with the odour of ancient Bibles. It did not tell me by any outward sign that the Word had been made flesh … nothing told me that Christ was born in the flesh and had lived on the earth.

In Rome that image was to be seen everywhere, not only in churches but on the walls of houses, at cross-roads in the suburbs, in wayside shrines in the parks, and in private rooms … A religion that dared to show forth such a mystery for everyone to see would have shocked the congregations of the north, would have seemed a sort of blasphemy, perhaps even an indecency. But here it was publicly shown, as Christ showed himself on the earth. That these images should appear everywhere, reminding everyone of the Incarnation, seemed to me natural and right …

George Brown, in his drawn-out movement towards Roman Catholicism, would certainly have lauded these sentiments. He would also have approved of Muir's summing-up of his life:

As I look back on the part of the mystery which is my own life, my own fable, what I am most aware of is that we receive more than we can ever give; we receive it from the past, on which we draw with every breath, but also – and this is a point of faith – from the Source of the mystery itself, by the means which religious people call Grace.

This was the man who, accompanied by his wife Willa, interviewed George in the Stromness Hotel in the summer of 1951 about the possibility of studying at Newbattle Abbey College. George was so nervous that he had a couple of pints of beer in the bar before the meeting. In a privately printed memoir prepared for a young French student who was working on a thesis about Muir, GMB described what happened at this first historic meeting between two men who are now regarded as giants of twentieth-century Scottish letters:

I was introduced to a rather small man with a large graying head. He walked in a kind of slow glide. His face was remarkable. One noticed first of all the gentleness and serenity. He wore glasses; it was only when he took them off – which he always did to read – that you noticed how large and brilliant and blue the eyes were. He had a poet's mouth too – full, sensuous, fastidious lips. I was nervous of meeting a man whose work I admired so much, but he put me at my ease immediately, he had so much charm and gentleness. Early on he said he had read one of my short stories in a magazine and that he had liked it. Of course I was flattered, and my nervousness vanished ... Before we parted that afternoon he told me that he accepted me as a student at Newbattle, when the College resumed in October.

GMB never consciously imitated Edwin Muir's style as a poet. He did, I am convinced, assimilate, at a conscious or unconscious level, some of Muir's themes and emphases.

It is impossible to understand George Mackay Brown's spiritual journey from now on without paying close attention to the work and assumptions of the quiet man from Wyre.

CHAPTER 5

'Men of Sorrows and Acquainted with Grieve'

A Bible college in the US Midwest used to advertise itself as being 'situated forty miles away from any known form of sin'. Newbattle Abbey might have made a similar (equally dubious) claim in the Middle Ages, isolated as it was in acres of rolling pastureland; but the college built on the same site had a pub close at hand. George Brown knew what it was to make the journey from the Justinlees Bar to the austere, cold college dormitory in horizontal mode.

George regarded the Newbattle year 1951–2 as the happiest in his life. He was pleased to find himself, for the first time, among a group of contemporaries whose interests were much the same as his own. He later jotted down some impressions. Here are some: *A shyness, broken tentatively with poetry and politics, sometimes mixed. A left-wing group mostly, but none of the dour leveller ascetic kind. Poetry, Labour, beer. A group emerged, including me. In the Justinlees we raised glasses for the first of a hundred times. Then the poetry came, eager and urgent.*

Edwin Muir took it upon himself to promote George's work. As a result, some of the younger man's poems appeared in journals such as the *New Statesman* and the *Listener*. If someone was going to advance his poems, who better than one of Scotland's finest writers? *There is no doubt that the influence of Edwin Muir ... helped to make me a writer. If I had stayed in Orkney, I would have gone on writing, to 'be for a moment merry' in the desert of boredom and poverty. But Newbattle stimulated me, and gave me a sense of purpose and direction.*

An insight into George's view of Edwin Muir is to be found in a one-man play, *Edwin Muir and the Labyrinth*, which George wrote in 1987 for John Broom, a friend who was struggling to become an actor. The play has never been published, nor – as far as I can ascertain – performed.

'The Labyrinth' is one of Muir's best-known poems. It envisages life as a maze from which it is difficult, if not impossible, to escape. After describing the complexities and hazards of the labyrinth, the poet says he could not live if this were not an illusion. He has glimpsed another world. In a dream or trance, he saw the gods on high, looking down on human life. Their eternal dialogue was peace, 'where all these things were woven'. The poem closes with these words:

> That was the real world; I have touched it once,
> And now shall know it always. But the lie,
> The maze, the wild-wood waste of falsehood, roads
> That run and run and never reach an end,
> Embowered in error – I'd be prisoned there
> But that my soul has birdwings to fly free.
>
> Oh these deceits are strong almost as life.
> Last night I dreamt I was in the labyrinth,
> And woke far on. I did not know the place.

The poem entranced George. The image of life as a labyrinth filled with wrong turnings and deceptions spoke to him, as did the dream-like intimations of another world, in which the gods converse about peace while they weave their tapestries. Such pagan-sounding mythologising was attractive to an Orkney poet steeped in the Viking sagas. George was captivated by the notion of divine creativity in the weaving of tapestries, the threads of which were the raw material of human life and history. In pagan theologies, the weaving of tapestries by the gods is related to the issue of Fate.

The tapestry motif, with its long and varied pedigree, is still sometimes employed as a creative response to what is known in technical theology as the 'theodicy' problem – the presence of evil in a world run by God. If divinity is all-good, all-powerful and all-knowing, why is there evil at all? Why is there so much suffering in the world? One frequently given answer is that human beings are not equipped to respond adequately to such a question, which ultimately lies in the realms of mystery. On this reckoning, faith is trust that behind and beyond space and time, divine creativity is weaving a pattern from all the elements of human life, one that will be revealed in all its beauty at the end of time.

Is this a satisfying answer from a philosophical point of view? Let's just say that it appeals to poets more than it does to logical positivists. Grounded in a devotional spirituality which begins in humility and ends in a blaze of divine glory, it is an aesthetic resolution of what is, humanly speaking, an insoluble philosophical problem. The continual reworking over centuries of the old pagan notion of the eternal weaving of a tapestry beyond time is integral to GMB's spiritual understanding. His conviction was that there was a shaping divine intelligence at the heart of the universe, one which operated beyond the reach of a rationalist mindset.

The one-man drama, which tells us as much about GMB as about Muir, is set in Muir's study at Newbattle Abbey College in 1952. In this excerpt, the warden is musing about the nature of poetry:

> *A great mystery, poetry.*
>
> *It is the greatest of joys. It is the golden key that unlocks all doors. Lets me out of the labyrinth when the walls begin to close in on me … Bird wings, throat of a bird. I fly free …*

The writing of poetry would, in time, let George out of the labyrinth of his life.

A dreamy Muir meditates on the theme of time; and, as he does so, he is soon back in the beloved Orkney of his childhood.

Time is the enemy. Time begins to build the labyrinth about us, while we play in our dream of childhood.

In a lonely island in the north.

Outside time. In a region of unsullied purity. Innocence and Eden …

There's a long line of writers that goes right back to the author of Genesis. They tell, over and over, the same fable. We begin in the Eden of innocence, before clocks and calendars and sundials. We go, like creatures fated, into the world of 'getting and spending' – the iron gate clangs behind us, we're in the labyrinth then, for good.

But we never forget. However terrible the times, the poets keep the vision in its purity. If the vision of Eden goes, everything is lost; the world is open to the Fascists and the Communists, the cold, bleak, heartless swarms. Regan, Goneril, Cornwall. They keep the gates.

Thank God, then, for Isaiah and the Psalmist. For Shakespeare. For Vaughan and Traherne. For Wordsworth. Thank God for Dylan Thomas, that boy genius who tries to numb the pain of the labyrinth with drink.

It was not just Dylan Thomas who tried to numb the pain of the labyrinth with drink. The Justinlees Bar, not far from the college, was a place of both stimulation and temptation. When George sat round the table with his friends, the discussion sparkled. He remembered it later as 'a kind of literary revivalist meeting, tinged with politics and philosophy'.

Sometimes the conviviality got out of hand. A post-pub game of football in the street ended in a police caution down at the station. Edwin Muir was concerned enough about the level of George's drinking to raise the matter with him in his typically gentle way.

Reflecting on that stage of George's life, Morag MacInnes told me: 'When he did go to Newbattle, he had that whole adolescent, "being a student" thing, and of course he was mature, so it sat very uneasily and he got into lots of trouble. He was the wicked boy getting drunk and doing silly things – quite often rather adolescent things. You can't grudge him that, because he had missed out on all of these things. Also, there's the summer-school syndrome: sitting up late and talking about poetry with pretty girls and boys and not having ever done that.'

I asked Morag how she saw Edwin Muir's influence on George, both in terms of his development as a writer and as a troubled man on a spiritual quest. 'Muir's ascetic take on poetry and his particular brand of spirituality were fascinating to George,' she said. 'The whole ambience of Newbattle was spiritual, and for him it was a hallowed kind of place, a safe place, a place where reading was paramount, where you got your second chance. There was a lot in Muir that George assimilated, and I think Muir helped with George's style too, because the overt romanticism in the early stuff disappears round about 1951/2 – that's when the poem about Peter Esson was written, and some of the best ones, like "Hamnavoe". The other thing that Muir did was to introduce George to the European writers – and that opened a lot of gates for him as well. The European dimension is important for George's development as a writer.'

The sonnet, 'The Death of Peter Esson: Tailor, Town Librarian, Free Kirk Elder', is a good example of George's style, early though it is. George's father used to do some tailoring work at Peter Esson's shop, which was a gathering point for local worthies. George and Ian MacInnes used to play there as children – picking up not just bits of cloth, but bits of stories as well. Here is the poem:

> Peter at some immortal cloth, it seemed,
> Fashioned and stitched, for so long had he sat
> Heraldic on his bench. We never dreamed
> It was his shroud that he was busy at.
>
> Well Peter knew, his thousand books would pass
> Gray into dust, that still a tinker's tale
> As hard as granite and as sweet as grass,
> Told over the reeking pipes, outlasts them all.
>
> The Free Kirk cleaves gray houses – Peter's ark
> Freighted for heaven, galeblown with psalm and prayer.
> The predestined needle quivered on the mark.
> The wheel spun true. The seventieth rock was near.
>
> Peter, I mourned. Early on Monday last
> There came a wave and stood above your mast.

The poem is marked by economy of words, and by vital images. The tailor is 'heraldic on his bench'. You can imagine him straight-backed, cross-legged, a serene Presbyterian yogi with a calm authority. 'We' never dreamed it was his own shroud he was working on. Did Peter? His solemn theological books will not last as long as a tinker's tale – and the apparently unflinching, upright, Protestant man knows this in his heart. The 'predestined needle' is an allusion to Peter's unadorned Calvinism. Resistance to God's plan is not just blasphemous but also pointless. The image of the wave standing above the mast is both awesome and immediately recognisable in a community that prays for those in peril on the sea.

At the end of term in June 1952, George said his farewells and headed up to Orkney, uncertain of his future. Back home, he picked up where he had left off, being pampered by his mother and firing salvos in the *Orkney Herald*. He was out of kilter with a post-war Orkney that rather enjoyed its better roads, new agricultural machinery, electricity and television.

George's rants against 'progress' were not appreciated. Dispirited by what he saw around him, he had fallen out of love with Orkney. He was delighted when he was awarded a grant of £150 for a second year at Newbattle.

At the beginning of the spring term of 1953, he became ill again and had to go back to Orkney. The tuberculosis had returned. He would remain in Eastbank Sanatorium for fifteen months. By this time, new drugs for the treatment of TB were very promising, and George was one of the guinea pigs for the testing of new treatment options.

His spirits were lifted by visits from Robert Rendall. He described the situation thus: *Robert Rendall came to see me regularly, bringing like apples and flagons his latest enthusiasm – a drawing, a discovered shell, a plan to visit Italy. His gaiety dispelled the sombre moods that gather about a long-term patient. He would read me a fragment or draft of a new poem. He recited like an old skald, in a high piercing chant; everyone in the hospital*

could hear him; next morning the patients would recite over their breakfast
Robert's latest:

> *Lord we are thine, the captives of Thy bow:*
> *Fast as we fled, thine arrows laid us low.*
> *We found thee Friend who feared thee once as Foe …*

There is something touching about these bedside poetry readings, with the excitable Rendall screeching his newly composed sonnets in the direction of the stricken younger poet, while the bemused horizontals take it all in. GMB himself wrote a new poem that was published in the Eastbank magazine, *Saga*. It is called 'The Stoic', and it tells us something about the state of GMB's soul.

> *The wind has fallen, the rain keeps on.*
> *My torn feet on the road*
> *Go quietly, doggedly onward*
> *To emptiness, or God.*

This verse is not packed with the power of positive thinking. The journey is a dogged one, and the pilgrim's feet are bleeding. The destination will be a place either of desolation or of divine revelation. His other writings at the time express a similar state of mind. 'Many of the poems that appeared in *Saga* evoke spiritual journeys or ordeals,' write Rowena Murray and Brian Murray on page 52 of their book, *Interrogation of Silence*. 'Brown's raging and ranting against society was transformed into a quest to find meaning and salvation through writing.'

Edwin Muir sent George parcels of books from time to time, and wrote letters of encouragement:

> Forgive me for preaching, but let me say that you are lucky in one way, that you have a gift that most people pass their lives without having, and that even in Orkney, even without the atmosphere which would help to nourish it, it is yours, and you can do something with it, to our good and your own.

When George was feeling low, the letter in his locker from a writer of such eminence must have been a ward against despair. Muir, never a flatterer when it came to literature, was both shrewd enough to know this and kind enough to take the time to write such an affirming letter. For a man searching for meaning and direction, this was the confirmation George needed as he passed the long days in the sanatorium. In encouraging the languishing Orcadian poet and reinforcing the importance of his gift and his vocation – to do something with his talent for the benefit of others and himself – Edwin Muir was a key actor in the sometimes tortured drama of the redemption of George Brown.

George had written enough decent poems to have his first collection of poetry published. In a letter from Eastbank on 14 February 1954 to Ernest Marwick – who was, on George's recommendation, studying at Newbattle – he talked about getting his own poems ready for the press. There was an interesting PS at the end: 'I want a name to put to my poems. Shall it be George Brown (which sounds too ordinary) or George M. Brown (which is hardly better) or George Mackay Brown, which I favour at the moment?'

The Storm and Other Poems was published at the author's expense, under the name of George Mackay Brown, in June 1954. He had progressed from being Georgie Broon, the sweet but sometimes fearful boy, to George Brown, the talented but troubled young man. With the publication of *The Storm*, George Mackay Brown, the gifted writer, was born in a sanatorium. He was 32 years old.

Muir wrote a generous introduction to the new poetry book. Saying that GMB had the gift of imagination and the gift of words – 'the poet's endowment' – Muir observed that GMB's poetry was imbued with a strangeness and a magic 'rare anywhere in literature today'. He added that, in GMB's poetry, he found himself impressed 'by something which I can only call grace. Grace is what breathes warmth into beauty and tenderness into comedy; it is in a sense the crowning gift, for without it beauty would be cold and comedy would be heartless.'

The Storm sold out its 300-copy print run within two weeks. It is noticeable that several now-familiar George Mackay Brown themes are already in place. Tinkers and saints, St Magnus and St Rognvald, monks and drunks, kirks and alehouses, and fishermen, crofters and lifeboatmen all make an appearance. The Scottish Reformer John Knox also shows up.

There is one particularly religious poem in the collection that I relish. It is part of a series called *Orcadians: Seven Impromptus*, which is dedicated to Edwin Muir. It is simply called 'Saint':

When Peter, orraman at Quoys
Was 'saved' by Pentecostals
They dipped him in the sea.

'Peter's gey simple.'
Round blue eyes
Aimless amble of plouting feet
Bird cries on his tongue
Laughing among bairns
simple Peter.
He knew nothing of justification,
Election or original sin,
But that morning on the beach
He heard the rocks cry out
GLORY TO GOD!
Each wave had a trumpet on its lips.
The caves were strewn with weeds and shells of praise.

Peter's mouth brimmed with psalms like a bell,
His knees bored holes in the wet sand,
His hands shivered with blessing.
For O, that ploughmen's boots upon the road
Rang fire from the cobbles of New Jerusalem!

Peter the Saint
With thirty shillings a week (all found)
And his peerie black Bible.

Simple Peter
Talking to a thrush on the telegraph wire.

I like George's celebration of the simple faith of a simple man with 'bird cries on his tongue'. As a minister, I have known such people. The poet does not patronise this daft man who knows nothing of theology and laughs among the bairns. In the poem – which demands to be read aloud – Nature rejoices with simple Peter, and, like Gerard Manley Hopkins, trumpets the glory of God.

George was discharged from Eastbank in the summer of 1954. 'Once more into the desert,' he wrote. What to do, though? Not strong enough to take up his place at Newbattle, he went back home to be looked after by his mother. He went back to the pub. He went back to the *Orkney Herald*, where once again he railed against the modern trends which he saw as destroying Orkney. He identified television as an enemy. *Will it give a death-blow to the already dying art of conversation and story-telling? Will it cause the dust to gather even thicker on the fiddle on the wall? Will it make books and reading old-fashioned? Will it give our sons and daughters a still greater thirst for the bright lights of the city, and accelerate depopulation? I think I hear the trows* [trolls] *on the hill-tops sniggering sarcastically and withdrawing deeper among their shadows.*

The depressions which continued to haunt him worsened after 24 March 1956, when his brother Hughie died of a heart attack at the age of 43. George was stricken. He felt guilty for still being alive. At the same time, he knew he had to get out of Orkney again. *After the death of my brother Hughie I fell into one of those troughs of depression that have irked me from time to time; and still persist. Then I remembered that I still had in my keeping a term's grant from Newbattle that hadn't been used up. I wrote to the new warden, Edwin Muir's successor, and was accepted for the summer term.*

It was good to be back. It was good to be away from Orkney.

Writing to Ernest Marwick, who was by this time back in Orkney, George rhapsodises about Newbattle Abbey College. *Here I am perfectly happy, I only wish it was 600 years ago so that I could have taken vows and become a monk (one of the Browning-esque kind that keeps a secret still buried under the beech tree).* Maybe. Had he been serious, there was nothing to stop him joining an order at the age of 34. He certainly admired – and sometimes envied – monks in the silent orders.

One memory of a disastrous evening stood out. He had been asked to record a talk about Edwin Muir for the BBC in Edinburgh. As well as taking a friend from Newbattle, Edward McLaughlan, with him for support, he downed a few drams before going into the studio. The recording did not go well. He blew his BBC fee on a drinking spree with Edward. The two of them were roaring drunk by the time they arrived back at the college.

Unfortunately, a group of foreign students from Edinburgh University was being entertained there, in the hope that they might spread the word about what the college could offer. Let George tell what happened: *The two drunk students arrived, rising and falling, just as the colonial students were about to leave on their bus. The carefully planned visit was a ruin. Next morning, when I was sitting wretched with hangover in the library, the new college secretary arrived to tell me that the new Warden wished to see me at once in his office. I was curtly told to pack my bags and go. Edward McLaughlan was let off with a severe reprimand. I was considered to be the chief culprit, and so I was. Still, I was stunned and shaken by this expulsion.*

On hearing the news, the students threatened to leave the college and to publicise what had happened. George was saved by the intervention of a Church of Scotland minister: Rev. James Campbell, who was doing further study at the college, went 'carrying the palm branch, between the Warden's office and the crypt'. George was reprieved on the understanding that for the rest of his time at Newbattle he would never darken the door of the Justinlees or any other pub.

After Newbattle, George decided to apply to become a student of English language and literature at Edinburgh University. He was accepted, and was given a grant by the Orkney Education Committee. He found digs in Marchmont in Edinburgh, an area of handsome tenements separated from the main city by a great open park called The Meadows. *Studies start in earnest on Tuesday,* he wrote to Marwick. *It's all a game really: I have no ambition towards academic honours whatsoever. But I felt I had to get out of Orkney for a while – I was beginning to droop and wither there.*

The Catholic question remained unresolved. He had been to Mass in Dalkeith once or twice when he was at Newbattle, but had been disappointed by the services. He was much influenced by a fellow student, John Durkin. *In his house I experienced the closeness and kindness of Catholic family life. His mother was like one of those generous indomitable women that Sean O'Casey writes about in his plays. Catholicism was worked into the texture of their lives: it wasn't the kind of self-conscious piety that is often to be found in respectable Presbyterian households, for there was no objection to drink and fun (so long as they were kept within bounds). There was a wild free Irish extravagance in John Durkin's gaiety that leavened any dour Scottish company he found himself in. And yet we had quite serious talks together, and we troubled with delight the deep waters of poetry and speculation.*

John Durkin no longer went to Mass, but when one has been bred a Catholic, one can never rid oneself of the essence of it. A cradle Catholic is quite different from a convert.

George said that, more than the lecture halls of the university, it was the pubs that drew him. One particular pub attracted him. It was frequented by some of the great names of what became known as the Scottish Renaissance. *I must go to the Abbotsford some evening,* he wrote to Ernest Marwick, *to meet Gavin, Sydney Smith, MacDiarmid and the others who haunt that temple of Dyonisius.*

One evening, he plucked up the courage to go to the Abbotsford Bar in Rose Street, a long, cobbled alley which runs between Princes Street and George Street. Norman MacCaig and Sydney Goodsir Smith and a few friends were clustered at one corner of the counter. *Simply to be there, watching that famous huddle, was a delight. I drank my beer but dared not go near them ... The same scene, with different groups of writers and artists, was repeated over the weeks and months that followed.*

Sydney Goodsir Smith: whether it was that he had noticed my perpetual timid hoverings in their vicinity, or whether he had been told that I had been at Newbattle under Edwin Muir, I don't know, but one day he crossed over and spoke to me, and invited me to join the group. I was so confused that I shook my head; I would stay where I was. And yet the fact that he had spoken to me was a joy. After the poet had rejoined his friends, I could have kicked myself. In time, however, and in my own devious way, I drifted into the company of the Rose Street poets, and got a civil acceptance.

It is interesting that, in his iconic painting of the Rose Street poets, *Poets' Pub,* Alexander Moffat places GMB in the centre of the picture. In fact, there are three poets at the centre: MacDiarmid and Smith are on either side of GMB, who has a pint glass in one hand and a cigarette in the other. The quiet man who had been too shy to join the group, then 'drifted' in from the edge, is now close to the heart of things – in his own devious way. The others who are in Moffat's painting are Iain Crichton Smith, Norman MacCaig, Edwin Morgan, Sorley MacLean, Alan Bold and Robert Garioch.

I like Sydney Goodsir Smith's talk of GMB in his poem 'Kynd Kittock's Land'. Placing him in Milne's Bar, another favourite Rose Street haunt of the poets, Smith says that

> Brown leads wi his Viking chin
> And winna be rebukit.

In these few words, Smith, who wrote in Scots, affectionately captures George's quiet stubbornness. The Orkney man means business with that jutting Viking chin. He might be gentle, but he should not be underestimated. Once he had, by stealth and attentiveness, found acceptance in the midst of these greater luminaries, GMB was not intimidated in the debates that went on. After all, he was used to Ian MacInnes and friends in Stromness. He was never the kind of person who would dominate discussion, but his perceptive interventions would make people think. His quick wit endeared him to the others, as did the mimicry which only emerged when he was emboldened by drink.

Sydney Goodsir Smith was the Rose Street poet for whom GMB felt most affection. A gregarious and kindly man, he was a dazzling raconteur. GMB admired MacCaig's brilliant gifts, but, even in his appreciative comments about him, there are reservations about MacCaig's sarcastic tongue. Almost against his will, GMB grew to like Hugh MacDiarmid (Christopher Murray Grieve), the leading figure in the Scottish Renaissance movement. George's first encounter with the great man was in a toilet. They had both been to see a play, *Uranium 234*. George wrote: *At the interval I stood in the toilet stalls next to a kilted man with a terrier-head, Hugh MacDiarmid.*

His wariness of the great man had its roots in MacDiarmid's well-earned reputation for invective. MacDiarmid famously called Edwin Muir 'a paladin in mental fight with the presence of Larry the Lamb'. *I had been prepared, on first meeting MacDiarmid, to find the same kind of man who expressed himself with such violence in his essays and articles. And would I dare to say that I was an Orkneyman? I found myself talking to a quiet courteous humorous man, who listened attentively to my half-baked opinions and observations, and showed nothing but encouragement and goodwill.*

Edwin Muir was never part of the Rose Street scene. 'Men of sorrows and acquainted with Grieve' was his sardonic parody of Isaiah's poetic description of Israel's prophesied suffering servant, 'A man of sorrows and acquainted with grief'. (It was not, one suspects, a spontaneous throwaway remark.) George Mackay Brown, though, gained a great deal from the discussions, both in the pubs and at the parties afterwards, most often in MacCaig's flat. *Some of the happiest hours of my life have been spent in these two poets' pubs … never did the bird of poetry sing so sweet and true!*

The bird of poetry certainly sang sweetly in GMB's second collection of poems, *Loaves and Fishes*, which was published in 1959 by the Hogarth Press of London. The person responsible was, unsurprisingly, Edwin Muir. He had written to Hogarth enclosing some of GMB's poems. GMB often acknowledged the formative role of Edwin Muir in the development of his career as a writer. Being naturally disinclined to promote himself and his work, he regarded Muir's patronage as akin to a gift from the heavens.

As well as poems such as 'Hamnavoe' and 'The Death of Peter Esson', the new collection contained more overtly religious poems –

about the Nativity, St Magnus and the Virgin Mary. Perhaps inspired by MacDiarmid, he essayed a poem about the Nativity in Scots, simply titled 'Stars':

Tae be wan o them Kings
That owre the desert rode
Trackan a muckle reid star
The herald o God!

Tae swivel a crystal eye
Abune a mountain place
And light on an uncan star,
A tinker in space! –

Thought Tammas, rowan his boat
Fae creel tae creel aroond,
When Venus shook her hair
Owre the Soond.

One particular poem in *Loaves and Fishes* showcases both GMB's increasing mastery of his craft and his maturing spirituality. A recording of GMB reading this poem, called 'Elegy', is playing as I write this. No matter how often I listen to these words, the poem still moves me:

The Magnustide long swords of rain
Quicken the dust. The ploughman turns
Furrow by holy furrow
The liturgy of April.
What rock of sorrow
Checks the seed's throb and flow
Now the lark's skein is thrown
About the burning sacrificial hill?

Cold exiles from that ravished tree
(Fables and animals guard it now)
Whose reconciling leaves
Fold stone, cornstalk and lark,
Our first blood grieves
That never again her lips

Flowering with song we'll see,
  Who, winged and bright, speeds down into the dark.

Now let those risers from the dead,
  Cornstalks, golden conspirators,
    Cry on the careless wind
      Ripeness and resurrection;
        How the calm wound
      Of the girl entering earth's side
Gives back immortal bread
    For this year's dust and rain that shall be man.

GMB makes sacred that most familiar sight of the ages, a simple ploughman turning the soil. Preparing the ground for the eventual making of bread is a hallowed task, a vocation. GMB links this primal earthly activity to the Church's Easter liturgy, including the sacrament of broken bread and shared wine. The earth's wounding by the plough will allow the buried seed to flourish, in the ripeness of time, in a resurrection that will produce physical and immortal life-giving bread. The whole poem should be read aloud slowly to savour the hidden rhymes and the alliteration.

With the publication of *Loaves and Fishes*, George Mackay Brown made the transition to being a public poet of note on the UK stage. Of course *The Storm* was a public event in Orkney, and the scattered poems which appeared in literary magazines had given his name a wider recognition in certain circles – but a collection launched by a respectable British publishing house marked the emergence of a serious poet.

For all GMB's insistence that he did not care what the critics said, I don't believe him. The reception for *Loaves and Fishes* was mixed, and he was hurt by some of it, particularly John Wain's assertion in the *Observer* that the poems had been influenced by Edwin Muir. *In fact, no two kinds of poetry could be more different. Muir adventures deep and far into the racial memory, and the treasures of image and symbol he brings back are steeped in the beauty and light and tranquillity of the beginning. My poems have a much narrower range of time – a thousand years maybe – and they celebrate as best they can 'whatever is begotten, born, or dies', generation by generation, until they stop with memories of my father and his letters and tailors' shears … It is the modern world that provoked Edwin Muir and me into poetry. His adolescence in Glasgow, his 'expulsion' from Prague in 1948 when the Communists took over; those dreadful experiences he set against his childhood in Orkney. Without that contrast, he would have been a different kind of poet, and a lesser one. I hadn't experienced such wreckages in my life; rather, the slow seepings and rottings of the new age.*

There is much truth in this; nevertheless, both Muir and GMB are poets of Eden and the Fall. They express their vision in heraldic terms. The opening lines of the second stanza of 'Elegy' express some of this: *Cold exiles from that ravished tree / (Fables and animals guard it now) / Whose reconciling leaves / Fold stone, cornstalk and lark.*

GMB was impressed by Muir's writing about his childhood. The Wyre man said that his father and mother were fixed allegorical figures in a timeless landscape.

> We begin life not by knowing men and women, but a father and a mother, brothers and sisters … When I was a child I must have felt that they had always been there and I with them, since I could not account for myself … Where all was stationary my mother came first; she certainly had always been with me in a region which could never be known again. My father came next, more recognizably in my own time, yet rising out of changelessness like a rock out of the sea. My brothers and sisters were new creatures like myself, not in time (for time still sat on the wrist of each day with its wings folded), but in a vast, boundless calm.

Note the heraldic nature of Muir's account. His parents were fixed allegorical figures in a timeless landscape. George himself would write: *Much has been written about the heraldic element in Edwin Muir – his preoccupations with emblems, shields, fabulous beasts. The fact is that the landscape of Orkney looks heraldic – hillsides quartered with tilth and pasture, beasts against the sky, the solitary falcon above the hill. Everywhere there is the feeling of timelessness that heraldry seeks to impose on the chaotic flux.*

In the same review of *Loaves and Fishes*, John Wain said that GMB was a poet to be watched. Most critics, in fact, were of the opinion that this island poet with a distinctive voice was a promising newcomer. With the publication of his new collection, GMB's stock rose even further in Rose Street. Sydney Goodsir Smith, in his review of the new collection, said that out of the ruck 'a name is beginning to emerge'.

George Mackay Brown, the writer, was one to watch; George Brown, the man, was in turmoil over a relationship with a vivacious young woman who haunted the Rose Street pubs and the lives of some of Scotland's finest poets.

She was one to watch, too. She was a star.

CHAPTER 6

The Odd Couple

S he was stunning, she was vivacious, she radiated sexual energy, she was 'like a Botticelli painting'. And she was engaged to George Mackay Brown. For a short time, at least.

When Stella Cartwright first encountered George Brown, in the Abbotsford Bar, she thought the shy man in the roll-neck sweater was a fisherman. Well, the fisherman was hooked. Here is how he remembered that first fateful meeting: *this girl with the sweet-smelling honey-coloured skin and the sweep of bright hair was delightful to talk to. She laughed a great deal – not the empty half-nervous spasmodic spillings of many young women, but out of a deep well of humour that was forever renewing itself.*

Expensively educated and a bit spoiled, Stella was paraded around the Rose Street pubs at the age of 17 by her draughtsman father, who seemed to regard her as a kind of 'trophy' daughter. She was certainly a trophy some of the leaders of the Scottish Renaissance fought over.

They were an odd couple, this shy, coughing poet from a poor island background, and this upper-class lover of poetry and of certain poets. He was 36 years of age, she was 20.

Their next meeting was at a party at the MacCaigs' house. After midnight, the only guests left were Stella and George. *Even our hosts had gone to bed. I remember nothing of our dialogue but the laughter and delight of being in her company. At dawn Stella had run out of cigarettes – we spent a while looking here and there for a half-smoked one in an ashtray, or one forgotten in a packet. When the shops opened, I went out and bought cigarettes for Stella. It was a joy to give her things.*

Stella would be necessary to this story, of course, because she awoke in me a delight I had not known before. But she had a wider richness. Charles Senior the Glasgow poet wrote a poem about her called 'The Muse in Rose Street'. The title describes her perfectly; it was on poets that this extraordinary girl cast her spell. It could almost be said that all the contemporary poets in Scotland were in love with her, at one time or another. That future Scottish literary historian will have a busy winter's work, discovering how much poetry was written about Stella in the 1950s and 1960s.

She was very beautiful. She was intelligent, but not to the extent that it becomes a strain or a pose. She liked art and music and literature, but not sufficiently to make a kind of religion of it, as happens so often nowadays (for everyone must give allegiance to some 'reality' outside the cave of shadows that is oneself). What emanated from her was a kind of radiance, a rich essence on which poets and artists feed to sustain themselves. It is a rare mysterious innate quality, that cannot be acquired.

There was great happiness, simply to be with her: at Cramond, in her parents' garden at Juniper Green, window-gazing along Princes Street, drinking coffee in the Laigh, or Crawford's, travelling in buses and trains.

I think he liked her.

There is an idyllic, filmic quality about that description of George's early infatuation with Stella Cartwright. However, after his account of the effect Stella had upon him, he immediately alludes to a darker aspect of the story. *She suffered, because of her endowments. Beneath the radiance and the serenity was a deeply vulnerable person. The passing sorrows of the world she was compelled to endure with a double or triple intensity. She was open, to a dangerous extent perhaps, to the sufferings of others; she made instant instinctive response to a torn bird, or some old one too sick to do housework or shopping.*

In this way, Rose Street was a dangerous environment for her. She drank, to begin with, because she loved people, and a little whisky put glancing edges on stories and talk and poetry. She drank, in the end, to dull the pain of life. She was so loved by so many in those taverns that her glass was rarely empty for long. Alcohol, that at first is a place of laughter and heightened sensation, becomes in the end a prison.

It is a sorrow to think of her and what she might have been. She had all that was necessary to be a good wife and mother, and a leaven in any community ... It was not to be. The sweetness that most women keep for husbands and children she gave to the poets of Scotland, and to the helpless and the suffering.

I have problems with the gushing 'Muse of Rose Street' rhetoric of the poets, but I will come back to that later.

How did those who were not among the poetic giants of the land perceive Stella? I arranged to meet Stanley Roger Green, a charming man now into his eighties. In the 1950s, he was a rookie poet on the edges of the Rose Street scene.

'People thought Jack Cartwright was an idiot, taking this lovely girl round the pubs, showing her off,' he told me in Waterstone's tea room in Edinburgh. 'I always felt Stella was more sinned against than sinning. She didn't set out to ensnare or seduce anyone; she was just so full of life. The fact is that poets are a flirtatious lot. Sydney Goodsir Smith, Tom Scott and Norman MacCaig were outrageous flirts. Norman could charm the birds from the trees. He was very witty, but he could be cruel. Tom Scott was a very striking-looking man. He looked like a Border raider. He regarded himself almost as a secular prophet, an evangelist.'

In his book about the Rose Street scene, *A Clamjamfray of Poets: A Tale of Literary Edinburgh*, Green tells of his own relationship with Stella, whom he had first met in another Rose Street pub, Paddy's Bar. He wrote:

She at once asked me if I'd read *Crime and Punishment* and when I shook my head and admitted I could hardly spell the author's name, I was peremptorily told to repair this deficiency in my education without delay. 'It is an experience,' she stressed, looking solemn and meaningful.

And, I should add, as lovely and adorable as if she had just stepped out of a canvas by Botticelli, all ovals and curves, honey-coloured tresses loosely restrained by a gauzy snood, framing a face to haunt a poet's dreams. Which, as it happened, proved to be the case only too often in the years to come.

Alarm bells are ringing. What is it with these poets and Botticelli, and honey-coloured skin and tresses? Green now tantalises:

Then, after we had dealt with Dostoyevsky, and poetry and music … she asked if she could read my poems. She had heard quite good reports from the *Lines Review* grapevine. So we went to my pigsty of a bed-sit near the art college. Over coffees I learned that Stella had recently left her school (for young ladies), that her handsome father was an architect and artist and was pally with Norman and his circle. She had been so accustomed to arty parties since childhood that for a while she thought everyone's house was like that! Her laughter was spontaneous and musical, and I cancelled my initial impression she was a blue-stocking. Meanwhile it was late, the last tram-car had rattled off to the depot, and I couldn't afford a taxi to her home at Juniper Green.

The problem didn't arise. 'If you've no objection, I might as well sleep here,' she said, and my heart leapt; 'if you promise to keep to your side of the bed, that's to say. I haven't taken the plunge yet, you see. Sorry. I'm supposed to be staying with a school-friend, so she'll cover for me.' We undressed shyly without a word and lay in bed about a foot apart. A brief kiss was exchanged then she turned away and fell asleep. I did my best to comply with her proviso as wintry rains lashed the window-panes for hours.

Quite so. It took a poet to be in bed with Stella at all. It took a poet to describe the encounter in such an artful way: 'as wintry rains lashed the window-panes for hours'. In these words – linked to Stella's 'If you've no objection, I might as well sleep here' – a whole film script lies.

Some months after that night of bridled passion, Green was recovering from a tempestuous affair with a girl called June. As he reflected upon it, he realised that June and Stella had a lot in common. He wrote:

They were temperamental, given to sudden switches of mood, quickly bored by the humdrum and both had a sharp eye for fakes and pretentious behaviour. They were, in their different ways, disturbingly attractive females and exuded a latent sensuality that was like a dangerous scent, a feral musk. They shared another trait, one less easily defined, a sort of *carpe diem* fatalism, as if, in the words of Fitzgerald's Omar Khayam, 'The bird of time has but a little way to fly, and lo! the bird is on the wing …'. A sense of desperate haste to sample what life had to offer before the curtain came down. I must have intuitively recognised in Stella's nature the potentially damaging idiosyncrasies of June's, which is how I resisted her magnetism.

Even from this distance in time, there is an air of child-like vulnerability about Stella Cartwright. Sensitive to the world's ills, and bored with her less sophisticated peers, she inhabited a social milieu that could inflict great damage upon her. Looking at her in Rose Street, you want to shout 'Beware!' Tellingly missing from Moffat's painting, she is like a butterfly, somehow both on the edge of and at the centre of things. The men were drawn to her; and Stella, her glass regularly refilled, was bewitched and flattered by the high priesthood of modern Scottish poetry. Crucially, too, she was not a poet, and therefore not a threat intellectually. She bolstered the poets' egos and confirmed for them their power as males.

Reading various accounts of the Rose Street scene, I was struck by how masculine a world it was. In the late 1950s, largely unreconstructed Great Men were not subjected to serious challenge on matters to do with gender. It was a boozy, male-dominated, Scotch-fuelled, flirtatious, strutting scene. Saul Bellow's view that all a writer had to do to get a woman was to say he was a writer fitted that era.

I close my eyes and imagine the likes of Carol Ann Duffy, Kathleen Jamie, Liz Lochhead, Meg Bateman and Jackie Kay – five Scottish poets with substantial reputations – in Milne's Bar in that company. There would have been much-needed mayhem.

Why, then, was the glittering, sometimes exuberant Stella Cartwright drawn to the introverted, self-effacing George Brown?

It is impossible to explain this without describing what it was like to meet him. A decade and a half after his death, the sense of George Mackay Brown's presence is easier to conjure up than to describe.

I used to drop in and see him when I was in Stromness. He would hum, or sing, while the kettle boiled; the hot water would be poured into a china teapot, and the tea would be offered in a china cup. In conversation, he was pleasant and courteous. He would always ask after my wife and children, and was genuinely interested in what we were doing. He was an agreeable, humorous man (though one had to be alert to catch the humour sometimes).

'Bigsy' is a word used by Orcadians to describe someone who is rather pretentious and overblown; well, George was the opposite of bigsy. There was an endearing kindness about the man. I liked his shy manner. I noticed that he didn't much care to be looked at; when he caught your eye, he would look away quickly. When he said something that might be construed as being controversial, he would glance in your direction to catch your reaction, then avert his eyes. Despite his coyness, or maybe because of it, I was comfortable with him and enjoyed the visits.

When I visualise George, I see a certain wistfulness. A look of sadness, pain even, would visit him from time to time; yet the mournful shadows would soon be chased away by a disarming, boyish smile, with a hint of mischievousness.

Would he like water in his whisky? 'If there's room,' he would reply with a grin.

My guess is that it was precisely because he was so different from the others in the Rose Street bars that Stella was attracted to him. The fact that he was a socially awkward man with a quaint manner may have been part of his attraction.

He paid attention rather than played footsie. He was interested in what she had to say. No doubt he used her name a lot at the end of his soft, musical sentences. 'What do you think of that, Stella?'

He had an intriguing spiritual hinterland. He seemed to be a still centre of safety in the midst of exciting but dangerous waters. His craggy features and blue eyes were attractive. With enough whisky flowing through his veins, his humour and mimicry were a joy. And he was a coming man in the world of poetry: she had Sydney Goodsir Smith's word for that.

My sense of this was confirmed by Irene Dunsmuir, my informant about George's fleeting career as a roadman on the island of Rousay. Irene was about 10 years old when her family went to live close to the Browns in Stromness. She only really got to know George, who was more than twenty years her senior, when she moved away from Orkney. After college, she went to Edinburgh to work, and she met up with people who had Orkney connections, including would-be actor John Broom. She connected with George again, and the shy Orkney girl was introduced to the leaders of the Scottish Literary Renaissance in Milne's Bar. As she knew little about them, she was not overwhelmed.

I talked with Irene at her home in Stromness. In our conversations, I was impressed by her wisdom, gained over a life that has not always been easy. She has never spoken before about her relationship with the Rose Street scene – and in particular with Stella Cartwright.

'At that time, I never looked on George as a writer, other than the man who wrote for the *Orkney Herald*,' she told me. 'When you are 20, people over 40 are very old. I was always aware that George was my mother's friend rather than my friend, he was more her age group. I was fortunate to get to know a lot of the Rose Street gang through George. I went in with a fairly open mind. I felt quite at ease with them, and judged them in my own naïve way. I certainly wasn't influenced by who they were.

'I remember Hugh MacDiarmid. I wasn't just too sure of him; I think it was my age. It took me a good wee while to come round to MacDiarmid; I was a bit in awe of him. Communism was a fairly new word in my vocabulary at that time. It meant a Russian with a red flag, something to be scared of! I met MacDiarmid several times, but he was a distant kind of man. He was very, very dogmatic. That spoiled him, he was too dogmatic. I think I only took to him if we all had a drink – it relaxed things a bit.'

What about the others?

'I liked Norman MacCaig because he was a gentler being altogether. He was a very imposing man, he did take your attention.'

How did George fit into the Rose Street scene?

'Milne's Bar was really a small pub, full of beer-drinkers, mostly broke, a right Bohemia. George was very shy, even in that company, and he was very willing to listen. He and Sydney Goodsir Smith would end up in a corner on their own, deep in conversation, and George was all ears. He had an amazing memory. Say or write the smallest thing to George, and he would remember it if he felt it was important at all. He could pick out what was important and what wasn't – that was a big part of his gift. He was very turned on to other writers. He was very patient. He was interested in everybody else's work, and he was quick to recognise any wee hint of genius, anything out of the ordinary. George seemed to be able to pick out the ones who were going to make it.'

And Stella Cartwright?

'Stella was quite a character. George was very, very fond of her. She was the bright button in the box, and George no doubt would have been charmed, thrilled by the fact that she would pay attention to him. You can see why he was captivated. It was flattering for him.

'I liked Stella, I loved her. She was a lovely person. It's very difficult to describe Stella. She could be quite an imposing young woman, she could be a very angry young woman, she was a very proud young woman – and yet she was a modest person. She was very sensitive, willing to listen.'

She seemed to be a great favourite with all the poets?

'She was indeed. They were all in love with Stella at some point or another. They all seemed to flock to her. I've seen Stella in so many different moods, I've seen her so pleasant and charming and absolutely delightful, but at the turn of a switch she could go the other way. I think she felt a little bit frustrated, because she tried to write, but she was too influenced by too many people. She never found her own voice. And being in that kind of company was enough to turn anybody's head. She maybe came to expect too much of herself – in that field, you definitely have to crawl before you can walk. In that kind of company, people could take advantage of you, use you.'

Indeed they could.

Irene gave me some surprising information. She told me that she shared a flat with Stella in two different places, and that Stella was bridesmaid at her wedding.

'I moved into Naismith Place in Edinburgh with Stella and Sydney Goodsir Smith and John Broom, then I lived with them all down in a house in Dundas Street for a while. George visited there. It made a special bond between George and me, in a way. It deepened our friendship because I now knew a bigger circle of friends, and, once we were both back in Stromness, there were so many things and people we knew in common. We used to laugh and speak about all that.

'The flat in Dundas Street belonged to Sydney Goodsir Smith. Sydney spent a lot of his time at Dundas Street, and he certainly thought a great deal of Stella. He used to call me "Abigail"; I was the maidservant!

'I didn't know Stella's mother very well. She was just a lady who visited Dundas Street now and again, very disapprovingly. The Cartwrights reckoned they were a bit higher up the social scale. I often think it was Stella's breakaway from that kind of life that led her to Dundas Street. But her father, Jack, and she got on very well together. If you think on it from the Cartwrights' point of view, their daughter was a fairly young woman, and the situation she was getting into was not what they'd maybe hoped for their daughter, especially from the kind of social circle they were in. Her parents would regard that as Bohemian. They would have wanted her to marry well, preferably to another architect or banker.'

And Irene's wedding? A close eye had to be kept on Stella because her drink problem made her somewhat unreliable. The wedding turned out to be a real Orkney occasion.

'We weren't going to have a reception, but my brother insisted that we went to a hotel in the West End for lunch. The hotel was run by Orcadians. It turned out that Edinburgh Orkney was there – it ended up being quite an Orkney wedding! The Rose Street–Dundas

Street crowd were there, too. It wasn't really their scene, they weren't too happy out of their own territory. Sydney was there, and I think John Broom. We had planned this very quiet thing, and suddenly we had a full Orkney wedding on our hands!'

I asked Irene if she thought a George–Stella marriage would have worked. 'It would never have worked,' she said. 'Stella was such a complex character in a lot of ways. She could be so easy and yet … There's no doubt in my mind that George really loved her, and in a deep way.'

She also believed he would have been afraid of the commitment that a serious partnership would have demanded. 'When you do go into a deep and what you hope is a lasting relationship, you have expectations and demands. A woman tends to think, I'm not just your partner, I'm your friend, your confidante. She wants the lot, the full package. That would have been frightening to George. You couldn't go through life as friends – never mind being married – without having a disagreement about something. George would have shied clear of that.

'He knew how important his time on his own was, too. That would have been the selfish part of a relationship. Everyone likes a certain degree of privacy; maybe that privacy extends into your mind, that there are things that you regard as being private to yourself. Maybe George realised he couldn't afford the luxury of a wife.'

George had sometimes talked about having children. Would he have liked that? Irene thought it would have been fine in the realm of imagination, but not in the reality of his life as a writer. 'Possibly, at some stage in the thinking process you might turn your art into your babies, but before you know where you are it's too late to have the real thing. I'm sure that Stella would have married George, but he might have felt total commitment frightening.'

Stella comes over as a very sexual being. Would that have been intimidating for George?

'This is interesting now. I don't know if Stella was such a sexual being. She was searching for something that she never achieved. She dulled it with drink. She could drink, and then different things became a priority – i.e. where her next drink was coming from! I would say that Stella had problems with sexuality and commitment too.'

Irene's view, based on day-to-day knowledge of Stella, provides a new angle on the breathless sexual dynamics of Rose Street. To what extent has Stella Cartwright's public profile been defined and distorted by projections made by the frustrated alpha – or would-be alpha – males of the Scottish Renaissance?

When you look back on it, I asked Irene hesitantly, could you imagine yourself being married to George?

'No,' she replied firmly. 'Someone who married George would have to be completely selfless.'

When George was under pressure in a relationship, Irene told me, he used to go on binges. 'When it would stop, he would be home and in bed for a week. Was it ill-health that was putting him there, or was it "I'm getting into deep water here, slow down boy!"? Maybe the staying in bed was the cooling-down period – "They are encroaching on my space!"'

Every time I have talked with Irene Dunsmuir, she has given me a great deal to think about. Do women, I wonder, have a deeper understanding of George? And, indeed, of Stella?

Another perceptive woman, Morag MacInnes, has an interesting take on the subject. 'George wasn't happy at university,' she told me. 'What he was happy with was Rose Street. He was much more lonely than people think, and he was older again – younger students regard mature students as ancient! Then Stella waylaid him, and that caused such a lot of pain and anger in him. He wanted to be what she wanted him to be; but he couldn't, and it's ever so sad.'

I asked Morag why she thought women were attracted to George. 'I don't think he was gay, I think he was asexual,' Morag said. 'Women get fascinated by hermits and asexual people, for some of the same reasons that they are attracted to gay men. It's a challenge, on one level, because they think "I can fix him". It's a real impulse that women have: "No woman's ever been able to touch this guy, but I'll do it!" On another level – it's a safe relationship, to some extent, precisely because sex isn't a big part of it. I think there was a bit of that in Stella. Her alcoholism often led her into ill-thought-out sexual adventures – but that wasn't the case in her relationship with George. It was a see-saw – when the drink made her too needy, George withdrew. Crucially, he learned how to be controlled. She didn't. His drinking came in binges, like lots of alcoholics, and then there would be a withdrawal and an abstinence, and frenzied work to absolve himself. Religion fed into that, too.'

It may also be that George's 'monkishness', and the possibility that he might be celibate, were also both attractions and challenges for women.

Could George and Stella ever have been able to work things out between them? Morag didn't think so: 'The relationship with Stella was very poignant, because it could never have come to anything. So it resolved itself in an almost poetic, celibate kind of end. George turned Stella into a metaphor, Stella for star, because then she was nice and safe, just like the Virgin Mary. Writing letters to her was a way of holding things at a distance. By doing that, you can live your life in a more ritualised way.'

It would hardly be surprising if his bouts with TB gave him a distaste for the physical. That is not to say that George did not get into bed with Stella. One woman in Stromness, who is an entirely reliable witness, told me about a party she attended in an Edinburgh house. Feeling hungry early in the morning, she went to look for food. She opened one door and discovered George and Stella in bed. George shouted at her to get out. But – as Stanley Roger Green has already established – being in bed with Stella was quite different from bedding Stella.

One man who knew George as a student was David Campbell, a charming, kilted storyteller with a ponytail. I have known David for some years. As a BBC producer, he had encountered George quite a bit; but he also encountered him when both were students. We talked over a beer in Milne's Bar.

'I found myself in the same year as George at university,' he told me. 'I was considerably younger. What used to amaze all of us was that, while most of us hated Old English and Anglo-Saxon, George used to say: "Oh, I really like that, I like to get to the roots of things". He was crazy about Beowulf and Gawain, and the Dream of the Rood: all these things were his cup of tea.

'I'm quite forthright and mischievous, and I tried to be that with George – but I could never really get anything out of him to do with sex. I had the feeling that one way or another it was something that frightened him or there was not such a huge impulsion – people vary hugely in their drives. He said to me that he looked like Pinocchio! If you really feel uncertain about your physical appearance, any serious illness that leaves you feeling weak takes away any sexual "attack" that you have in life. I never heard him make any kind of statement that would be interpreted beyond liking people. Never. Most men at some stage will say something about a woman being really attractive, but George didn't do that. He wasn't flirtatious in that way.'

The engagement in the summer of 1960 was short-lived. Nearly two years later, Stella would write a very sad note to George (who was by this time back in Orkney) in response to a letter in which George had expressed his hurt over something Stella had said or done. 'My dearest George,' Stella wrote on 21 March 1962, 'Your lovely letter filled me with a deep sadness. I was never unaware that I had hurt you but probably never flattered myself by realising how much I had done so. I truly suffer a great deal whenever I know I have hurt anyone, so to have wounded someone I love as much as you makes me feel utterly wretched. All I want is to help people and give them happiness – yet I seem to bring such sorrow. As you said recently, we might have been married for almost two years now. Did you not find me physically attractive, honey?'

That final, needy, plaintive note is so sad. The wounds inflicted on George Brown's body and his psyche cost him dear.

That body and that psyche let him down in 1960, necessitating a return to Orkney for rest and recuperation. His mother was glad to attend upon him with her usual loving care. 'Dear, dear George,' Stella had written on 15 March, 'you are such a good and gentle soul, and a real delight to me. I am missing you already. Thank you for saying such sweet things in your letter – it makes me both glad and sad for I want always to be kind to you and make you happy, but there are things which can hurt you and I do not control the universe. But I pray you will be happy, sweetheart and have enough peace within you to tackle everything and grow stronger through every difficulty. Bless you for being you. With my love, Stella. PS Write soon!'

Two days later, Stella wrote: 'I will write you a long letter at the week-end. I will not get drunk on Saturday dearest George because I will be thinking mostly of you. You are a presence in my heart, and do not ever quite disappear. I have been very unhappy very often sweet, and you, I think, have not always bubbled with joy. But you, by being you, and by loving me, have changed a lot of that ... We have both seen enough insecurity and felt enough of it, to know how cancerous it can be, but if we really love each other wholly we will grow beyond all that, and exist within ourselves and our love, warmly and happily ... My own dear George please always tell me how you feel physically or spiritually because I care about you and all your joys and sorrows. If you are unhappy or depressed or unwell I will want to try and help you however I can.'

George's spirits were lifted by an event in Orkney of great spiritual importance. The fabric of the Italian Chapel, which was now a place of pilgrimage, had been deteriorating for some years. In July 1958, Father J. Ryland Whitaker, who was based in Kirkwall, initiated the formation of a preservation committee, which contained members of different Christian denominations. Some necessary repairs were carried out. A BBC programme about the Chapel was broadcast in Italy, and its inspirational artist, Domenico Chiocchetti, was traced to Moena, a village in the Dolomites. In March 1960, Chiocchetti came to Orkney for three weeks, a visit funded by the BBC and the PoW Chapel Preservation Committee. Chiocchetti, who restored the Chapel's artwork, was deeply moved by the whole experience.

When the Chapel had been completed in 1945, George had written an article in the *Orkney Herald*, in which he fired another broadside at Calvinism. He also made a scathing comparison: *The*

Italian soldier is a far more spiritual being than his British counterpart. Where the English captive would build a theatre or a canteen to remind him of home, the Italian, without embarrassment, with careful devout hands, erects a chapel.

GMB makes an amusing point here about the building of a theatre or a canteen, but I'm tempted to add – and indeed will give in to the temptation – that the same unworthy, apparently unspiritual British soldier whom George denigrates fought body and soul against the vicious Fascism which was disfiguring Europe, and by so doing helped to preserve freedom of worship.

On the last Sunday of Signor Chiocchetti's visit, 10 April 1960, around 200 people of all denominations crowded into the little chapel for a rededication service. In his homily, Father Whitaker said:

> Of the buildings clustering on Lamb Holm in wartime only two remain, this Chapel and the statue of St George. All the things which catered for material needs have disappeared, but the two things which catered for spiritual needs still stand. In the heart of human beings the truest and most lasting hunger is for God.

From Moena there came a gift of a carved figure of the crucified Christ. It remains to this day in front of the Italian Chapel. It is interesting that two of the buildings most loved by Orcadians, St Magnus Cathedral and the Italian Chapel, stand as testimonies not only to Catholic inspiration, but also to ecumenical co-operation. The artist charged with responsibility for the Chapel's artwork over many years, Gary Gibson, is a member of the Presbyterian congregation that worships in St Magnus Cathedral.

By now, George was well enough to return to Edinburgh to sit his finals, and in July 1960 he graduated Master of Arts with second-class honours. At the graduation ceremony in the McEwan Hall, Mary Brown looked on with pride as her 38-year-old son received his degree certificate. How proud John Brown, the postman of Hamnavoe, would have been.

Because his course at Edinburgh University had been funded under the National Teachers' Training Scheme, George enrolled at Moray House College of Education in September. As part of his training, he taught at Boghall School in Bathgate. For a man who recoiled from any form of public performance, the experience was traumatising. He knew in his heart that teaching was not for him, but how could he withdraw from the teaching course? His body responded to his 'get me out of here' prayer, and he suffered a collapse. In November 1960, the university doctor arranged for him to go to Tor-na-Dee Sanatorium, near Aberdeen.

Living in the sanatorium was preferable to facing a classroom full of Bathgate youngsters. He had the leisure time to read and write again. 'Last week I did a short story with an Orkney setting for the fourth centenary of the Reformation, in which of course the whole sordid conspiracy is shown up in repellent detail,' he wrote to Ernest Marwick. 'I hope to get an X certificate for it – maybe a trial at the Old Bailey.' On 13 January 1961, he wrote to Marwick from Tor-na-Dee saying he was sorry about the news that the *Orkney Herald* was closing down. He added: 'I am quite well again. The cavity left by pneumonia has closed up, and in fact never was infected with the tubercle. There must be something tough about Brown, hidden deep down, a spring that keeps bubbling up when all seems lost. I should have been dead for about a decade, by all the medical rules.'

Although their engagement was over by this time, Stella Cartwright wrote anxious letters to him. The patient was not entirely responsive. 'My dearest George,' Stella wrote, 'are you trying to give me a taste of my own medicine by remaining enigmatically silent, or are you angry with me, or worse than all are you ill?'

George was refreshed as much by his reading and writing as by his medical treatment. It was like a Sabbath for him – a 'time out' for the works of the imagination and for reflection upon his own life. It confirmed for him – if he needed any confirmation – that writing was what he was meant to do for the rest of his life. Approaching his 40th birthday, in addition to feeling guilty about the effects of his behaviour on his mother, he reproached himself for having wasted so much of his life. It was his Richard II moment: 'I wasted time, and now doth time waste me'.

He also recognised his craving for solitude. He knew that he needed well-defended space and time if he was to fulfil his vocation as a writer – almost certainly as a celibate writer. The crisis provoked by another breakdown in health, and the time it afforded him for contemplation, made him sure he wanted to place that vocation within the security and richness of a well-grounded religious system, which for him could now only be Roman Catholicism. The sheer scariness of the Protestant alternative, with its strong emphasis on individual decision-making before God, meant that it could not compete with the emotional security of an all-embracing Catholic Mother Church. George's attraction to Roman Catholicism was an intuitive and aesthetic impulse that had grown stronger over two decades – but he had not yet taken decisive action.

Sabbaticals do not last forever. Dues must be paid. In March 1961, George was back, trembling, in the Bathgate classroom. It was – as he knew it would be, and probably contrived to make it so – a disaster. Teenage pupils could easily spot weakness or unease, and their student teacher's heart was not in the job. Chaos was the result when George was left alone with a class. The authorities and the student came to the same conclusion: George Mackay Brown would not a teacher make. Not a schoolteacher, at any rate.

George's decision disappointed his teacher brother Richard, who was always known as Norrie. Allison Dixon, Norrie's daughter, told me: 'I think my father felt that, if he had the time that George had to just read, he might be a writer too. The thing that disappointed my father most was George giving up on teaching so easily. I think he felt that it wasn't a very good example to set us. I can remember feeling like running away from my first teaching practice, and yet you can understand that George wouldn't have coped. He was too fragile.'

But what could he do? After four decades, his health was unstable and he was distinctly lacking in qualifications for any job. The royalties from his poetry would, as he often said, not feed a cat. There was nothing else for it but to head back home to Orkney, where his long-suffering mother was ready and waiting.

He was also going home in a different sense, to a different mother. He would become a Roman Catholic.

In Edinburgh, doing research for this book, I go into Milne's Bar. Memorabilia cover its walls. A portrait of Hugh MacDiarmid accompanies his poem 'Old Wife in High Spirits in an Edinburgh Pub'. Sydney Goodsir Smith is pictured, sitting, cigar in mouth. Norman MacCaig's poem, 'November Night', is beside his portrait.

There is also a painting of the outside of Milne's Bar. 'Ten o'clock was chuck-out time in the mid-Fifties,' says the accompanying text, 'but it didn't stop the arguments spilling out into Rose Street.' The characters emerging into Rose Street are Hugh MacDiarmid, Norman MacCaig and a rather shadowy George Mackay Brown.

I move over to the snug, and sit and sip my beer. The inscription in this room says: 'So many writers and students wanted to sup at Milne's Pub in the late 1950s it was decided that the poets' circle were to be given their own room at the far side of the bar. The left-wing politics discussed inside earned it the nickname The Little Kremlin.'

As I sip my pint, while revellers clink glasses and shout, a film about Milne's Bar in the late 1950s starts in my head. I hear the passionate arguments, dominated by a piercing Hugh MacDiarmid and a loud Tom Scott, while a smiling Norman MacCaig slips in brilliant, sometimes savage, interjections. George Mackay Brown and Sydney Goodsir Smith are engaged in close conversation. Stella Cartwright, whisky glass in hand, watches them both. All of the poets, at some stage, fix their gaze on Stella.

I am more and more repelled by all this 'Muse' talk. It strikes me as both sexist and exploitative. The romanticising of a vulnerable young woman, who is increasingly dependent on alcohol and who can never live up to the drink-fuelled fantasies of the poets, is beyond distasteful. Or am I just too Presbyterian and judgemental for my own good?

Put together Stella's youthful, teasing beauty with sexually frustrated, middle-aged, sometimes self-obsessed writers; add breathless, impossibly idealised accounts of an adoring and adored 'Muse'; then throw in liberal quantities of alcohol: all the elements are there for an emotional crash, with Stella Cartwright as the principal casualty. Our already physically and emotionally damaged man from Orkney will crawl out from the wreckage, bearing wounds that will never heal.

I think of the haunting verdict of Stanley Roger Green, spoken to me in Waterstone's tea room: 'It was tragic. They were both lonely. George and Stella clutched each other in order to save each other, and they went down all the quicker.'

I feel sad. I slip out, through the 'chuck-out' door of the painting, into Rose Street, accompanied by Hugh MacDiarmid, Norman MacCaig and George Mackay Brown. I wish I could ask them questions.

CHAPTER 7

A
Knox-ruined
Nation?

It is evening in Rackwick in late autumn, 1961. Ian and Jean MacInnes, as they often do, are spending the weekend on Hoy. They make a social call at a cottage belonging to Sylvia Wishart. George Mackay Brown is staying with Sylvia for the weekend; they have both been drinking and are rather merry. They greet the MacInneses with some unexpected news.

'Guess what?' says George, 'We've both decided to become Catholics!'

So, that is how George Mackay Brown became a Roman Catholic? No, of course not. He had good reasons for finally coming to this point of decision. Nevertheless, the cameo embodies an aspect of GMB's life and character, and should be placed alongside the more high-minded, well-rehearsed narrative of George's journey to Catholicism.

Sylvia Wishart was brought up next door to the Browns. A talented artist who underestimated her own ability – George had described her in the *Orkney Herald* as 'a gifted child artist of whom Orkney will not be ashamed in the years to come' – she was persuaded by Ian MacInnes, himself an artist of considerable skill, to study at Gray's School of Art in Aberdeen. She flourished there.

When she was a postgraduate student, she visited George's ward at Tor-na-Dee Sanatorium. As the visits became more regular, a friendship developed between the two, based on respect for each other's art, and increasingly on mutual affection and even attraction. Sylvia, who was fifteen years younger than George, also had a great love for Rackwick, and she spent many weekends at the cottage which she had had restored. Like him, she was interested in exploring, in her art and in her life, the spiritual dimension of human life.

Given the views he had expressed quite early on – and the fact that he had kept newspaper and magazine articles about prominent Catholics, published in the 1940s – it is not at all clear why it took George so long to make the move. He simply said that no Scotsman takes precipitate action. That is a bit lame.

Was it because Catholicism was seen as something strange, alien even, in Stromness, and it required courage to make such a controversial public move? He would write in his autobiography: *We knew little about Catholicism. There were no Catholics in the little town I was brought up in, except an Italian ice cream seller and an Irish barber … The Orcadians had never been 'enthusiasts' in religion; and I never heard Catholics denounced or reviled; still, there was something sinister in the very word Catholic; all the words that clustered about it – rosary, pope, confession, relics, purgatory, monks, penance – had the same sinister connotations. I can't remember that we were ever instructed to hate Catholicism or Catholics; it was just that Catholicism and its mysteries lay outside our pale, and it was better so. We Presbyterians, so it was implied, were enlightened by comparison, and had travelled on far beyond mediaeval idolatry and superstition.*

I doubt very much that the minority status of Roman Catholicism in Stromness was the reason for George's indecision. He could be thrawn; and strangeness would probably be more of an attraction than a barrier. Or was the delay down to a worry that his Free Presbyterian mother might disapprove of any move in the direction of Rome? This is more plausible. But, if this was the reason, why make the step in 1961? My guess is that his spell in Tor-na-Dee, where he had time to reflect on his life – including his broken engagement and his failure as a teacher – pushed him towards decision.

Whatever the reason or reasons, the time has come to put George Mackay Brown's journey towards Roman Catholicism into a more comprehensive frame.

There are two key polarities: GMB's increasing distaste for, and even detestation of, the Presbyterianism of his forebears, and his growing attraction to, and love for, Roman Catholicism. His early revulsion against what he saw as the destructiveness of the Reformation in Scotland can be seen in markings on the subject that he made on books in his house. The impact of the reading of Francis Thompson's poem, 'The Hound of Heaven', upon him has already been noted, as has the fact that his attraction to Catholicism was confirmed by his reading of the *Orkneyinga Saga* – especially the story of St Magnus – in 1946. I have already drawn attention to what I believe is a key marker on the road of disenchantment with the Calvinist world-view – namely, his letter to Ernest Marwick of 1947 in which he expresses his disgust at the Calvinism of his day. The passages in his *Orkney Herald* columns in which he rails against what he regards as the malign effects of Protestantism are key pieces of evidence.

George's linking of judgemental small-town gossip to the culture of Presbyterianism, whether justified or not, certainly made his growing aversion to Presbyterianism highly charged. It is also, in my view, grounded, much more than has been acknowledged, in the writing of Edwin Muir. As I read again Muir's *Collected Poems* and his *Autobiography*, and looked at George's journalism and early religious writings, I became more aware of Muir's influence on the Stromness man's religious world-view. George, I believe, 'inhaled' some of his mentor's spiritual tropes.

Muir attacks Calvinism for turning the Christian mystery of the Incarnation into a set of wordy creeds and confessions. A shorthand version of how he understands the matter might run like this: the eternal Word of God became flesh in Palestine, in the shape of a Jewish teacher who was known to history as Jesus of Nazareth, and to theology as Jesus Christ (Jesus the Anointed One). Under the baleful influence of Calvin, the embodied Word has been unmade, sundered into banal pieces. The Word that became flesh has been reduced to mere human words.

The two opening stanzas of Muir's poem, 'The Incarnate One', say a great deal:

> The windless northern surge, the sea-gull's scream,
> And Calvin's kirk crowning the barren brae.
> I think of Giotto the Tuscan shepherd's dream,
> Christ, man and creature in their inner day.
> How could our race betray
> The Image, and the Incarnate One unmake
> Who chose this form and fashion for our sake?
>
> The Word made flesh here is made word again,
> A word made word in flourish and arrogant crook.
> See there King Calvin with his iron pen,
> And God three angry letters in a book,
> And there the logical hook
> on which the Mystery is impaled and bent
> Into an ideological instrument.

In Muir's understanding, John Calvin, with his iron pen and his angry God, has turned the central Christian mystery into a controlled and controlling ideology. Muir sees Calvinism as being as ideological and repressive as Marxism. The poem goes on:

> There's better gospel in man's natural tongue,
> And truer sight was theirs outside the Law
> Who saw the far side of the Cross among
> The archaic peoples in their ancient awe,
> In ignorant wonder saw
> The wooden cross-tree on the bare hillside,
> Not knowing that there a God suffered and died.
>
> The fleshless word, growing, will bring us down,
> Pagan and Christian man alike will fall,
> The auguries say, the white and black and brown,

The merry and sad, theorist, lover, all
Invisibly will fall:
Abstract calamity, save for those who can
Build their cold empire on the abstract man.

A soft breeze stirs and all my thoughts are blown
Far out to sea and lost. Yet I know well
The bloodless word will battle for its own
Invisibly in brain and nerve and cell.
The generations tell
Their personal tale: the One has far to go
Past the mirages and the murdering snow.

In Muir's eyes, pagans were more enlightened – because less tainted by theological corruption – than Calvinists. He sees the dilution of the mysterious divine Word into bland bloodlessness as a catastrophe, one which ultimately undermines resistance to the politics of totalitarianism. Muir had seen totalitarianism up close in Europe, and he felt that Protestantism was ill-equipped to provide spiritual resources for the struggle against ideological despotism.

I am not so sure about that. Take Germany, home of the Reform movement. While many German Christians did capitulate, the courageous and costly stances made by Protestant theologians like Dietrich Bonhoeffer, Martin Niemöller and the other members of the Confessing Church who openly opposed Hitler and the Nazis, were heroic. Niemöller is famous for his public warning against refusing to speak up against tyranny: 'They came first for the Communists, and I didn't speak up because I wasn't a Communist; then they came for the Jews, and I didn't speak up because I wasn't a Jew; then they came for the trade unionists, and I didn't speak up because I wasn't a trade unionist; then they came for me, and by that time no-one was left to speak up'.

Bonhoeffer, who had called Hitler 'the anti-Christ' in 1933, was executed in Flossenburg concentration camp in 1945. Karl Barth, the greatest Protestant theologian of the twentieth century, was another leader who took a courageous stance against the Nazis in the 1930s. Hailed by Pope Pius XII as the most important theologian since

Thomas Aquinas, Barth had to leave Germany in 1935 after he refused to swear allegiance to Adolf Hitler. He had also been influential in the writing of the Barmen Declaration, which argued that German Christians should stand up for Christ and oppose the influence of other 'lords', such as Hitler.

The Roman Catholic record in relation to publicly opposing the Nazis shows a similar mixture of heroism and complicity. Father Maximilian Mary Kolbe is a good example of bravery and self-sacrifice. In Auschwitz, he took the place of a condemned man who was married with children. After his execution, the story of his unselfish act spread throughout the camp. One of the prisoners commented: 'In those conditions ... in the midst of a brutalization of thought and feeling and words such as had never before been known, man indeed became a ravening wolf in his relations with other men. And into this state of affairs came the heroic self-sacrifice of Father Maximilian.' The Polish priest was canonised in 1982.

Much as I admire both Muir and GMB as writers, I am troubled by their lack of rigour in both theology and history. I do not think it is an exaggeration to say that Edwin Muir was fixated on Calvinism to the point of obsession. Calvinism was the dominating element of his continual worrying over the centuries-old problem of determinism versus human freedom. This gnawing concern runs through his work. (I was interested to learn, later, that the person who knew Edwin best, Willa Muir, used the vocabulary of 'irrational obsession' to describe her husband's preoccupation with the theology and culture of Calvinism.)

One of Muir's greatest poems is 'Scotland in 1941', with its memorable opening lines: 'We were a tribe, a family, a people. / Wallace and Bruce guard now a painted field, / And all may read the folio of our fable, / Peruse the sword, the sceptre and the shield'. The poet sees the radical Scottish Reformation of 1560 as setting in motion a period of decline in the nation's life. He deftly paints a romantic picture of life in Scotland before the Reformation 'Fall' – 'A simple sky roofed in that rustic day' – and castigates leaders of the Scottish Reformation such as John Knox and Andrew Melville. In Muir's eyes, the consequences of the Scottish Reformation both made Scotland a nation, and robbed Scotland of a nation. Calvinism, having stripped bare the altars of Scotland, also had, he was convinced, a destructive effect on culture. The decline is inexorable: 'Now smoke and dearth and money everywhere, / Mean heirlooms of each fainter generation, / and mummied housegods in their musty niches, / Burns and Scott, sham bards in a sham nation, / And spiritual defeat wrapped warm in riches, / No pride but pride of pelf'.

This is controversial stuff. Robert Burns and Walter Scott, with their synthetic Scots, are 'sham bards in a sham nation'. Well, well. Muir's account of Scotland's peculiar Eden and Fall is eloquent and searing. But is it true?

GMB certainly agreed with Muir about Presbyterian verbosity. Like his father before him, he was unimpressed by the words he heard from the pulpits of Stromness. He also assented to Muir's thesis that the Reformation sparked a decline in Scottish life and culture.

Muir's biography of Knox, *John Knox: Portrait of a Calvinist*, is a biting piece of work. The Orkney man's Knox is an unremitting tyrant with few redeeming features. In a letter to his friend Sydney Schiff, Muir said of the biography that it was

> more particularly written for the purpose of making some breach in the enormous reverence in which Knox has been held and is still held in Scotland, a reverence which I had to fight with too in my early years (so that I really feel quite strongly about it) and which has done and is doing a great deal of harm.

Whether or not John Knox was held in enormous reverence in Scotland in 1929 when Muir wrote the letter is a matter for debate; uncritical adulation of Knox was certainly not the norm in the 1950s. As I read Muir's biography, I was struck by its lack of balance. It is high on rhetoric and low on contextual analysis. Muir gives the game away in the preface to his book. Despite the fact that *John Knox* is the book's title, he says: 'With the historical figure I am not particularly concerned, and I have filled in only such a rough sketch of the sixteenth-century Scottish background as I thought necessary to make the Calvinist comprehensible'.

This is an astonishing statement for a biographer to make. When Edwin Muir and George Mackay Brown meet on the subject of John Knox, scouring their work for facts is a task which throws up scant results. After all, why bother with facts when you can make the story up out of your head and keep your prejudices intact? For all his flaws, John Knox, one of the makers of modern Scotland, deserves a better-researched and more profound commentary than that offered by Edwin Muir.

It is significant that, in the prologue to GMB's first published collection of poems, *The Storm*, for which Muir wrote such a generous preface, GMB immediately turned his attention to Knox and the Scottish Reformation:

> For the islands I sing
> > and for a few friends;
> not to foster means
> > or be midwife to ends.

> For Scotland I sing,
> > the Knox-ruined nation
> that poet and saint
> > must rebuild with their passion.

The Knox-ruined nation? Well, maybe. There is no evidence that George ever read a word of Knox. (That, of course, does not mean that he was wrong about him.) The Scottish Reformer is a bit of a bogeyman for GMB, a symbol for everything he hates. GMB describes the Scottish Reformation as 'Knox's wild Hogmanay'. It is a brilliant phrase; but the Reformation did not happen simply because some crazed characters decided to stage a rebellion. It happened at least partly because the Catholic Church was in need of reform. The leading Reformers in the early period of the Protestant movement were Catholic priests who saw what they were doing as attempting to restore what had been lost, rather than to create something new and separate. In Scotland, as on the continent of Europe, there were good reasons why the Reformation became a popular movement.

To understand Knox, it is necessary to know something of his context. Ordained to the Catholic priesthood in 1536, he was influenced by humanist learning and the growing Reform movement in Europe. Like his fellow Reformers, he felt that the original simplicity of the gospel of Christ was being obscured by a Church that was obsessed with worldly power and status.

On the run, Knox was captured by the French and made to work as a galley slave for two years. After his release from the galleys in 1549, he became a minister of the Church of England, which was undergoing its own reformation. When Mary Tudor, a zealous Catholic, ascended to the throne in 1553, Knox departed England for continental Europe. He eventually moved to Geneva, where he came under the influence of John Calvin. He returned to Scotland in 1559 when Mary of Guise was ruling as Queen of France and Scotland.

Believing that all were equal in the sight of God, Knox refused to bow the knee to people because of their rank. He supported Martin Luther's doctrine of 'the priesthood of all believers', which asserted that every person had a ministry, not just those who were ordained. The Scots preacher with an English accent preached fiery sermons around Scotland, winning support for the Reformed cause, while Mary's French troops tried but failed to defeat the English-backed Protestants. Mary of Guise died in June 1560, and in August of that year Scotland was declared Protestant by an Act of Parliament.

Knox was a very uncomfortable radical. He was not, perhaps, the first choice for company down at the tavern – although he was a more convivial character than the stereotypes allow, and certainly not teetotal. When he was a 51-year-old widower, and regarded as a Scottish hero, he married 17-year-old Margaret Stewart, daughter of a Protestant aristocrat.

Knox wanted to see an egalitarian Kirk, one which would, in the words from the 1560 Scots Confession, seek to 'save the lives of the innocent, repress tyranny, and defend the oppressed'.

117

The Reformation in Scotland was achieved with much less violence than elsewhere in Europe. The most notable exception was the assassination of Cardinal Beaton in St Andrews in 1546. Beaton could hardly be represented as an innocent saint, given his role in the killing of leading Reformer George Wishart in St Andrews earlier that year.

Could Scotland be just as legitimately described as a 'Cardinal Beaton-ruined nation?' In *Reformation: The Dangerous Birth of the Modern World,* Dr Harry Reid examines some old stereotypes. Here is how he characterises John Knox:

> He learned much from Calvin during his time in Geneva, yet he was never a zealous follower of the Frenchman; for example, he was much more radical in his belief in the legitimacy of revolt against tyrants. Knox was emphatically not the killjoy of popular caricature. Despite his ill-advised 'blast of the trumpet' against rule by women, he was always something of a ladies' man. He appreciated wine and good fellowship … He was a social as well as a religious visionary, and the blueprint that he and five colleagues drew up for the new Scotland was centuries ahead of its time in its democratic integrity and its emphasis on education and social welfare.

To help me look further at these issues, I went to see the eminent Scottish Catholic historian Professor Tom Devine, whose magnum opus, *The Scottish Nation,* became a best-seller. I wanted to know what he made of GMB's phrase 'the Knox-ruined nation'.

Devine was more equivocal than GMB. 'I wouldn't say it was ruination,' he said. 'I would say it was probably diversion into certain channels. It's quite remarkable, when you look at the period over the late sixteenth, seventeenth and early eighteenth centuries, to see the dearth in science and philosophy. I think it would be very hard to argue against the view that, but for the long-term impact of the Knoxian revolution in education, you wouldn't have had the Enlightenment flowering of the eighteenth century in the particular form it took. So, in that sense, I think it was a major factor in Scottish development, and a positive factor, arguably. The three great influences on the making of modern Scotia were the Reformation, industrialisation/ urbanisation as a totality, and the Empire. I wouldn't include the Enlightenment, because I think the European Enlightenment was just as important as the Scottish dimension.

'I think it's easy to understand why the Reformation is now un-fashionable; it's more difficult to understand why something like the Enlightenment, which wasn't even known about until the last thirty years in terms of popular culture, is just so popular. Obviously it panders well to our modern secular society, which again totally distorts it, because it was essentially a Christian Enlightenment. You could argue that the particular "colour" of the Scottish Enlightenment could not have been there without the Reformation. There were aspects of the Scottish Enlightenment which were specifically Scottish rather than simply being the European Enlightenment in Scotland. A shaper of that kind of development was undoubtedly the Reformation and its long-term effects.'

What about the Catholic Church in Scotland at the time of the Reformation? 'As far as the Scottish Catholic Church in the period was concerned,' said Devine, 'there certainly were attempts to reform from within, but it was too little, too late. The striking thing about mid-sixteenth-century Scottish Catholicism is the incredible speed of collapse. The Scottish Reformation was virtually bloodless, and that wasn't necessarily because of the kid gloves of the Reformers. It was because the Old Church didn't seem to ... well, its spine was broken. It didn't seem to have the capacity. There wasn't any kind of national counter-revolutionary process, so I think one would have to acknowledge – and I say this from a Papist perspective – that the Old Faith in Scotland was pretty rotten from within. And it didn't take much to push the whole rotting edifice over.

'The other thing to bear in mind is that obviously the Reformers consisted of those who were former Catholics, including former Catholic priests such as John Knox, so one of the reasons why there was a fairly bloodless transition might be to do with the very strong kindred and associational relationships there were in Scottish society.'

How would he characterise John Knox?

'I think I would be quite sympathetic. Knox had courage, and I think he was … I suppose the modern term is "very focused". He could have been a bit more flexible – yet, if he'd been a bit more flexible, he wouldn't have been a revolutionary! That's the conundrum. The other thing that's very important is that we now know that a lot of the things that we used to associate with Knox are totally false. We know that Knox's attitudes – and indeed the attitude of all the Reformers – to the sensual arts was quite different from what we had previously assumed. Some of the things that we assumed about Knox and the Reformers were not really in place until the 1630s, 1640s.

'The statues let Knox down! Especially the one at New College. Knox liked a good drink. If you read what scholars have said about him, and then look at that statue, it's almost a metaphorical inverse, and that is the image that's constantly portrayed when Knox's name comes up. It's fascinating the way fashion changes, especially in terms of heroes. I was recently a member of a panel which was responsible for bringing the "Top 100 Scots Ever" down to a shortlist of thirty. Knox wasn't even in the top 100! Today's context is not fertile for a generous reassessment of the realities of the Knox persona. It's back to this whole issue of the stereotyping of the Scottish Reformation, which I have argued against in print.'

I asked Professor Devine about George Mackay Brown's position. 'From my limited knowledge, I would go along with the view that GMB was probably thinking about the more aesthetic area, and there he may well have a point. But I think human endeavour is broader and deeper than the aesthetic area, and in terms of the extraordinary achievements in science, medicine and philosophy, both natural and moral, then that's definitely part of the equilibrium.'

There is no doubt that, in their impatient desire to rid the Church of what they saw as idolatrous art which contravened the commandment against making graven images, the Reformers, or at least some of them, removed or destroyed some fine visual art. Stained-glass windows and representations of traditional religious images such as the Virgin and Child were disfigured or smashed, causing grief to

Catholic believers who had found inspiration and solace from such well-loved aids to devotion. With their fierce commitment to the pure Word over against the Image, some Reformed preachers incited their followers to go on cleansing missions which were seen as attacks on the piety of believers, many of them unlettered and poor.

Yet, to portray the Reformers as simply an iconoclastic and intolerant rabble wreaking destruction on an unwilling Scotland does justice neither to the humanistic learning and desire for genuine religious faith of the Catholic leading lights of the Reformation period in Europe, nor to the depth of the yearning for religious renewal among many ordinary believers. What was also welcomed was the strong commitment of the Reform movement to social action on behalf of the poor. 'Social disorder', said Calvin, 'is first and foremost disdain for the poor and oppression of the weak.'

Still on the John Knox trail, I took my microphone to the Edinburgh home of George Rosie, an award-winning journalist, author, broadcaster and television documentary-maker. He began the interview by saying that he wanted to make it clear that he was 'an unrepentant atheist'. So, what, I asked him, did he think of the description of Scotland as a 'Knox-ruined nation'?

'I think it's bullshit sentimentality,' he said. 'In general, there's an Anglo-royalist cast to British popular history – not real history, but popular history. An image has been created – especially in this century – to the effect that all Knox ever did was to upset poor dear Mary Queen of Scots. But poor dear Mary Queen of Scots was a fairly hardline Catholic who'd been brought up by the Guises in France, who engineered the anti-Protestant Massacre of St Bartholomew's Day in 1572.

'We talk today about Knox's anti-Catholicism as if he was complaining about a twenty-first-century churchman like Cardinal Keith O'Brien; Knox was talking about the Catholic absolutism of the sixteenth century when the Catholic Church was burning people for reading the Bible. It was a different world then. In my view, the Renaissance begat the Reformation and the Reformation begat the

121

Enlightenment. I know that's crude, it's a bit of a generalisation, but I think that, by and large, that was the intellectual progression.

'Professor Gordon Donaldson, who's no great admirer of Presbyterianism, makes the point that the Reformation in Scotland came from the bottom up, from the people up, and not from the top down as it was in England. If you look at the *Book of Discipline*, you find Knox and the Reformers giving every congregation the power to elect their minister. OK, let's not get too starry-eyed about this, it was the men of the congregation, it wasn't everybody. You're talking the sixteenth century here. But, as a political and philosophical step forward, it was a huge jump and a precious thing. And, as Donaldson points out, Knox is always portrayed as a harsh, unforgiving figure, but the Reformation in Scotland was almost entirely bloodless. It was an extraordinarily benign affair compared to what happened in England, where it was bloody.

'But somehow Knox gets the reputation of being a sort of monster, which I think is outrageous. This idea that Knox ruined Scotland really angers me. The Reformation improved Scotland enormously in that it created the atmosphere in which intellectual debate could flourish and people had the freedom to do that kind of arguing. It took a long time. I'm not saying that in 1560 opinions were as free as they are now, but it started something. I would even argue that Knox is maybe the most important Scotsman of the last 1,000 years. It seems like a large claim to make for a Kirk minister, but I think it's true. I do think that the rubbishing of Knox which has gone on, especially in the last century, is just ignorant. There was a Catholic–Anglican distaste not just for Knox but for Presbyterianism in general that produced a completely bogus picture of a harsh, repressive, dismal, art-hating thing, which is nonsense. George Mackay Brown obviously bought into the Knox myth.'

No controversy there, then.

Many people, even in Scotland, labour under the misapprehension that they actually know about John Knox. They think the most tempestuous of the founding fathers of the modern Scottish nation was some kind of morose Scottish Orangeman. They may know that he was stern and demanding and that he reduced Mary Queen of Scots to tears, but that's about it. Far from being revered, Knox has had a terrible press in Scotland for years. The received modern view of Knox is that he was a dour Scottish ayatollah who was at his most fulfilled when he discovered people enjoying themselves and put a stop to it.

The whiskery stereotypes are hauled out at regular intervals and pressed into even more tired and tiresome service. No less a personage than Scotland's Chief Medical Officer, Dr Harry Burns, declared that Scotland should throw off the burden of 'doom and gloom' imposed by John Knox and pursue happiness for the sake of its health. He said a number of studies had found that anxiety, pessimism and a sense of hopelessness had serious effects on health and could shorten a person's life by up to fifteen years, and added that Knox was partly to blame for a certain negativity in Scots culture.

While I warm to the picture of Scotland's Chief Medical Officer of Health poring over Calvin's *Institutes* or Knox's *Book of Discipline*, what he is really doing is reheating old Scottish mince.

Like all stereotypes, the notion of Knox and Calvin as merchants of misery has a degree of truth in it. No-one could mistake them for stand-up comedians. They were serious men about serious business. Knox's passion for education and his desire to raise funds so that even poor ploughmen's sons could go to university did not represent a desire to destroy people's confidence. He was all for giving people from a wide social background the resources to stand on their own feet.

The kind of pessimism Dr Burns attributes to the likes of Knox and Calvin is not restricted to Scotland. It tends to be more prevalent in northern climes – though not exclusively so – where climate and shortage of daylight have an effect on people's outlook. Is John Knox to blame for that as well? In one survey, the UK was placed forty-fourth in a league table of the happiest countries. Switzerland came top of the league. Geneva is the second biggest city in Switzerland. Who was its most influential historical figure? Step forward a smiling John Calvin. Maybe Calvin was Switzerland's first Happiness Tsar.

'Knox' as a swearword is surpassed only by the naming and perpetual shaming of the theology which informed the Reformer's passion – Calvinism. This is modern Scotland's Big C – the dreaded cancer which is believed to have destroyed the vitals of Scottish life. Calvinism is blamed for Scottish dourness and melancholy. It is credited with destroying Scottish cultural life. It is held responsible for everything from football hooliganism to drizzle and midges.

I do not seek to present John Knox as a saint. He was a man of his bloodthirsty times; and yet, on occasion, he transcended his times. He was brave and passionate. As well as laying the foundations of the educational system of Scotland, he helped to give the national Kirk its democratic shape. For these achievements alone, he deserves an assessment which is at least intellectually rigorous.

So, is that it, then? Has GMB, following Edwin Muir, got John Knox and Calvinism all wrong?

If only things were so simple. While I am glad to have contended for plain Mr Knox and the Scottish Reformation, I am not entirely satisfied with what I have written. My account, I fear, is too much 'in the head' and 'in the gut'. Something in the heart zone is missing. It has to do with the acute sense of loss and dislocation that many people must have felt at the time of the Reformation in Scotland.

I need some help here. In the conversational spirit of this project, I turn to Jocelyn Rendall, who lives on the Orkney island of Papa Westray. (The island's name suggests a historic connection with priest-missionaries; St Boniface Kirk on Papay, as the island is known locally, is the only church in Orkney, apart from St Magnus Cathedral, to survive the Reformation and remain in use in the present day.)

Jocelyn helps her Orcadian husband Neil run a 400-acre farm on the island. A graduate in English, theology and political philosophy from Durham University, she is also a historian and author – her book *Steering the Stone Ships: The Story of Orkney Kirks and People* (Saint

Andrew Press, 2009), is a highly regarded study. I asked Jocelyn about George Mackay Brown and the Scottish Reformation.

'I think the question is not so much "Why did GMB become a Catholic?" but "Could one imagine him not becoming one?"' said Jocelyn. 'I think that the Catholicism was almost an inevitable result of his idealised view of the past – that safe place where all is continuity, tradition – and that he saw the Reformation as a catastrophe for Scotland because it tore apart the social fabric of custom and belief. His poem "Chapel between Cornfield and Shore" says it all: the grey uprooted wall of the old chapel had once been solid and reassuring, but the ebb tide had taken away all the things of the past, and the wall had not merely fallen down or been knocked down but been violently uprooted. For someone who found so much inspiration in belonging to a particular place with its particular past, to be uprooted must have been the worst possible calamity he could imagine. He saw all the goodness and wholesomeness in life as deriving from continuity, living physically and spiritually in the footprints of the ancestors who had gone before us.'

Was GMB's understanding of history realistic?

'Of course he viewed the past through very rose-tinted spectacles, but, despite being a card-carrying Protestant, I have a lot of sympathy with him in this. It is true that Scotland was "reformed" with little opposition or bloodshed, but I doubt that much of Luther's theology percolated down to the peasants of Orkney. Mans and Hild [an old couple who feature in GMB's novel, *Magnus*] didn't get "good news" of salvation by grace, they got witch-hunts and whippings and the repentance stool and those ghastly joyless Sundays; and they lost the consolation of their saints and the festivals that brought some colour and merriment – one of George's favourite words – into their backbreaking, hungry, squalid lives. You only have to look at how tenaciously people clung to their "popish superstitions" to see how desperate they were for something more emotionally fulfilling than the Discipline inflicted on them by the Kirk. Two or even three hundred years of rebukes and punishments didn't stop the pilgrimages to holy lochs and wells and rituals at "popish chapels"!

'One of George's stories I love is *A Treading of Grapes,* where the ever-so-dull sermons of the sceptical Presbyterian ministers are contrasted with that of the pre-Reformation priest who preaches the reality of the miracle of the Incarnation to the merriment of the children of God. Of course it is another fictional rewrite of the past, there probably never was a priest who preached remotely like Halcro – most of them didn't preach at all – but miracles are important to GMB, he is alive to them, and what he sees around him is a busy, sceptical, materialistic world that has shut out the possibility of miracles. The thing that knocks at one's mind is that he was writing in his letters to Stella about his suicidal depression at the same time as he wrote about finding merriment in faith.'

What about John Knox?

'I may be wrong, but I don't picture GMB sitting down and weighing up the pros and cons of different theological doctrines before he converted. The Knox in his poems is a figurehead to be punched, not a serious collection of ideas to be intellectually challenged. It's easy to understand what he was reacting against – what he saw in Stromness was not the liberating "justification by faith" message of the Reformers but the censorious old women gossiping on the pier. But I find myself resenting the way he – and Catholic admirers – treat the miracle of the Incarnation as if it were somehow exclusively Catholic property instead of the cornerstone of Christianity. Perhaps he didn't find much sense of the wholeness of Creation, the cycles of bread and life and so on in the Calvinists of Stromness, but you certainly don't have to enter the Catholic Church to get there!

'I see his conversion as having less to do with Knox or Calvin versus the pope than with his own sensibility, and the vulnerability that made him frightened of many things: of women and relation- ships, modern technology and all that was noisy, fast, materialistic in modern life. The pace of life in the past seemed slower and less threatening, with time and space for mystery and the imagination, and Catholicism a quiet place in the past. Perhaps even a place where you could find merriment without a hangover next day.'

Yes, that is what is missing in my account so far.

As I look at the sources, I can see more clearly that George Mackay Brown's distrust of, and distaste for, the Reformation had a great deal to do with the sense of uprooting and dislocation triggered by the Protestant revolution. His spiritual and aesthetic sensibilities were offended by the seismic shift which the Reformation represented. Not much interested in theological debate, and alienated from the culture of early to mid-twentieth-century Scottish Presbyterianism, George mourned the loss of an all-embracing pre-Reformation Catholic culture with its clear structures of authority.

He would not have been impressed by the argument that the Scottish Reformation paved the way for the Scottish Enlightenment, with its exciting explorations of physical, scientific, intellectual and spiritual territory. George was not an Enlightenment man. His sympathies lay with the common people who tilled the soil and fished the seas and whose symbols of comfort and consolation were taken away from them. Their familiar churches were not so much destroyed as denuded. The colour had given way to greyscale.

Reading GMB's stories and poems and reflecting upon these conversations has exposed me to the sense of grief which many ordinary people must have experienced as the foundations of their way of being in the world were shaken. I have always believed that the Reformation was a necessary tragedy; my focus has been on the intellectual issue of necessity, but I have not, until now, engaged with the felt sense of that tragedy. Even taking into account George's admitted romanticising of the period, I am moved by the sense of loss which rolls down four-and-a-half centuries.

I remain drawn to the values of the Scottish Enlightenment, and to the radical, egalitarian nature of the Scottish Reformation. But, on this conversational passage around George Mackay Brown, I am increasingly attracted to the notion of a Reformed, inclusive Catholicism.

It is a dream, a chimera perhaps.

This walking alongside George Mackay Brown, notebook and microphone in hand, is turning into something of a personal quest for me. Such a venture can damage your certainties. Who knows where this exploration will end?

George Mackay Brown was a poet, not a historian. Nor was he a philosopher; in fact, he went out of his way to eschew the label 'intellectual' – though I think that is a little disingenuous. As the expression of his spirituality took a specifically religious shape, he was working out of his experience, his gut instinct and his poetic imagination.

In addition to Edwin Muir's influential work, there were other writings around at the time which may have been an influence on George. The novels of Fionn MacColla (Tom Macdonald), a contemporary and friend of Hugh MacDiarmid and a convert to Roman Catholicism, highlighted the harshness of Calvinism. His best-known novel, *And the Cock Crew*, published in 1945, took the Highland Clearances as its subject. At its heart is an encounter between Fearchar, the Gaelic poet, and a minister, Maighstir Sachairi. The Established Church does not come out of it well.

Despite my defence of John Knox and John Calvin against lazy and modish thinking, I am not a Calvinist. (Indeed, neither was Calvin.) I have unresolved questions about the Protestant tradition in which I was raised. The state of the late medieval Catholic Church and the desire for reform may partly explain the success of the Protestant Reformers, but it does not follow that the theological agenda of Scottish Reformers such as John Knox and Andrew Melville was justified in every aspect. While the central Reformation doctrine of salvation by grace through faith is fundamentally liberating – salvation as a freely given gift from a loving God, rather than the consequence of a series of moral and spiritual tests that one fails at one's peril – it has been historically problematic. The man carrying the banner reading 'How can I be sure about my status before God?' has been, and still is, the ghost at the Protestant feast.

One attempt within Protestantism to answer the salvation question led straight to the Calvinist doctrine of Predestination, which stated that while God's salvation was a free gift of grace, it was restricted to the 'Elect', the chosen ones. But how could one be sure that one was part of the 'Elect'? And, if you were sure that you were among the Elect, irrevocably chosen by God from before the womb, what was to stop you from behaving amorally? After all, your eternal salvation was secure by divine decree. This question lies at the heart of James Hogg's classic novel, *The Private Memoirs and Confessions of a Justified Sinner* (1824). Anxious introspection, rather than assurance, became part of the Protestant baggage carried down through time.

Another problematic part of the Reformed tradition is the doctrine of Scripture alone. Individual judgement before God – especially when holding a copy of the Scriptures in a language you could understand – felt hugely liberating to many when it was first preached. But what if your neighbour, reading his or her Bible in the vernacular, came to a different conclusion from you on matters of Christian life or doctrine? Protestant individualism, freed from Church authority, has proved to be a very mixed blessing; it has led inexorably to further divisions and splits in the Presbyterian community. (Nevertheless, faced with the scandal of disunity, the Presbyterian movement in Scotland in the twentieth century saw reunions of some of its main branches. Stromness now has only one Presbyterian congregation, part of a more inclusive Church of Scotland.)

My difficulty with George Mackay Brown, and with Edwin Muir, is certainly not a matter of total disagreement with them. It has to do with the inadequacy of their treatment of John Knox and the Scottish Reformation. The work of these two rightly respected writers on this subject is simply not up to standard.

I was interested to read Peter Butter's biography of Muir, *Edwin Muir, Man and Poet*. Speaking of Muir's biography of Knox, Professor Butter says that Muir lacked the detachment and the historical knowledge to paint a fair and comprehensive picture. Butter accuses Muir of hauling Knox into the twentieth century and arraigning him from the point of view of a modern liberal, making little apparent effort to get into the mind of Knox.

George Mackay Brown was not a writer who overburdened himself with research. When challenged about this in several interviews, he simply replied that he was too lazy. The received view is that this is false modesty. I am not so sure. No notebooks filled with jottings about subjects which he had investigated were found among his papers. He was not a regular visitor to the archives of Stromness library. His strengths lay elsewhere, in the depths of his imagination.

George MacLeod, founder of the Iona Community (which rebuilt the living quarters of the abbey on the island of Iona as a post-Second World War sign of renewal), would sometimes talk about Einstein, and about matter as light energy. When he would start on this topic, his wife, Lorna, would mutter with exasperated affection: 'Einstein! Einstein! He hasn't read a word of Einstein!' The old Celtic mystic proved that one could be lazy – or careless – and still be maddeningly right. Whether or not GMB comes into this category is a matter for a debate that can have no easy closure.

No, George Mackay Brown did not convert simply because he got drunk one night in Rackwick. But what was it that finally pushed him to 'take the plunge' – to borrow Stella Cartwright's words from an entirely different context – and become a Roman Catholic?

CHAPTER 8

Home
at Last

It was books wot did it, as the *Sun* newspaper might say in big, brash letters. George Mackay Brown put the matter more deftly: *In the end it was literature that broke down my last defences. There are many ways of entering a fold; it was the beauty of words that opened the door to me:*

> *'Love bade me welcome; yet my soul drew back,*
> *   Guilty of dust and sin ...'*

In quoting the opening words of a poem by the seventeenth-century Anglican divine, George Herbert, and putting them at the heart of his account of the breaking-down of his resistance to becoming a Roman Catholic, GMB was placing himself within a broad Christian tradition which saw beauty as the key to unlocking the door to truth.

Described by Dr Rowan Williams, Archbishop of Canterbury, as an 'iconic figure in the Anglican imagination', Herbert is regarded by many as the finest religious poet in the English language. A contemporary of Shakespeare, he was one of a loosely connected group of what became known as the 'Metaphysical Poets'. Writers such as Herbert, John Donne and Thomas Traherne wrote lyric poems characterised by wit, irony and serious intent. Interested in the earthy and the physical and the sensuous, but also in what lay beyond earthly realities, they took on big themes such as love, humanity, transience and divinity. They explored these topics in intense, brief meditations, written in striking language.

George Herbert, a gifted, Oxford-educated scholar who was marked down early for a political career, was in turmoil for several years over his sense of calling to the priesthood. The struggle was not resolved until his ordination to the Anglican ministry at the age of 36. Out of this inner conflict and bouts of ill-health, some exceptional religious poetry emerged. Far from becoming a public figure, he buried himself in the wondrously named rural parish of Fuggleston-cum-Bemerton in Wiltshire, where he was a revered vicar until his death at the age of 39. Several of his poems have been set to music and used in public worship. 'Let all the World in Every Corner Sing', 'Teach me, my God and King' and 'King of Glory, King of Peace' are much-loved classics.

GMB greatly admired Herbert. He knew by heart his best-known poem, 'Love':

> Love bade me welcome, yet my soul drew back,
> Guilty of dust and sin.
> But quick-ey'd Love, observing me grow slack
> From my first entrance in,
> Drew nearer to me, sweetly questioning
> If I lack'd anything.
>
> 'A guest,' I answer'd, 'worthy to be here';
> Love said, 'You shall be he.'
> 'I, the unkind, the ungrateful? Ah my dear,
> I cannot look on thee.'
> Love took my hand and smiling did reply,
> 'Who made the eyes but I?'
>
> 'Truth, Lord, but I have marr'd them; let my shame
> Go where it doth deserve.'
> 'And know you not,' says Love, 'who bore the blame?'
> 'My dear, then I will serve.'

'You must sit down,' says Love, 'and taste my meat.'
So I did sit and eat.

In this poem, Love is introduced as a person of unknown gender, one who initiates the encounter with a welcome. The narrator immediately feels unworthy, but Love, who is revealed as the divine Creator, puts him at his ease – 'You shall be he', a guest worthy to be in Love's presence. Rather than reinforcing the narrator's language of blame and guilt, 'sweetly questioning' Love points to the liberating sacrifice of Christ – 'who bore the blame?' – and issues an invitation … to dinner. Herbert's line '"You must sit down," says Love, "and taste my meat"' brings to mind the mystery-laden words of Christ in John's Gospel 6:55–6: 'For my flesh is meat indeed, and my blood is drink indeed. He that eateth my flesh, and drinketh my blood, dwelleth in me, and I in him.' The words from Psalm 34:8, 'O taste and see that the Lord is good: blessed is the man that trusteth in him' – spoken at communion services in many tongues over nearly two millennia – are also implicit.

Herbert's placing of the spiritual at the heart of the material attracted and fascinated George Mackay Brown, the man and the poet, until the end of his life.

GMB was drawn to the Christian mystical tradition – particularly in its poetic form – exemplified by Herbert's work. What was the primary attraction? Both from my knowledge of George and from a study of his writings, I believe it to be the notion of the divine nature as unconditional love. The mystical sense of encounter with a divine love which slips incognito into the human dimension held great appeal for George, even though he simply admired the Metaphysical Poets without seeking to emulate them. In 'Love', Herbert presents the divine as mysterious, personal, welcoming and disarming. The one who encounters the divine presence feels unworthy, but these feelings are dismissed almost casually. The work of God in the sacrificial love of Christ has taken care of that – so, now let's eat! A prodigal hospitality which sets no entrance exams is audaciously placed at the heart of the divine nature.

This was spiritual balm for George's psychological wounds. The simple and beautiful language of this seventeenth-century rural writer spoke directly to the twentieth-century Orkney man's poetic heart.

George also admired Herbert's friend and fellow Anglican divine, John Donne. The Jesuit-educated poet, a convert to Anglicanism, became Dean of St Paul's Cathedral in 1621. The father of twelve wrote erotic poetry of intense power, as well as religious verse which has stood the test of time. Lines from his *Holy Sonnets* continue to excite interest from modern writers and composers, especially 'Death, be not proud, though some have called thee / Mighty and dreadful, for thou art not so', and 'Batter my heart three-personed God'. Donne's much-quoted sentiments about death and community were entirely agreeable to GMB:

> No man is an island, entire of itself; every man is a piece of the continent, a part of the main. If a clod be washed away by the sea, Europe is the less, as well as if a promontory were, as well as if a manor of thy friend's or of thine own were: any man's death diminishes me, because I am involved in mankind, and therefore never send to know for whom the bell tolls; it tolls for thee.

Yet another of the Metaphysical Poets who inspired GMB was Thomas Traherne. The seventeenth-century Anglican priest's almost-pantheistic Nature poetry spoke to the heart of the post-Rackwick GMB. Traherne delighted in the created world. He believed that, since God had put human beings in the world, it would be ingratitude not to exult in God's creation:

> Our blessedness to see
> Is even to the Deity
> A Beatific Vision! He attains
> His Ends while we enjoy. In us He reigns.

Traherne's almost child-like view of the divine at the heart of the created world gladdened George Mackay Brown's soul. Here was a God who actually wanted human beings to rejoice in and enjoy the gifts of life and nature. This felt much more like 'good news' than the sometimes moralistic tidings delivered sonorously by black-gowned Presbyterian preachers. As Traherne put it:

Long time before
I in my mother's womb was born,
A God preparing did this glorious store
The world for me adorn.
Into His Eden so divine and fair,
So wide and bright, I come His son and heir.

Traherne was to influence twentieth-century Christians as diverse as Roman Catholic contemplative monk Thomas Merton and Protestant Christian apologist C. S. Lewis (who described Traherne's *Centuries of Meditations* as 'almost the most beautiful book in English'). As I turn the pages of Herbert, Donne and Traherne, I find personal refreshment as well as examples of the kind of generous spirituality that appealed to GMB.

The three gifted Anglicans link into the more restrained of the later Romantic poets whom GMB admired, especially Wordsworth, whose 'Ode: Intimations of Immortality from Recollections of Early Childhood' sees human beings as God-forgetting, God-haunted creatures:

Our birth is but a sleep and a forgetting:
The Soul that rises with us, our life's Star,
Hath had elsewhere its setting,
And cometh from afar:
Not in entire forgetfulness,
And not in utter nakedness,
But trailing clouds of glory do we come
From God, who is our home:
Heaven lies about us in our infancy!

It is interesting that Herbert, Donne and Traherne were from the Anglican tradition. Anglicanism saw itself as a Reformed Catholicism, and sought to position itself between Roman Catholicism and Protestantism.

Protestantism has its own mystical and devotional traditions. Anne Fremantle's anthology, *The Protestant Mystics*, introduced by W. H. Auden, includes Herbert, Donne and Traherne among many others. Traherne opposed both Roman Catholicism and Non-conformist Protestantism. GMB would have agreed with the seventeenth-century philosopher Peter Sterry, who declared that the stream of the divine love is the source of 'all truths, goodness, joys, beauties and blessedness'. Sterry himself was a radical Puritan preacher and a chaplain to Oliver Cromwell.

Reflecting with me on the influence of the Metaphysical Poets, Orkney-based novelist and English teacher John McGill pointed out that they were out of vogue for a good 200 years – appealing neither to the rationalist temper of the Enlightenment nor to the emotional excesses of Romanticism. They are virtually absent from the definitive lyric anthology of the Victorian age, *Palgrave's Golden Treasury*.

'Then came Herbert Grierson's *Anthology* of 1921,' John told me, 'and suddenly they were the most interesting strand of English poetry, the corrective to post-Keatsian sugariness as exemplified by Tennyson. Their endorsement by T. S. Eliot helped to secure their place, and it's easy to see a path – intellectual, spiritual and linguistic, even socio-political – from Eliot to George Mackay Brown. George and my father-in-law, Ian MacInnes, loved listening to LPs of Eliot droning his stuff, and loved even more reciting chunks of *Four Quartets*. Anyone coming to Donne and company from the diet of virtually unleavened late Romanticism that prevailed in school poetry would have a sense of shock and awe.'

Given that he was spiritually nourished by Anglican poets, some with Protestant tendencies, why did George Mackay Brown become a Roman Catholic?

One reason, I believe, is that he regarded the Roman Catholic Church as a more reliable custodian of mystical traditions. It is a matter of record that after the Reformation, both the Roman Catholic Church and Protestant churches regarded mysticism with suspicion. They were wary of claims about the authority of personal spiritual experience, over against the authority of the Church or of the Bible.

Protestant mystics tended not to use the terminology of mysticism, partly because the word 'mysticism' itself was of pagan origin. Protestant preachers such as Jonathan Edwards, John Wesley and George Fox emphasised inner spiritual experience, but they carefully avoided talk of mysticism.

In the Roman Catholic Church, mysticism began to be the province not of prominent bishops or theologians, but of less powerful figures, particularly women in religious orders. Nevertheless, the Catholic Church preserved greater access to the riches of the mystical traditions of the past, associated with the likes of St Augustine and the brilliant fourteenth-century German Dominican friar Meister Eckhart. (Eckhart's career illustrates some of the pitfalls of the mystical tradition. He was a popular preacher in the German vernacular; his boundary-pushing emphasis on personal experience led to him being tried as a heretic by Pope John XXII. Eckhart's pupil, Henry Suso, engaged in masochistic mortifications of the flesh. He wore a vest studded with sharp nails, and for twenty-five years declined to have a bath.)

Another poet who nudged George along the road to Roman Catholicism was Gerard Manley Hopkins, who had also been influenced by Thomas Traherne. George was so intrigued by Hopkins that he did some postgraduate research on him, beginning in 1962; but he found literary criticism deadening, and his study grant was not renewed two years later. For those unfamiliar with Hopkins, one of his best-known poems, 'Pied Beauty' – which GMB would start reciting for no particular reason – will provide a startling introduction, especially if read aloud.

> Glory be to God for dappled things –
>   For skies of couple-colour as a brinded cow;
>   For rose-moles all in stipple upon trout that swim;
> Fresh-firecoal chestnut-falls; finches' wings;
>   Landscape plotted and pieced – fold, fallow, and plough;
>   And all trades, their gear and tackle and trim.
> All things counter, original, spare, strange;
>   Whatever is fickle, freckled (who knows how?)

With swift, slow; sweet, sour; adazzle, dim;
He fathers-forth whose beauty is past change:
Praise him.

Like Traherne, Hopkins exulted in the glory of creation. He did so with fresh, dazzling language. Brought up by devout High Church Anglican parents, he wrote Nature poems which reflected not only a Romantic perspective but also something of the outlook of the Metaphysical Poets. In 1866, at the age of 22, he was received into the Roman Catholic Church by John Henry Newman, the nineteenth century's most high-profile convert from Anglicanism to Catholicism. Hopkins' decision to convert devastated his parents. Two years later, he entered the novitiate of the Society of Jesus. When he became a Jesuit, he burned all the poems he had written – though he would later return to writing poetry. Ordained a priest in 1877, he was appointed Classics Professor at University College Dublin. (James Joyce was one of his students.) Nothing of Hopkins' poetry was published during his lifetime. It first appeared in print in 1918, published by poet Robert Bridges some nineteen years after Hopkins' death at the age of 44.

Saying that no English poet ever fell upon the language with such skill, sweetness and boisterous daring, GMB continued: *It was a heroic lonely attempt to put song back into a language grown thin and washed-out. Somewhere literature had left the high road and smithy and market-place for the salon and the university, and grown anaemic.*

It was necessary, Hopkins thought, to go right back to the beginnings, to rediscover a lost power and beauty. He strove to enter the first 'house of making', where word-men worked with all the excitement of men discovering ore in the rocks, and realising what marvellous artefacts could be made: crude, perhaps, but resonant with possibilities. He strove to make himself one of the ancient smelters and smiths of poetry.

What he made was utterly new, and so had no place in the mainstream of late Victorian literature.

It certainly was new. Hopkins' poetry should ideally be read aloud to catch its 'sprung' rhythms, its alliterations and assonances, its power and originality. His poem, 'God's Grandeur', is one of the finest religious poems of the nineteenth century.

The world is charged with the grandeur of God.
    It will flame out, like shining from shook foil;
    It gathers to a greatness, like the ooze of oil
Crushed. Why do men then now not reck his rod?
Generations have trod, have trod, have trod;
    And all is seared with trade; bleared, smeared with toil;
    And wears man's smudge and shares man's smell: the soil
Is bare now, nor can foot feel, being shod.

And for all this, nature is never spent;
    There lives the dearest freshness deep down things;
And though the last lights off the black West went
    Oh, morning, at the brown brink eastward, springs –
Because the Holy Ghost over the bent
    World broods with warm breast and with ah! bright wings.

As well as being struck by Hopkins' distinctive poetic style and his celebration of God-in-Nature, the Orcadian poet was moved when he learned of the Jesuit priest's black depressions. Hopkins suffered from anxiety and a sense of abandonment by God. George identified with the Jesuit's self-hatred; his account of Hopkins' profound melancholy is written with a sympathy born of personal understanding.

What is clear is that George Mackay Brown's appreciation of Catholicism was primarily aesthetic and intuitive. Intellectual argument was not his way to truth. (He used to say that when he was directed, as a student, to read some of the work of the eighteenth-century German philosopher Immanuel Kant, it could have been written in Chinese for all he could make of it.)

Beauty and literature hooked him and reeled him in. It was what he saw as the beauty of the Christian doctrines of the Incarnation and Christ's Passion which made him a believer. *Nowhere in all created literature, not in Homer, Dante, Shakespeare, Goethe, is there anything of such awesome majesty and power as the drama of the Passion. The imagination could never compass that – it* must *be true.*

139

He loved to quote the words 'Beauty is truth, truth beauty', from the final stanza of Keats' 'Ode on a Grecian Urn'. The last two lines are as follows:

'Beauty is truth, truth beauty' – that is all
   Ye know on earth, and all ye need to know.

GMB talked of how glimpses and revelations in literature moved him in the direction of conversion. *The mystery and the beauty increased, as I read more widely. Graham Greene's* The Power and the Glory *impressed me deeply; for here was a hunted and driven priest, and in many ways a worthless one, who nevertheless kept faith to the end, as better martyrs had done in other places. From every age and airt of literature, poems and prose swarmed in to increase the beauty and the mystery I had wandered into, it seemed by accident, so long ago. If 'beauty is truth, and truth beauty', here were beauty and truth beyond price. A few fragments of such truth and beauty, like treasures long lost, were sufficient … Can it be that those beauties of literature and all the arts are a striving to return to that immaculate beginning? – the word lost in The Word?*

Is 'Beauty is truth, truth beauty' really all you need to know? Certainly not for those whose approach to ultimate reality is scientific or philosophical. It is not a compelling argument for those engaged in disputations in today's somewhat testy intellectual wars between religion and atheism. But, for George Mackay Brown, it was not an argument or a form of proof at all. It was for him an unadorned aesthetic appreciation. It was akin to standing in front of a great painting, or listening to great music, and allowing oneself to be addressed at the core of one's being. To this degree, its authority is personal and subjective.

The Orcadian storyteller also fell in love with the parables of Jesus. Why? Because he found them beautiful. In his imagination, he transposed the archetypal characters in the first-century Biblical stories into the Orkney landscape. He was also moved by the words of Jesus as recorded in John 12:24: 'Verily, verily, I say unto you, Except a corn of wheat fall into the ground and die, it abideth alone: but if it die, it bringeth forth much fruit'. It was the Biblical text that George repeated most often. *The beauty of Christ's parables was irresistible. How could they fail to be, when so many of them concern ploughing and seedtime and harvest, and his listeners were most of them fishermen? I live in a group of islands that have been farmed for many centuries; all round me in summer are the whispering cornfields turning from green to gold. 'Except a seed fall into the ground, and die.' Those words were a delight and a revelation, when I first understood them. And at piers and moorings in every village and island are the fishing boats, and the daily venturers into the perilous west, the horizon-eyed salt-tongued fishermen ('The kingdom is like a net ...'; 'I will make you fishers of men ...'). The elements of earth and sea, that we thought so dull and ordinary, held a bounteousness and a mystery not of this world. Now I looked with another eye at those providers of our bread and fish; and when I came at last to work as a writer, it was those heroic and primeval occupations that provided the richest imagery, the most exciting symbolism.*

GMB was always more interested in farmers and fishermen than in theologians. While he admired John Henry Newman, he confessed that he found much of his written work boring. George exalted farm workers and fishermen, seeing them as essential figures in a universal salvation story, heroic and heraldic against their backgrounds. *That the toil of the earthworker should become, in the Mass, Corpus Christi, was a wonder beyond words, and still is. That one of the Pope's titles is The Fisherman, an acknowledgement of his descent from Simon Peter the fisherman, was an added delight to the mind and spirit, and still is.*

The story of Magnus was also for George a wonder beyond words – though he spent many words attempting to capture aspects of the life and death of Orkney's saint. Magnus himself was, of course, a Catholic Christian, and the fact that Orkney's 'glory and wonder of all the North', St Magnus Cathedral, was built as a place of Catholic worship made a big impression on George. It is not surprising that he felt his devotion to St Magnus would be easier to express within the framework of Catholicism.

Another aspect of Roman Catholicism which attracted George was its appeal for ordinary working people. Like Edwin Muir before him, he was moved by the devotion of poor people as they attended Mass and knelt at the altar rails to receive the sacrament. Again like Muir, he contrasted this with the somewhat bourgeois Presbyterianism he encountered in Orkney, where not many poor people attended public worship.

I encountered this myself in my ministry in the Glasgow housing scheme of Easterhouse. People on the margins of society would look at the Church and say: 'It's no' for the likes o' us'.

George saw the Catholic Mass as beautiful and majestic – particularly in its Latin form; he lamented the sidelining of the Latin Mass – celebrated on countless altars all over the world. In this, he was certainly not alone. The Catholic faith, with its rituals and rich imagery, had an appeal for a number of writers who converted to Catholicism in the twentieth century, including Graham Greene, Muriel Spark, Thomas Merton, G. K. Chesterton, Evelyn Waugh and Oscar Wilde.

We have tracked George Mackay Brown's aesthetic journey of the spirit from his upbringing in, and growing antipathy to, the Presbyterianism of Stromness, through the pagan and Christian spirituality of the Norse sagas (with particular reference to St Magnus), on to the Nature-spirituality evoked by Rackwick, then the Christian mysticism of the Anglican Metaphysical Poets and the brilliance of the Catholic convert Gerard Manley Hopkins.

So, what was the clinching attraction of a move to the Roman part of the wider Catholic tradition? I believe the answer was the authority, unity and long history of the Catholic Church. George was disturbed by Protestantism's divisions, which he witnessed close at hand in Stromness. The continued existence of the Roman Catholic Church, with its global reach and claim to be the one true Church, provided, for George, a resolution for the problem of competing assertions.

But what about some of the grislier characters who have stalked the life of the Catholic Church down through history? George was not deterred by that difficulty. Earlier in his life, he had read Lytton Strachey's *Eminent Victorians*, with its iconoclastic attack on

Cardinal Manning, another high-profile Anglican convert to Roman Catholicism. Manning, unlike Newman, strongly supported the doctrine of papal infallibility and an extension of the powers of the pope. Strachey pilloried Manning.

The more he read, the more George Brown became incensed. Strachey, he said, *demonstrates gleefully how the dogmas and utterances of one pope were contradicted out of the mouth of another pope. What could any average rational being make of such a morass of error and human frailty and pretension? And yet the whole pageant that Strachey unfolded before me – intended to make every reader chuckle scornfully – gave me one of the great thrills I have got out of literature.*

That such an institution as the Church of Rome – with all its human faults – had lasted for nearly two thousand years, while parties and factions and kingdoms had had their day and withered, seemed to me to be utterly wonderful. Some mysterious power seemed to be preserving it against the assaults and erosions of time.

At first sight, there is something perverse about George's position. It is as if the worse the sins of the institution are, the more convincing is its claim to supremacy. I believe George's stance is a sound one. Over the generations, there have been various breakaway movements seeking to create ever purer versions of the Church. In some cases, dissident groups have claimed that the sacraments of the Church have sometimes been invalid because of character flaws in the celebrant. Once that line is taken, there is no end point in the process. The 'purer than thou' argument is ultimately destructive. George would have concurred with the view of Catholic writer Hilaire Belloc that, if the badly run Roman Catholic Church were not the work of God, it would not have lasted a fortnight.

Having reread Greene's *The Power and the Glory* after a gap of more than thirty years, I'm not at all surprised that GMB loved the book. The whisky priest on the run from a totalitarian government is not a virtuous man in conventional terms; yet he can still offer up the bread and the wine for poor and desperate people at makeshift altars. If the validity of sacramental action depends upon the spotless character of the presiding minister, then – in the words of Private

Fraser in the TV series, *Dad's Army* – 'We're a' doomed!' The doctrine of the perfectibility of man should be left to the righteous modern priesthood of tabloid editors.

To a large degree, in its journey through history, the Catholic Church has managed to contain its divisions. The two major splits – the separation of the Eastern churches from the Western Church in the 'Great Schism' of the eleventh century, and the Protestant Reformation of the sixteenth century – had devastating impacts, but, given the propensity to human divisiveness, the Catholic track record on unity has been far better than the Protestant equivalent. Mind you, my colleague in Easterhouse, Father Tom Connelly, who went on to become director of the Catholic media office in Scotland, had an interesting view on this. On the subject of splits in Presbyterianism, Tom would say: 'When you guys fall out, you go away and form another denomination. When Catholics fall out, we go away and form another order. It's the same thing!'

Well, it's not quite the same thing, since the Roman Catholic Church manages to keep its various orders – despite historic rivalries – within the body of the Kirk, so to speak. The Kirk has even failed to keep itself in the body of the Kirk at times in its turbulent history.

Through its sacramental system, particularly the sacrament of penance, the Catholic Church has also provided a remedy for guilt feelings. (There is a flippant Protestant reaction to this: 'All Roman Catholics need to do is to say a few "Hail Marys" and then go back to sinning'. This dismissiveness would have fed GMB's rejection of Protestantism and drawn him towards Catholicism. It would also have added to his feelings of being an outsider in his own community.)

With its emphasis on the individual before God, Protestantism has insisted that there is no need for priestly intervention in the matter of the forgiveness of sins. This theological high-mindedness fails to take account of human psychology. The Roman Catholic ceremonies surrounding the confessional and the ritualised pronouncing of the words of absolution – what Professor J. L. Austin called 'performative utterances' – provide a more embodied and accessible route to a feeling of deliverance from guilt. It is no surprise that the poet who was still being assisted home from the pub felt drawn to the more generous spiritual rituals of the Catholic world-view.

If I were asked to take a short-cut through the reasons why George Mackay Brown became a Roman Catholic, I would express the heart of the matter in these crude and simplistic terms: George viewed the Presbyterian tradition in which he had been raised as being essentially life-denying, whereas he saw the Catholic tradition as being essentially life-affirming.

Looking at George Mackay Brown's decision from a Protestant perspective, I am persuaded by parts of the case he makes. But he is, in my view, excessively hard on the Presbyterianism he grew up with in Stromness. While I am not under any illusion about some of the weaknesses of the Presbyterian world-view and practices, my day-to-day experience of the Church of Scotland over many years gives me a more positive perspective than GMB (and Edwin Muir) would allow. That may simply be down to different experiences at different times. I can only testify to the fact that, despite the Kirk's Presbyterian sins, I have also found in its congregational life a depth of Christian commitment and a warmth and generosity of spirit that are missing from GMB's and Edwin Muir's accounts of Presbyterianism.

But, while I recognise the deficiencies in the Protestant tradition which he highlights, and the strengths of the Roman Catholic tradition, I find George's view of Catholicism to be a romanticised, idealised one. I would contend that this sprang from a lack of acquaintance with the day-to-day life of the Roman Catholic Church. George's Catholicism was a Catholicism of the mind and spirit. Nothing wrong with that. But inheriting his father's scepticism about the lived Presbyterian tradition, and encountering some of its worst aspects in Stromness, George had no corresponding engagement with the Roman Catholic community. He was dealing with the best of Catholicism and the worst of Presbyterianism.

I have been rereading John McGahern's searing novel, *The Dark*, about a young boy growing up in Catholic Ireland. Arguably Ireland's finest twentieth-century novelist, McGahern, a Roman Catholic, was dismissed from his post as a teacher, and the book was put on the index of forbidden publications. The treatment of McGahern makes me wonder how George would have reacted if brought up in a similar environment. McGahern presents a Roman Catholic Church which is every bit as stifling and life-denying as GMB's experience of Presbyterian church life in Stromness. The Irish writer said that, when he was in his twenties, it occurred to him that there was something perverted about an attitude that thought that killing somebody was a minor offence compared to kissing somebody.

Even so, McGahern is grateful for some aspects of his Catholic upbringing. Towards the close of his *Memoir*, he writes: 'Through the violent history of Catholicism run the two dividing movements: the fortress churches with their edicts, threats and punishments; and the churches of the spires and brilliant windows that go towards love and light'.

'Fortress churches with their edicts, threats and punishments': isn't that like the Presbyterianism that George so much despised?

My viewpoint is admittedly biased, but I have found no evidence that George Mackay Brown applied anything like the same rigorous critique to Roman Catholicism that he did to Presbyterianism.

Were there other reasons for becoming a Roman Catholic that GMB either omitted from his public account or was not even aware of at a conscious level? I suspect that there were. My experience as a biographer tells me that one has to be wary of autobiographies – however candid they appear to be – especially those written by skilled wordsmiths. What is concealed may be as important as what is revealed.

I wonder if, by becoming a Catholic, he might identify himself, almost defiantly, as an outsider in his own community. Orcadian novelist Alison Miller has an interesting take on the subject.

'George carved out a life of the mind, a made-up Orkney, and lived there, rather than in the "real" community,' she told me. 'He had to in order to write, I think; he wrote it in order to live there. I have no evidence, but it seems to me that George had a need to keep himself apart from (he'd have been upset at the notion of "above") the daily workings, gossip, jealousies, relationships, scandals, down-and-dirty business of being human. I suspect Catholicism offered a way of doing that – a legitimate way, difficult to question or challenge, a safe retreat. It's a Catholicism of the mind, located in an Orkney of the mind, an escape from, rather than an engagement with, the local community. It's harder to avoid being pigeon-holed in a place like Stromness. People tend to know a lot about you – and about your family and your forebears. I-kent-his-faitherism is bad enough in Scotland as a whole, but in a small place it can be crippling.

'Maybe his shyness and other-worldliness engendered in him a need to escape even from – especially from? – Stromness. Catholicism offered a way of doing that and in turn enriched his imaginative life. He then "wrote" the Orkney he wanted to live in, shot through with the golden threads of the romantic Catholicism he embraced. That's far too schematic, I know. The interplay in GMB's work between his life, his artistic vision and his faith is far more complex than can be tied down in such a neat formula, and I don't doubt for a moment that his faith was genuine. But a writer needs some distance from what he/she is writing about. George's way of achieving that in the town where he was born and lived all his days was partly an escape into his imagination, into Catholicism, partly his creation of archetypes. It had to be Catholicism for George, because hardly anybody else in the community was Catholic. Maybe it also offered a way of legitimising his dreaminess, his difficulties with women, his apartness.'

This view was confirmed by Rowena Murray, Reader in the School of Applied Social Sciences, Strathclyde University, and author, with her father, Brian Murray, of *Interrogation of Silence: The Writings of George Mackay Brown*.

'Without wanting to be disrespectful to anyone else's faith, I'm not sure that it was about faith in a God personally,' she told me. 'It might have been about being different in some ways, outside of the majority in Stromness and Orkney. Maybe that's taking it a bit far, but I always felt it was about positioning himself in Orkney society. When he was in the sanatorium, he was apart from everyone else; when he was in Edinburgh, he was out of Orkney, not hugely part of the student body. When he came back to Orkney, this was another way to stand apart.

'He knew he was going to be different from everybody else, he knew he wasn't going to be the fisherman with a plough or the farmer with a boat, he knew he wasn't going to be the postman, he wasn't going to be close to anyone up there. It's not simply a statement of defiance against whatever anyone else thinks, but it's in that direction; it's saying he was going to do something quite different. It is the writer thing as well, needing to be solitary.

'His emotional difficulties were always going to prevent him from bonding with anyone. Loneliness comes through in his writing sometimes. There are stories about lairds who live on their own. Then there's the Andrina story about an old man, and a young girl coming in and out. The loneliness isn't just about the climate or the drink, it's about the person. It was very difficult for people to get close to him other than on his terms. He had determination – you'll not get to know him, in the way you might get to know your other friends. He kept himself hidden away. In letters to me, he would tell me stuff about his life, but when we would sit down and chat, it was different.

'It's important to make clear that he himself did not say these things – they are my views, based on reading his works, more than anything else, and my take on his views, since religion was one of many things we did not discuss explicitly.'

I asked Irene Dunsmuir for her view. She said: 'It's not that becoming a Catholic would have solved all his problems, but it gave him a reference point. When the subject of religion came round, he could say: "I'm a Catholic". People wouldn't want to go there. It would have been like George having his own religion, his own space, where he could work things out. It was a crutch to get him through things. It was a support.'

Irene remembered George going to the Roman Catholic church in Kirkwall before he finally committed himself. She sometimes went with him and Sylvia Wishart.

'George played about with religion quite a bit,' she said. 'I went several times to the Catholic church with him. There was an old man in Stromness called Attie Campbell. He always drank at the Royal Hotel, so George probably knew him from there. What a character he was! He had a big brown coat and a brown felt hat. He had been around – in the navy in the war, and so on. Attie had a car, and he was most obliging with lifts so long as you paid petrol. We would all go to Kirkwall to the Sunday Mass.

'Every pound was a prisoner with Attie! To get a drink out of Attie – that was almost unheard of! Then there was Sylvia, and she was a character too, she was a very strong character in a quiet way, very opinionated. She opened up a world to George, perhaps – the world of art. Sometimes the company would change. We all met up in the pub in Stromness before we left. It would be a case of: "Do you fancy going to the Catholic church?" "Oh yes, why not! Wait till I get another dram!" Attie would charge 10 shillings for his petrol, for his return trip, whether that trip meant right round the West Mainland … we ended up in all kinds of strange places! Straight from the Catholic church to the Standing Stones of Stenness or the Ring of Brodgar!

'I went to the church purely to see what this was all about. I didn't understand it at all. Maybe I was looking for something more in my life. The pomp and ceremony of the Catholic church was theatre to George. I used to wonder if it was the performance that attracted him. He could let his imagination run away. He could remember the Church of Scotland minister in Stromness banging on the pulpit and screaming, and the comparison must have been so joyful. I found out that there was something good in this, even if it was just the ceremony that he was admiring.

'For a long time, there was the newness of it all, getting this new experience in Orkney, not having to go in search of it – and a character to take him to the church on Sundays, who filled him with stories. This is the thing with anyone who changes their religion. They're apt to take the bits out of both that they like, and they leave behind the bits they don't, and marry the two together. I think that that is a luxury that we as islanders are afforded. We get off with it, whereas in a city you are black and white, you're Protestant or Catholic.

'I don't think that someone who leaves the Protestant Church leaves behind all the trappings, and likewise, anyone who leaves the Catholic Church. But to mingle them both together seems to be a compromise that a lot of folk fall into, and maybe George did that. George was a complex character, and yet he was a simple man in many ways. That's the beauty of him. There's a whole lot of things about George that I don't understand, and never will now.'

I love these Orkney stories. You start off talking about lofty aesthetic reasons for joining the Catholic Church, and soon you are into a well-told story about a man with big brown coat and a brown felt hat driving a fairly tipsy crew to Mass in Kirkwall, followed by a trip to one of Orkney's historic monuments.

I also love the poem that George wrote about Attie, after the driver's death in 1967. It's simply titled 'Attie Campbell, 1900–1967':

Where do you wander now, old friend?
Where do you drink?
Few inns better than Hamnavoe bar,
Few better stories, I think.
Is there a star
Stirred with laughter that has no end

A million light-years beyond the Milky Way
Where Villon and Burns,
Falstaff and slant-eyed Li Po
Order their nectar by turns
(No 'Time, gents' there, no drinker has to pay)
And words immortal gather head and flow?

For that far glim you'd crank your aged car,
But that the faint bell-cry
Of tide changing in Hoy Sound,
The corn surges that salve the deep plough-wound,
Would draw you home to where you are
At Warbeth, among the dead who do not die.

How did George's decision to convert go down with other family members? That was the question I asked Allison Dixon. She said: 'It was the first time that I was aware within my family that there was a feeling that to be a Catholic was not like being a Protestant, so what on earth was he doing? A bit inferior? This was on my mother's part. It was unheard of within the family. How could he do this, and how could he do it to his mother? But my father was very different. He explained to us that Uncle George had read deeply, read into it, and he knew what he was doing. So, all my life when people have said to me: "What possessed George to become a Catholic?", I always said: "Oh well, he thought deeply about it, and read into it".'

How did George's mother take it?

'My sister Ros said she remembers how unhappy Granny was. I don't remember that – I wasn't aware of it. But Father Bamber in Kirkwall won Granny round. He was absolutely charming, and she loved Father Bamber, so he made it all alright. We came to Orkney in 1968 and got to know Father Bamber as well. He never passed you in the street, and he wanted to know all about what was happening. He was quite a flirt!'

Father Bamber was much loved in the Presbyterian congregation of St Magnus Cathedral, and indeed in the whole community. To mark his 80th birthday, I invited him to come up from his place of retirement to Orkney and preach at the Church of Scotland morning service in the cathedral. He preached a brilliant ten-minute homily. He came to the manse for lunch after the service, along with two women from the cathedral choir. He charmed them both. I can well imagine him charming Mrs Brown and getting her 'on side'.

Conversions can be complex, slow-moving dramas, ranging all the way from agonised high-minded theological reflections to the chatting-up of anxious mothers by scholarly, slightly flirtatious priests.

Decision time has arrived, then, for George Mackay Brown. His Presbyterian-sceptic of a father had never taken him as a child to the Kirk for baptism. George is now ready to bring his prevarication to an end, and make up his adult mind.

At the Church of Our Lady and St Joseph in Kirkwall on 23 December 1961, the sign of the Cross is made in water on his furrowed brow. At Midnight Mass on Christmas Eve, he kneels to receive communion for the first time as a Roman Catholic. He is home at last.

This promising Orkney bard is still a man troubled by drink, depression and nightmares. Though half in love with easeful death from time to time, he is not fated to be Orkney's dying Keats. He is 40 years of age: too old now to die young. The best years of his writing are to come.

PART 2

Transfigured by Ceremony

CHAPTER 9

Poet of Silence

It was in the 'Swinging Sixties' that George Mackay Brown made his name as a writer. The promise that he had shown in his two poetry collections, *The Storm* and *Loaves and Fishes*, and in his poems in various magazines, came to fruition in a flurry of publications which earned him awards and critical praise. Three new poetry collections, *The Year of the Whale*, *The Five Voyages of Arnor* and *Twelve Poems*, marked his continuing development as a skilled poet with a distinctive voice, and further raised his national profile.

In an interview in 1964 with Peter Orr, a British Council representative, he talked about the influence of his religious faith upon his work. Asked if he was a religious man, GMB replied: 'Well, when you say that, in a way I suppose I am, more than anything else – though I'm not a moral man, but I'm a religious man, if you can bridge the gap between these two!'

In less tortuous terms: the poet has a religious belief, but this is not to be confused with a moral system. And he knows himself too well to claim to be a moral exemplar.

Did his religious faith come into his poetry? His reply was unequivocal. 'Oh, very much, yes. In fact, it's the whole foundation of my poetry.' Writing poetry, he said, was what he wanted to do more than anything. It was the greatest happiness he knew, under the circumstances in which he lived. Asked about the sort of things he wanted to write about, he replied: 'Well, fishing and farming and – though I'm not a very good person, morally – religion: Catholicism especially, which is religion for me. These are the things – nothing else.'

Asked if he would be a 'smaller man' without the writing of poetry, he replied: 'Yes, well, I'd be a sort of bewildered person – I wouldn't know what was happening at all, you see, but now I have a rough idea of the way things are – what's going to happen to me, and time and eternity – whereas if I didn't do that, I don't know what I would do. I would be a man sort of waiting for the football results on Saturday night, the dogs, and the horses and all that. But of course, I don't care about these things. I have a sort of deeper perspective.'

That sounds more arrogant than the George I knew. Maybe it was true of the man twenty years or so before I knew him. Or could it be simply that his unease when faced by a microphone made him express things awkwardly?

I smiled when I read that without poetry he would have been a man waiting for the football results on a Saturday night; that is exactly what the poet I knew did! He *needed* to know how Celtic had fared. And he needed to watch the football highlights on the monster he excoriated – the television set in the living room.

He certainly needed to write. Poetry was his passion, his vocation, his salvation.

Now that the decision about religious allegiance had finally been made visible in his own community, he was much more settled in terms of the direction of his life and work. His collection, *The Year of the Whale*, published in 1965, consolidated some of the religious themes evident in his earlier writing. Over the next three decades or so, in his desire to express the spiritual at the heart of the material world, GMB would ransack the Catholic tradition for themes and images. Rather than simply repeating these images in traditional ways, he would refresh them, time and again.

Roland Walls, an Anglican divine who converted to Roman Catholicism and became a monk and a priest, was a theological mentor of mine at Edinburgh University. He used to say that reading George Mackay Brown was like breathing fresh mountain air or drinking fresh mountain water. George's capacity for taking well-worn religious themes and expressing them in new idioms is exceptional. He found the Catholic tradition of spirituality to be an inexhaustible seam which he mined until the end of his days.

GMB was much drawn to Mary, the Mother of Christ; and she appears under a multitude of titles. In the poem 'The Statue in the Hills', which appeared in his collection *Fishermen with Ploughs*, published in 1971, he throws titles into the wind. Here are a few: Our Lady of the Silver Dancers, Our Lady of Oil and Salt, Our Lady of the Inshore, Our Lady of Querns, Our Lady of the Last Snow, Our Lady of Quiet Waters, Our Lady of Vagabonds, Our Lady of Fishbone and Crust, Our Lady of Dark Saturday, Our Lady of Kneeling Oxen.

In my conversations with him, George showed a deep interest in the Celtic traditions of Iona. The spirituality of Celtic Christianity – sets of practices found in Ireland, Scotland and other parts of Europe in the early Middle Ages – is marked by a reverence for the created world; it saw God as being everywhere, in everything. The Book of Nature sat alongside the Book of the Bible as sources of knowledge of the divine. Lovely Celtic poems and benedictions also pointed to the presence of God in domestic routines and relationships. The blessings were passed on orally; many poems, prayers and benedictions were gathered from the Gaelic tradition by folklorist Alexander Carmichael in the Highlands and Islands of Scotland. His collection, *Carmina Gadelica*, was published by Floris Publications in 1992. Contemporary Celtic prayers, based on the older styles and themes, are popular. Here is the Rune of the Peat Fire:

The Sacred Three
to save, to shield,
to surround the hearth,
the house, the household,
this eve, this night;

Oh, this eve, this night,
and every night,
each single night.

The very elements are seen as conveying the grace of God, as expressed in the Iona Blessing:

Deep Peace of the Running Wave to you.
Deep Peace of the Flowing Air to you.
Deep Peace of the Quiet Earth to you.
Deep Peace of the Shining Stars to you.
Deep Peace of the Son of Peace to you.

The first stanza of GMB's poem, 'Our Lady of the Waves', shows a Celtic influence:

The twenty brothers of Eynhallow
Have made a figure of Our Lady.
From red stone they carved her
And set her on a headland.
There spindrift salts her feet.
At dawn the brothers sang this
  Blessed Lady, since midnight
  We have done three things.
  We have bent hooks.
  We have patched a sail.
  We have sharpened knives.
  Yet the little silver brothers are afraid.
  Bid them come to our net.
  Show them our fire, our fine round plates.
  Per Dominum Christum nostrum
  Look mildly on our hungers.

George attributed 'a vein of Celtic mysticism' in his writing to his mother.

The title poem of *The Year of the Whale* brings together one of the poet's most persistent themes – the transience of human life. Here is the first stanza:

The old go, one by one, like guttered flames.
  This past winter
    Tammag the bee-man has taken his cold blank mask
      To the honeycomb under the hill,
    Corston who ploughed out the moor
  Unyoked and gone; and I ask,
Is Heddle lame, that in youth could dance and saunter
      A way to the chastest bed?
The kirkyard is full of their names
  Chiselled in stone. Only myself and Yule
    In the ale-house now, speak of the great whale year.

George Mackay Brown's signature is all over this poem. In GMB's world, loss has to be named in specific, personal terms. While, like Edwin Muir, he is drawn to the heraldic and the ritualistic, he differs from Muir in his emphasis on the personal and the peculiar. Reading that first stanza, one can picture the characters, even though they are conjured up in such economic, compressed terms. Tammag the bee-man, Corston the ploughman, Heddle the sauntering philanderer: they have had their moments in earthly time. Only Yule and the narrator can talk in the pub about the great whale year, and they too will soon pass into legend.

Another poem in *The Year of the Whale* names two themes that will engage GMB's attention for the rest of his life: the importance of silence and the true vocation of the poet. His poem 'The Poet' is of particular interest:

Therefore he no more troubled the pool of silence.
But put on mask and cloak,
Strung a guitar
And moved among the folk.
Dancing they cried,
'Ah, how our sober islands
Are gay again, since this blind lyrical tramp
Invaded the Fair!'

Under the last dead lamp
When all the dancers and masks had gone inside

His cold stare
Returned to its true task, interrogation of silence.

The first word of the poem, 'Therefore', creates the sense that this is part of an ongoing conversation. The poet leaves his private 'pool of silence' to do his very public duty. For this, he needs his mask and cloak and guitar. This familiar, strange outsider, 'this blind lyrical tramp', enlivens the feast. But, after the revellers have gone inside, his 'cold stare' returns to its proper business, interrogation of silence. This is the 'true task', the poet's solitary vocation. While he can engender a convivial atmosphere, this weird tramp is inwardly a recluse. He is in the world of masks and music, but he is not of it.

George enjoyed convivial company, especially when drink had been taken and his inhibitions were loosened. Yet, even in the midst of merriment, there was a detachment about him, an inwardness that kept him at several removes. He was more observer than participant; there was something of the solitary monk about him. In the raging discussions at Thistlebank, the MacInneses' home, he rarely entered the fray.

Silence mattered to him. It was essential for his psychological, spiritual and artistic survival. Regular retreat into himself was an essential part of his defence against an intrusive and threatening world; it released the pressure in his life and gave him space in which he could repair his protective shield. The withdrawal into his own imagination was as good as a vacation; the man who suffered from agoraphobia and rarely travelled from his native Orkney was a world traveller in the kingdoms of the mind.

Yet there may be a different drive at work here. A friend of mine who read this part of the text immediately recognised George's over-whelming need to have time alone frequently; it described her own youth.

'If it is the same mindset – and it might not be! – then I'm inclined to think that it's not about self-protection or, if it is, that's not the main reason,' she said. 'I'm wondering if GMB's desire for silence/time alone was more to do with a great drive within himself: to reflect and grow his thoughts and express himself in writing – a key part of his make-up and of the writing process. In my case, I completely withdrew involuntarily from conversations when I was with people after an hour or so if I didn't get frequent time alone through the day. I just took the alone-time, whatever was happening and even if I was in a group of people – and I couldn't prevent it. It was an overwhelming and overriding need. For me, it more or less disappeared in my late teens and early twenties, and it was part of my own development – but for GMB it was much deeper and stronger and lifelong. If I do understand it myself, it's an overwhelming need to reflect particularly on what life is all about and to write, write, write ... speaking isn't enough. It's the writing that matters. That drive is largely gone or temporarily submerged for me, but I remember the strength of it very well.'

As ever, I am made to think and think again by the conversational partners in this book. What is being said here is an important angle on George Mackay Brown's need for silence. I don't feel a need to choose between this view and the view I have already expressed about silence being a hidden sphere of psychological defence and repair.

While extended times of solitude were essential for the functioning of George Mackay Brown, man and poet, the notion of silence itself increasingly held a metaphysical meaning for him. Or, to be more precise, it had metaphysical – literally, beyond the physical – meanings for him. As Rowena Murray and Brian Murray show in *Interrogation of Silence*, GMB came back repeatedly to the subject of silence in order to wrest new meanings from what was, for him, an inexhaustible topic. Silence was not just the welcome absence of sound: it lay at the heart of his maturing spirituality as well as his work as a writer. In solitude, he meditated upon the significance of silence. In silence, silence itself developed into a primary spiritual category of his life and of his work.

But, it may be objected, what on earth can silence possibly 'mean'? Silence is silence is silence. Silence can be a blank screen upon which every human longing is projected. Silence, by definition, cannot reveal itself in words. Silence literally has nothing to say for itself;

consequently, any meaning claimed for silence must have been imputed by the claimant.

GMB was not interested in such philosophical arguments. His emphasis on silence pre-dated his conversion to Roman Catholicism; he was used to the geography of ceilings. Now, silence was nourished and enriched by his adopted faith. In GMB's understanding, his poetry – and indeed his life – came from what he called the 'pool of silence', to which it would eventually return.

There is something elemental in his understanding of silence; it is out of silence that the originating Word is spoken. The opening of the book of Genesis put it thus:

> In the beginning God created the heaven and the earth.
>
> And the earth was without form, and void; and darkness was upon the face of the deep. And the Spirit of God moved upon the face of the waters.
>
> And God said, Let there be light: and there was light. (Genesis 1:1–3, KJV)

The brooding, creative spirit of God hovers silently over the waters before the generating, divine Word is uttered. But what of the silence which preceded the Word? I was helped to understand something of this by the Israeli pianist and conductor Daniel Barenboim. In the first of his Reith Lectures – which was titled 'In the Beginning was Sound' – delivered in the Cadogan Hall, London, in 2006, Barenboim talked about the importance of the silence before the first sound.

'The first thing we notice about sound, of course, is that it doesn't live in this world,' he said. 'Whatever concert took place in this hall earlier today or yesterday, the sounds have evaporated, they are ephemeral. So, although sound is a very physical phenomenon, it has some inexplicable metaphysical hidden power. The physical aspect that we notice first is that sound does not exist by itself, but has a permanent constant and unavoidable relation with silence. And therefore the music does not start from the first note and goes on to the second note, etc. etc., but the first note already determines the music itself, because it comes out of the silence that precedes it.'

For GMB also, silence had 'some inexplicable metaphysical hidden power'. Just as there are times when he comes close to confusing God and Nature, there are times when he comes close to confusing God and silence. From a philosopher's point of view, his thinking is somewhat fuzzy. He is not much interested in definitions and boundaries, and is content to live with mystery. Silence, for him, is the sphere of God; religious wordiness is therefore inappropriate. He would have understood theologian Robert Funk's observation that when the gods are silent, man becomes a gossip. In E. M. Forster's *A Passage to India* – a book that GMB said he had read about ten or a dozen times – Mrs Moore, a lifelong but troubled Christian, has come to India to try to find new meaning and purpose in her life. On a trip to the echoing Marabar caves, she reflects on the faith she has grown up with, and describes it as 'poor little talkative Christianity'.

All creativity, GMB believes, begins and ends in silence. When writer and ecologist Satish Kumar pressed him about the relationship between the 'pool of silence' and the interrogation of silence, he replied: 'Of course there must be relationships, because life wouldn't continue without them, but all relationships and all words end in solitude and in silence. I am interested in human relationships, but in the end it's the solitude which is my destination. I am trying to say something which is almost impossible to say. I cannot explain silence in words.'

The difficulty inherent in 'trying to say something which is almost impossible to say' troubled GMB all his life. As he struggled to explain the inexplicable, he linked silence to perfection. 'I think the only perfect poem or piece of music is pure silence, and a very good poem or a very good piece of music approaches this silence,' he told Kumar. 'But the silence that comes after a good poem or a good piece of music is quite different from the silence that went before it. The silence which follows a beautiful piece of music or poem is richer and more perfect – something towards which the music or poem aspires, but never quite achieves.'

There are echoes of Plato here. The Greek philosopher put forward the notion that heaven was the sphere in which 'pure forms', of which earthly things were mere shadows, existed. In other words, only in the transcendent realms, the place of the silence of the gods, was pure perfection and originality to be found. Earth-bound creativity aspired towards perfection but could never attain it.

George certainly would have understood these words from St Paul, when the apostle contrasted the shadowy nature of human knowledge on earth with the clarity of the divine encounter after death: 'For now we see through a glass, darkly; but then face to face: now I know in part; but then shall I know even as also I am known' (1 Corinthians 13:12, KJV).

GMB believed that, while the poet's true vocation was to interrogate the silence in which the perfect poem resided, he or she could never quite get to its core.

> Its secret is always beyond your deepest
> > Questionings,
> > That rune.

As critic George Steiner put it: 'Language can only deal meaningfully with a special, restricted segment of reality. The rest, and it is presumably the much larger part, is silence.'

This contrast between imperfection and perfection, between provisionality and completeness, lies at the core of GMB's mature spiritual vision and his work as a poet. He is always seeking after the perfect poem and the perfect story, even as he knows that perfection is unattainable. He articulates this through a variety of voices in his poems and stories. *In the morning I will bring a work of great beauty to the prince, a blank paper, silence. After the perfect poem – which no poet will ever write – the second-best poem is silence.*

Yet, despite its limitations, an exceptional poem could be almost sacramental. *The poem was, as never before, a cold pure round of silence; a fold; a chalice where, having tasted, a man may understand and rejoice.*

A Catholic tradition of spiritual theology that has some similarities with the poet's quest is called the *Via Negativa*, the way of negation. It is most commonly explored by theologians who are sympathetic to mysticism.

The argument goes something like this: God, by definition, is absolutely 'other'. Human minds are limited. It is therefore very difficult to make positive statements about the divine. Those theologians who walk the *Via Negativa* – also known as the 'apophatic' (negative) tradition – insist that it is important to say what God is *not*. God is not another 'thing' in a universe of things. God does not exist in the same sense as everything else exists. God's 'goodness' is not the same as human goodness. And so on.

There is an obvious problem here. In a provocative essay, 'How to Be an Atheist', the Catholic philosopher Denys Turner, Norris-Hulse Professor of Divinity at Cambridge University, UK, talks about the problem of 'deferral' – that is to say, by continually concentrating attention on what God is not, one defers saying anything positive about God at all. God is thereby rendered effectively redundant. Mystics tend to respond that the only way to bridge the human–divine knowledge gap is by direct personal experience. This internal experience should be expressed in chaste language; God can be spoken of only by way of analogy and metaphor, and even then in very limited ways. The allusive language of poetry rather than prose is best equipped for the impossible task.

This comparatively modest style of Christian thinking and behaving is quite different from the Stand Up and Be Counted school of religious proselytising – and also from those who refer to God as if he were the pal next door. At all costs, the mystics would say, the mysterious 'otherness' of the divine must be protected. They point to Scriptural texts such as the Old Testament story of Moses and the burning bush; when Moses asks God what name he should call Him, God answers enigmatically: 'I am what I am'. God reveals himself to the prophet Elijah not in a great wind, or earthquake or fire, but in a still small voice. This theological approach emphasises asking the right questions over against delivering the right answers. GMB's view that the task, the vocation, of the poet is the interrogation of silence belongs in the same spiritual territory.

George would not have entered these debates. His embrace of Catholic Christianity did not come out of a philosophical inquiry which established that Catholicism was the one true faith or even that Christianity was the repository of everything that could be said about God. For GMB, Catholic Christianity was a rich, comprehensive, spiritually authentic resource, a treasury that would take many life-times to explore. It was more than enough for the poet to be getting on with.

GMB put these words in the mouth of a poet in 'The Seven Poets' (from *The Sun's Net*): *I think often of the boundless power of words. A Word made everything in the beginning. The uttering of that Word took six days. What is this poetry that I busy myself with? A futile yearning towards a realisation of that marvellous Word. What is all poetry but a quest for the meaning and beauty and majesty of the original Word? Poets all over the world since time began have been busy at the task of re-creation, each with his own little pen and parchment ... I think that Shakespeare in his lifetime made perhaps the millionth part of a single letter of the Word. Will the complete Word ever be spoken for the second time? ... This is my contribution to the Word – such a sound as a speck of dust might make falling on grass – no more.*

George's constant tinkerings with even published poems were not evidence of an obsessive-compulsive disorder; his quest for a perfection which he knew to be impossible to attain stemmed from a humility which was an integral part of his religious view of life. It also explains why he returned to the same themes time and again; there were always, always, new ways of approaching the same subject. Even if the poet could never say it *right*, that did not mean that he or she could not learn to say it *better*. And better again. The Nobel Prize-winning Polish poet, Czesław Miłosz, says that the enigmatic impulse that does not allow a poet to settle down in the achieved, the finished, is, quite simply, a quest for reality.

Unsurprisingly, there were times when GMB drew out very little fresh water after returning with his bucket to the same well too often. Some well-worked phrases – such as 'turning the salt key', 'tongue of malt', 'a tumult of roofs' and 'harp of the sea' – are over-used.

As his work progressed, it showed more and more structure and pattern, largely drawn from the Catholic spiritual tradition.

Through the 1970s and 1980s, and into the 1990s, his collections such as *Fishermen with Ploughs*, *Winterfall*, *Voyages*, *The Wreck of the Archangel* and *Following a Lark* show his fixation with forms and numbers: the twelve months of the year, the fourteen Stations of the Cross, the seven days of the week. The number seven, a sacred number in Jewish and Christian lore, keeps appearing. His poem titles include 'The Seven Houses' and 'Seven Translations of a Lost Poem'. He loved to construct poems in units of seven: *In the making of a story or a poem, the number seven has extraordinary power. The writer can look at a character or event, or a place from seven different viewpoints. It is obviously impossible to hope to grasp and hold a totality; art imposes a pattern on the endless flux. My particular pattern is the heptahedron* (a solid figure with seven faces).

There are Stations of the Cross with Orcadian or Scottish references. His Pieta in his poem 'Stations of the Cross' reads thus:

> *Mother, fold him from those furrows,*
> *Your broken bairn.*

In his poem 'Stations of the Cross: The Good Thief', the thief is told by the Roman soldier:

> *'You carry your own tree, Jimmy ...'*
> *Another gallowsbird behind.*
> *One ahead, burdened, a bruised brightness.*

Jimmy? This must have been Glasgow Cross.

GMB returned repeatedly to the Nativity story, and to Christ's Passion. In poems about Christ's Resurrection, daffodils proliferated. Far from being the cruellest month of T. S. Eliot's imagination, April was George Mackay Brown's favourite month. He could not keep himself away from interlinked talk of Resurrection, April, daffodils and earth's springtime renewal. His delightful poem 'Daffodil Time' begins:

> *Ho, Mistress Daffodil, said Ikey (tinker)*
> *Where have you been all winter?*

There was snow in the ditches last night
And here you are.
Did you light your lamp in that blizzard?

When Ikey came back
Next day, with his pack, from windy Njalsay
The yellow hosts
Were cheering and dancing all the way to the inn.

There are hints of paganism in GMB's spiritual understanding of the Resurrection. One of the attractions of the Catholic world-view was that it was broad enough to incorporate and baptise pagan sentiment. The more austere Biblical Protestantism did not do daffodils – or Easter bunnies – in its discourse about Christ's rising from the dead. Nor was it hospitable to Christmas trees and gaudy decorations. In Presbyterian Scotland, Christmas Day was not a public holiday until 1958. The Protestant churches, ever watchful for hints of idolatry, were sniffy about the fact that the date of Christmas had been chosen by the early Church to replace the popular pagan midwinter solstice. Until the mid-twentieth century, Presbyterian churches tended to view Christmas as a Popish jamboree, and largely ignored it. The result was that Scotland's midwinter celebrations were focused on New Year's Eve, with not always happy consequences. Catholicism, with its ancient rituals for each part of the Christian Year, has always done fasting and feasting much better – a fact which was appreciated by George, who fought his own losing battles with the darker side of the Scottish Hogmanay revels.

To select from the treasury of GMB's religious poems is very difficult. For me, one of the most exquisite is 'The Harrowing of Hell'. It is an imaginative construction of Christ's descent into hell after his Crucifixion and before his Resurrection. This day in the Christian Year, known as Holy Saturday, is a time not just for holding vigil, waiting for Easter morning, but for reflecting on the text from 1 Peter 3:19, which says that Christ 'went and preached unto the spirits in prison'. Some early Christian legends said that Christ rescued many just and good people from previous ages. GMB's poetic account sees Christ releasing Solomon, King David, Joseph, Jacob, Abel and Adam.

He went down the first step.
His lantern shone like the morning star.
Down and round he went
Clothed in his five wounds.

Solomon whose coat was like daffodils
Came out of the shadows.
He kissed Wisdom there, on the second step.

The boy whose mouth had been filled with harp-songs,
The shepherd king
Gave, on the third step, his purest cry.
   At the root of the Tree of Man, an urn
   With dust of apple-blossom.

Joseph, harvest-dreamer, counsellor of pharaohs
Stood on the fourth step.
He blessed the lingering Bread of Life.

He who had wrestled with an angel,
The third of the chosen,
Hailed the King of Angels on the fifth step.

Abel with his flute and fleeces
Who bore the first wound
Came to the sixth step with his pastorals.

On the seventh step down
The tall primal dust
Turned with a cry from digging and delving.
   Tomorrow the Son of Man will walk in a garden
   Through drifts of apple-blossom.

In rereading GMB, I came across a little jewel of a poem, simply titled 'Shroud', which he omitted from his *Selected Poems*. In compressed and dazzling form, it provides an unusual angle on mortality. It manages to introduce the number seven, and finishes on a breathtaking note.

Seven threads make the shroud,
The white thread,
A green corn thread,
A blue fish thread,
A red stitch, rut and rieving and wrath,
A gray thread,
(All winter failing hand falleth on wheel)
The black thread,
And a thread too bright for the eye.

As GMB developed as a poet, his Catholic faith gave him not only 'a swarm of images' but also a freedom to experiment within a hallowed tradition.

I asked Stewart Conn, one of Scotland's finest living poets, to talk to me about religion in GMB's poetry. Conn's work has been widely anthologised. He was made Edinburgh's first Makar (poet laureate) in 2002. When he was BBC Radio Scotland's senior drama producer, he worked closely with GMB. I arranged to meet him in the café of the Scottish Storytelling Centre in Edinburgh's Royal Mile. A distinguished-looking man with a sweep of silver hair, he is a son of the late Dr John Conn, a minister of the Kirk.

'Your invitation made me realise I hadn't focused on George's religion,' he said. 'I'd taken it for granted, because it's a trope that covers the entire work. Looking over the plays and stories and poems, I find it incredibly difficult to unravel religion, spirituality, mythopoeia, timelessness and a bleakness, the "skull-and-hourglassness". The amalgam is what makes him unique, is it not?

'I took the religious part for granted, as part of the texture of what he was writing. But is that not the success of it? – because I never felt I was being preached at; if someone else had been using the same degree of religious reference, as a son of the manse I would have run away as if my pants were on fire!

'Thinking about his life and his relationships, it's almost as if he had a destiny of celibacy. For instance, retracting the proposal to Stella. There's a link to his religion there. He uses the monks – e.g. the Voyage of St Brandon, and the monks in Eynhallow, because what they're doing is down to earth, and they were ordinary people despite the miracles that were happening through them.'

In a memoir, *Distances*, Stewart Conn wrote shrewdly of GMB:

> With his conversion to Catholicism came a consolidation of Christian ritual and symbol, often in incantatory form. At the same time (and especially in the authorial voice prevalent in his masterly stories) I sensed something of a residual Calvinism on the cusp of his Catholicism. And alongside his hierarchy of creatures with Christ at its summit, his work embraced images of the paganism so dominant in Orkney's Viking inheritance.

Back in Stromness, George's long-standing friend and literary executor, Archie Bevan, told me that, despite GMB's apparent insularity, he was always something more than just a very good regional writer. 'What set him apart was the transcendent vision by which he transformed the familiar Orkney scene into something timeless and universal. His work is imbued with a deep sense of compassion, a gentle humour and a quiet assurance that all shall be well and all manner of things shall be well. He was a religious poet who achieved some of his finest work in a non-religious context.'

But was he GMB the poet, or GMB the religious poet, or something in between – and does it matter? Archie told me that, a number of years ago, he was invited to discuss GMB with postgraduate foreign students. Virtually the first question they asked was whether he considered George to be a religious poet.

'I was inclined to side-step the question, because I suspected the answer they were looking for was "yes". However, I conceded that George was a religious poet in much that he wrote, but that he had more than one string to his bow, and could make them all sing with the greatest sweetness and strength, not only those which were overtly religious. The students responded politely, but I don't think I convinced any of them!'

Did he think of George as a religious poet in his earlier days? No, said Archie. 'To me he was quite simply a master craftsman with the magic touch in virtually everything he wrote, regardless of subject matter. There was indeed no shortage of spiritual content in his work at this time – especially in many of the short stories. A slight concern of mine is that, in some quarters, there seems to be a process of sanctification abroad in relation to George and his writing, particularly with respect to his mysticism and symbolism, which might lead to some diminishing of his massive overall achievement. George was resistant to the idea of dichotomies in human life – between sacred and secular, carnal and divine, between the spiritual and the corporeal. I am certainly left with the unflinching view on George – that he was undoubtedly a writer of supreme quality in whatever genre he chose to practise.'

I would agree with Archie that George Mackay Brown should not be typecast as a 'religious poet'. His range was much broader than that. Nevertheless, especially from the time of his conversion, his Christian faith informed all his work. His writing sings of transcendence. He was not a poet who was seeking to propagandise or to win converts; he was simply trying to tell it as he saw it. In his vision of the mundane as well as the spectacular world, the material and the spiritual could not be separated. This is epitomised in the last lines of an early poem, 'Port of Venus':

> *They trembled as their lips*
> *Welded holy and carnal in one flame.*

Since writing poetry was what George enjoyed doing most, he was very encouraging to promising young poets who asked for his advice. George was helpful to Pamela Beasant, a poet living in Orkney, who would in time become the first George Mackay Brown Fellow.

'I was very young when we first came to Orkney, and I was in awe of him,' she told me. 'I met George very soon after we arrived, in 1986. I certainly didn't come here following George's star the way some people did, though I really loved his poetry. I sent him poems fairly innocently, not realising how many people did that – the awfully boring thing, sending him poetry! I got a lovely letter from him. He took my poems to Rackwick and read them there, and then we met on and off for the last ten years of his life.'

What about George's religion?

'There's something very powerful about Catholicism, the beauty of it, the ritual, but there are all sorts of difficulties as far as I'm concerned: the Catholic Church's position on contraception and women – things that maybe George didn't spend much time on. Certainly those issues didn't stop him becoming a Catholic, but it would stop me becoming one.

'Another of my great poetic heroes is Norman MacCaig. I've thought about this often because I really love MacCaig's poetry, but there's something missing in it, ultimately. I think it's the spirituality. He was such a committed atheist. But when George achieves that real purity of emotion and when it all comes together – sometimes I think he over-used religious imagery – it's wonderful, and it works on more levels and wider and deeper levels than MacCaig's do.

'MacCaig's poems do achieve a complete honesty that I really admire, but there's another level which they don't have, which George's do have, when everything comes together; it's an acknowledgement of something outside the self, something wider, and for George it was pretty clear what that was and who he wanted to symbolise it – all these figures that came together for him: Rognvald and Magnus and Christ. At the other end, and just as important for George, there were the drunks and all the rest of it – he was one of them! He identified with the outsiders in the community, which seems to be something he always felt himself to be in some degree – sometimes quite proudly.'

His religious faith gave him a structure for his life, didn't it?

'Yes, the ritual of the Catholic faith and the ritual of his own days and the little things he was attached to – these were important in allowing him to achieve the discipline he needed to become a writer instead of a drunk.'

He was more serene later in his life?

'Yes – although he did have that look about him. If I hadn't known him, and someone had pointed to him and said "That man has depression", I'd have said "Yes, he looks like he does". Although he had the serenity, there was a melancholy sometimes – until he smiled and stuck his chin out, and then he looked like a naughty schoolboy!

'It annoys me when people speak about George as a mystic sage, which is all wrong. It wasn't that. But he definitely had a greatness of the kind which is always linked to complexity and trauma and difficulty, and things that you have to struggle with all your life.'

Another promising writer who was encouraged by George was Christopher Rush, who has since gone on to establish a reputation as a fine poet, short-story writer and novelist. He was introduced to George's writing in the late 1960s.

'I was bowled over by what I read,' he told me. 'He seemed to me to be head and shoulders above the whole Scottish literary establishment. As a student, I had studied Old Norse in Aberdeen, and I'd read the Icelandic sagas. I was struck by how George had adopted that narrative mode and had woven into it a poetry of his own. Nobody could create an atmosphere, a character, a place, a narrative, a starting point, a whole drama, using half a dozen words, but he could do it just in a sentence. It was his economy that impressed me – every sentence was bursting with juice on the inside, but the outside was polished and smooth.

'So he became a hero, and I just read everything he wrote. There is no question about it, when I started writing, I was a disciple, and George was my model. I wrote a few poems and I wrote a short story, and I sent it up to Stromness, not thinking I would necessarily get any reply. But there was a reply within a few days, and he gave a great response. He said: "You have the gift, keep it alive". So I carried on. I was inspired by this, and in due course I sent in a whole collection of short stories. My first published collection was called *Peace Comes Dropping Slow*. George wrote a foreword for it in which he said some nice things.'

Rush had been brought up in the Calvinist tradition. He wrote memorably about his experiences in his memoir *Hellfire and Herring*. 'George said to me that, although the Calvinists proclaimed joy in being saved, it was a very bleak kind of joy. It had no poetry in it. Religion is a sort of poetry and a leap of the imagination. What George and I originally had in common, a Presbyterian upbringing, lacked the poetry he was finding in Catholicism.

'When I spoke to him in the early 1980s, he said that he'd spent a lot of time drinking and partying. He said it was a complete waste of time, and he wished he'd never been sucked into that way of life. And the same goes, he would say, for these stupid literary cocktail parties where people stand around scratching each other's backs and telling each other how wonderful they are, when they should be just sitting at their desk just writing – doing the job they're supposed to do.'

The two poets carried on a correspondence that lasted about twenty years. 'In his letters, he never talked about formal religion. He would talk about religion in a kind of pantheistic sense. One quite interesting thing he wrote to me was that he only felt alive when he was writing. The rest of the time, "I'm dead, I'm going through the motions, the outward flourishes of life, but as soon as I sit down to write I come alive".'

In the silence of his Orkney 'cell', writing poems on metaphysical yet local themes in the compressed style of the Saga writers, George Mackay Brown was a cross between a monk and a skald (a Scandinavian or Icelandic poet writing in Old Norse in the Viking age). His was one of the most distinctive voices in the whole of Scottish literature. Seamus Heaney said of him:

> His sense of the world and his way with words are powerfully at one with each other. His vision has something of the skaldic poet's consciousness of inevitable order, something of the haiku master's susceptibility to the delicate and momentary, and since the beginning of his career he has added uniquely and steadfastly to the riches of poetry in English.

And GMB was clear about his vocation: *The main business of any poet is to keep the roots and sources clear. He starts with language, since that's the material he works in – 'purifying the dialect of the tribe' – restore images, use words sparingly and accurately. For if the language gets fouled, then all values go – people think wrong, or sloppily, then all proportion and values are lost, life becomes meaningless or a nightmare. Under the present-day prosperity of Orkney, and indeed the Western world, terrible negative forces are at work. I have tried to open a few of the old springs that have been choked and neglected, in the hope that one or two folk, here and there, might taste and think again …*

As a writer informed by his Catholic faith, GMB was a poet of the sacrament of the present moment. He saw divine grace in Nature, in human relationships and in the simple rhythms and rituals of the seasons: on land and sea, in church and pub.

Our Lady of Cornstalks
Our Lady of the Flail
Our Lady of Winnowing
Our Lady of Querns
Our Lady of the Oven
Blue Tabernacle
Our Lady of the Five Loaves

> *Take the ploughman home*
> *from the ale-house sober.*

George Mackay Brown pointed quietly to the sacred in the midst of the ordinary. And he did it without donning a black teaching gown. For him, the geography of faith was not just Bethlehem and Nazareth and Jerusalem, but also Stromness and Hoy and Kirkwall. They were *all* places of revelation, places where the rumour of God could be heard, places where the glory could be glimpsed.

CHAPTER 10

Tell Me
the Old,
Old Story

The din of rattling cutlery, the clinking of glasses and the crying of babies threaten to overwhelm the little digital recorder that is lying on the table in Jolly's Restaurant in Edinburgh's Elm Row. The man I am having lunch with, Father Jock Dalrymple, was much influenced by George Mackay Brown. Jock and I have a common spiritual mentor in Father Roland Walls; Jock gave me some help with a book I wrote about Roland, who died on 7 April 2011.

Father Dalrymple is about 50. His beard is greying, and his face is creased. Sometimes a look of sadness flits across his face. He has a vigour about him, and also a sense of the spiritual. I know him to be a wise and compassionate man.

I want to ask Jock this question: given the fact that the Catholic Church contains within itself a wide range of interests and emphases, how would he characterise George's understanding and living of his faith? But first, I ask him about how he came under the spell of the Orkney writer.

'I first read George in 1987,' he tells me. 'My grandmother had died a few years before, and she had a copy of George's novel, *Magnus*. It had been on my bookshelf for quite a long time. I can't remember why, but I picked it up one day. My brother was being married in

London, and I took the book on the train with me. From the first few pages, I was right in there, touched by the magic of it.'

The following year, Father Jock went on retreat to St Beuno's, the Jesuit spirituality centre in Wales where Gerard Manley Hopkins spent years of study and contemplation. On the way there, Jock went into a bookshop in Crewe and found two other GMB books, the novel *Time in a Red Coat* and a collection of short stories. From then on, George Mackay Brown, through his writings, was a companion for Father Dalrymple, especially when he went on retreat.

I ask Jock how he would characterise George Mackay Brown, the Roman Catholic. To explain it, he talks to me about 'exclusive Catholicism' and 'inclusive Catholicism', with the caveat that what he is giving me is 'a very simplistic caricature'.

'Exclusive Catholicism tends to define who's in and who's out,' he says, 'and gives you a clear identity, characterised by a certain approach to morality. I find it a rather narrow and life-denying approach to life. The big fear among exclusive Catholics, understandably, is that if you are totally open, you lose your identity. The problem is that they tend to seek identity within morality, particularly sexual morality, rather than in service to the poor. But there's also a broader position that is inclusive of people, more compassionate, but also linked in with an appreciation of the sacramental dimension of all of human life. It emphasises the sacrament of creation, and of God's presence in the lives of all human beings, particularly those who are struggling. George tuned into this broader stream. He's never narrowly confessional in his faith at all. His Catholicism is much less judgemental than the kind of Catholicism that tends increasingly to get preached from pulpits these days.

'Exclusive Catholicism would see the sacramental in terms of the seven sacraments of the Church – for those who are fit to receive them – over against this much broader sacramental approach which is less concerned with people's past misdemeanours or situations than with the needs of the fragile human spirit. George had a basic sympathy for people who were on the outside, and people who were a bit broken in their lives. Even before he became a Catholic, he seemed to identify himself in that way as an outsider. Becoming a Catholic reinforced that aspect and gave him a framework for the whole non-judgemental thing.'

As Jock is speaking, the words of the lay Indian theologian, M. M. Thomas, come into my mind: 'The Church is defined by its centre, not by its circumference'. In other words, the Church should focus on its centre (Christ) and not on who is in and who is out.

'Quite often, George portrays women gossiping about people,' Jock continues. 'He had sometimes encountered that in the Presbyterian Church – a Presbyterian exclusivism much like Catholic exclusivism, which put everything in a moral, rather than a spiritual, framework. I wonder how fair he was to Calvinism – Catholic communities can be just as negative, but he didn't have first-hand experience of it!'

Jock's thinking about exclusive and inclusive Catholicism is reminding me of John McGahern's talk of the Roman Catholic Church's fortress churches and churches of the spires and brilliant windows.

What was the essence of George's Catholic spirituality, and how did it compare with his understanding of Presbyterianism?

'At a deep theological level – and here I might be doing Protestantism a disservice – my understanding is that, deep down, Catholicism has a slightly more optimistic understanding of human nature than Calvinism has. It wasn't just that God decides not to look on our depravity, it is that He thinks humans are capable of some good! George was very aware of human frailty and weaknesses, and his own weaknesses in particular, but he also had a great appreciation of all that is good and brave in human beings. One of the lovely things about his writing is his sympathy.

'Roland Walls taught me about the importance of where you feel at home. When people come to see me about becoming Catholic, they sometimes say, unprompted: "I feel at home here". There was an intellectual element in George's conversion, but ultimately he became a Catholic because he felt at home – and nourished – in Catholicism: in the final pages of *For the Islands I Sing*, he says that the simple country

Mass is one of the most beautiful things imaginable. Ultimately, it was the beauty of the Eucharist that drew him to Catholicism and confirmed him there. It was the route of beauty. I never heard of him reading holy books or spiritual writings – that didn't seem to be part of it.'

Did George have struggles over his Catholic faith?

'I think he struggled with the change from the Latin Mass to the vernacular after Vatican II. It wasn't to his instinctive taste, but it didn't seem to provoke a crisis in faith. He struggled with his own depression, but that was a slightly different struggle; it probably affected his faith to some extent, but it didn't seem to lead to any major doctrinal doubts.'

What was the main influence of GMB on Father Jock's personal faith?

'One can project things, but I find him a help to my faith because of his emphasis on the beauty of the ritual – although I lack the kind of poetic dimension to really appreciate it on quite the level he did – and his sense of history. Also his sense of the beauty of creation – the whole Celtic, or neo-Celtic, stuff. But he was realistic, too, about the dark side of creation. His appreciation of Nature wasn't in any way gooey – there was a real sense, for instance, of the darkness of the sea, and how it often took people's husbands – and, with them, their happiness.

'Above all, there was his understanding and appreciation of human nature with all its foibles – the goodness and the beauty of the simple person, at the same time as their frequent narrow-mindedness. His belief in the Incarnation – the idea of God becoming a human being and sanctifying human life – wasn't an other-worldly ignoring of the darker side of life; yet he was able to believe that the created world is a place where the grandeur of God is seen, particularly in human beings. It's very much a kind of Christian humanism – it's not life-denying at all.'

Intriguing. I want to think more about this. The notion of 'Christian humanism' interests me primarily as a way of under-standing and describing GMB's maturer spirituality, but also as a tentative way of categorising this stage in my own quite different faith passage.

I want Jock to develop his understanding of Christian humanism.

'On one level,' he says, 'Christian humanism, a broader sacramental approach, and inclusiveness rather than exclusiveness, are three facets of the one single thing. For me, inclusiveness rather than exclusiveness includes always having a place for "the little ones". Our value doesn't depend on how we behave. There's a place for everybody – perhaps less of a place for the self-righteous and those who feel they've got it made – but certainly a place for everybody who wants to belong, rather than defining who's "out". Some takes on Christianity can be fairly life-denying, and for me Christian humanism is the opposite of life-denying. I suppose it would focus on the Incarnation, and take from that the fact that each human being matters. It would incorporate a kind of wonder at the human spirit and its potential, as well as its foibles. Christian humanism for me would be very – though not 100 per cent – focused on this life, with the kingdom of God being recognised as often present here and now.'

As opposed to life being a vale of tears?

'Yes. There is a prayer traditionally attributed to the great twelfth-century Cistercian monk, St Bernard of Clairvaux, which begins: "Hail, Holy Queen, Mother of Mercy, hail our life, our sweetness, and our hope. To thee do we cry, poor banished children of Eve; to thee do we send up our sighs, mourning and weeping in this vale of tears." That would be the opposite of a Christian humanism.'

I see what Father Jock is getting at. It does strike me now, though, after reading George's letters and rereading his autobiography, that he sometimes did see the world as a vale of tears from which he wanted to escape. There were agonised spells in his life when he longed for oblivion. At these times, he saw death as a blessed relief, something to be desired. What it was that kept him going in these bleakest of times will be discussed later; certainly, the dark clouds would eventually lift, and cheerfulness would break through again.

I ask Jock to say more about the sacramental spirituality that he sees at the heart of GMB's view of faith. And what exactly is a sacrament?

It seems rather surreal to be having an earnest discussion about sacramental theology in this busy restaurant. (On reading this part of the manuscript, writer and robust atheist friend, John McGill, interjected: 'What, aren't you guys forever swigging wine and chewing bread?')

'A sacrament may be defined as "a living sign of God's love",' says Jock. 'More recent sacramental theology would start off with Jesus as the sacrament of God. Jesus is the primary sacrament. The Church as the body of Christ, called to be Christ in and for the world, is a secondary sacrament. One of the ways the Church does that is by celebrating the seven sacraments (Baptism, Confirmation, Holy Communion, Confession, Marriage, Holy Orders and the Anointing of the Sick).

'The notion of the sacramental is much broader than that, though. A friendship can be sacramental, a sunset or a rainbow can be sacramental, a view can be sacramental, a person saying sorry can be sacramental. George wouldn't use that kind of language, but it's about seeing signs of God's presence in the ordinary things of everyday life, and not just in church things.'

When I was a minister in Easterhouse, Glasgow, I got to know some nuns who belonged to an order called the Little Sisters of Jesus. They had a flat in the middle of the housing scheme. They believed that a contemplative life could be lived in the midst of the ordinary life of people who were the opposite of celebrities. The sisters, too, believed in 'the sacrament of the present moment'. They were living out something that had been said by St John Chrysostom during the first centuries of Christianity: equal attention must be paid to Jesus present in the poor as to Jesus present in the Eucharist.

Some things are coming together for me in Jolly's Restaurant. GMB's perception of the sacred in the midst of the ordinary is a key part of his 'signature' as a writer, as is his ability to express this insight in fabulous language. Another thing which has impressed me about

George is his concern for outsiders and those who are vulnerable, alongside his love for children. Reading his letters to James Maitland, I was struck time and again by the tenderness of his concern for the Maitlands' grandson, who had Down's Syndrome.

'I am sorry that little Andrew will have from the beginning to overcome difficulties,' George wrote on 18 June 1987. 'But there is a core of resilience in even tiny children – may he live and grow to enjoy the many bounties of earth. Many "Down's" children are delightful and happy, and give much happiness to others.' On 26 January 1989: 'Andrew is a lovely boy. I am so glad he's so much better. I won't be forgetting to light a candle in the spirit for him.' Almost every single letter contains a kind word for, or about, Andrew.

A child howls at a nearby table in the restaurant. Our talk about the sacrament of the poor and vulnerable leads us to reflect on the life and work of another Catholic thinker who has been influential for both of us, and whose writing resonates with some of GMB's themes. His name is Jean Vanier.

Son of the Governor-General of Canada, he was deeply moved, at the age of 17, when he accompanied his mother to meet starving Holocaust survivors. He went on to teach philosophy in Paris, but a visit to an institution for people with psychological or physical difficulties changed his life. Disturbed by the dreadful conditions in which the inmates were living – locked away from the rest of society, and leading dismal, unproductive lives – Vanier decided to follow his heart. In 1964, he bought a small house in a French village and invited two inmates from an institution to share it with him. He called the house 'L'Arche', after Noah's Ark. Today, there are 130 L'Arche communities in thirty countries on five continents.

Never ordained, Jean Vanier is a brilliant theologian and an irreverently joyful prophet for our time. As well as his caring work, his profound spirituality has made him one of the most loved and admired figures in the ecumenical movement today. Now in his eighties, he still shares his day-to-day life with people who have learning difficulties. Vanier's God, like George Herbert's, is a vulnerable deity, one who slips into the margins of human life. In his experience and in his reflections, Vanier expresses a religion of the heart, one which embodies the theology of the second-century theologian Irenaeus: 'The glory of God is a human being fully alive'.

George Mackay Brown took up writing short stories because he needed money. His career as a schoolteacher was over before it started. Physical work was out. Poetry paid poorly. To make a living as a writer, he would have to produce material that would pay better.

He also turned to writing short stories because he was a natural storyteller. He knew the power of stories. *In Scotland*, he said, *when people congregate, they tend to argue and discuss and reason; in Orkney, they tell stories.*

His first two collections of short stories, *A Calendar of Love* and *A Time to Keep*, published in the late 1960s, heralded the arrival of a gifted storyteller. His book about Orkney, *An Orkney Tapestry*, showcased his gifts as a poet and prose stylist; and his broadcast play, *A Spell for Green Corn*, produced by Stewart Conn, was well received. He was awarded a Scottish Arts Council grant for poetry, a Society of Authors Travel Award and a Scottish Arts Council Literature Prize. This productivity continued – and indeed increased – in the 1970s, 1980s and 1990s, right up until the time of his death.

The short stories sold well, increasing GMB's national profile. Some critics preferred his stories to his poetry. One such person, whose work I have admired for some time, is Kenneth Steven, Scottish poet and fiction-writer. He writes out of an explicitly religious tradition. I had a chat with him when he came to Orkney to make a programme about GMB for BBC Radio 4.

'I still struggle a bit with George's poetry,' he said, 'especially the later poems, which I feel almost to be like bare bones. It's the stories I relate to first and always. And the fact that they're not didactic. That's what I'm always seeking as a writer with faith, ways that are not didactic. I'm terrified by didacticism, haunted by it.'

If he were sitting down with GMB now, what are the questions he would want to ask him as a fellow craftsman with words, and also as a fellow religious believer?

'Can I have an hour to think? I'd want to talk to him about the question of the didactic. That would be at the core of it for me. George reaches so far down into people, into their spirits. It frustrates me greatly when evangelical people pick up books of mine and they turn round to me and say: "It's a shame that you don't write more religiously". I could go away and weep at that point. My religious intention is with everything I write, but I want to write differently. I'm a writer who is a Christian, but I don't like to be described as a "Christian writer" – because that seems to immediately characterise one as writing devotional things, which I run a mile from, for the simple reason that it's preaching to the converted. Often the evangelical writers are providing the answers, whereas a writer like GMB is providing the questions, and he's letting the echo of those questions live long after the last word has ended.

'I'd also want to ask George about writing to do with the land, which is always my starting point, since I've grown up in relative wildscape. There's a very strong umbilical there, which is why I'm always drawn to his writing. It is lyrical. He's always a poet, in a sense, whatever it is that he's touching in terms of genre. There's a song-like quality behind so much of the writing.'

As a short-story writer himself, how would he evaluate GMB?

'There's a bareness, a sparseness, about his work. It just conveys so much, so deftly, so succinctly, and I am left reeling with envy. He conveys so much with a scattering of a few jewels of words. I envy that. I know I'm guilty of purple prose – though not so much as I used to be – but I'm still in love with descriptive writing and I can't resist three sentences when one would do! There's such a richness in George's work. It's rich and redolent and so evocative. He's painting with words.'

Any other things to learn from him?

'Humility.'

Given GMB's resolute refusal to pay attention to the fashions of his day, it seemed strange to me that the 'Swinging Sixties', with its exuberant rebellion against social and cultural conservatism and institutional religion, should be the era of his first public flourishing. It was hard to see how the unflamboyant and apparently conservative Orkney writer connected with the era.

Morag MacInnes helped me to see that my view of this particular period in history was simplistic. 'Publishers like a unique selling point,' she said, 'and George had something of the monk about him. As his body of work grew, he also luckily came into the Sixties, that time of innocence and hope and mysticism. The ground was ripe for some sort of celebration of Nature, and of course George does that beautifully. It was also ripe for young people coming up to islands and looking for solitude, and all these values of the Sixties that now appear innocent and naïve. The Beatles and the Maharishi and all that. I think it would be fair to say that publishers probably thought: "Oho, here we have something really good".'

It is still hard to imagine George going along with that, surely?

'The whole Sixties revolution actually fitted with George's way of thinking about life. He was very kind to all the people that I brought up to Orkney, because I was a roaring hippy at that time. He loved them. He loved the idea that I had pals who were walking down the street barefoot, going to Rackwick and dancing in the moonlight, going round the standing stones, all that sort of thing. The era certainly had an atmosphere that made him likely to be successful, likely to sell.

'From the publisher's point of view, George had to be marketed because he was such a shy man. There's no way he could have marketed himself. In the Sixties, there's that kind of innocence and search, and suddenly this voice comes in from the islands, so you've got everything: the island thing, and this poet who's talking about religion in fairly general terms – he hasn't yet moved into the very circumscribed world of poetry that he moves into later where he does become obsessed with the Stations of the Cross and the syllable-counting and all the rest; he's still groping towards a way of finding it. I think it comes through the stories and through the novels. The short stories are interesting if you look at them in terms of a growing understanding of something spiritual happening.'

Alison Miller's view was that a lot of George's appeal then was linked to a romantic view of Orkney. 'It was a kind of amplified Lake Isle of Innisfree, where "peace comes dropping slow",' she thought, 'and he clearly captured a yearning in people all over the world for such a place.'

The pagan strands in George's spirituality and in his Nature poetry in the 1960s and 1970s would certainly have found resonances. GMB's developing critique of modern progress and technology would also have fitted the mood of the times, as would his somewhat romantic nostalgia for simpler days. Whether GMB ever read Theodore Roszak's 1968 cult classic, *The Making of a Counter Culture*, is not known, but he would probably have agreed with many of its sentiments. He was a counter-cultural man himself. So, it is not really so surprising that he liked Morag MacInnes's hippy friends and was sympathetic to their thinking, though he was never likely to be seen wearing beads and sandals. Certainly not in Stromness. What would the pierhead chorus have made of that?

It is also fair to say that George was never likely to be an un-qualified cheerleader for the shaking of the cultural foundations in the 1960s and 1970s. He disapproved of the excesses of the counter-cultural movement, especially in terms of sexual freedom and the taking of drugs (other than alcohol, of course).

My gut feeling is that George's sympathy for the Sixties' and Seventies' emphasis on personal liberation stems less from ideological reflection than from his experience of life-threatening illness. Feeling himself to be an outsider in his own community, he knew what it was to be in opposition to a culture that he perceived to be repressive.

I think it goes even deeper than that, though. His lack of physical confidence made him yearn for a more spontaneous life in the flesh. This can be seen in his attitude to the tinkers who appear and reappear in his stories. At the same time, his childhood fear of tinkers was not entirely absent. On one level, he identifies with them in their status as condemned outsiders. But he also envies their freedom from convention and their (perhaps imagined?)

187

uninhibited sexual energy. He both disapproves of sexual liberation and is attracted to it, despite – or probably because of – his physical frailty. This conflict shows up in his work, and presumably in his soul, though how much of it surfaced in his conscious mind is impossible to tell.

Of all the interviews I read in researching this book, the most penetrating was that conducted by Isobel Murray and Bob Tait. Professor Murray's friendship with George went back to the time when they were both students at Edinburgh University. In the interview, George was asked about his fascination with tinkers. Was it because he thought that their view of everything was somehow detached, somehow truer?

'Well, they're on the edges of society,' he replied, 'they're not part of the establishment, you see, and they have a sort of wild freedom of their own, I think. And they're able to behave in a distinct way from us, who are part of the framework of the community. We are sort of restricted compared with these people.'

Pressed by Isobel Murray, George admitted that he was envious of some aspects of tinkers' lives, even though he recognised that he could not live in a quarry or in a tent in winter.

Bob Tait said: 'On the one hand, there's a very strong feeling from your work of a desire for a very stable social order, where everybody does have their place and their function, and they're known from generation to generation almost *by* their function; and on the other hand, this interest, this appeal of those who are on the margins and enjoy a freedom. Are you conscious of playing this paradox?'

'I think so, I think you're quite right, Bob,' George replied. 'And then the fishermen, the local fishermen too, well, they *are* part of the community, but are still in a way, they are not quite so free as the tinkers, but they behave in their own – they have their own rules and laws, you know – they fight and get drunk and all that sort of thing, but they're fascinating people too, you know, and their wives.'

In his memoir, *For the Islands I Sing,* GMB returned to the subject of tinkers. *I mention those trivial events because later, when I first began* to write, tinkers and drinkers entered frequently into my stories and poems – too frequently, for many readers. One reason, I think, is that such people are possessed of a wild precarious freedom denied to most people who are on the diurnal treadmill of money-making and expected behaviour and whose days are folded grayly together.

With all this at the back of my mind, I was intrigued to come upon a GMB story about a boy's encounter with a tinker girl. Called 'Five Green Waves', it appears in George's first book of short stories, *A Calendar of Love*, published in 1967. It tells of a schoolboy making his way along the shore as he heads for home after school. Checking that there is no-one around – apart from a gravedigger at work in the kirkyard – he takes his clothes off and runs into the sea. He loses himself for an hour in the cry and tumult of the waves. Birds soar past him, and seals bob up and down like bottles. Then he runs wild and shouting up the beach, and falls gasping on his heap of clothes.

Suddenly three words drifted from the rock above me: 'You naked boy.' I looked up into the face of Sarah, Abraham the tinker's daughter. She rarely came to school, but whenever she did she sat like a wild creature under the map of Canada. She was sprawling now on the rock with her legs dangling over. Her bare arms and her thighs, through the red torn dress she wore, were as brown as an Indian's.

Sarah said, 'I come here every day to watch the boats passing. When the sun goes down tonight we're moving to the other end of the island. There's nothing there but the hill and the hawk over it. Abraham has the lust for rabbits on him.'

The tinkers have curious voices – angular outcast flashing accents like the cries of seagulls.

She jumped down from the rock and crouched in front of me. I had never seen her face so close. Her hair lay about it in two blue-black whorls, like mussel shells. Her eyes were as restless as tadpoles, and her small nose shone as if it had been oiled.

'Sarah,' I said, 'you haven't been to school all week.'

'May God keep me from that place forever,' she said. With quick curious fingers she began to pick bits of seaweed out of my hair.

189

'What will you do,' she said, 'when you're a tall man? You won't live long, I can tell that. You'll never wear a gold chain across your belly. You're white like a mushroom.' She laid two dirty fingers against my shoulder.

'I'm going to be a sailor,' I said, 'or maybe an explorer.'

She shook her head slowly. 'You couldn't sleep with ice in your hair,' she said.

'I'll take to the roads with a pack then,' I said, 'for I swear to God I don't want to be a minister or a doctor. I'll be a tinker like you.'

She shook her head again. 'Your feet would get broken, tramping the roads we go,' she said.

Her red dress fell open at the shoulder where the button had come out of it. Her shoulder shone in the wind as if it had been rubbed with sweet oils.

She stretched herself like an animal and lay down on the sand with her eyes closed.

I turned away from her and traced slow triangles and circles in the sand. I turned a grey stone over; a hundred forky-tails seethed from under it like thoughts out of an evil mind. From across the field came the last chink of the grave-digger's spade – the grave was dug now; the spade leaned, miry and glittering, against the kirkyard wall. Two butterflies, red and white over the rockpool, circled each other in silent ecstasy, borne on the stream of air. They touched for a second, then fell apart, flickering in the wind, and the tall grass hid them. I turned quickly and whispered in Sarah's ear.

Her first blow took me full in the mouth. She struck me again on the throat as I tried to get to my feet. Then her long nails were in my shoulder and her wild hair fell across my face. She thrust me back until my shoulder-blades were in the burning sand and my eyes wincing in the full glare of the sun. She dug sharp knees into my ribs until I screamed. Then she ravelled her fingers through my hair and beat my head thrice on the hard sand. Through my shut lids the sun was a big shaking gout of blood.

At last she let me go. 'Next time I come to the school,' she said, looking down at me with dark smiling eyes, 'I'll sit at your desk, under the yellow head of the poet.' She bent over quickly and held her mouth against my throat for as long as it takes a wave to gather and break. Her hair smelt of ditch-water and grass fires. Then she was gone.

190

I put on the rest of my clothes, muttering through stiff lips, 'You bitch! O you bloody bully, I'll have the attendance officer after you in ten minutes, just see if I don't!'

As I left the beach, walking slowly, I could see her swimming far out in the Sound.

She waved and shouted, but I turned my face obstinately towards the white road that wound between the kirkyard and the cornfield. The salt taste of blood was in my mouth.

What a strange, highly charged story! A psychoanalyst would make much of such a striking tale, one which was played out in the theatre of GMB's mind. I am not about to commit the critic's sin of treating all writing as directly autobiographical, but I agree with Martin Amis's view that the writer's spiritual thermometer gives its true reading in the fiction. In the story of the boy and the tinker lass, the spiritual thermometer's reading indicates a significant disturbance, a woundedness that makes for inward mourning. It is not implausible to suggest that this tale of envy, yearning, fear, rejection and humiliation may represent the acting-out of an elemental spiritual struggle in George Mackay Brown's psyche.

The tinker girl is the stronger of the two characters. She is always in charge of the action. The story is told from the point of view of the boy, and it is literally a fearful story. While the schoolboy is drawn to the wildness of the tinker girl, he is also wedded to a more ordered and more defended way. The presence of the gravedigger is not an accidental detail. When the boy has turned away from Sarah, who is stretched out like an animal on the sand, he lifts a grey stone: 'a hundred forky-tails seethed from under it like thoughts out of an evil mind'.

Calvin could not have put it better. The last chink of the grave-digger's spade tells him that the grave is dug, waiting for its occupant.

The boy is both attracted to and repelled by the tinker girl whose hair smells of ditch-water and grass fires. (What did he whisper in Sarah's ear, provoking such a savage response? Was it something sexual? The writer withholds the information.) After beating him

191

up, she holds her mouth against his undefended throat, like a dog that has conquered its rival. In the face of this abject humiliation, the boy who would be a wild man turns into school attendance officer. Taunted from the sea, he makes his way home along 'the white road that wound between the kirkyard and the cornfield'. This is GMB's public personal territory, situated between eternity and the fecund earth, with all its rituals, liturgical and otherwise; in his more private personal territory, he is both excited by and fearful of the tinker girl and all she represents. Drawn to, and repulsed by, the unconventionality and primitive sexual energy of Sarah, his chastened story boy – who had earlier joyously lost himself for a whole hour in the sea, accompanied only by birds and seals – must walk the white road from now on, albeit sometimes with a heavy heart. The open grave in the kirkyard can only be faced while uttering incantations drawn from a more ordered, ritualised world.

The image of the uninhibited tinker girl haunts the imagination of George Mackay Brown. The wild dance exists in an inner room that might be labelled 'the unlived life'. Neither Presbyterianism nor Roman Catholicism could have accommodated such a dangerous, out-of-control swirl. Physical capacity or incapacity would have had its powerful say as well. We do not know.

The elevation of George's public profile in the 1960s and 1970s was not without its problems. He was in demand. Interviewers headed northwards. People in the arts world wanted to have a piece of this distinctive writer who was winning prizes. In Orkney, some feared that George's head was being turned and that he was being taken over by movers and shakers in the wider cultural world.

'In the mid-Seventies there was a shift in the dynamics of the artistic community in Stromness,' Alison Miller told me. 'Where once Ian MacInnes, with his expansive personality, his warmth and generosity, had kept uproarious open house, now the quiet, retiring, reclusive George was taken up big style.'

There were grumbles in Stromness about some of his stories. He was accused of giving Orkney a bad name. Stewart Conn told me: 'I was very aware of feedback about George being very offensive to Orkney and undermining Orkney's reputation – quite vehement criticism – I suppose it was an image of drunkenness they were objecting to.'

Christopher Rush recalls being in the Stromness Hotel one evening when three GMB films were due to be shown on television. *Celia*, which was based on Stella Cartwright, was one of them.

'I thought, Oh my goodness me, what a fortuitous thing! Here am I in Stromness sitting in the Stromness Hotel, and it just so happens that on comes a trilogy of GMB films!

'Then the barman reached over and turned it off. Nobody among the drinkers objected. It was quite an interesting moment that, just seeing it being switched off. An unspoken statement. This typified that early hostility, which GMB told me about personally. "Hostility" was the word he himself used, and he warned me that I'd get the same treatment when I started writing about the East Neuk of Fife in the early 1980s. And right he was! Now there are so many modern incomers it doesn't matter any more. But I'm told that among the locals I'm currently ahead, with 60 per cent in favour and 40 per cent still complaining about "the lies".

'There is no absolute truth, as we know, merely the moody accounts of individual witnesses. But George told me it wasn't about truth or lies, it was about local people feeling that a writer had no right to be opening the community windows for a curious outside world to be peeping pruriently in. In time, of course, he became a well-kent figure and respected in Orkney, but there was that period of hostility.'

The critics, though, praised GMB's brilliance as a storyteller. In the *Dictionary of Literary Biography*, Thomas J. Starr called GMB 'a prose stylist with a poetic vision'. He thought that George's novel *Greenvoe* 'ranks with *The Great Gatsby*, *Mrs Dalloway* and *The Spire* as among the great prose poems of this century'.

What GMB brought to the telling of tales was the craft of a maturing poet. He said that the short stories he wrote were 'sort of poems', though he felt that the rhythms were 'wider and looser'. He also said that it was much more difficult to write a poem than a short story – the poem had to be more or less perfect, whereas the writer had more leeway with a story.

If there is anybody who knows about stories, it is Dr Donald Smith, director of the Scottish Storytelling Centre on Edinburgh's Royal Mile. Donald, who is very much involved in the Scottish literary scene, is an admirer of GMB, and the Centre has a George Mackay Brown room. I had a coffee with Donald and asked him if GMB himself can be seen in his work.

'If one was looking in George's work for things that were an expression of the writer's individual self in a more direct or revealed kind of way,' he said, 'the stubborn dogged misfit ne'er-do-well character regularly surfaces in the stories – like the old, dour crofter who won't take help and he'd rather expire in his bed … he spurns the woman's help and he puts up with it eventually and he doesn't speak to her; and then when he dies he's left all his money to her so that she and her husband can buy a new fishing boat. I think George was a much more stubborn, stronger person than the slightly saintly image of this poetic recluse and charming man would indicate. Clearly there was charm; but in that kind of society, to have managed to endure through the drink, the illness and unemployment, and hang out for his vocation, ultimately must have taken real determination.'

George could certainly be thrawn. The word used in Orkney is 'dugged'. That very characteristic probably helped to save him. Donald went on: 'I think it is fascinating the number of times the stubborn individualist, in quite an unattractive element, surfaces in George's work – and that's one of the interesting sources that generates the necessary conflicts needed for the stories. If it was all gentleness and peace and the rhythms of the seasons and whatever, there couldn't be great art, because you need drama and conflict.'

What about George's Catholicism?

'His great legacy is the work, and when you look at that you can see two strong reasons why Catholicism would be a home for George.

On the one hand, there's the continuity of tradition, with all those aspects of ritual, pattern, whatever, which is very important to George; but also Catholicism would be a personal, symbolic, Romantic choice. His Catholicism never comes across to me as a "preachy" thing in the books. I never ever felt in George's own work that there was an abandonment of the art in favour of the evangelist.

'What you find is the rhythm of the sacred, which is something that is bigger than the individual self, it's bigger than human beings, it's bigger even than the community of human beings – it's a big rhythm in which we all play a part. That's expressed in George's work in the patterns of Nature; but it's not just that, it's in the psychological neurones, in the patterns of psychology, it's in the three great transformational mysteries of birth, love and death. Everything in George's art is saying: "Look at the poetry of what's around us". He achieves it effortlessly, and with this extraordinary assurance: it's the voice of the skald, the voice of the saga-teller – it's not an antiquarian voice, it's a "now" voice, and for me that's the huge note.'

Iain Crichton Smith, himself a fine short-story writer and novelist, had this to say about GMB, the teller of stories:

> Local, though not parochial, he has remained. Orkney is his world, and a curt, terse lapidary Norse background can be seen behind it. Not for him, as for Muir, the myth of Troy but rather the recreated history of the Vikings; voyages, seas, deaths and marriages. He has, as Faulkner did, created a fictional universe which feels authentic. You strike it and it rings back pure gold … He has not gone abroad for renewal of the imagination or for fresh stories. He is and has been a continually renewed well. He has never been seized by the fatigue of the familiar, which appears to him to be sacred … Unlike Muir, his is not an enquiring mind in the world of ideas: unlike Muir he is not a traveller. Like Muir he is a fabulist, but with a gift for the story and the novel that Muir never had. Like Muir, however, he is a mystic, a religious person.

This chapter opened with a conversation with Father Jock Dalrymple about what kind of Catholic George Mackay Brown was. As we were leaving the restaurant, Jock casually threw in the remark that he had bought a painting by Stella Cartwright.

It is interesting how, even from this distance, Stella still attracts and fascinates.

She would continue to play an important part in George Mackay Brown's life after their parting in Edinburgh, and even after her death.

We will return to her.

CHAPTER 11

Making the Terrors Bearable

B efore Edith Sitwell sat down to write each day, she would lie in an empty coffin. The intention was presumably to focus her mind on her own mortality and to place her day's writing in the context of human frailty and impermanence. (When he heard of this ritual, one poet who had experienced the lash of the grand Dame's notoriously waspish tongue is reputed to have wondered aloud why no-one had taken the opportunity to nail down the lid.)

While George Mackay Brown did not begin his writing day with such a dramatic piece of psychic theatre, the coffin was certainly part of his internal furniture. His adolescent familiarity with the gravestones at Warbeth and his Keatsian dance with the Grim Reaper in Eastbank Sanatorium gave him an awareness of human transience that remained until he himself joined the silent conquering army at Warbeth cemetery.

The themes of human contingency and mortality run through his oeuvre. Dust and skulls keep showing up:

A hundred Lents from now
  Who will remember us?

What is a carved name, some numbers?

Sand sifts through the skulls.

Who shall know the skull of a singer?
Silence is best. Song
Should be rounded with silence.

Another tongue of dust will rejoice
A hundred springs from now.

With his focus on mortality, GMB was, of course, speaking out of a long Christian tradition, and indeed from a long pre-Christian tradition. The slaves tasked with whispering 'Memento Mori' ('remember death') in the ear of a victorious Roman general were going about the traditional business of reminding successful people that they, too, would face death and judgement.

In mid-eighteenth-century England, two-thirds of babies failed to reach their second birthday. Even as late as the Victorian era, large families could be reduced by more than a third as a result of disease. There were many chastening sermons on the theme of death.

Advances in public hygiene, diet and personal medical care in the twentieth century dramatically reduced infant mortality in the Western world and increased average adult life expectancy. This meant that many people first encountered mortality at a personal level when elderly grandparents died.

In a rural community like Orkney, in which agriculture is still the biggest industry, death, whether of livestock or human beings, is seen as being part of the natural order. Of course there is distress over an untimely human death – the fishing industry has traditionally had a relatively high death rate – but evidence of mortality tends to be treated with stoical acceptance rather than with Dylan Thomas's raging against the dying of the light. Acceptance is not the same as passive resignation; it is a stronger notion, perhaps informed in the Northern Isles by the Norse concept of 'fate'. As a minister conducting funerals in Orkney, I noticed the difference – 'Ah, weel, we'll just hiv tae get on wi' it' – from more troubled attitudes on mainland Scotland.

In his youth, George Mackay Brown would regularly hear sermons about accountability for one's life right up until the Last

Judgement. He imbibed the heavy Calvinistic version of the Socratic insistence that the unexamined life is not worth living. There was a similar stress within his adopted Catholicism. One of the most oft-repeated phrases in Roman Catholic devotion is the prayer to the Blessed Virgin Mary, the mother of Jesus: 'Pray for us sinners, now and at the hour of our death. Amen.' Many Catholic devotional books and websites advocate contemplation of death as a way of ordering life priorities. It can be stern stuff. One website declares: 'The stench and corruption of the grave in which the pampered body is the prey of the lowest vermin show us the folly of carnal pleasures'.

This is out-Calvining Calvin. Mind you, the vocal un-Presbyterian part of my mind intervenes to suggest that bleak talk about the corruption of the grave might actually serve as an incentive to cram in as many carnal pleasures as possible before death.

When George was a student at Edinburgh University, he was introduced at an early stage to the work of the eighth-century Northumbrian monk known as the Venerable Bede, best known for his study *The Ecclesiastical History of the English People.*

In his magnum opus, Bede cites the words of a counsellor at a meeting designed to persuade King Edwin of Northumbria to convert to Christianity: 'It seems to me, O King, that the life of man on earth is like the swift flight of a single sparrow through the banqueting hall where you are sitting at dinner on a winter's day with your captains and counsellors. In the midst there is a comforting fire to warm the hall. Outside, the storms of winter rain and snow are raging. This sparrow flies swiftly in through one window of the hall and out through another. While he is inside, the bird is safe from the winter storms, but after a few moments of comfort, he vanishes from sight into the wintry world from which he came. So man appears on earth for a little while – but of what went before this life, or what follows, we know nothing.'

Bede's story about the transience of human life preoccupied GMB, whose poem 'Bird in the Lighted Hall' was published in his 1985 collection, *Voyages*:

The old poet to his lute:
'Bright door, black door,
Beak-and-wing hurtling through,
This is life.
(Childhood lucent as dew,
The opening rose of love,
Labour at plough and oar,
The yellow leaf,
The last blank of snow.)
Hail and farewell. Too soon
The song is mute,
The spirit free and flown.
But you, ivory bird, cry on and on
To guest and ghost
From the first stone
To the sag and fall of the roof.'

One way to understand the spiritual vision at the core of George Mackay Brown's work is to see it as an extended meditation, in a variety of forms, on the image of Bede's bird's swift flight through the banqueting hall.

The Gaelic language has a word, *seannachie,* which means 'storyteller', a bard who safeguards and passes on the traditions of the tribe. His role is to tell vivid stories of the community to the community. His tales, repeated and repeated, help to give the community its identity.

George Mackay Brown was such a man. His stories are largely set in a ritualised Orkney of his own creation. Above all writers, including Edwin Muir, George Mackay Brown created the modern myth of Orkney. In his early stories, usually set in the past, his characters tend to be archetypical. Critics have pointed out that this was GMB's way of putting himself at an artistic distance from them. There is some truth in this, but I think there was another reason, one that had less to do with aesthetics. In a close community like Orkney, well-known people might be identified as the models for unedifying characters in his stories. And his critics knew where he lived.

GMB's saga style, his humanity, and the religious world-view that undergird his stories, make his writing distinctive and immediately recognisable. In his tales, everything is seen from the vantage point of his understanding of eternity. Contingency, loss and death are never far away. This does not mean that his stories are gloomy and morbid; indeed, there is a fair bit of holy and unholy joy abroad in the world according to GMB.

Reading and rereading the short stories and novels of the mature GMB, I see his generosity of spirit everywhere. While there is a moral dimension to his work, the spiritual – expressed in non-judgemental terms – is primary. His writing is grace-full, in both style and content.

This quality marks the collections of GMB's tales that appeared from the 1960s until the 1990s. Wedded to a high craftsmanship, his Christian humanism – to borrow Father Jock Dalrymple's suggestive terminology – is, for me at any rate, a deeply attractive religious force. A prose stylist with a poet's gift for the right word in the right order, GMB pulled off the considerable feat of appealing to, and often enthusing, literary critics while at the same time gaining a sizeable popular readership.

The growth in his reputation continued despite his refusal to do public readings. He said that, whenever he had to utter anything in public, his tongue would stick to the roof of his mouth. His reticence was not totally due to shyness, though. He was a man of genuine Christian humility. Posturing and self-aggrandisement were anathema to him. He did not want any fuss made about himself. Since he believed writing to be a craft like carpentry, plumbing or baking, he condemned the tendency to look upon artists as a new priesthood of an esoteric religion. Unimpressed by social status and public image, he was not bothered by accusations of insularity. He knew his land, and he knew his place in his physical and metaphysical territory.

He was disturbed by what he saw as a steady erosion of community. Attributing this loss to a love affair with technology, he was drawn to the mythical as a way of repairing the fragmentation that so distressed him. The modern world, he felt, was suffering from a debilitating amnesia – a lethal forgetting of older wisdoms (including, but not limited to, Catholic Christianity). While he believed that his own childhood days exhibited at least some elements of an older, tested wholesomeness, he felt that these were being lost.

Many stories in the GMB corpus invoke a sense of loss, none more so than the one titled 'Master Halcrow, Priest'. The tale is told by an Orkney cleric in 1561, the year after Scotland was declared a Protestant nation. Responsible for Masses in Stromness, Master Halcrow is not, by his own admission, a very diligent priest. *My kirk, St Peter's, is built above the rocks at the shore. My people are fishermen and crofters. A few women come to my Mass each morning, and when I confess to God at the altar, to these also I confess – I fish too long at the rock, I pray only a little, I drink too much of the dark ale that they brew on the hill.*

The priests round about are no better. One lives openly with a concubine. *In Stenness John Coghill gabbles his Latin like a duck, yet because he is bastard son to the prebend's cousin, a place therefore had needs be found for him. St Magnus, pray for the Church. Pray for an old man whose throat is dry, though not with praying. And pray also for the good and worthy priests that are everywhere in the islands, true guardians of the Word. Easy it is to write of wickedness; their goodness is hidden with God.*

Master Halcrow has visitors who bring him bad tidings, including the learned Bishop whose seat is in St Magnus Cathedral in Kirkwall. The bishop gives him disturbing, though not entirely unexpected, news. *'The Government of Scotland has passed a law. The Pope's authority is put down. All bishops and priests are abolished, and also the Mass. Relic and image and altar must be removed at once from our kirks. The word of God is become the sole guide. Every man will discover the truth that his own soul requires in holy scripture. Henceforth every man is his own priest.'*

Halcrow's colleagues decide to renounce their priesthood and become Reformed ministers. Asked to hand over the keys of his church, Halcrow refuses. When he is shown the bishop's writ that spells out what has to happen, he surrenders the keys. *They waited for me to leave the kirk. I bade them look well to the building, for it was a place dear to me, I having been a priest here fifty years until now. Every stone was become precious to me ... He who now had charge of the parish, the new minister, fearing violence, came between us and said beseeching that now it was time for me to go. Thereupon I bowed my knee to the altar where lay the Body of Our Lord, and turned my back on those men and left the kirk.*

As he walks along the coast, ruminating about his position, he suddenly thinks about the Blessed Sacrament. What might these men have done to the Bread of Heaven? He rushes back to the church to find the statues of Mary and St Peter and St Magnus thrown down. The crucifix lies broken at the base of the baptismal font. He asks Master Anderson, the former priest who lived with his concubine, about the Blessed Sacrament. Anderson draws from an inner pocket the bright pyx which contains the holy wafers. Explaining that he intended to consume the communion elements himself, he asks Master Halcrow to pray for him. Halcrow in turn asks Anderson to pledge that he will come with oil when he hears of Halcrow being on his deathbed. Halcrow puts the round white circles of the Host into his mouth.

Thus transfixed, I crossed myself and walked out of the kirk. The stooks were rising bright in every field. There were two fishing boats off the Graemsay rocks. Jean Riddach was at the well with a bucket.

Saint Peter, pray for us.

This is a touching story about the grievous fracture precipitated by the Scottish Reformation. GMB does not romanticise the priests, who are the objects of local gossip because of their public sins. Halcrow and Anderson acknowledge that they have fallen well short of the demands of their calling; perhaps they and their brother priests bear some responsibility for the speed and strength of the Reform movement. Yet there is also goodness in the two men. Master Halcrow refuses to renounce his priesthood and take the Protestant shilling. Though Master Anderson is prepared to turn his coat, he preserves the Blessed Sacrament and promises that, when the time comes, he will go secretly to Master Halcrow's deathbed and anoint him with oil.

The ending of the story is very significant. The two men's determination to protect the Host, and the pragmatically Protestant Master Anderson's pledge to go to Master Halcrow's deathbed to perform a Catholic ritual, are GMB's way of signalling that though Protestantism was now in the ascendant, the Old Faith would survive in Scotland. This would be for two reasons. Firstly, the words GMB puts into the mouth of the Bishop – 'The word of God is become the sole guide. Every man will discover the truth that his own soul requires in holy Scripture. Henceforth every man is his own priest' – go to the core of Protestantism's most vulnerable area. Secondly, GMB has always believed in the importance to ordinary people of the rituals associated with the cycle of the agricultural seasons, whether pagan or Catholic. He knows that word-based Protestantism, with its hard, linear notion of time and technological progress, will ultimately be unable to satisfy the communal need for symbol and ritual, particularly with regard to the fertility of both human beings and the earth itself. It is no accident that, as Master Halcrow leaves his church, the stooks are 'rising bright in every field', there are two fishing boats off the Graemsay rocks, and a woman is at the well with a bucket.

Another story from the same collection that deals with losses inflicted by the Scottish Reformation is one simply titled 'Witch'. It is a chilling story, told from the point of view of one of the interrogators, and set out in the form of a drama script. It is about Marian Isbister, an 18-year-old servant woman who is accused of witchcraft. She is interrogated by a cast of characters including the laird, a factor for the Earl of Orkney and a Protestant chaplain to the earl.

At the Earl's Palace in Kirkwall, Marian is stripped naked in front of the men, where she endures the humiliating 'witch's test'. *Then the probe was put into the said Marian's body, in order to prove an area of insensitivity, the devil always honouring his servants in that style. These parts were probed: the breasts, buttocks, shoulders, arms, thighs. Marian displayed signs of much suffering, as moaning, sweating, shivering, but uttered no words. After the seventh probe she lost her awareness and fell to the ground. They moved then to revive her with water.*

Another visitor is introduced – Master Peter Atholl, minister of the parish. He sits companionably beside Marian and takes her hand into his. He tells her that he is sent to her by his masters, and that she is accused of 'corn-blighting, intercourse with fairies, incendiarism, the souring of ale, making butterless the milk of good cows', and much else. At a sign from the minister, three men enter the prison. Bearing wine and a lamp, they unlock Marian's wrist-chain. Marian weeps for joy, and they all drink the wine that Atholl reveals to be a gift from the earl himself. When Marian asks if she is at liberty to walk free, Atholl says that she first has to put her mark on a piece of paper. She lets the quill fall from her fingers.

Witnessing this, Atholl gives her a warning. *You deceive yourself. Sign this paper and all that will happen to thee is that thou shalt be tied to a cart and whipped through the street of Kirkwall, a small thing, and Piers the hangman is a good fellow who uses the scourge gently. But if thou art obdurate, that same Piers has strong hands to strangle thee, and a red fire to burn thee with, and a terrible eternity to dispatch thee into.*

Marian tells him to take the paper away. *Then was the chain put back on Marian Isbister's wrist, and the lamp darkened on the wall, and Master Peter Atholl left her, a silent man to her from that day to the day of her death.*

After a travesty of a trial, in which the sheriff shows himself to be in the power of the hated Earl Patrick Stewart, Marian Isbister is sentenced to death. After her toenails have been extracted, she makes her way through the jeering crowds to the place of the gallows, where Piers the hangman mercifully gives her a speedy death to spare her further suffering.

There are many thought-provoking aspects to this story. The role of the parish minister is particularly significant. He is answerable more to the earl than to God. GMB is saying that this is what happens when the power of the Church is subverted: John Knox's democracy degenerates into a value-free tyranny. The sexual dynamics of the probing of the naked woman in front of men who are strangers to her are evident in a 'cool' narrative that requires no comment. Marian Isbister's acceptance of her fate and her staggering through the drunken crowd towards the stake have an understated Christ-like dimension. Piers the hangman, like Lifolf, the reluctant executioner of St Magnus, exhibits compassion – showing himself to be a more Christian man than the parish minister and the sheriff in the brave new world of post-Catholic Orkney.

Among the many poems, short stories and novels in the extensive GMB corpus that express his religious sentiments, is there any single work that goes right to the heart of his spiritual under-standing?

I think there is. In his collection titled *Hawkfall*, there is a story called 'The Tarn and the Rosary'. GMB normally keeps out of his own stories – though he is powerfully present in his absence – but I think there are compelling reasons for regarding this beautifully crafted tale as at least partially autobiographical.

'The Tarn and the Rosary' tells the story of Colm, a young boy growing up in the mythical island of Norday. At school, things are learned by rote; poetry is murdered – just as GMB described his experience at Stromness Academy. And, like Georgie Broon, Colm regularly produces the best essay in the class. There are poor kids there, including the elemental Phil who comes bottom of the class and is a figure of ridicule, much like the tinker outsiders in GMB's school experience. In the community, there is a bitter (Protestant) chorus of women, and there is prejudiced discussion about Catholicism among the men.

'It's the Pope that decides,' said Corporal Hourston sententiously. 'The Pope decides the date of Easter every year for the whole world.'

They pondered this, gravely.

'The Pope' said Mr Smith, offended. 'The Pope. The Pope has no authority over us.'

'No, we're Presbyterians.' said Timothy Sinclair. 'We threw off that yoke a long time ago.'

... *'No doubt but it is a great abomination,' said Andrew Custer solemnly. 'It is The Scarlet Woman spoken of in the Bible. It is the Whore of Babylon. It is the abomination of desolation.'*

Colm befriends an atheist, Jock Skaill, an outsider in the community who is much gossiped about, though Colm's mother makes a kindly assessment of him (much like George's mother did when gossip was going the rounds in Stromness).

Like George, Colm eventually leaves the island to live in Marchmont, Edinburgh. Colm is a writer. He suffers from a debilitating lung condition. He is lonely in the city. He converts to Roman Catholicism. He eventually decides to return to Norday, a move which allows him to breathe more easily, literally and metaphorically.

Several familiar GMB themes are present in this story. Jock Skaill – sounding a bit like John Cleese in the 'What did the Romans do for us?' skit in Monty Python's *Life of Brian* – describes progress as a modern curse. *'This island is enchanted with the idea of Progress. Look at what we have now – reapers, wireless sets, free education, motor bikes, white bread. Times are much easier for us than for our grandfathers. So, they argue, we have better fuller richer lives. It is a God-damned lie. This worship of Progress, it will drain the life out of every island and lonely place.'*

What is most important for our present purposes is a letter that Colm writes to Jock Skaill, justifying his decision to become a Roman Catholic. Skaill had written protesting against Colm's decision in favour of what he called 'idolatry'. He had said: 'I will never never understand why you have been enchanted by that mumbo-jumbo to such an extent. Giving up old Calvin and his works, that was well done, but you have opened your door to seven devils worse than the first.'

In his response, Colm articulates what I regard as the heart of George Mackay Brown's approach to religion. It certainly fits well with fragments, hints and allusions from GMB's other stories, poems, novels and interviews.

'I will try to tell you now, in writing, for I have as you know a heavy awkward peasant tongue. You always beat me in an argument. If I have to

argue, all I can offer is an unfolding sequence of images: stations that lead to a stone, and silence, and perhaps after that (if I'm lucky) a meaning. Where can I make a start? It isn't too easy, trying to assemble your thoughts at half past five in the morning in a cold Edinburgh bedroom, with the prospect of another day of hurt breathing.'

Colm begins by citing Tom Sanderson, a peasant in Norday who is well known to Skaill, pointing out that Sanderson lives a monotonous life. Colm reads a deeper significance. *'Tom Sanderson is a simple self-effacing man. In this evil time, indeed, he is ashamed of his coarseness and earthiness when he compares himself with such folk as grocers and clerks and insurance-men. He is, after all, bound upon the same monotonous wheel year after year. There is nothing alluring about the work he does. He wrestles with mud and dung to win a few crusts and flagons from the earth.*

'Yet see this peasant for what he is. He stands at the very heart of our civilization. We could conceivably do without soldiers, administrators, engineers, doctors, poets, but we cannot do without that humble earth-worker who breaks the clods each spring. He is the red son of Adam. He represents us all. He it was who left the caves and, lured on by a new vision, made a first clearing in the forest. There he began the ceremony of bread. He ploughed. He sowed seed. He brooded all the suntime upon the braird, the shoot, the ear, the full corn in the ear. He cut that ripeness. He gathered it into a barn. He put upon it flail and millstone and fire, until at last his goodwife set a loaf and an ale-cup on his table.

'He exists in a marvellous ordering of sun and dust and flesh. I can hear Mr Smith the merchant saying, 'Nonsense – it's simply that man has learned how to harness the brute blind forces of nature ...' I can hear, among the cloth clippings and shears of Norday, a wiser explanation, 'Man and nature learned at last to live kindly and helpfully with one another ...' But that for me is simply not good enough; it leaves too much out, it doesn't take account of the terror and the exaltation that came upon the first farmer who broke the earth. It was a terrible thing he had done, to put wounds on the great dark mother. But his recklessness and impiety paid off at the end of summer when he stood among the sheaves. Soon there were loaves on his table; he kept every tenth loaf back – the set-apart secret bread. Why?

Because he sensed that there was another actor in the cosmic drama, apart from himself and the wounded earth-mother: the Wisdom that in the first place had lured him on to shrug off his brutishness – the quickener, ordainer, ripener, orderer, utterer – the peasant with his liking for simplicity called it God. Man made God a gift in exchange for the gifts of life, imagination, and food. But still the primitive guilts and terrors remained, for the fruitful generous earth would have to be wounded with the plough each spring-time.

'In the end, to reconcile the divine and the brutish in men, that Wisdom took on itself to endure all that the earth-born endure, birth and hunger and death.

'You have read and digested all those Thinker's Library books on your mantelpiece – Robertson, Ingersoll, Reade – and so you know that no such person as Jesus Christ ever walked the earth; or if indeed some carpenter at the time of Tiberius Caesar left his work-bench to do some preaching in the hills, that doesn't mean that he was an incarnation of God – that was the fruit of a later conspiracy of priests and potentates, to keep the poor in thrall.

'But I believe it. I have for my share of the earth-wisdom a patch of imagination that I must cultivate to the best of my skill. And my imagination tells me that it is probably so, for the reason that the incarnation is so beautiful. For all artists beauty must be truth: that for them is the sole criterion (and Keats said it 150 years ago). God indeed wept, a child, on the breast of a woman. He spoke to the doctors of law in the temple, to a few faithful bewildered fishermen, to tax-men and soldiers and cripples and prostitutes, to Pilate, even to those who came to glut themselves on his death-pangs. With a consummatum est *he died. I believe too that he came up out of the grave the way a cornstalk soars into wind and sun from a ruined cell. After a time he returned with his five wounds back into his kingdom. I believe that a desert and a seashore and a lake heard for a few years the sweet thrilling music of the Incarnate Word. What is intriguing is how often the god-man put agricultural images before those fishermen of his: 'A sower went forth to sow ...' 'First the blade, then the ear, after that the full corn in the ear ...' 'The fields are white towards harvest ...' 'I am the bread of life ...' No writer of genius, Dante or Shakespeare or Tolstoy,*

209

could have imagined the recorded utterances of Christ. What a lovely lyric that is about the lilies-of-the-field and Solomon's garments. I'm telling you this as a writer of stories: there's no story I know of so perfectly shaped and phrased as The Prodigal Son or The Good Samaritan. There is nothing in literature so terrible and moving as the Passion of Christ – the imagination of man doesn't reach so far – it must have been so. The most awesome and marvellous proof for me is the way he chose to go on nourishing his people after his ascension, in the form of bread. So the brutish life of man is continually possessed, broken, transfigured by the majesty of God.'

And here comes the key passage:

'It is ceremony that makes bearable for us the terrors and ecstasies that lie deep in the earth and in our earth-nourished human nature. Only the saints can encounter those 'realities'. What saves us is ceremony. By means of ceremony we keep our foothold in the estate of man, and remain good citizens of the kingdom of the ear of corn. Ceremony makes everything bearable and beautiful for us. Thus transfigured by ceremony, the truths we could not otherwise endure come to us. We invite them to enter. We set them down at our tables. These angels bring gifts for the house of the soul ...

'It is this saving ceremony that you call "idolatry" and "mumbo-jumbo".

'Here, in a storm of mysticism, I end my homily for today.'

This is not simply GMB, the writer, creating an imaginative fiction: this is George Brown, the man, justifying his Roman Catholic beliefs – to his own community? To Ian MacInnes? (The iconoclastic MacInnes could easily floor George in debate; to respond to him adequately, the poet would have had to think for hours in solitude, before reaching for his pen.)

George Mackay Brown is here setting out his credo with eloquence and supreme craftsmanship. The notion of unendurable truths being made bearable by being 'transfigured by ceremony' encompasses older pagan religions, as well as the Christian religion. It is a more all-embracing spiritual category than that of the specifically religious; yet, for GMB, it includes and is perfected by the Christian – particularly the Catholic Christian – view. The 'ceremony of bread' is ancient and primitive, healing the wounds of the earth and putting life-giving food on the table; it also puts physical soul-food on the holy altar for the healing and salvation of the world.

Thus the earthbound peasant with his outwardly monotonous life is invested with dignity and a heavenly vocation. He is an indispensable figure in the economies of both human survival and eternal salvation. He is Nature's priest, preparing the earth for the miracle of seed-growth, and offering up the fruits of the earth for the healing of the death-dealing sicknesses of human hunger and human sin. Down through history, he is called by life, by the gods, and then by the God of Abraham, Isaac and Jacob, to be a master of magical, life-giving ceremonies.

I try to imagine saying all this to my neighbouring farmer here in Orkney. He would laugh, would be astounded. Pretty much every peasant farmer and his wife in every generation would probably have a similar reaction. The backbreaking task of wresting a living from the sometimes unyielding earth might feel more like a burden than a vocation.

Nevertheless, even modern farming, with its dependence on sophisticated labour-saving technology, is characterised by rituals and superstitions. It is still better to keep on the right side of the gods. There are muttered prayers as well as imprecations. There is a human need to give thanks for the miracle of the harvest in secular as well as religious ways. The 'harvest home' celebrations, with wine and music and dancing, and the harvest thanksgiving services with their familiar hymns, are still regular parts of the seasonal calendar in any farming community.

The important thing for our purposes is not how the tillers of the soil see themselves, but how the writer by the name of George Mackay Brown sees them and presents them. GMB is a poet-seer who ritualises the world and invests simple ceremonies with sacramental significance.

In 'The Tarn and the Rosary', GMB is not saying that ceremony *explains* the terrors of life, nor does it provide answers to the eternally recurrent question: if God is both loving and all-powerful, how can

He permit so much suffering? Appropriate ceremony, GMB believes, does not make these things comprehensible, but it may help to make them bearable.

George Mackay Brown is highlighting something very important here. In the course of pastoral visitation as minister of St Magnus Cathedral, I often found that members of the congregation carried around with them heavy burdens of loss, particularly bereavement, sometimes stretching back decades. Those who belong to the Reformed tradition are told that comfort is to be found in the Scriptures – and that is true. But sometimes people who are bereaved want to *do* something. The Roman Catholic believer may slip into a church and light a candle. He or she knows that it will not solve anything; that is not its purpose. It is a gesture, an intention, a prayer.

As a parish minister, I learned repeatedly about the importance of funeral services. When bereavement strikes, families often feel helpless and disorientated. It may be the first time they have encountered the death of a loved one – or even a hated one – close at hand. When assisting families to prepare for the funeral service, I have often been moved by their memories of, and stories about, the deceased. These have been woven into the funeral liturgy.

At their best, funeral services are both personal and universal. On many occasions, those who have been bereaved have dreaded the day of the funeral service; yet they have often found themselves strangely comforted and given new strength by the simple ceremonies in church and at the graveside or crematorium.

Some deaths – particularly those of children or young people – shock the community. On many such occasions, I have seen people crowd into the great shelter that is St Magnus Cathedral. The rituals of the bringing-in of the coffin by the pall-bearers, the lighting of a candle, the reading of familiar and sometimes unfamiliar Scriptures, the solemnity of the organ music, the incantatory prayers, and – in the Roman Catholic tradition – the ceremonial sprinkling of holy water on the coffin, help mourners to release their beloved and place him or her beyond time.

It might be protested that ceremony changes nothing. The beloved dead remain dead. One of the most powerful books I have read in recent years is Joan Didion's *The Year of Magical Thinking*. The American essayist talks about the devastating impact of the sudden death of her husband, a Catholic, while their daughter was in a coma in hospital. After her daughter came out of hospital, a funeral service was held in the Cathedral of St John the Divine in New York. A Catholic priest and an Episcopal priest conducted the ceremony. The efficacy of ceremony does not consist in producing a Lazarus effect. It could not bring Joan Didion's husband back. Yet the impression remains from her book that, while there was no miracle, the ceremony gave a bit of order to the difficult days of overwhelming grief.

Ceremonies that avoid the stark reality of death are unhealthy. Families sometimes seek to make the funeral service exclusively a celebration of the person's life. Of course, it should be that; but at the heart of the service there has to be an acknowledgement that a death has taken place. The irreducible fact is that there is a still and silent body in a wooden box. I have heard of clergy being pressured to keep the coffin out of the church, on the grounds that such a public intrusion of reality would interfere with the upbeat talk!

Hymns can be powerful parts of ceremonies of both consolation and celebration. Every parish priest or minister knows that hymns matter to people, even to Presbyterian and Roman Catholic atheists. Hymns stay in the memory bank, strengthened by deeply felt associations with past funerals or weddings or baptisms. Life-long agnostics can find themselves suddenly reduced to tears when, on the car radio on the way home from work on a dark December evening, a boy soprano moves effortlessly and beautifully into 'Once in royal David's city'. Unbelieving mourners can become distressed because, at the cremation of a dear friend, their favourite hymn was sung to an unfamiliar tune.

Religious believers are obviously helped most by these traditional ceremonies, but my experience as a minister is that many who claim no religious faith are also comforted. They may regard the Scripture readings simply as beautiful poetry and choose, with integrity, to withhold assent to the doctrines expressed in some of the hymns; nevertheless, some will find the solemn ceremony consoling. You can see it in the faces of people. Eyes will mist over as images of special funerals show up in the theatre of the mind, when the familiar soundtrack of Psalm 23 – 'The Lord's my Shepherd' – begins.

The same holds good for baptismal and wedding services. The years will melt away as mourners go back in time to baptisms at which 'By cool Siloam's shady rill' caused a mass reaching for hankies. Old men will become young again, remembering Boys' Brigade camps at which 'Will your anchor hold?' stirred the blood. Wistfulness clouds the faces of people who recall hymns at weddings which sadly and painfully ended in tears. It is the shared, communal nature of hymns that makes the difference.

In her book, *Glorious Things*, BBC presenter Sally Magnusson points out that favourite hymns are often associated with life-changing events. She reveals that 'Fight the good fight' is one of her favourite hymns because it was sung at the funeral of her 11-year-old brother, Siggy, who fought for life for three days after being knocked down by a lorry outside his school playing fields.

> It was only when I rose to sing it in tiny Baldernock church, stricken at the sight of the small coffin resting at the spot where parents normally stood to bring their lively children for baptism, that I realised what the rest of the hymn was telling us to do. Amidst the waste of death, we found ourselves singing 'Lay hold on life'. Deep in the misery of the sight of that still coffin, we heard ourselves murmuring, 'Lift up thine eyes'. In a haze of grief we sang of trusting to the love of Christ and a meaning to human existence where there seemed at that moment to be none at all. Sometimes a hymn gets there before you.

During the season of Lent one year in St Magnus Cathedral, I decided to light a candle each Sunday after the sermon. I explained to the congregation what I was doing and why I was doing it. The theme for the season was 'darkness and light'. I knew from experience that some Protestants are made uncomfortable by a gesture as simple as the lighting of a candle (seeing it as 'the thin edge of the Scarlet

Woman', as one colourful preacher put it). I said we would review the situation at the end of Lent. As I lit the candle, the cathedral choir sang a chant from the ecumenical community of Taizé, 'Bless the Lord my soul', while I said these words: 'We light this candle of Remembrance and Hope to call to mind Magnus and Rognvald and all the saints, and all those dear to us who have gone before: and as a sign of hope to future generations yet unborn. Jesus said: "I am the light of the world. Whoever follows me shall not walk in darkness, but shall have the light of life."'

The effect of this simple ceremony was to slow the service down and to allow worshippers time and space in which to name their losses and their yearnings. Far from being discomfited, the congregation found the ceremony helpful, and looked forward to that meditative time and space every week.

GMB saw the Eucharist as the supreme foundational ceremony. He saw shadows of it everywhere: in nature, in agriculture, in fishing and in human relationships. Holy communion was at the heart of his spiritual vision. For GMB, the Reformation itself represented a breaking-up of sacramental allusions and archetypal patterns in the everyday world. The Reformation, in his eyes, was an assault upon the imaginative elements of good religion. Communion every three months in his home Presbyterian congregation failed to satisfy.

Within mainstream Protestantism, the ceremonial has been downgraded in the name of the elevation of the Word. This lack of a proper respect for appropriate ceremony has been costly. I believe that one of the reasons why the ecumenical Iona Community has grown in numbers over the past seven decades has been because simple ceremony has remained at the heart of its worship.

In Iona Abbey, there is a weekly service of prayers for the sick. People come forward and kneel to hear words of absolution and receive the laying-on of hands. There is also a weekly service of commitment. Those who wish to make a personal commitment are invited to come forward and kneel in front of the communion table. A saying of Jesus is spoken for each person. On Good Friday in Iona Abbey, worshippers are given the opportunity to write down the things in their lives that trouble them. The sheets of paper are then ceremonially burned in the flame of the Paschal candle as appropriate Scriptural texts are read out.

Commenting on the value of ceremony, Rev. Kathy Galloway, a former Leader of the Iona Community, says this:

> It allows us as individuals to relate to our own lives in a way which takes us beyond meaningless-ness and despair, a way which allows us to pose a question, and, if not an answer, a resolution. And this in forms and modes which draw on all the creativity of the human spirit, in art and music and drama, in architecture and the work of our hands, in words and movement and silence; and in the use of all the symbols which have ancient and ever-new power – light and darkness, colour, procession, withdrawal and the ordinary things of life – the table and the basin, the bread and the wine. All this to express something that is not different or detached from everyday life, but which transfigures it with significance and meaning.

Alison Miller drew my attention to a poem titled 'Out of This World' in Seamus Heaney's 2006 collection, *District and Circle*. Here is the first section, titled 'Like everybody else …':

> 'Like everybody else, I bowed my head
> during the consecration of the bread and wine,
> lifted my eyes to the raised host and raised chalice,
> believed (whatever it means) that a change occurred.
>
> I went to the altar rails and received the mystery
> on my tongue, returned to my place, shut my eyes fast,
>   made
> an act of thanksgiving, opened my eyes and felt
> time starting up again.
>
>   There was never a scene
> when I had it out with myself or with another.
> The loss occurred off-stage. And yet I cannot
> disavow words like "thanksgiving" or "host"
> or "communion bread". They have an undying
> tremor and draw, like well water far down.'

I am not sure to what extent this poem is autobiographical. The narrator, 'like everybody else', bows his head during the consecration of the communion elements. He believes – 'whatever it means' – that a change has occurred – though whether he believes that the bread and wine have been transubstantiated into the flesh and blood of Christ is left deliberately unclear. The narrator has lost his faith at some stage, 'off-stage'. It's all a bit fuzzy. And yet, and yet ... the sanctified words cannot be dismissed. 'They have an undying tremor and draw, like well water far down.'

Alison Miller connected the poem with an experience of her own at a communion service in St Magnus Cathedral when I was minister.

'When the cup came to me, I passed it on to the woman on my right without drinking from it. My view was that – well, I don't believe in the wine as the blood of Christ, and, out of respect for other people's belief in it, I should not take part in that ceremony. My thinking on that has changed. Even at the time, it felt like a strong rejection of the people around me – I will not drink from the same cup as you – a breaking of the link in our shared humanity. By the time I read the Seamus Heaney poem, I realised I'd moved away from my earlier position.

'It is partly because the sense I had of Christianity had changed from it being entirely a tool of the Establishment, to a set of beliefs that attracts a wide range of adherents from utter bampots to extremely decent human beings that I would trust with my life. What's more, you could find a similar range of humanity attached to most sets of beliefs. There is still a difference, though, in that the Church – and the Kirk – are linked to royalty and the ruling elites; the power of the all-male clergy in the Catholic church is immense. Christianity, by my reckoning, is a long way from being entirely a force for good in the world. But then, no other set of beliefs I can think of, put into practice by human beings, is free from taint. My view now – and I know this sounds simplistic – is that we are in deep trouble when any creed has followers believing it is the one and only truth; that they, by dint of their beliefs, are all good, and those who don't

217

believe must therefore be bad. That's when we start piling up the kindling round the stake.'

Alison's reflection reminds me of the words of another mentor of mine, the late Professor Robert Carroll of Glasgow University:

> If the definition of the divine is to include that which is beyond human comprehension, then any account of God which knows as much as traditional religions claim to know about such a being offends against that principle. Creeds and confessions, Bibles and Korans, all appear to be able to specify the inside-leg measurements of their god to such a degree of accuracy that they can persecute and prosecute any who differ from them in any detail. Religious history is filled with the corpses of people who knew less about the god than the creeds or sacred books permitted, or who knew other than was asserted in such sources.

And again from Bob Carroll: 'Everywhere we look, ideology slouches along the freeways and autoroutes, sometimes carrying a cross, sometimes a sickle, sometimes a crescent, but always busy doing somebody in somewhere, somehow'.

Near the end of GMB's novel, *Magnus*, there is a scene of unspeakable beauty. The tinkers, Jock and Mary, are in Birsay. Mary is blind. Her feet are hurting her, and she does not want to go any farther. She is hungry, and wants fish. Jock is hungry for something else, something indefinable, and he urges her on, towards the kirk. He keeps checking that something he has placed in the pocket of his coat is still there. He stops Mary from stealing a white chicken. There's to be no thieving, says Jock; they need clean hands and clean hearts for what they are about to do. Suddenly a church comes into view. It is the church in which the bones of the slain Earl Magnus are interred.

The kirk is deserted. The monks are asleep in their beds. Jock puts his fingers in a stone hollow at the porch and crosses himself with holy water. Then he bends a stiff right knee in the direction of the red light of the tabernacle in which the consecrated Host rests. He goes forward tremulously, down the nave. In the centre of the aisle, there is a square of new sandstone with a carved cross. It is the tomb

he is looking for. The tinker prays for Mary. Then he readies himself
for the act he feels impelled to perform.

*Jock felt in his coat pocket and brought out a hunk of tallow. He held it
for a moment at the dying votive candle, till it took light. He dribbled hot
grease on to the tomb and set his offering up, a reeky flame.*

*– Beeswax. I'm trying to mind on a prayer. Light for light, Magnus. Ask
the Lord God to put a glimmer back in her skull.*

The pleep of the old woman entered the kirk on a stir of night wind.

– How much longer do I have to bide out here in the cold!

*– A small blink only, Magnus. I'm asking no more. She was as shining
a lass as ever walked the roads. You must have seen her in her best days,
many a time, going to the Dounby Fair with pans and laces, among the
ponies and the fiddles and the tilting bottles. She could see in them days like
a hawk through crystal.*

*Stone and silence. His knees and hands and mouth were beginning to
be numb.*

But Magnus has heard the tinker's prayer. The story moves on:

*This man was now in two places at once. He was lying with a terrible
wound in his face in the kirk near where the old man and the old woman
were girding themselves for the road: Birsay, place of his beginning and
end, birth and sepulchre. Also he was pure essence in another intensity, a
hoarder of the treasures of charity and prayer, a guardian.*

*This fragrant vivid ghost was everywhere and always, but especially he
haunted the island of his childhood. That morning he had been summoned
by a candle, a small pitiful earth-to-heaven cry; its flame quickly quenched,
and seemingly futile.*

The saint – in the novel first described as such by Jock, who
shouted 'Saint Magnus the Martyr, pray for us' – had been summoned
by an unlettered tinker. Jock had dragged old, blind Mary to that
sepulchre because some deep instinct told him that he should perform
a little ceremony at that sacred spot. Magnus was summoned and
sainted not by a prelate but by an outcast with a candle in his pocket
and a prayer in his heart for a blaspheming and blinded old wife.
Jock the tinker sought to make the terrors bearable, by the simple
act of lighting a candle on the tomb of a holy warrior. This unlikely

scarecrow was driven by a profound urge to make a feeble offering with 'a small pitiful earth-to-heaven cry' in the shape of a piece of tallow. He trusted that by some miracle of grace the truths he could not otherwise endure would be transfigured by a simple ceremony of guttering light beside the relics of a saint.

George Mackay Brown would say the Prayer to St Magnus every day until he died.

CHAPTER 12

Orkney's
Still Centre

We are now deep into the heart of George Mackay Brown's mature spirituality. The central figure in his mythologisation of Orkney is Magnus Erlendson, the Norse earl who walked solemnly towards his dreadful destiny one Easter Monday morning in history and legend.

The time has come for a fuller reflection upon the importance of Orkney's saint for the life and the work of Orkney's bard.

The *Orkneyinga Saga*, in which the Magnus story is enshrined, was George's constant companion from the day that the would-be poet with a smouldering fire in his chest first opened its pages. 'A whole new world lay before me,' he would later write. 'I have exploited it to the full.'

Indeed. No-one who has read GMB's output could regard that last sentence as hyperbole. The *Orkneyinga Saga*, with its compressed, sometimes incantatory approach, had an easily discernible influence on his writing style. A later saga, the *Longer Magnus Saga*, goes so far as to claim divine warrant for its narrative style: 'For the Lord made short discourses, so we make this story plain with clear words and pure telling, as God hath granted us to discern'.

Scholars propose that the *Orkneyinga Saga* was written around the year 1200. The *Shorter Magnus Saga*, which was written around 1250,

221

was basically a rewrite of the *Orkneyinga Saga*. Also known simply as *Magnus' Saga*, it was republished in a special illustrated edition by the kirk session of St Magnus Cathedral in 1996, when I was minister. The *Longer Magnus Saga* is believed to have been written around the year 1300.

While many of the elements of the story remain the same in the three accounts, there is, through time, a gradual progression of Magnus from political Viking warrior to gentle saint. In the *Longer Magnus Saga*, the emphasis is upon the religious aspects of the life of Magnus. When he came to write his 1935 biography of St Magnus, Kirkwall historian John Mooney made the *Longer Magnus Saga* his preferred source. In *St Magnus Earl of Orkney*, Mooney presents a fairly sanitised, passive figure.

The sagas tell us that, early in the twelfth century, Orkney was ruled by two cousins, Hakon Paulson and Magnus Erlendson. There was tension in Orkney between Hakon and Magnus. It was decided to hold a peace conference on the island of Egilsay immediately after Easter in the year 1117. It was agreed that each earl should bring only two ships and an equal number of men. Magnus got to Egilsay first. When he saw eight warships on the horizon, he knew that he was doomed. He made three offers to Hakon: to go into exile, to be imprisoned for life, or to be maimed and blinded. Hakon was inclined to accept, but his chieftains insisted on execution. Hakon chose Lifolf, his cook, to do the evil deed. Lifolf was reluctant, and he began to weep out loud.

> 'You mustn't weep,' said Magnus. 'It's not manly. A deed like this can only bring fame. Keep a steadfast mind. You can have my clothes and weapons according to the laws and customs of our ancestors. Don't be afraid, you're doing it against your will, and the man who gives the orders sins more gravely than you.' Then Earl Magnus took off his tunic, gave it to Lifolf, and asked leave to pray. This was granted, whereupon he prostrated himself on the ground, committing himself to God and offering himself as a sacrifice. He prayed not only for himself and his friends, but for his enemies and killers, forgiving them with all his heart for their crimes against him. He confessed his own sins before God, praying that his own

soul might be washed clean by the spilling of his own blood, then placed it in God's hands, praying that He would send his angels to meet him, and bear him to the Heavenly Paradise. As he was being led to his execution, he spoke to Lifolf.

'Stand right in front of me,' he said, 'and strike me a hard blow on the head. It's unfitting for a chieftain to be beheaded like a thief. Take heart, poor fellow, and don't be afraid. I've prayed God to grant you his mercy.' With that he crossed himself and stooped to receive the blow, and took a single stroke in the middle of his head, and so his soul passed away to heaven.

George Mackay Brown never lost his fascination for the story of the execution of Magnus Erlendson. *These historical events form the backdrop to much of the narrative and verse that I have written. Without the violent beauty of those happenings eight and a half centuries ago, my writing would have been quite different. (I was almost going to say, it would not have existed; but of course the talent that will not let one rest would have had to latch on to other themes. There are, fortunately for me, many legendary and historical sources in Orkney from later centuries that any native-born writer can seize on with delight – but still the great story of Magnus and Hakon is the cornerstone.)*

GMB's preface to *A Calendar of Love* expresses his attitude eloquently: *Orkney is a small green world in itself. Walk a mile or two and you will see, mixed up with the modern houses of concrete and wood, the 'old farmhouses sunk in time'; hall and manse from which laird and minister ruled in the eighteenth century; smuggler's cave, witch's hovel; stone piers where the whalers and Hudson's Bay ships tied up; the remains of pre-Reformation chapel and monastery; homesteads of Vikings like Langskaill where Sweyn Asleifson wintered, the last and greatest of them all; the monoliths of pre-history; immense Stone Age burial chambers where the Norse Jerusalem-farers broke in and covered the walls with runes.*

Dominating all the islands is the rose-red Cathedral of Saint Magnus the Martyr in Kirkwall, called 'the wonder and glory of all the north'.

This Magnus was a twelfth-century Earl of Orkney, in a time of terrible civil war. One April morning he heard Mass in the small church of Egilsay;

then he walked out gaily among the ritual axes and swords. Next winter the poor of the islands broke their bread in peace.

Round that still centre all these stories move.

The phrase 'then he walked out gaily among the ritual axes and swords' signals that what is being talked about here is not history. Or rather, it is more than history. The 'still centre' of which GMB writes, and around which his stories move, lies at the core of a mythic Orcadian salvation history which was crafted with the language of fable at a table in Stromness. In this story, the ritual axe which brings to an end the earthly life of Magnus leads to a welcome outbreak of Biblical 'shalom' – peace with justice – throughout Orkney, followed by strange happenings at the martyr's burial place.

Magnus' Saga recounts:

> Not long after the burial, a bright, heavenly light was often seen at night over the grave of Magnus. Then people began to pray to him in time of trouble when they found themselves in peril, and for those who prayed, all difficulties were soon overcome. People would be conscious of a heavenly fragrance over his grave, and recovered their health there, so the sick began coming from Shetland and Orkney to keep vigil at his graveside, and they were cured of their illnesses.

What is known about Magnus Erlendson, and what was the role of the mythologised Magnus in the imaginative spirituality of Orkney's gospel-writer, George Mackay Brown? Here is what *Magnus' Saga* says about Magnus: 'As a leader, Magnus was outstanding, courteous in manner and strict in morals, wise, victorious, eloquent and majestic. Everyone sang his praises. He was open-handed with money and sound with advice, brave in battle and loyal to his friends.'

In his days as a journalist, George was contemptuous of attempts to fill out the saga record. In an article in the *Orkney Herald* on 9 January 1945, he was fiercely critical of an anonymous account of the life and death of Magnus in *The Orkney Book*, published in 1909. He highlighted one particular sentence in the book: 'St Magnus, the isle earl, was the most peerless of men, tall of growth, manly, and lively of look, virtuous in his ways, fortunate in fight, sage in wit, ready-tongued and lordly-minded'. Commenting on this, GMB went on: *Now the truth is that the character of St Magnus can never be certainly known. He may, for all we are aware, have been a moral coward and a hypocrite. In the above quoted passage the author, conscious that he must supply Magnus with some kind of character, brought forth all the noble, abstract epithets in his vocabulary; and cluttered up the page with them. Much better had he confessed to the general hazy ignorance which shrouds the subject.*

This prim lecture about the difference between real history and made-up history is not without irony, given George's later treatment of Magnus. There would be no possibility of mistaking Mackay Brown's Magnus for a moral coward and hypocrite. He was – well, manly. And virtuous in his ways.

To learn more about the historical Magnus Erlendson, I am driving down to Burray – an island until it was linked up to the Orkney mainland by the Churchill barriers – to visit Orkney's pre-eminent historian, William P. L. Thomson. His *New History of Orkney* is the standard text. I was a chaplain to Kirkwall Grammar School when Willie was rector, so I know him well. I am curious to know whether he and George Mackay Brown argued about the historical Magnus.

'I never spoke to George about Magnus,' he tells me. 'He didn't really want to know too much about the historical detail. And I didn't want to be too much influenced by his image of Magnus, so I would steer round it. If I found out a single fact about Magnus I would be excited by it, but George was the opposite. He was trying to simplify his own image of Magnus.'

Was GMB more interested in the imaginative action going on in the theatre of his own mind than in the Magnus of history?

'Not just with Magnus,' says Willie, 'but the whole nature of Orkney society! Look at the way he avoids dialect in his writing. He might not have been a fluent dialect-speaker. Many writers would have written in accessible Orcadian, to give a bit of flavour.'

In his autobiography, GMB defends his lack of interest in accurate history. *I used to reproach myself with being too lazy to research a situation thoroughly before writing about it. But now I'm sure that this is not how the creative energies work. All that is required is a suggestion, a flavour, a rhythm, an aroma. The imagination seizes on such intangibles and creates upon them living forms which are more real than a first-hand account by the best journalist – I was tempted to say, than history itself, but the reality of history and the reality of literature are quite different, each being one facet of the truth.*

If ever I have attempted to research the background to some story I was getting ready to write, I have found that the spirit of the story was always crushed under accumulated facts and figures. I know it is not the fashion nowadays for novelists and playwrights to work in this way, with intangibles and the free play of the imagination. They must go and see for themselves, taste the salt of a strange sea or catch as well as they can the rhythms and intonations of an exotic dialogue. Something in the spirit of modern man demands this, the factual more emphasised than the imaginary. If so, laziness and timidity and distrust of 'the real' have left me stranded centuries back ... Realism is the enemy of the creative imagination.

Interesting, but not entirely convincing. GMB is right to distrust what is confidently presented as 'real'; but surely a writer does not have to make a stark choice between facts and creative imagination?

Willie Thomson talks about the various ways in which the sainthood of Magnus has been seen. 'I present him as a warrior saint,' he says, 'but people like John Mooney present him as reacting against violence – which I think would be difficult to sustain. John Mooney was just too nice a person to write properly about Magnus. His book is splendid – he was the first person to gather together all the different sources, including some pretty obscure ones – but he believes everything he's told. He wouldn't hear a bad word said about Magnus or Bishop William or Rognvald. To him, they were like nineteenth-century missionaries to India, or something like that.'

What is beyond dispute – realism? – is that Magnus Erlendson knew how to use his sword in those bloodthirsty times. His reputation as a pacifist – promoted by John Mooney and GMB – rests primarily upon one story in the *Orkneyinga Saga*. It concerns an expedition made by the king of Norway to the Hebrides and on to Anglesey in Wales. When the order was given to attack the ships of two Welsh earls in the Menai Strait, Magnus remained seated on the deck. Here is how *Magnus' Saga* tells the tale:

> When the King asked why he was sitting down and not seeing to his weapons, Magnus replied that he had no quarrel with anyone there. 'So I'm not going to fight,' he said.
>
> 'Then take up your weapons for your own protection,' said the king.
>
> 'God will shield me,' answered Magnus. 'I shall not be killed if he wishes me to live, but I'd rather die than fight an unjust battle.'
>
> Magnus took out his psalter and chanted psalms throughout the battle, and though he refused to take cover, he wasn't wounded.

What does Willie Thomson think about the role of Magnus in the battle? 'It's not even certain that Magnus was at the Menai Strait,' he says. 'He might have been on a later expedition, but not the one described.' He takes me through a debate about Magnus that raged in the *Orcadian* newspaper in 1994. It was sparked by an article – provocatively titled 'Well, is St Magnus really a saint?' – by Eric O. Paulsen, a historian and journalist in Bergen, Norway. Paulsen argues that, to be a proper saint in the Church, a candidate had to go through a long process before eventually being proclaimed a saint by the pope. When Magnus was canonised in 1135, there were three rival claimants for the Holy See, and Magnus was not proclaimed by any pope. Outside of Norway and Orkney, few people had heard of him.

There is some truth in what Paulsen is saying, but the process of canonisation in that era was often irregular.

Paulsen moved from historical process to theology, raising the question of whether Magnus could be described as a martyr, in the sense of dying for his faith:

> If we read the Orkney Saga, it is rather obvious that Earl Magnus was killed not because he was a Christian (though he was praying when Earl Hakon and his men came), but because Earl Hakon, after much trouble with his cousin, wanted the political power on Orkney ... I can't find any evidence in St Magnus' history that makes him a martyr – killed fighting for the Faith. And with that lack of evidence it's pretty difficult to consider him a saint.

Three weeks later, on 3 November 1994, George Mackay Brown –
keenly disappointed that no other Orcadian had spoken up on behalf
of their saint – came to the defence of St Magnus.

*Mr Paulsen argues his case well enough, but it is at best a grey un-
interesting case. It is the view of very many educated modern people who
are in thrall to the idea of progress and continuous enlightenment, and the
triumph of technology. The scientist has taken the place of the artist and the
contemplative nowadays. No doubt science and technology have brought
many benefits to many people on earth; but with every step forward it has
brought us nearer and nearer to the brink of world-wide disaster.*

*Every war since the time of Magnus and Hakon has become increasingly
savage and destructive; so that the very idea of a nuclear war is too hideous
for the world's statesmen to contemplate. And yet small countries are getting
the means to make nuclear weapons, increasingly. It seems to some of us
that the unthinkable event in the future is more than a possibility. To such a
perilous state have science and enlightened secular thought brought us.*

Mr Paulsen must have been more than a little bewildered to be
cast in the ranks of those who were rushing the world into a nuclear
holocaust.

GMB ploughs on: *We should think of Magnus as a man of pure vision,
who saw inevitably what would happen in history if the impulse to violence
and 'real-politik' – so lauded by the Vikings – was not to be confronted
and denied. Every human situation is a complication of good and bad; is
inextricably knotted in individual human nature and in societies.*

*Here in Egilsay was an unravelling of the knot, a simplification, good
faith and bad faith face to face, in the persons of Magnus and Hakon. They
had met to settle their differences by a peace treaty. The knot indeed was
untied, not by any mutual unravelling, but by a single axe-stroke. This
solution had been decided on by a gang of men (held in contempt at last
even by Earl Hakon, their leader).*

*Drastic and bloody as it was, it seemed, from the political point of
view, an ideal solution, at least for that generation. Orkney was to be ruled
by a single strong earl; instead of the double-rule or even treble-rule, that
had been such a curse in Orkney's governance in past generations – a
situation encouraged by successive Norwegian kings, who could, and did,*

play one Orkney earl off against the other time and again, to their own advantage.

This murder was not so much an event in history as a symbolic act, a ritual, a timeless moment, a sacred dance, a pure imitation of Christ.

GMB observes that a political miracle was the very first fruit of the killing on Egilsay: Earl Hakon became a resolute leader who brought unity and prosperity to Orkney. He also made a penitential pilgrimage to Jerusalem. GMB argues that saints were created not by prelates or popes but by the acclamation of the common people, as well as by the evidence of miracles. *The Magnus miracles were manifold and immediate. You can read about them all in our own Saga, together with the names and times and places of this cure and that. They were all there, to be verified. The Magnus poem – for that is what it is – went like a flame through all the northern parts of Europe.*

The Orcadian poet's defence ends with a typically defiant flourish: *We live in a dull prosaic time, when most people get their nourishment from the tabloid press, and TV soap operas, not from the great life-giving legends. We Orcadians ought to be saying 'Long live Magnus Erlendson' – because that Easter Monday on Egilsay was the greatest day in all our island history.*

GMB does not so much defeat Eric Paulsen's argument as bypass it. His objection to the Norwegian's case is not that it is unsound, but that it is 'grey and uninteresting'. The two men are talking different languages. Paulsen is looking at the historical evidence, whereas GMB is talking past him about poetry and symbolism.

When GMB says that the miracles are recorded in the *Orkneyinga Saga* with the names and times and places 'all there, to be verified', he is not thinking like a historian. He simply ignores the contentious question of the historical reliability of the Saga material itself.

A couple of months after the GMB rejoinder, Willie Thomson entered the public debate with a measured analysis:

I join this controversy with a certain diffidence, for George Mackay Brown has explored the Magnus story in a way, and to a depth, which is beyond the reach of a historian. But it may be that Eric Paulsen and

George Mackay Brown are looking for different kinds of truth. I would like to put forward the idea that Magnus's sainthood needs to be understood at more than one level. Sainthood after all is a complicated business.

Full marks for diplomacy.

Magnus's elevation to sainthood could be described, he said, as a 'political fix'. Among his many qualities, he went on, Rognvald was a supreme manipulator of public opinion, and it was very much to his advantage to promote the cult of his murdered uncle. Willie pointed out that such a move, with the prospect of a magnificent new cathedral – well endowed with land, and attracting pilgrims – was also to the benefit of Bishop William of Orkney.

This makes sense. Bishop William, a learned man who would not normally have been counted upon to support popular enthusiasms, may well have been prepared to lay aside his scruples when it came to stories of strange happenings at the burial place of Magnus. The twelfth-century equivalent of the Kirkwall Chamber of Commerce no doubt joined the good bishop in crying: 'Praise the Lord!'

On the question of whether the canonisation of Magnus was essentially a political and economic miracle, Willie Thomson is circumspect.

> The cults of mediaeval saints were often manipulated by politically astute people for their own ends, but saints are not easily created out of nothing just because it is convenient for the rich and powerful. The process of 'acclamation' – the widespread acceptance of his cult – was an important ingredient of Magnus's sainthood. Rognvald might take advantage of popular acclaim, he might encourage it, he might even ensure its success, but he was unlikely to have created it.

It is easy to see that Magnus fits precisely into the pattern of the Scandinavian patron saints, St Olaf of Norway, St Cnut of Denmark and St Erik of Sweden, all of whom came to represent a growing sense of national identity. These royal patron saints, like Magnus, met violent deaths at the hands of their own people. The creation of an Orkney saint in this fashionable mould can be seen as an assertion of the quasi-royal status of the earls of Orkney. Perhaps it tells us more about the nature of the earldom than about the actual life and character of Magnus. I suppose it could even be argued that Magnus's personal qualities might not have been the most important factor in his sainthood. It is not difficult to connect these royal saints to pre-Christian concepts of sacral kingship – the idea that the king is the priest but, if things go wrong, he may suddenly become the sacrifice. There are pagan accounts of semi-mythical Scandinavian kings who were killed by their subjects 'for good crops'. The Magnus cult is full of fertility and protection symbolism.

Willie Thomson then introduces an absorbing new theme into his analysis. He points out that the Magnus story has echoes of the pre-Christian Balder myth. The Norse god Balder had a miraculous immunity from injury from spears and arrows – as had Magnus in the *Orkneyinga Saga* Menai Strait account – but he was eventually betrayed by a close relative in 'a place of peace'. Balder suffered death – like Magnus – from a terrible wound as 'a bleeding offering'.

'It is clear,' writes Willie, 'that on a literary level the Christian saint was described in terms of motifs, mental patterns and archetypes drawn from a pre-Christian mythical past. Whether ordinary folk also understood Magnus's martyrdom as a re-enactment of that eternal myth is less easy to know.'

What of George Mackay Brown's depiction of the saint as a kind of Viking pacifist? Willie Thomson found it difficult to reconcile it with the medieval Norwegian statues of the garlanded Earl, sword in hand, or with the legend of the ghostly Magnus of 1314 galloping north in full armour to bring news of Bannockburn, or his visionary appearance at Summerdale in 1528 to encourage the Orkney men in their fight against the Caithness invaders. Then there is the inconvenient description in the *Orkneyinga Saga* of Magnus surrounding the house of the Viking Thorbjorn and setting fire to it, with the hunted man inside.

So, have we come nearer to unveiling the historical Magnus? A bit, but not too much. It is clear that GMB is happy to leave aside troubling questions about historical veracity and to allow his imagination to work on the material.

Willie Thomson's multi-layered analysis is judicious and convincing. He regards Eric Paulsen's questions as legitimate but finds his approach to be too one-dimensional; he respects and admires GMB's aesthetic and spiritual understanding of Magnus, but he has questions to ask about his pacifist saint in the light of the known evidence.

This search is reminding me of the 'Quest for the Historical Jesus' which exercised Biblical scholars and theologians for much of the late nineteenth and twentieth centuries. Questions were asked about who the Jesus of history actually was, and how a wandering, unconventional Jewish rabbi came to be worshipped as the Christ of faith, the Son of God, the Second Person of the Holy Trinity. (One or two scholars have questioned whether Jesus of Nazareth ever existed outside of the imagination of the Gospel-writers. Professor John Allegro famously argued that the name of Jesus was actually a code for magic mushrooms. The good professor himself seems to have over-indulged; very few reputable scholars have agreed with him.)

Jesus of Nazareth lived and died in human, recorded history, as did Magnus Erlendson. Both have had post-mortem existences of sorts. Dr Albert Schweitzer concluded his groundbreaking study of the Jesus of history, *The Quest of the Historical Jesus*, in these words:

> He comes to us as One unknown, without a name, as of old, by the lake-side; He came to those men who knew Him not. He speaks to us the same word: 'Follow thou me!' and sets us to the tasks which He has to fulfil for our time. He commands. And to those who obey Him, whether they be wise or simple, He will reveal Himself in the toils, the conflicts, the sufferings which they shall pass through in His fellowship, and, as an ineffable mystery, they shall learn in their own experience Who He is.

In the face of questions about historicity, what I think we can say about Magnus Erlendson is this: down through the mists of time, the lineaments can be traced of a winsome earl who attracted admiration and loyalty – so much so that he became a figure of legend. The story of the death of Magnus in the sagas is patterned on the death of Christ in the New Testament. Like Christ, Magnus is betrayed. Like Christ, he chooses to go willingly to his death. Like Christ, he forgives his executioners. Like Christ, he dies at Easter. How much is imaginative improvisation on the Biblical narrative and how much is grounded in the facts of twelfth-century Northern history is hard to say.

George Mackay Brown, the writer and the believer, the legend-lover and the legend-maker, sees the pattern of Christian redemption all around him, in human life and in Nature. In his kitchen-table reimagining of the world, Magnus Erlendson is a type of Northern Christ. It is stretching, but not breaking, the evidence to say that, for GMB, Magnus is Orkney's saviour. Not only does his death bring peace to the Isles, but also his watching presence from beyond space and time nourishes Orkney's health. When Orkney, seduced by the treasures of technology and a naïve faith in progress, loses touch with the living spirit of Magnus, it becomes drained of spiritual energy and lives inauthentically.

For George Mackay Brown, the death of Magnus, like the death of Christ, stands outside of time. When Christ died at Golgotha, says the New Testament, there was silence, and a great darkness came over the land. When the blinding flash of metal in the sun was followed by the red staining of the green sward of Egilsay, GMB imagines ships standing still in the sea. In Hamnavoe theology, this ritualistic murder is the turning point in Orkney's history.

The killing, for GMB, is crucial not only because it is an act of martyrdom, but also because it is an act of sacrifice. This theme lies at the heart of GMB's novel, *Magnus*. It is a strange book, with features that would now be described as 'post-modern'. There are various narrative voices – including a piece of shock journalism from Egilsay – as Magnus moves in slow motion towards his execution. Timothy Baker puts it thus in his persuasive study, *George Mackay Brown and the Philosophy of Community*:

> by interweaving a variety of styles and perspectives, Brown demonstrates the apparent timelessness of the story by using both archaic and contemporary narrative styles. The mixture of styles in 'The Killing' is Brown's attempt to open the novel up to include far more of the world than might originally be seen in an historic tale.

233

On one occasion, I wrote to George and asked if he might write a St Magnus Prayer which might be used sometimes in the Church of Scotland morning service. 'I don't know if I'm any good at that sort of thing,' he replied, 'but I'll give it a try.' Here is the prayer he wrote:

ST MAGNUS PRAYER

St Magnus offered his
transient power and
riches in this world for the
glory of God's kingdom: not
for himself only but on behalf
of the people of
Orkney and the north, and of
all people everywhere:

So we now offer
thankfully the fruits of our
various labour.

Magnus the novel is, in part, an extended meditation on sacrifice. Noting that, from early times, men offered slain animals as sacrifices to the gods, GMB talks about the first Old Testament offering of bread and wine at the altar – in place of animals – by Melchisedec the Israelite as 'a thrilling moment in the spiritual history of mankind'. Yet even the making of bread, from earliest times, required a form of sacrifice. The perennial 'wounding' of earth and sea is a common – indeed, overworked – theme in GMB's writing. *Nor was the pattern unaltered in the concert of god and man and the animals: for the earth had to be wounded in order to contain the seed, and the ripening corn drew its sustenance from the same deep sources that nourished the animals. Moreover it was a clean sacrifice, not the deluge of blood over the altar and the desperate flailing of hooves. Instead bread shone on the tongues of the worshippers and the redness that stained the brim of the chalice was wine. Also the god of the tribe, it seemed, was well pleased with the silence and immaculateness of the new offering made by Melchisedec.*

But what if the god were to choose to play a more active part, and come to the altar stone, himself the deity and the priest and the victim? GMB points the reader in the direction of the birth and life and death of Christ. *The tribe must have fallen into a deep dark pit to require such unique assistance. Yet to bring this about a man and a woman and a hidden one stood one night at an innkeeper's door in a village. And in the fullness of time the same hidden one endured gladly the fourteen stations of his death-going.*

That was the one and only central sacrifice of history. I am the bread of life. All previous rituals had been a foreshadowing of this; all subsequent rituals a re-enactment. The fires at the centre of the earth, the sun above, all divine essences and ecstasies, come to this silence at last – a circle of bread and a cup of wine on an altar.

For GMB, the Christian Eucharist exists both inside and outside of time. *At the moment of consecration, the bread – that is to say, man and his work, his pains, his joys and his hopes – is utterly suffused and irradiated with the divine.* He sees the pagan sacrifices offered by the ancients as being bound up spiritually with the contemporary offering of the Mass. The bread and wine of the altar point to the sacrifice of Christ, which itself refers back to the ancient Hebrew ceremony of the scapegoat: the sins of the community were ritually placed upon a goat that was then released into the wilderness.

This movement back and forth in time is a feature of George Mackay Brown's spiritual understanding. While he sees the sacrifice of Christ as the supreme fulfilment of the pagan and Old Testament instincts for sacrifice to the divine, he does not play down or put down the older understandings. He is interested in the continuities of earlier and later theologies, pagan, Jewish and Christian, and in their common understandings. *A festival, a shared meal, a song of praise, a death and a renewal, a dancing together: every sacrifice has these elements in it.*

This is orthodox Catholic theology, but it is expressed anew in imaginative and profound ways. George Mackay Brown is a metaphysical poet – whether he accepts that description or not – even when he is writing prose.

In the novel, more attention is paid to Magnus at Mass on Egilsay than to his execution. The narrator watches the dead man walking, one who has a taste of ashes in his mouth. The Gospel lesson read by the old priest is the parable in which Christ compares the celestial kingdom to a marriage feast, and how it is good for a guest to wear to the feast a wedding garment lest, having some inferior garment on, he is put to shame and cast out into the darkness.

GMB talks a lot about a symbolic coat. It means different things at different times. Sometimes it refers to the earl's ceremonial coat for public occasions. Sometimes it represents community. In addition to 'the seamless garment', there is 'the red coat of martyrdom'. Sometimes it stands for Christianity itself, as in 'the long white weave of innocence'. It also represents justice. In *A Spell for Green Corn*, this poem is to be found:

> Listen: somewhere a loom is set
> Beyond moth and rust.
> Fall, tissue of peace, from the loom,
> A single fold of light,
> That the just man
> May walk at last in a white coat among his people.

The parable of the wedding feast and the correct garment for the occasion is one to which George Mackay Brown returns again and again. It almost seems to spook him. (Did he, out of his abiding sense of personal unworthiness, harbour fears that he might miss out on the celestial kingdom? He was certainly a man of many nightmares.)

The Magnus of GMB's novel had had a dream about that very parable on the boat taking him on the fateful sail to Egilsay. *He had experienced this dream a few times in the past winter; it was not a pleasant dream, it was touched always with shame and loss and sorrow, but always when he opened his eyes afterwards he found that his mind was trembling with expectation ... The dream intermeshed with his diurnal existence: and it came, as he knew it would, in the form of an invitation – he was summoned in no uncertain terms to attend a marriage, first the ceremony and then the feast.*

In the dream, the man – who had no name – looked with a surge of shame at the clothes he was wearing. His coat was all stained and torn. He felt he was not properly dressed for the wedding, but the summons had been loud and imperious, and he dared not ignore it. He could not find the festal hall. He suddenly remembered with joy that he had ordered a coat at a little weaver's shop – surely it would be ready? He remembered, trembling, that to get to it he has to pass through a terrible street – a shambles with the reek of guts and blood, a place of fires and burning. Beyond those dangerous doors was the tranquil loom …

The man, to distract himself, sought to enter deeper into the significance of what was happening at the altar. The Mass was not an event that takes place in ordinary time … it takes place both in time, wherein time's conditions obtain, and also wholly outside time; or rather, it is time's purest essence, a concentration of the unimaginably complex events of time into the ritual words and movements of a half-hour … All time was gathered up into that ritual half-hour, the entire history of mankind, as well as the events that have not yet happened as the things recorded in chronicles and sagas.

GMB then goes on to spell out his understanding of the sacramental life, which he links to the whole of nature. *The sacrament deals with the actual sensuous world – it uses earth, air, water, fire for its celebrations, and it invests the creatures who move about among these elements with an incalculable worth and dignity. Sacramentally seen, the poorest beggar is a prince, every peasant is a lord, and the croft wife at her turning wheels of stone and wood is 'a ladye gay'. From the christening water to the last oil those immortal creatures move about in a world unimaginably rich; and the most precious times of the turning year are the feast days when these peasants with the stigmata of labour on their bodies enter as noblemen into 'the kingdom of the ear of corn': that is, when they experience with their actual senses the true dignity of the work they do, kneeling and receiving their own bread, made divine, into their mouths.*

In the dark church, the man dreams again. It is a resumption of the dream that haunted his mind on the Egilsay-bound ship, 'but touched with deep sorrow and denial'. It is a nightmarish scene. He has become one of a great shoal of mouths drifting in front of a magnificent courtyard. The mouths long for the food that is being served inside to sounds of merriment and music. The dreamer concludes that none of the excluded is worthy to taste the king's bread; he knows that unless he and all the others taste it they will drift about forever outside, citizens of a 'defeated allegiance'.

When a royal horseman comes out to sweep them away, the dreamer protests that he is invited to the feast and is simply waiting until his new coat is ready for him to wear; but his voice is lost in the tumult. Not only that, a voice that utters nothing but toneless obscenities and blasphemies follows him around.

My strong sense is that there are autobiographical elements in this writing. The despair and hopelessness have echoes of George's Dante-esque nightmarish hangovers and depressions; and the harsh, critical voice, with its obscenities and blasphemies, may not be unconnected to the cruel and foul things that the poet would sometimes say – and later repent of – when he was drunk.

The dreamer tries to answer the voice, but his lips are frozen. Suddenly, the sound of the sacring bell summons the man out of his dream. He knows that he will not leave the island alive. He knows that his life has been something of a failure, and that he has come with empty hands to the feast.

In that dark kirk, as he turns back to the theatre of the Mass, he offers all that he has left: the peace and the pain.

The gnarled old priest raises high the Bread of Heaven, followed by the chalice. The acolyte goes down on his knees to receive the Host on his tongue.

Suddenly, the man hears a stir behind him.

There was somebody else in the kirk, kneeling by the door. The man trembled with cold and expectation. The priest looked at him, touched with one finger a Host in the paten: he was being summoned again to a feast of unimaginable splendour and majesty. Dare he go, empty-handed and naked as he was? This much was true, the priest had shriven him before the Mass; he had laid aside the patched filthy coat of sins that he had brought with him to the island.

His mouth had been among hosts of evil; it had been one of them; it had shaken clear. Might it not still be capable of experiencing this good before it died (but in a veiled way, since human flesh would shrivel in that other flame, glory)?

The presence behind him and a little to the right, in the darkest corner, said in a clear voice, 'go now, man.'

The man rose from his knees. He went up to the altar rail. A coarse oaten crumb – Corpus Christi *– shone between his lips for a moment. He was a part of the feast.*

The man knelt, smiling, his eyes veiled with blue lids. He felt secure then, like a guest in a lamp-splashed jubilant castle.

Christ around me
Christ before me
Christ beside me
Christ above me

It pleased him to think that when he turned away from the altar he would see, standing at the back of the kirk, the unknown friend. He imagined hands smelling of sandalwood and oil-of-wool.

The man crossed himself. He rose from his knees. He turned. The kirk was empty. His friend was not there. Instead he saw, in the shadows of the porch, the quick flash of a sword and a livid mask above it. Sword and face withdrew at once into the darkness. He listened. A voice called from the next field. The syllables fell among the tombstones. A nearer voice answered.

Ite, missa est, *sang the old priest.*

The Mass was over. The priest stepped down from the altar and approached the man and said to him, Ite, missa est. *That is to say, my lord, 'go now, carry the peace of Christ into the world.'*

The priest then suggests that the man stay in the kirk, for in the sanctuary no-one could harm a hair of his head. The man says he thinks he will stay until morning. He asks the priest whether he has seen another man in the church, kneeling somewhat behind him, a man with a very sweet and comely countenance. *The priest said with a shaking of his head that there had been nobody in the kirk but three of them – priest, acolyte, worshipper. Sometimes it happened, in a time of trouble, that a man would know the palpable presence of the good guardian angel at his shoulder. The priest said that neither had he seen a soldier with a sword in the porch.*

Magnus must go to his death, to make a sacrifice which echoes that of Christ at Golgotha, the 'central sacrifice of history'. Despite the carpenter of Nazareth's submission to the will of the Father, the need for new sacrifices continues. *At certain times and in certain circumstances men still crave spectacular sacrifice. When there is trouble in the dockyards and there is no sound from the weaver's shed; when theologians brood over the meaning of such words as 'justification' and 'penance' beside dribbling waxflames; when the frontier tower becomes a strewment of stones; when black horsemen and red horseman ride through the hills and the heavy heraldic coat is riven; when the deep sources are seemingly hopelessly polluted – then bread and wine seem to certain men to be too mild a sacrifice. They root about everywhere for a victim and a scapegoat to stand between the tribe and the anger of inexorable Fate.*

So Magnus Erlendson, when he came up from the shore that Easter Monday, towards noon, to the stone in the centre of the island, saw against the sun eleven men and a boy and a man with an axe in his hand who was weeping.

It is fated.

Then in the light of the new day, 16 April 1117, there was a blinding flash of metal in the sun.

The tyrant dies, says Kierkegaard, and his rule is over; the martyr dies and his rule begins.

In the appendices to *A Spell for Green Corn*, the archetypal poet Storm Kolson notes: *A few must vanish in terror to keep the nets full. When the wounds of Christ are forgotten, a new saint must offer hands and feet and side.* It is no surprise, then, that GMB takes the theme of sacrifice in *Magnus* into the twentieth century. Herr Lifolf is a chef in a concentration camp. He is commanded to execute a man who is regarded as very dangerous because he spoke about 'the universal kingdom of love' and had sheltered Jews and spies in his church. *We wish to show this pure spirit,* says a Nazi officer, *by means of the butcher's hook, that he is, after all, when all is said and done, an animal like other men.*

Herr Lifolf protests. But he must do his duty, play his allotted part. He recognises the condemned man – a Lutheran pastor whose books were burned at the start of the war. The man stands reading out of a prayer book. He says to Lifolf: 'You don't look like a hangman'. He gives Lifolf his prayer book. Thus is Dietrich Bonhoeffer slain.

Many critics feel that the novel is disjointed and that the shift to Bonhoeffer does not work. I disagree. I would also concur with GMB that some of his best writing is in *Magnus.* What does intrigue me is why GMB chose a Protestant icon to make his point. He leaves no clues.

Bonhoeffer, a brilliant theologian in the church of Martin Luther, had been in America when war was declared, and he could easily have continued his academic career in the USA. Instead, he chose to return to Germany to take part in the underground resistance to Hitler, with inevitable consequences. He was led naked into the yard of Flossenburg concentration camp at dawn on 9 April 1945 – four weeks before Germany surrendered – and executed by hanging. The camp doctor later wrote:

> I saw Pastor Bonhoeffer kneeling on the floor praying fervently to God. I was most deeply moved by the way this lovable man prayed, so devout and so certain that God heard his prayer. At the place of execution, he again said a short prayer and then climbed the few steps to the gallows, brave and composed. His death ensued after a few seconds. In the almost fifty years that I worked as a doctor, I have hardly ever seen a man die so entirely submissive to the will of God.

There seems to be a deep psychological human need for saints and scapegoats. Psychologist and theologian Robert A. Johnston is of the view that saints are people who take on the projection of unlived holiness from a group of people, whereas scapegoats are singled out to carry the dark side of other people's personalities. The sacrificial burdens carried by saints and sinners may be the death of them.

Probably in response to critics, GMB explained in his autobiography why it was important to him to talk about sacrifice in a contemporary context. *In the novel* Magnus *there is another chapter I am glad to have written. Re-telling the story of Magnus and Hakon is well enough; but quite suddenly one morning, as I was thinking of ways to tell the story of the actual martyrdom in Egilsay in 1117, it occurred to me that the whole story would strike a modern reader as remote and unconnected with our situation in the twentieth century. The truth must be that such incidents are not isolated casual happenings in time, but are repetitions of some archetypal pattern; an image or an event stamped on the spirit of man at the very beginning of man's time on earth, that will go on repeating itself over and over in every life without exception until history at last yields a meaning. The life and death of Magnus must therefore be shown to be contemporary, and to have a resonance in the twentieth century. I did not have far to go to find a parallel: a concentration camp in central Europe in the spring of 1944.*

I have quoted so much of the text of the novel for two reasons. The first is that the story of Magnus is central to GMB's personal religious faith, and also to his work as a poet, short-story writer and novelist. It is therefore a key source for the delineation of George's mature spirituality. The second is that these Magnus passages are, I believe, among the finest pieces of religious writing in the English language in the twentieth century. They illustrate again how GMB can take traditional religious themes and, passing them through the lens of Orkney's saga-inspired history, breathe new, distinctive life into time-honoured tropes.

For Orkney's bard, Orkney is a microcosm of the world. The ritual execution of Magnus Erlendson echoes an earlier foundational sacrifice that speaks of a blood-red love at the heart of the cosmos.

In the world according to George Mackay Brown, St Magnus Cathedral itself is a stone ship of salvation, a heavenly Northern ark 'freighted with psalm and ceremony, blissward blown'. And, in *Magnus*, Orkney's bard places every human thing in the context of eternity: *For the generations, and even the hills and seas, come and go, and only the Word stands, which was there – all wisdom, beauty, truth, love – before the fires of creation, and will still be there inviolate among the ashes of the world's end.*

CHAPTER 13

Heidegger's Biro

Was George Mackay Brown simply a reactionary curmudgeon who hated the world he lived in? Was he an unreconstructed Luddite who loathed modern technology, even though its labour-saving devices made the hard, backbreaking work of farm workers, and women with large families, much easier?

Some critics thought so. Poet Alexander Scott accused the Orkney man of living in a medieval religious dream, out of touch with modern sensibilities. There is some truth in this: remember how George wrote to Ernest Marwick from Newbattle Abbey College, saying that, although he was perfectly happy, he wished it were 600 years ago so that he could have taken vows and become a monk. Poet and critic Robert Fulton accused GMB of making his reference back in time in order to dismiss with a grand gesture the kind of society in which most people in the West live. Poet Alasdair Maclean accused GMB of holding the notion that one can will oneself into primitivism.

There is something in these criticisms. GMB's acknowledged laziness in terms of research left him ill-equipped to defend himself against accusations that he did not know what he was talking about when he turned his attention to science and technology. Indeed, another of his critics is his nephew, who is a scientist.

Yet GMB's view of things is richer and more complex than straightforward reactionary Luddism. His critique of the modern myths of progress and technology – expressed sometimes in ranting form – is grounded not simply in wistfulness but in his deeply held religious outlook. To put it in theological terms, he sees the obsession with technological advances as a form of idolatry.

Asked by ecology journalist and campaigner Satish Kumar if he felt that industrial progress had gone too far, and did not know its limits, GMB replied: 'Exactly, yes. It has gone far too far and it shows no signs of letting up – and of course we can see the final result is coming into view now with nuclear power and nuclear weapons. The human race has never been in danger of complete extinction before, but we are faced with that possibility now.'

How had this situation developed?

'There's a kind of imbalance somewhere. I think humanity had kept an instinctive wisdom that kept a balance between materialism and spirituality, but somewhere way back, 300 years or so ago, the balance tipped finally on the side of materialism. We opted entirely for material existence and that's the road we are still taking, I'm afraid.'

Asked why people were no longer so keen on poetry, George replied that so much human energy and drive had gone into mechanical and scientific invention that the energy for poetry was much more diminished. 'The number has taken over from the word,' he said. 'Number has become more important than the word. The real creative thing is the word … Yet it's very ambivalent, because it has brought prosperity to great masses of human beings; people are better clothed, they have more to put in their bellies. So this numbers game comes to us in these two faces, which can be very confusing. It gives an illusion that you are comfortable; so you might be happier. The Great Deceiver can be very subtle. If it was pure destruction, we could see it for what it was, but it comes masked as a great benefactor to the human race. It is like Doctor Faust, who sold his soul to the devil. The devil promises Faust anything his heart desires for, but in the end his soul is forfeit of course. That is a kind of parallel to the modern materialistic progress – that we have actually sold our souls.'

In GMB's collection *Hawkfall*, there is a thought-provoking story called 'Sealskin'. Simon Olafson works on his father's farm on the island of Norday. His mother does not want him to marry – at least until after her death – because she does not want another woman in the house.

When Simon goes down to the rocks one day, he sees a naked girl kneeling among the waves. He rushes to the house to get a coat for her; he covers her and takes her home. His father insists that the girl should be allowed to stay in the croft house. We're supposed to be Christian, he says. The mysterious girl knows no English. Simon marries her after his mother's death. They have a son, Magnus. It is only when Simon is at a stonemason's yard in Kirkwall, ordering a stone for his parents' grave, that the reader learns that Simon's wife has disappeared as mysteriously as she had arrived.

Magnus Olafson becomes a musician and composer, and is soon a celebrity in Europe. At the height of his powers, he travels to Norday. He visits his father's grave. The return to the simple rural community in which he was reared is, for Magnus, a dislocating experience. When he goes back to Europe to the discussions about music and art with his sophisticated friends, he is aware of a disturbance in his spirit. *He often felt, in moods of depression, that he was caught up in some meaningless charade in which everyone, himself included, was compelled to wear a mask. He would take part in the passionate midnight arguments about socialism, the ballet, anthropology, psychology, and he would put forward – as well as his clumsiness with German or French allowed him – a well-ordered logical argument. But deep down he was untouched. It didn't seem to matter in the slightest. It was all a game, to keep sharp the wits of the people who had not to contend with the primitive terrors of sea and land. So he thought, while the eyes flashed and the tongues sought for felicitousness and clarity all around him. He was glad when the maskers had departed and he was alone again among the cigarette ends and the apple cores ... And his guests would say, going home in a late-night tramcar, 'Is he not charming, this Magnus? And how shy! And underneath, such talent!' What they were describing was the mask; few of them had seen the cold dangerous Orphean face underneath.*

This passage immediately calls to mind GMB's poem 'The Poet', in which the wandering bard puts on his mask and cloak and dances among the people. At the end of the revelry, when all the dancers and masks have gone inside, the poet returns to his true task, interrogation of silence.

There is, I believe, a close kinship connecting the wandering poet and Magnus Olafson and George Mackay Brown. The faster GMB's reputation grew, the more he tired of discussions about culture. He saw the masks that people put on – and that he put on himself – in social intercourse, and he longed for the authenticity that he associated with silence. Writing was his way of expressing this; and, even though he knew he had a gift, there were times – especially after much drink had been taken – when he felt he was worthless. He would have sympathised with the greatest theologian of the medieval Catholic Church, St Thomas Aquinas, who, after a profound experience of transcendence during Mass, said: 'All that I have written seems like straw to me'.

George tired of himself as much as he tired of others; his own razor tongue, after drink had loosened his inhibitions, depressed him. When he was drunk, his mother was offended more by the foul language he used than by the drunkenness itself. 'Is he not charming, this George? And how shy! And underneath, such talent!' What they were describing was the mask; few of them had seen the cold dangerous Orphean face underneath.

Back to 'Sealskin'. In the library of Trinity College, Dublin, Magnus Olafson is shown an ancient Gaelic manuscript. It tells of a tradition in which young men of the West and North find 'shy cold creatures of no tongue or lineage', with whom they have children. Magnus is moved by the story's quaintness and innocence, and by the light it sheds on the mystery of his parents' situation. It makes him think about the contrast between his life back home in Norday and the sophisticated conversations about cultural matters with his European friends. *He thought of the men who had thrown off all restraint and were beginning now to raven in the most secret and delicate and precious places of nature. They were the new priesthood; the world went down on its knees before*

every tawdry miracle – the phonograph, the motor car, the machine-gun,
the wireless – that they held up in triumph. And the spoliation had hardly
begun.

This is not simply grumpiness about the modern world and
nostalgia for 'the good old days', though there are elements of
both. His complaint against what passes for progress stems from a
spiritual understanding that sees an uncritical adulation for modern
technology's bounty as dangerous to the soul. Magnus Olafson/
Mackay Brown fears for the consequences of a technological revolution
that, while delivering many good things, also threatens humanity,
paradoxically in the name of humanity. GMB's Christian humanism
supports the flourishing of human life; his Christian apocalyptic sense
makes him tremble for the fate of humanity in a future dominated by
technological innovation.

The horizontal bard who had spent time staring at the ceiling
of a sanatorium ward contemplating his own mortality could run a
masterclass in the envisaging of scenarios of catastrophe, especially
in an era in which dazzling technology had offered up the gift of the
nuclear bomb. He feared for a world enchanted by technology while
turning its back on its own traditions of wisdom. He would have
agreed with Catholic philosopher René Girard's view that the most
frightening thing of all in the modern world was the conjunction of
massive technical power and the spiritual surrender to nihilism.

For GMB, then, the use and abuse of technology was a spiritual
matter. He believed that the speed of technological advances was
provoking a spiritual crisis. Technology, he believed, when harnessed
to the seductive notion of inevitable progress, was not simply a
neutral use of tools. It had become a runaway utilitarian ideology
in which things should be done simply because they could be done,
with damaging consequences that imperilled not only the life of the
individual soul but also the very planet itself.

While agreeing with much of what George says, I would have liked
to ask him how he squared his views with his own practices. After
all, he loved his gramophone and he enjoyed watching television. He
also relied on Attie Campbell and his motor car to get him to Mass

in Kirkwall. Did he not enjoy these 'tawdry miracles', even while he denounced them?

In the interview with Isobel Murray and Bob Tait (see Chapter 10 above), GMB appeared to modify his position, even seeming to suggest that he made some statements on the subject primarily for effect. When Murray said that one of the central planks of the Mackay Brown legend was an antipathy to progress, he replied: 'Oh, to progress. Ah, well, if it wasn't for medical progress, I would probably have been in my grave twenty years ago; so it's just a sort of stance that you take up, really, in order to fight for something that you truly believe in. People are worshipping all these false gods nowadays, progress and money and mammon; everything, even in Orkney. These television advertisements and that, you must get a better car, and a better washing machine and all that sort of thing. Terrible!'

> IM: I was perhaps surprised to see the television set in this room at all.
>
> GMB: Ah well, the only concession I've made is that it is black and white, you see. I keep one step behind. I'm not in the vanguard of culture.
>
> IM: You wouldn't see that as hypocritical compromise?
>
> GMB: Oh well, I suppose it is. I do enjoy some plays, I must say. No, I'm not against progress, or I wouldn't have a coal fire – I suppose I'd have peats, and I'd be living in a little croft on the edge of the moor with a few hens around the door, so no. But it's just that you've got to take up a certain position I think, and keep people in touch with their roots and sources.

Murray pressed GMB on Orkney's place and meaning in his work: 'So, it's not necessarily an insistence on Orkney itself. It's: sometimes Orkney is a symbol of basic simplicities and realities?'

> GMB: Not now, fifty years ago it was.
>
> IM: OK. It's precisely this Orkney of fifty years ago you're talking about. It's a symbol.
>
> GMB: That's right! That's why I like to write about people who lived then that I knew when I was a boy, and their language was far richer then,

most Orcadians still are. But I don't know: they've lost something that their grandparents had: there's no doubt about it.

IM: Don't you think that it's partly also, the coincidence of what you knew when you were a boy – the vision you saw them with – that everybody has perhaps a time when they see more clearly, more freshly, more intensely the people around them?

GMB: I suppose, maybe it's distorted a wee bit to that extent, you know, that you see through the rose-tinted spectacles and that. But I don't know ...

IM: Not distorted, that's a bad sense ... You see better, truer, perhaps.

GMB: Ah, that's right, yes. I think you're quite right. Because the people were very much poorer in those days too. But somehow they were more real human beings than, well – I hate to make comparisons too – and the people nowadays are all right really, but it's just that they've let the world come in a bit too much, you know.

George's nephew, Dr John Flett Brown, who is a geologist, backed up his uncle's statement about his position on technology being 'just a sort of stance'. I chatted with John – not in the sauna this time, but in his house – with GMB's rocking chair in front of us.

'I tackled George about his views on technology,' John told me. 'I wanted to debate it with him, but he wouldn't be led on it. He refused to debate it. "Ah, John, it's just a device," he said. He felt that it went with the persona that he had built up. He was in the past – they didn't have technology then – but George loved his technology.'

Sometimes GMB rails against technology *per se*, at other times his position seems to be a bit more nuanced. What he is definitely against is technology-as-ideology. So, he takes his stance against the myth of progress and pitches his battle tent in the Orkney of his childhood, a time of greater innocence.

Does he romanticise that era? Of course he does. In fact, he admits it himself. In an interview, he was asked if there was anything positive to be said for progress. He responded: 'Oh, yes, I'm sure there's quite a lot to be said for it. I sort of over-emphasise things ... I think I have tended to romanticise the past a bit. It must have been a very hard life that the farmers and fishermen had in Orkney a hundred years and more ago.'

In the 1960s and 1970s, when GMB was denouncing technology and progress – in *Fishermen with Ploughs* he talked about girls who are 'nothing but giggles, lipstick and gramophone records' – Orkney was enjoying such technological gifts as television, affordable motor cars, washing machines, tape recorders, tractors and combine harvesters. In some respects, George Mackay Brown was Orkney's Don Quixote, tilting at technology-driven windmills.

But, while he could be mocked for enjoying some of the fruits of the technologies he condemned, the gaunt ghost at Orkney's technological feast was on to something important. The task of artists and poets, he said, was to keep reminding people of their roots, of their humanity. In his essay 'The Broken Heraldry', published in a book called *Memoirs of a Modern Scotland*, GMB provides a more integrated account of his thinking about technology, progress and loss of humanity. He begins with a story that an old man had told him about the inauguration of the motor-coach service between Stromness and Kirkwall early in the twentieth century.

On the first day the horse-coach ran too (it generally took three hours to cover the 15 miles to Kirkwall). In the motor-coach were the young, the daring and the modern; the horse-coach was full of old-fashioned, conservative, sceptical people. Horse-coach and motor-coach left at the same hour, and at once the horse-coach was left far behind. At Stenness the motor-coach broke down, and presently the mocking horse-coach passed it. But the engine was repaired and before Finstown the motor-coach, full of cheering 20th-century people, fumed and rattled past the patient horse-coach. Beyond Finstown it broke down again … But eventually the motor-coach reached Kirkwall first. It was the end of an old song.

What caused the breach? Enter on left, wearing a black hat, the scowling figure of Mr John Knox.

Formerly a people of strongly-marked individuality, the Orcadians are gradually losing their identity – or rather they have willingly merged their identity with the rest of the western world. Many things contribute to this loss: wireless and television, compulsory education, newspapers, the insidious notion that urban ways of life are necessarily superior to rural ways. A town like Stromness, even 30 years ago, used to be alive with 'characters', the kind of delightfully surrealistic folk you read about in Russian novels. There are less and less of them now. It is as if people were ashamed to be different from one another.

One senses a growing coldness – the coldness of people who have received the fatal blessing of prosperity. The old gentle courtesy of country people, though it exists, is no longer so apparent; nor are the simple natural services they used to render each other in the harvest fields; nor is the gathering together in houses for fiddle-music and story-telling in the winter.

This break-up, though it has accelerated of late years, has been going on for a very long time, before Edwin Muir was born, before the first paddle-ship churned its way across the Pentland Firth. The fissure reaches far back through many generations to the Reformation. It was then that the old heraldry began to crack, that the idea of 'progress' took root in men's minds. What was broken, irremediably, in the 16th century was the fullness of life of a community, its single interwoven identity. In earlier times the temporal and the eternal, the story and the fable, were not divorced, as they came to be after Knox: they used the same language and imagery, so that the whole of life was illuminated. Crofters and fishermen knew what Christ was talking about, better perhaps than the canons and prebendaries of St Magnus, because they bore the stigmata of labour on their bodies – the net let down into the sea, the sower going forth to sow, the fields white towards harvest. The miracle of the five loaves and two fishes must have been intensely meaningful to a people who, in spite of perennial poverty and occasional famine, saw the bannock and the salt on their winter table. Most marvellous of all was that their daily labours were a divine image for their strivings heavenwards, and were rewarded at last by the Bread of Heaven, the Blessed Sacrament, Christ himself dwelling in them. Here was the ultimate intermingling of the earthy and the holy. They saw it as the superlative wit and charity of Heaven.

They were sustained by an immense confidence and security. Ultimately all was well with them. They knew that an angel and a devil wrestled inside each of them for possession of their soul, and the outcome was uncertain until the moment of death. But the sacraments of the Church, particularly penance and the Eucharist, were an infallible remedy. Grey mediocre people that they were, they believed that a shining thread of immortality was ravelled through them. Poor people, they were yet lords and princes with heavenly treasures lying thick about them. These beliefs gave their lives gaiety and confidence, and this gaiety is expressed in the ballads and songs that have come down to us. There, earthiness and blessedness are inextricably merged.

> *Be ye maids or be ye nane,*
> *We're a' Saint Mary's men,*
> *Ye's a' be kissed or we gang hame,*
> *Fore wur Lady.*

What he called 'the catastrophe' of Calvinism was followed by the threat of a breakdown in community. *Perhaps this break-down is inevitable once the heraldic vision that holds a people together is shattered. The great paradox of our time in Orkney is that with increased prosperity and education and communications, the quality of life has grown progressively poorer. Whereas the medieval Orkney peasant lived among treasures of legend and faith, we stand like exiles among accumulations of expensive trash. Once more, unknown to us, the Castle has been silently breached.*

The humble peasants labouring in the fields might have been astounded by such descriptions of their beatitude. In GMB's idealised, under-researched and somewhat ideological view of the past, there is no possibility of corruption in the Catholic Church being labelled 'a catastrophe', one which might have helped trigger a popular radical revolt and thereby contributed to Scotland's 'broken heraldry'.

There is an apocalyptic strain in GMB's journalism and novels. In the face of the oil bonanza of the 1970s and 1980s and the possibility of extracting uranium in Orkney, he warned that these things would radically change the nature of Orkney, for the worse, forever.

The end of the world might not be quite nigh, but it was on the horizon. He worried about the end times. Alarmed by technology's grip on the imagination, he was in despair about what he saw as a diabolical compact between a dazzled people and demonic powers which taught the superiority of the number over the word. There would be a reckoning, he was convinced, unless the imaginative arts – including those of religion – were empowered to offer a pathway to salvation.

Greenvoe is an apocalyptic story. It presents a small island community that is devastated by the intrusion of a large and sinister hush-hush project called Operation Black Star. The fact that the author never discloses the nature of the project makes it even more threatening. Operation Black Star exacerbates divisions already evident among the islanders, and effectively destroys the community. When the intruders have completed their work, the locals are cleared off the island.

The novel warns about the power of technological forces to destroy the very foundations of communal life. It is a parable about the dangerous powers of technique and money, and about the black magic that seduces and then annihilates without pity. The subsequent return of some islanders, and the restarting of the old ceremonies, hint at a form of renewal.

As a man of religious faith, GMB strikes a note of hope. *Perhaps something we cannot imagine will flower out of this desolation; it may be that out of some total destruction a kind of resurrection will come. Edwin Muir imagined, in one of his poems, an atomic holocaust, and after it, the plough-horses of his childhood returning.*

> *Barely a twelvemonth after*
> *The seven-day war that put the world to sleep,*
> *Late in the evening the strange horses came ...*

What are we to make of all this? Ever since human beings started using stones as tools, technology has been shaping human life for better and for worse. New technologies drive societies in undreamed-of ways. Just as the wheel transformed transport, so the humble stirrup, which enabled the rider to stand upright on the horse and fire a weapon, revolutionised warfare.

The unpredictable consequences of the introduction of a new technology may be illustrated by the invention of the clock. In the

Benedictine monasteries of the twelfth century, bells were rung at the beginning of each of the seven periods of daily devotion. This desire for precision led to the invention of the mechanical clock. Who could possibly have foreseen how this much-welcomed invention in the cloisters would lead to the more efficient ordering of capitalist society? The mechanism for the precise timing of the daily call to prayer became an essential component of the modern tyranny of 'efficiency'. The Benedictine invention helped to unleash a torrent of 'time and motion' studies in the 1950s.

The steam engine not only speeded up transport, it also provided 'pressure cooker' metaphors – such as 'keeping the lid on things' – for human emotions. The invention of the motor car increased people's choices, but it also led to the development of new technologies for refining and transporting oil, and thus to the ecological and political crises we face today. Television has dramatically altered the ways in which we see our world.

It is in the area of warfare that technological developments have had their most spectacular effects. During the 2003 invasion of Iraq, you could sit in your living room, bowl of crisps at your side, and coolly watch missiles drop down chimneys in Baghdad. In his book, *Straw Dogs*, John Gray observes that

> it is not the number of sovereign states that makes technology ungovernable. It is technology itself. The ability to design new viruses for use in genocidal weapons does not require enormous resources of money, plant or equipment. New technologies of mass destruction are cheap; the knowledge they embody is free. It is impossible to prevent them becoming more easily available.

Jewish psychotherapist Viktor Frankl emerged from Auschwitz a changed man. Since Auschwitz, he said, we know what man is capable of. And, since Hiroshima, we know what is at stake.

The impact of the microchip has transformed our lives. Science writer Christopher Rowe reported in his 1986 book, *People and Chips*, that if the motor industry had developed at the same speed as the computer industry, a Rolls Royce would cost around £3 and would do three million miles to the gallon. If the aerospace industry had developed at the same pace, a Boeing 767 would cost £400 and could circle the earth on only five gallons of fuel. Computers also provide distorting modern metaphors for the human. These paradigm-changes dramatically alter our discourse about what it means to be human. The talk is no longer about 'keeping the lid on things', but about our brains being 'hardware' and beliefs being 'software'; what we then need, when our lives go awry, is to be 'reprogrammed'.

GMB is right to insist that the use of technology is a spiritual issue. While researching a book about Christianity and technology, I was introduced to the writings of the French lay Catholic philosopher, sociologist and theologian, Jacques Ellul. Like John Gray, Ellul was a pessimist on the subject of technology. He warned about technology becoming a new religion, saying that whatever desacralises a given reality becomes the new sacred reality. He prophesied that 'La Technique' as he called it – a wide-ranging term to describe all aspects of technology and methods which have greater efficiency as the goal – would take over almost all aspects of modern life and would undermine culture, religion and politics.

Computers are, above all, instruments of efficiency. What they do best is to count and sort very quickly – useful tools; but the apparently innocent driving force of efficiency soon becomes a powerful ideology with immensely distorting power. This has huge implications for society. GMB was right to beware of the dominance of numbers. High IQ scores are equated with 'intelligence'. Targets become the fixation of modern systems. Vast sums are spent by public bodies on IT systems that, more often than not, fail to work. The passion of politics gives way to a bloodless obsession with pointless information. Technology-as-ideology means that if something cannot be counted, it does not count.

The German philosopher Martin Heidegger also worried about the dehumanising effects of technology. He felt that the Western world was focusing on the extraction and storage of resources; as part of that process, humanity itself was being reconfigured as one more resource. He was concerned about the gradual diminution of meaning in human life. Our ancestors, he said, had a sense of awe about the world; now, we were preoccupied with controlling and manipulating the world. In this respect, technology was becoming tyrannical. The drive to extract the power of the world for instrumental purposes was itself a form of 'disenchantment', leading to the absence of meaning.

Heidegger believed that the twentieth-century concentration on immediate satisfactions had led to a lessening of human fulfilment and sense of purpose. In looking at different ways in which meaning had been manifested in older times, Heidegger referred to an old ruined Greek temple. He saw the temple as a communal place that drew people together and provided corporate meanings and rituals, as well as housing a 'god'. (He interpreted this god not in terms of institutional religion but as a sense of the transcendent that attracted people.) He argued the question of meaning was now seen through the lens of a pervasive technology that had gained primacy largely because of the loss of meaning.

For Heidegger, the current dominance of the technological framework to life – 'die Technik', which was close to Ellul's 'La Technique' – was essentially nihilistic. To see human beings simply as a resource was ultimately dehumanising, and it was important to recover a sense of human beings as what he called 'shepherds of meaning'. GMB would, I think, have agreed with the main thrust of Heidegger's thinking, although he himself expresses the matter somewhat differently.

Yet there is an irony here. To get to it, we need to go back to the immediate post-war period. Here is an item from the *Daily Telegraph* of 22 November 1946:

BIRO'S BALL GIVES NEW POINT TO PENS

A revolutionary new pen which writes 200,000 words without refilling, blotting or smudging, has gone on sale. The Biro, which costs 55s, is the creation of Hungarian journalist Ladislao Biro, who became fascinated by printers' quick-drying ink when he was an editor in Budapest. His invention combines a rotating ballpoint with a tiny capillary tube to hold the ink. Biro, who fled to Argentina to escape the Nazis, sold out two years ago to his English backer, H. G. Martin, who is now marketing the pens.

I had not realised that there was actually a Mr Biro. Anyway, George Mackay Brown was a devotee of Ladislao Biro's pens. When he famously said that 'all a writer needs is a cheap pad and a tenpenny biro', he was making a plea for a basic simplicity. Irony lies in the fact that Heidegger presented the ballpoint pen as an exemplar of the technological world! Anonymous and interchangeable mass-produced items like biros were, he said, characteristic products of modern technology.

So, GMB was writing diatribes against modern technology with one of the prime symbols of that technology, on a lined notebook which was the product of an industry that destroyed precious forests.

That is precisely the problem with pervasive modern technology: in order to write or speak against its dangerous omnipresence, the means of modern technology have to be employed. I write these words on the Orkney island of Westray, on a laptop computer that has an Internet connection. My mobile phone is on the table as I write. Living in the technosphere, there is no pure moral ground on which to stand and denounce the dangers of modern technology.

After reading this section of the draft manuscript, novelist John McGill e-mailed me in the following terms: 'As you frequently stress, GMB is a *storyteller* – it won't do to get too solemn about his religion, philosophy, politics, etc. As he admits himself in the interview with Isobel Murray, he was often taking up a pose, fashioning a persona for himself. Writing may be a craft, or even a task infused with holiness – but it's also a game.'

This book began with a radio being hurled against the wall of a sanatorium in Kirkwall. George wrote a charming but pointed story titled 'The Wireless Set'. It tells of the first wireless ever to come to the mythical valley of Tronvik, Orkney, in 1939. It was brought by Howie Eunson, son of Hugh the fisherman and his wife Betsy. There was great excitement in the valley when Howie returned with his gifts, and people crowded into the croft. Howie lifted the portable wireless out of a cardboard box and set it on the table.

For a full two minutes nobody said a word. They all stood staring at it, making small round noises of wonderment, like pigeons.

'And mercy,' said Betsy at last, 'what is it at all?'

'It's a wireless set,' said Howie proudly. 'Listen.'

He turned a little black knob and a posh voice came out of the box saying that it would be a fine day tomorrow over England, and over Scotland and south of the Forth–Clyde valley, but that in the Highlands and in Orkney and Shetland there would be rain and moderate westerly winds.

'If it's a man that's speaking', said old Hugh doubtfully, 'where is he standing just now?'

'In London,' said Howie.

'Well now,' said Betsy, 'if that isn't a marvel! But I'm not sure, all the same, but what it isn't against the scriptures. Maybe, Howie, we'd better not keep it.'

'Everybody in the big cities has a wireless,' said Howie. 'Even in Kirkwall and Hamnavoe every house has one. But now Tronvik has a wireless as well, and maybe we are not such clodhoppers as they think.'

They all stayed late, listening to the wireless. Howie kept twirling a second little knob, and sometimes they would hear music and sometimes they would hear a kind of loud half-witted voice urging them to use a particular brand of toothpaste.

At half past eleven the wireless was switched off and everybody went home. Hugh and Betsy and Howie were left alone.

'Men speak,' said Betsy, 'but it's hard to know sometimes whether what they speak is truth or lies.'

'This wireless speaks the truth,' said Howie.

Old Hugh shook his head. 'Indeed,' he said, 'it doesn't do that. For the man said there would be rain here and a westerly wind. But I assure you it'll be a fine day, and a southerly wind, and if the Lord spares me I'll get to the lobsters.'

Old Hugh was right. Next day was fine, and he and Howie took twenty lobsters from the creels he had under the Gray Head.

But things get sinister. Over the radio come messages by William Joyce, the traitor known as Lord Haw-Haw, who tells lie after lie about the progress of the war. One night, the wireless is switched off and ale is drunk, and stories that have nothing to do with the war are told until two in the morning.

The magic box that can bring music and good cheer can also transmit demonic lies. In this tale, GMB amusingly sets the new technology against the wisdom and social customs of the valley. The point is well made.

But did George Mackay Brown listen to the radio?

Of course he did. He loved it.

I'm sitting in the King Street Church in Kirkwall. It is a tribute night for the late Alan Plater, playwright and television scriptwriter, who wrote three plays for the St Magnus Festival. I am watching an abridged version of his adaptation of *Greenvoe* for the stage.

The capacity crowd is enjoying the play. They laugh at Mrs Olive Evie – played by local actress Margaret Hay – as she pronounces moral judgements from behind the counter of the Greenvoe store. Local actor Graham Garson makes an impressive Ivan Westray, the rough island ferryman. (Graham has just made the show with minutes to spare, having come over on the evening boat from the island of Westray, where he is a schoolteacher.) The audience laughs as Miss Agatha Fortin-Bell, niece of the laird, Colonel Fortin-Bell, brays on the pier. (*The islanders could never understand why the gentry spoke in such heroic voices*, wrote GMB; *their own speech was slow and wondering, like water lapping among stones.*)

The audience goes very quiet as the uniformed Lord of the Harvest and the Master Horsemen stand to attention. The novice (played by a young local man, Magnus Dixon) is blindfolded. He carries a horseshoe.

THE LORD OF THE HARVEST: We have come to the station of The Seed. What are you seeking here, Ploughman, among the Master Horsemen?

THE PLOUGHMAN: A kingdom.

THE LORD OF THE HARVEST: The man with a new bride, who has ploughed a field in March, what does he know of kingdoms?

THE PLOUGHMAN: Beyond the blood of beasts, further than axe and fire, there it lieth well, in the light, a kingdom.

THE LORD OF THE HARVEST: What hinders you from this kingdom?

THE PLOUGHMAN: Blindness. And it is a long road through the new furrows.

THE LORD OF THE HARVEST: Are you willing to enter the earth womb? Can you suffer the passion of the seed?

THE PLOUGHMAN *does not answer*.

THE MASTER HORSEMEN: Answer. Answer.

THE PLOUGHMAN: I am willing.
> *The Master Horsemen stretch the Ploughman supine on the floor. They lay a straw-woven seed-basket on his chest. They lift his knees and shoulders. They lower him through the opening in the floor. They stand like mourners about a grave.*

THE LORD OF THE HARVEST: Take him, earth. Receive the Sower.

The audience, many of whom are of farming stock, both know and don't know what this is about. They are awed by this commanding pagan ritual enacted before their eyes in a twenty-first-century Presbyterian hall-church.

Well-enacted ceremony, especially when open to transcendent mysteries, has a special power.

PART 3

The Wound and the Gift

CHAPTER 14

Lost in the Barleycorn Labyrinth

It is 3 November 1968. It is another time of crisis in the life of George Mackay Brown.

The poet gets out of the taxi at Warbeth cemetery. He stands at the grave of John and Mary Jane Brown, thinking, praying. He looks around at the elemental scene: the big sky, the scudding clouds, the wind-whipped waves of the sea, the cliffs of Hoy. His gaze takes in the serried memorials to the dead.

He lays a spray of flowers on his mother's grave. She was passionate about flowers.

It is the first anniversary of her death. At the age of 46, he is living on his own for the first time in his life. He hardly knows how to boil an egg.

His mother had been proud of her boy, her sick boy. She did everything for him. When he was destitute, she had kept him uncomplainingly, even bringing him cigarettes on Fridays. *For years – but for her protection – I was hardly better than a tramp.*

She had never liked his drinking. Her rebuke, 'Some Catholic you are', still wounds him. Standing there, protected from the wind by his duffel coat and scarf, he feels guilty about the way he treated his mother.

He has been having dreams about her, nightmares even. In almost every dream, Mary Jane Brown has been displeased with him. She has looked hurt and angry.

She had often been angry with him in the last few months of her life, for no reason he could identify. He remembers how, in her final weeks, he had spoken back to her harshly. He burns with remorse.

As she had become more confused and bewildered, he had felt it was as if she was learning a part in a frightening play – more a Beckett tragedy than the pastoral comedy she had played with such natural grace and gaiety all her days.

Yet he does not want to remember only these latter days of her decline, when she had worn 'the dark mask'. He smiles as he recalls going shopping with her on Saturday nights when he was a boy: he would have sold his soul for a pan drop or a brandy ball or a yellow butternut. He thinks with fondness of his mother's baking, in particular a sweet confection known as 'melting moments'. His father, ever the jester, had rechristened them 'sleepless nights'.

His mind turns to the day of his mother's death. Could it really be twelve months ago?

At her hospital bed, he had been disturbed to see how distressed and disorientated she was. *Now she was learning the confused mysterious language of the dying; through which we could guess at nameless (and doubtless imaginary) dreads.*

Towards the end, he was 'a shadowy vaguely hostile stranger' to her. How sad.

There had been an oxygen mask over her face. The ward sister had held her pulse.

Time passed.

At last, the sister had said: 'Now there's no pulse …'

Mary Jane Brown left an estate of £4.

The wind is getting colder. It will not be long until the northern November darkness comes down like a curtain.

He looks around at gravestones of people he knew. They are all dust now. As he will be, fairly soon he thinks, in this very place.

The simple ceremony of flowers is over. He will not return with flowers to that grave. He will be racked by guilt about that, too. He will believe that his mother comes back to censure him in dreams because he has, over the years, neglected 'the filial duty of flowers'.

Mrs Brown's Calvinistic Catholic boy turns and makes his way to the taxi. He knows that he has important decisions to make about his life.

A number of people who knew George well – or thought they did – told me that they were shocked when they read his autobiography. Even some family members and friends were unaware that he had been engaged to be married. They had no inkling about his depressions. When they read *For the Islands I Sing,* one or two thought that he had made it all up or had been exaggerating.

George's nephew, Dr John Flett Brown, is one who is sceptical about George's stories about being depressed. 'I think it's another of his artifices,' John told me, bluntly. 'Is he creating something? Is there anything dark in his poetry of the period? What is depression? Is it clinical bipolarity? That's a pretty debilitating thing. I, and most of the family, have no memory of George having any debilitation. Sometimes he drank harder than others, like everybody else, but it certainly wasn't clinical bipolarity. George also claimed that his grandfather was depressed. That was something that had never been spoken about in family circles. I asked my father about it, and he categorically said "No". My father wasn't very far away, only in the bank in Kirkwall, and home at the weekends. As far as he was concerned, his father never exhibited any depression, whereas his brother Jimmy was bipolar, and George would have been totally aware of that. Whether George thought he had some of that, and that it was a genetic thing, I don't know.'

Especially having read the correspondence between George and Stella, I am not persuaded by John's thesis. The letters are extraordinary source documents for this study. I had read about this correspondence in Maggie Fergusson's biography, but the availability of the letters had come too late for a full display and analysis in that work.

When I began to study them in the National Library of Scotland and Edinburgh University Library, the unremitting litanies about drink and depression were almost overwhelming. I used to reel out of these great institutions filled with melancholy, and with feelings of guilt about reading these sometimes excruciatingly painful letters.

Was I right to read these personal letters, never mind put extracts from them in print? This was – and still is – a troubling question for me.

In the libraries, I felt I was eavesdropping on a private and intimate conversation. Though they were nearly half a century old, the letters felt very immediate. I was deeply touched by them. I wanted to shout out to George and Stella at different points in the correspondence.

When I had finished reading and recording them, I felt it necessary to stand back and take a long view. I wanted this to be an honest book; and these letters were, to an extent, in the public domain. Extracts from a small number of them had already been quoted in the biography. Legally, there was no problem. But ethically? Not so simple.

Voltaire said: 'To the living we owe respect, but to the dead we owe only the truth'. Is this all there is to it? I don't think so.

In thinking the matter through, one crucial fact stood out for me: it was George Mackay Brown who chose to make public his troubled relationship with Stella Cartwright. It was also George who opened up the issue of his drinking and his sometimes suicidal depressions.

Why did such a reserved and well-defended man make the decision to expose himself in this way? I am not sure – just as I am still not sure why he chose to reveal his own self-loathing in the pages of the *Orkney Herald* when he was 26 years old: *But above and beyond everything I hate myself; everything about me revolts me beyond belief.*

Deeply aware of his own weaknesses, he certainly would have dreaded being 'written up' as some kind of religious saint.

As a biographer, I have learned to view autobiographies with some reserve. They are often a form of personal spin-doctoring. Even an ostensibly candid autobiography can be an instrument of concealment rather than of revelation.

It may be that George intended his autobiography to provide a way of 'framing' his life for future biographers. Aware of his national standing as a writer, he would have known that someone would want to write his biography.

He instructed his literary executors to ensure that his autobiography would not be published until after his death. It was as if he did not care what people said or thought about him after he was dead. Not only that, included among the papers he left after his death were many of the letters quoted in this book. There are gaps in the correspondence; George presumably destroyed the letters that he did not want to end up in the public domain.

What is beyond doubt is that GMB himself made the conscious decision to initiate the debate, on his terms. My judgement was that if I was serious about writing a book on the subject of George Mackay Brown's spiritual journey, the letters contained important information about some of the struggles within his soul, and that, however unflattering they might be, they would help to provide a more honest and complete picture. The letters certainly gave me a deeper understanding of the internal conflicts that kept George awake at night; they also drew from me an even greater admiration for his achievements as a writer of extraordinary power.

Does this mean that all of my qualms are resolved? If only life were so simple.

In the extracts that follow, I will allow the stark relentlessness of the darker themes to emerge. To do otherwise would be to turn a study of a gifted but damaged man's spiritual journey into a public-relations exercise.

I have, for reasons of space, not adhered to the original formatting of the letters in terms of paragraphing and spacing. As opposed to his public writing, where considered style is of the essence, what is most important here is the substance of what is being discussed. The letters from George to Stella are held in Edinburgh University Library, and the letters from Stella to George are held in the National Library of Scotland.

George told Stella that he was going to the wedding of Sylvia Wishart's brother. On 27 October 1966, he wrote about the event: 'I went to the wedding and got very drunk. Fought & insulted people.'

Stella had been seeing a psychiatrist, Dr Henry Walton, about her addiction to drink. (Dr Walton, an innovative professor of psychiatry at Edinburgh University, ran a unit for alcoholics. One of his strategies was to keep people up half the night in therapy groups.) George had told Stella a year earlier: 'I have been for some days past confused and in a cloud. This is caused by drink. I think I'll have to come to Edinburgh soon to see Dr Walton. Thank goodness the cloud is lifting a bit now. But it's worse I'm getting, with violent frequent outbursts. I know you will sympathise a little. When the worst is over it's horrifying to look back on. Then the clouds gather again. Last time – only a day or two ago – I lost friends with my carry on.'

On 15 December 1966, he wrote: 'Dearest Stel, Hope you are well – weller than Georgie Brown who is sick with excess alcohol, a trouble that came on him suddenly last Sat evening towards midnight and escalated (as they say) all day Sunday & Monday so badly that even now – on Thursday – I feel as if I was a big stone ruin inhabited by a hundred wee shivering spooks, all shiver! Excitement! & coldness! Remorse!! … So I'm warning you well, sweetheart, look after yourself, because that John Barleycorn is one treacherous bastard! Honest.'

It was not just in Orkney that George was sometimes out of control. On one occasion, he ended up in a police cell in Edinburgh after being arrested for being drunk and incapable in Hanover Street. He spent a day in the cell with two other drunks. Let him tell it in his own words. *We were, all three, in the miseries of withdrawal; yet what I remember about that day was laughter. One cell-mate was a sailor who had damaged his hand in a fight in a respectable Edinburgh coffee-house; I had to roll his cigarettes for him. The other drunk was an Englishman who happened to be in Edinburgh on holiday: he was mildly indignant because we didn't get a cup of tea. From time to time an elderly policeman came in and threw coal on the fire but, though appealed to, he brought no teapot or cups. The long day passed, in wretchedness and laughter. Late at night the cell door opened and a ragged dirty little man was pushed in. He kept shouting, 'I'll tell you this, I hate Catholics!' At last the sailor with the hurt hand remarked mildly that he was a Catholic. Then the Englishman who longed all day for a cup of tea said that he was a Catholic. And I announced that I too was a Catholic. (None of the three of us had known this before.) At once the ragged little drunk beat on the cell door with his fists and kept shouting, 'Let me out! Let me out! They're all Catholics in here! They'll kill me! ...' Eventually he was taken away to another cell. I think the laughter that broke from us then more than outweighed the degradations of the day.*

Late at night I was released on bail of £3.

I never saw my cell-mates again, whom I had liked so much. Next morning I had to appear before the magistrate, along with the previous day's haul of drunks and prostitutes. The little ragged anti-papist was tried before me. He demanded in a loud voice to be X-rayed. When my turn came, I was admonished. I have written so much about drink because it occupies an important part of my life and writing.

I got a different angle on the police-cell story from George's niece, Allison Dixon. Her father, Norrie, George's brother, had died in 1964. The family still lived in Oxgangs, Edinburgh. She remembers the day her sister Pamela answered the door and found two policemen standing there. They said they were calling about Mr George Brown. Allison told me: 'She said: "Oh, that's my uncle. What's he done?" They said he was in custody "for indecent exposure". They said he had peed in the street. "Oh, is that all?" Pamela said. "I thought he'd murdered somebody!"

'Anyone less likely to murder anybody, I can't think of. My mother had to bail him out. She was so furious about it that she donned her best fur coat to go and get him! She said: "There was I among all the prostitutes of Edinburgh ..."! My mother got more het up about it than she ever needed to be, but we thought it was hilarious! My mother treated George more like a son than a brother-in-law. He needed to be chastised on occasion.'

There was sweetness in the relationship between George and Stella. She wrote to him on 15 March 1960 (before their short-lived engagement): 'Dear, dear George, you are such a good and gentle soul, and a real delight to me. I am missing you already. Thank you for saying such sweet things in your letter – it makes me both glad and sad for I want always to be kind to you and make you happy, but there are things which can hurt you and I do not control the universe. But I pray you will be happy, sweetheart and have enough peace within you to tackle everything and grow stronger through every difficulty. Bless you for being you. With my love, Stella.'

On 10 August 1962, she wrote: 'It pleases me you are not getting so drunk. Up to a certain point drink is useful, beyond it is sheer destruction.' On 1 September 1963: 'How awful we are you and I, always having depressions and fits of blank melancholia. I've been feeling blue too, but the cloud is lifting – although I feel somehow disorientated. Things seem somehow unreal and insecure. I am getting old ...'

The first surviving letter from George to Stella, who by this time was engaged to a librarian by the name of Hugh Mackay, is dated 25 November 1963. 'My dearest Stella, We have given each other a lot of wounds just lately. I hurt you, you hurt me. Why this should be, when at the roots of it all we have such affection for each other, I just don't know. Like yourself, I have been deeply unhappy for the past week or more. If you want to see me, I will meet you anywhere and at any time but *please*, not in a pub. I want to give you whatever I can, but I'm afraid it may be too late to heal the breach between us. I hope not, with all my heart. Remember there is much poetry between us. That at least can never be taken away. With much love, George xxx'

George to Stella, 5 January 1964: 'I'm a bit tired after all that New Year revelling. The whisky went like a river in spate. I put my fist through a thick glass window (I don't remember how or why) and woke in the morning covered in blood, the blankets and sheets too ... I wish for you a very happy year, Stella dear. Of course we will always have love & tenderness for one another. Whatever little cruelties there are in our relationship are made more cutting by the fact that we truly care for one another and that love & affection is *the* important thing. Bless you my dear. Be good till I see you again. Please don't let us fight next time.'

There is heartfelt affection between George and Stella – yet, clearly, mutual wounding is going on.

George to Stella, 3 July 1964: 'So, my sweet friend, *don't* get despondent or unhappy. And don't make too big friends with John Barleycorn or Cissy Gin or Charlie Carlsburg because they always let everyone down, the devils.'

On 14 September 1964: 'Dearest Stella, I'm writing this in the midst of a deep depression caused in the main by our old enemy Barleycorn, but I think the weather and the futureless future (without money or prospects or any worthwhile objective) are a bit to blame, too.'

As this affectionate and painful correspondence develops, it is clear that the self-loathing that George wrote about as a young journalist has not gone away. He feels himself to be in some ways responsible for Stella's plight. This guilt fuels his drinking.

On 28 September 1964, George talks of his guilt about his mother, who has been ill. 'I'm so sorry for her, and yet sometimes I'm not very good to her. Last night I went out & had too much to drink, and that made her very unhappy. I'm not a very good person, I'm afraid. There's so much pain and sickness in the world. Suffering is a mystery, especially when naturally good people like yourself & my mother have so much to put up with.'

At times, George and Stella seem like two lost children trying to prop each other up. George to Stella, 8 November 1964: 'What a couple of old crocks we are! I got rid of my cold but then didn't bronchitis set in, and that was another confined week. Friday & Saturday, to restore the balance, I had a good drink; so today the writer of the greatest sonnet of the 20th century (and maybe of the entire 2nd millennium) has a bad stomach and a benumbed mind.'

Two weeks later, George's drinking is causing him more problems. 'Your Orkney friend has a very sore head because the silly fool, he went to the Royal last night on his tod and he drank pint after pint of heavy and then the idiot, on his way home didn't he call at Dr Johnstone's and drink homebrew and after that lot he didn't know whether he got home on his head or his heels ... Dear Stel, there's a wee man standing up inside my skull and he's delivering sledge hammer blows on it. If I get hold of that wee man I'll pulverise him. It's the drink … That wee man in my skull has got a brother sitting in my stomach and he's pouring acid all down my intestines, the little bastard.'

What is remarkable is that, in the midst of all this turmoil and illness, George continues to produce writing of high quality. On 27 November 1964: 'I've been busy all week at a long poem, that I guess won't be ready for a long time yet. But the writing of it keeps me from morbidity and despair.' Then he offers Stella a solution: 'If only you were a Catholic! At least it would give you firm ground under your feet. At best it would show you a great many things shot through with a new beauty.'

On 9 January 1965, George tells Stella about his New Year: 'As for me, you'll never guess! I got fou and at 6 am on 1st Jan I fell all the way downstairs and when I came to in the cold cruel light of day I had some broken ribs. So ever since I'm just a poor chap that groans about the house like an old man of 90. The worst thing is bed – it's terribly sore lying flat out. I don't get much sleep.'

On 23 January 1965: 'My ribs are getting better but they're still sore when I bend in certain directions. In bed I have to lie flat on my back, so I'm no good to any Orkney woman at the moment. Between now and the end of April I won't be able to father any children (poor little sods, they'll be better off in the darkness and silence anyway.) Unless, of course, I get raped. What wicked buffoonery!'

On 21 May 1965: 'My mother isn't speaking to me this morning so I must have been a bad man last night – goodness knows, I can't remember'.

On 18 June 1965, George turns pastoral counsellor: 'Please tell me how you got on in your interview with Dr Walton. All of us have relied too much on drink for satisfaction in the past. It's a deadly thing, "the smiler with the knife", if it turns against one. Think, you are a sweet & good person without whisky. Does it help you to know that?'

Probably not. Some of Stella's letters at this time are obviously written when she is drunk. The handwriting is awry. She has been going to the doctor about her drinking, and has been taking part in group therapy.

June 1965: 'Look after yourself. Don't drink *every* day. If only we did not have to hide our miseries, we would probably not need booze … My dearest George, why are you so sad? Are you lonely in a way? You struggle alone with many emotions that probably nobody can help you with – so it seems. I am thinking of you very often and tenderly. Maybe we are alike in many ways, my dear. We suffer, both of us, we also have great joys.'

On 6 August 1965, Stella is in hospital, having treatment for alcoholism. She writes: 'Please George do not let drink take you away …'

This is all terribly sad. George and Stella are saying one to another: 'Please stay off the drink, or you will become like me'. The self-delusion, collusion and co-dependency of serious drinking buddies is achingly obvious.

In that month, *The Year of the Whale* was published. The relationship with Sylvia Wishart had come to an end. Both George and Sylvia were talented creative artists, and they were equally determined characters. Both liked a drink; when in their cups, they could be verbally – and sometimes even physically – aggressive with each other. On one occasion, George had a kick at Sylvia on a bus.

George to Stella, 31 August 1965: 'I am in a curious mixed-up state. My friendship with Sylvia, which has been guttering for some time, expired in a violent flare-up a few nights ago. I expected I would be utterly desolated and miserable and suicidal, but in fact I feel free and gay and at peace with the world. I guess it would never have worked out between us anyway. So now, my dear Stel, I see I'm cut out only to be an old bachelor drinking pints at sunset at the door of pubs and wondering who will wash my shirt next week.'

George to Stella, 11 November 1965: 'There's a lot in what you say about fighting, etc. being a part of loving. But there are different kinds of fighting, there's a creative kind, positive & healing strife, & hard fusion. And there's the discharge of black hatred; and that's the kind that frightens me, though I know I'm one of the poles that generates

275

the voltage. You should know, my dear, that it's impossible for you not to love. As for me, I think now I'm quite incapable of it. So I plunge into a vortex of work, and in fatigue and in some species of small creation (for poetry and all art is a poor thing, set beside love) I get contentment (of a kind). It hurts me to think of you being unhappy, Stella. I think of how happy we might have been together, there was such tenderness & quiet joy.'

George knows what it is to be on the receiving end of 'black hatred'; he also knows that, when whisky gets the upper hand, he himself is capable of discharging black hatred on others, including his mother. It frightens him, gives him nightmares.

Yet the flow of poetry and stories continues. In December 1965, George is awarded a Scottish Arts Council bursary of £750.

The drinking goes on. And on. George to Stella, 3 February 1966: 'I was at a Burns Supper last night. Drank too much. Woke in a vile temper this morning, had a row with Mrs M. J. Brown. What about? Don't know. So here I sit in the bedroom, a poor thing ... did I tell you I wrote a lovely new short story? Well I have. If I behaved myself better I would write more. There are a thousand dry peas in my skull, rattling back and fore, fore & back, foreback, backfore, foba, fb, bf, bloody fool ...'

Whisky continues to push Stella into a spiral of decline. On 20 February 1966, she writes to George complaining of a lack of balance, impaired vision, shakes, palpitations and dizziness. She is going into hospital. She fears that she is dying: 'George, pray for me, I don't want to die yet – not before I have remedied some of my sins of omission. It helps to know that we think of each other kindly, and often. George my dear, dear friend, please take a warning from Stella: don't abuse alcohol. I would *hate* to have you in the state I am in. We have both had pretty hellish hangovers – some of which we have shared, but this is no ordinary over-hung hangover ... What an unholy mess I have made of my life – and what is more, maybe of other people's lives also.'

Stella may have been thinking here of her relationships with one or two of the married Rose Street poets.

George is getting desperate. He fears for Stella. His guilt over his perceived responsibility for her plight fuels his depressions. He feels powerless. All he can do, through the power of words, is to encourage her to see her life more positively. On 24 February 1966, he writes to her: 'You must not talk of your life being wasted. No person can say his life is a failure until the moment of death, and even then it is for God to say. Perhaps you – and this applies to me and a host of others – have gone about some things in a wrong way, not intending any evil. It is hard often to know the right way to act in this confused world. But this must be a comfort to you dear – I'm speaking as one who has benefited often from your kindness and love and sweet nature – you have given much happiness to people who were hungry for it.'

Maybe too hungry for it, devouring Stella herself. In the same letter, George calls drink 'the fatal Barleycorn labyrinth'. He talks of 'slaving away to get rid of depression'.

George to Stella, 30 September 1966: 'Dearest Stel, Nothing but rain and low clouds and increasing darkness, and the silver wings of the spirit furled in despondency'.

Despite the darkness and despondency, good writing continues to flow from the tip of his ballpoint pen. In February 1967, *A Calendar of Love*, containing some of his finest short stories, is published.

On 3 November 1967, George's mother died. No letters about his mother's death have survived. In September 1968, George moved to Mayburn Court, Stromness. He did not have a clue about how to organise a 'flitting'. His friends stepped in and took charge.

As I look at George's life and his relationships so far, a pattern emerges. All through his life, people have come forward when he needed help. Is this simply down to serendipity? I think not.

My mother used to say of a dependent person like this: 'He has the kind of face that would get a scone at any door'. George Mackay Brown had such a face. It was as if the words 'Feed Me' were imprinted on his forehead. The feeding could be both physical and emotional. Somehow, from a rather passive 'back' position, George drew people in to help him. Or to buy him a drink, or to give him cigarettes. His friends used to laugh about how difficult it was to get George to buy his round at the pub. It is possible that these subtle strategies were adopted, either consciously or unconsciously, in the days of his illness, when he had little money.

The day of his flitting from Well Park to Mayburn Court is a classic. Fraser and Allison Dixon, Ian MacInnes and Archie Bevan were on hand to help. The men did a lot of the heavy lifting. Allison's job was to clear up when items were removed, and to sort things out at the new house as well. Her baby daughter Judy was in the playpen in the middle of the floor. Friends hired a van for the move.

'When the time came for the move,' Allison Dixon told me, 'George was sitting having his breakfast, and he had to finish it. Then he got up from the table and went and stood at the back door staring out over the sea. He had lived in that house for a long time. Goodness knows what was going on in his head, but he spent a lot of time standing there. The men who were moving him just came and took the four corners of his table cloth, and lifted it up and took it to Mayburn Court like that!

'The Bevans very kindly gave us all lunch. George started drinking with Jimmy Isbister. In Greenvoe, there's a character that's very much "Jimmy I." – the Skarf. Fraser, who was supposed to put up light fittings, gave up. He went back in the evening to see if he could do it, but there was no point. It was all too much for George, I think.'

As I read the sources and talk to those who knew him, my sense is that the time after his mother's death was a critical period in the life of George Mackay Brown. Having been looked after by his mother from birth to middle age, he was at a bit of a loss.

His feelings about his mother's death were complicated. A ministering angel can produce ambivalent feelings in a dependent person. He loved his mother, but his need of her in times of illness and financial hardship stirred up feelings of anger as well as gratitude. His worries and fears about Stella – might she commit suicide, and would he bear some responsibility for that? – added to the crisis in the life of this most private of men. He could function socially, but, once he laid down the social mask, the demons were waiting for him.

Given the amount of drinking evidenced in the correspondence with Stella – and even allowing for some exaggeration – it is evident that, at this stage in his life, George could have chosen to – or, more passively, allowed himself to – languish in his own black Barleycorn labyrinth until he died. As a minister, I have presided at the early graves of people, including friends, who have done just that.

This, I believe, was the most dangerous stage in George Mackay Brown's spiritual journey. It was his 'change of life' time, a spiritual crisis requiring a resolution that could not be found at the bottom of a glass. He had to confront searching questions about values, meaning and vocation.

Living on his own, afflicted by self-loathing and guilt, spooked by his dead mother, in turmoil over a relationship with a suicidal woman whose actions he could not control, and drinking in ways that seriously damaged his physical and mental health, he was facing a defining moment in his life. It is not too dramatic to suggest that, at the age of 46, he had to make a choice between dying and living.

American playwright Edward Albee once said: 'I think everyone has a certain amount of alcohol in their life. I just drank it all very early.' Albee also said that there comes a critical time when an aspiring writer has to ask the question: do you want to be a drunk or do you want to be a writer?

That, I believe, is exactly what George Mackay Brown did. He looked death in the eye, and chose life.

In Australia in the 1960s, so the story goes, a community centre advertised a course of lectures called 'Sex Without Guilt', while across the road the local Roman Catholic church advertised a series titled 'Guilt Without Sex'. (Why is it that the apocryphal stories are the best ones, and often contain what Orcadians call a 'peedie grain' of truth?)

A recurring feature of George Mackay Brown's life was the presence of attractive women who were devoted to him. They brought scones – and sometimes sexual turmoil – to his door. One such person was Nora Kennedy.

Born Eleonora Berger, she had a troubled upbringing. (On his return from the Second World War, her authoritarian father – who was divorced from her mother – ordered that Nora's beloved pet rabbit be killed and cooked.) She trained as a jeweller in her home city of Vienna.

Separated from her Scottish husband, Nora came to Orkney in 1976. When she first encountered George in the bar of the Royal Hotel, Stromness, she was struck immediately by his frailty. He in turn was struck immediately by her beauty, by her intelligence and by her exotic allure. George, fourteen years older than Nora, was so smitten with her that for a spell he went every afternoon by taxi to South Ronaldsay to see her.

Such a bold move was out of character for George. Taking the taxi every day from Stromness to South Ronaldsay was a serious declaration of intent, especially in an Orkney where regular patterns of movement did not go unnoticed. Stories grew legs quickly. (There's a saying about Stromness: 'If you fart at the north end, by the time you get to the sooth end, you've shitten yourself'.)

The relationship became very intense. George wrote to Nora: 'You have taken me into regions where I never thought to go. I am half-enchanted, half-afraid.' Any competent film director could make a two-hour sweaty epic out of these two sentences. The relationship was, in his own words, 'a curious kind of rack of flowers to be stretched out on, so late in the day'. The power of Nora's allure both disarmed him and threw him into turmoil.

The evidence points to George's relationship with Nora being the most fully sexual relationship of his life. His talk of being taken into new regions and of being 'half-enchanted, half-afraid' does not feel like the stuff of a platonic relationship. The fact that George declined to go forward for communion at Mass in Kirkwall is significant. After all, Nora was still married; as a Catholic, George should not present himself for communion until he had confessed a mortal sin and promised to desist.

The pleasures of a physical relationship with such a good-looking woman gave him much joy, but the breaching of his carefully constructed defences also made him panic. What was particularly threatening was Nora's demand for commitment. Her own emotionally difficult upbringing and the failure of her own marriage gave her an overwhelming desire for emotional security. George experienced this as a need for a level of attention that he could not, or rather would not, offer.

Cyril Connolly famously said that for a writer 'the enemy of promise is the pram in the hall'; GMB probably felt that the enemy of his promise as a writer was a beautiful and intelligent woman who demanded from the relationship more than he was willing to give. (And my hunch is that there was also an inner celibate monk in the complicated mix.)

He did what he always did when things got too hot – he withdrew, both emotionally and physically. 'Do not expect a kind of love I am not capable of giving to anyone,' he wrote to her. The Muse, he said, demands all that there is.

I asked Morag MacInnes what she thought about the relationship. 'I think that with Nora he found himself in a situation where she was determined to make him have a relationship,' she said. 'That frightened him to bits, and he just withdrew. George says to her that, as a writer, he is giving everything and there's nothing left over. That's probably true, but it's also a way of holding somebody at a distance. You can see it both as a truth – the vocational thing is his priority – but also as a good defence against such a relationship.'

I sensed among George's friends an ambivalence about Nora Kennedy. Some felt she was a bit feckless, others thought that she was pushy. I asked George's niece, Allison Dixon, about all this.

'George liked attractive girls, it's true,' she said. 'Poor Nora. George was very infatuated with her when he first met her. He told us he had met this beautiful Austrian girl and she was coming to see him that evening. Could he bring her along to see us, because he didn't quite know what to do with her for a whole evening? That was the first time we met Nora. She was quite an enigma. She didn't want to be asked questions – you never got an answer from her. I just never knew how to take Nora at all.'

All this, though, didn't explain why George's relationship with Nora lasted for close on twenty years, with varying degrees of intensity. While I was writing the final draft of this book, I discovered, during the course of a casual conversation, that a near-neighbour of mine was Nora's best friend in Orkney. Christine Clarke was a successful businesswoman in Stromness and Kirkwall before her retirement. I asked her what Nora was like.

'She was a wonderful person,' Christine told me. 'She had an incredible knowledge of music, literary subjects, art and architecture. She was a mine of knowledge, and so interesting to talk to. I can understand George's fascination. We discussed so many topics. She was very political, a real socialist. She was like a breath of fresh air, just a fascinating person to be in company with.

'She was also very beautiful, with lovely dark hair. She was neat and delicate. Whatever she was doing, a lot of thought went into it. She was very gentle and sweet-natured. Mind you, if you got on the wrong side of her, she would let you know that she wasn't happy.'

Christine went to Vienna to stay with Nora.

'She was always saying to me: "I'm going to Vienna, Chris, when are you going to come?" I stayed at the family flat in Vienna. Her mother was dead by that time, and her father and his partner – they lived in Germany – came over, and I lived with them in the flat. It had been a family home for a long time.'

Christine showed me a film she had made about the visit to Vienna. Nora was certainly vivacious. Her heavily accented English was also attractive.

'George had so many things in common with Nora,' Christine said. 'There were also differences. She had travelled a lot and experienced different cultures in Europe. She worked in Scandinavia for a while. George and Nora had an admiration for each other. George was really, really good with her.'

If George had asked Nora to marry him, did Christine think she would have done so?

'That is a difficult question to answer. They both had their individual independent homes. Having their own place suited them both. George had his routine of writing every morning, then the afternoons and evenings were free. Nora was very Bohemian – she would rise, maybe, at half past ten, by which time George would probably have done two hours' work!

'It was a real twentieth-century relationship, in which people could live together and have a sexual relationship, yet keep their own homes. That wasn't frowned upon the way it used to be. Although she had her own home in Stromness, Nora would stay over at Mayburn Court sometimes. Later on, she moved from Stromness to Deerness, but she still made regular trips over to Stromness and stayed with George while there.

'The talk of George not liking women is a load of rubbish. I have no doubts whatsoever about it being a sexual relationship. Nora was very open about it; she would say: "I stayed at George's last night". She was a cultured lady who certainly wouldn't have been flinging herself around.'

On one occasion, Nora invited George to lunch along with a young artist friend of hers, Kenna Crawford. George took a shine to Kenna – who looked remarkably liked Stella – and wrote a poem for her. When Kenna left Orkney to travel in New Zealand, George wrote what were, in effect, love letters, telling her how he had been overwhelmed by her beauty. Kenna was flattered by the attentions of a distinguished writer who was nearly forty years older than she was – he dedicated his book *The Golden Bird* to her – though she was disinclined to escalate the friendship to something more intense. She did stay with him in Mayburn Court for a month after she returned from New Zealand, but she eventually left Orkney and got married.

Morag MacInnes told me that George received lots of letters from women. 'He was being bombarded by people who had an idea of him which he could never have lived up to. The other thing I'm beginning to see from some of the letters is that, between Catholics, there is a very private kind of language, about faith, underlying every issue; and you assume a kind of intimacy with another Catholic because they share your knowledge of this language and this world-view which underpins everything. Often it expresses itself in the ardent way in which some of these women write to him. "Darling George" and all that. People who write to poets also seem to think that they have got to write poetically as well – or have ambitions so to do! He was getting a lot of sustenance from this very emotive, rich language women were using to him, people who barely knew him but assumed kinship. Religious phraseology – "I'm praying for you", "I'm lighting a special candle for you …" seems to have provided him with a warm, non-threatening discourse.'

Was it like medieval courtly love, where people have a relationship but it's all in the imagination? 'Dead right, that's just what it's like. And you're allowed to talk this way, because you know it's not going to come to anything.'

It is odd that, in his autobiography, George said that one of the greatest experiences of most lives never happened to him – he never fell in love with anybody, and no women ever fell in love with him. *I used to wonder about this gap in my experience, but it never unduly worried me. There were girls that I thought pretty and attractive and sweet; but in their presence I was immediately awkward and withdrawn and put on a frown. I had no homosexual urges, apart from one, when I admired another slightly older schoolboy in my class, and for a while couldn't have enough of his company and his talk. I would seek him out by devious ways. To meet him on the street suddenly was a magical thing: I was shaken with sweet secret delight. This infatuation lasted for part of one summer, then broke like a bubble; and he who had been the adored hero went about in the light of common day again. Many adolescent boys, I think, have this experience. It never happened to me again.*

I asked Irene Dunsmuir why she thought George was so attractive to women. 'They wanted to mother him,' she said.

This, I suppose, is the 'face that would get a scone at any door' theory.

'But there was also George's child-like appreciation for what you did. Orcadians are very slow to give compliments or show gratitude, but George could do that. He also made you feel special, and believe that he really meant it. The fact that he saw you like that, that was good enough.'

While I was conducting research for this book, I read – for fun – Humphrey Carpenter's rollicking biography of Robert Runcie, the former Archbishop of Canterbury. One passage jumped straight off the page. Carpenter interviewed Lindy, Runcie's wife, and asked her about a relationship she had had before she married Runcie. Let the biographer tell the story:

> I said that Runcie had told me there was a bruising romance before he came along. 'Huh!' exploded Lindy. 'It wasn't bruising. I've seen him once or twice recently. I mean, he's very like Robert, same sort of lost little boy, you know.' A lost little boy? 'That's what women fall for. I mean, Robert's not allowed to go on a Swan Hellenic Cruise without me! And even so, I have had to step in. These lonely widows, or divorcees, and so on. Some of them are an absolute pain in the neck.' They think he fancies them? 'Well, he's so kind, and he looks at you with those blue eyes – Ol' Blue Eyes! – and you feel he's really interested in you. Of course, he's thinking of something else at the same time, or wishing they'd go away.'

I think now that I begin to understand George's apparently puzzling statement that he never fell in love with anybody, despite the fact that he was clearly besotted with Stella and Nora. My interpretation is that he was never so much in love with anyone that he felt he simply had to be with them for the rest of his life: perhaps because he was so fearful, or so protective of his solitariness as a writer, or even drawn to celibacy as a religious choice. It may be a combination of all of these factors. Certainly, when Stella or Nora made demands upon him, or became, in his eyes, too clingy or needy, he absented himself both physically and emotionally. When it came to intimate personal relationships that might threaten his autonomy, there was ultimately a cold centre – Nora said that there was something 'harder than diamonds' at his core – and a steely self-protecting determination.

Yet, there is another possible line of interpretation. In *Greenvoe*, there is a strange passage, in the voice of a 'Biblical' narrator, during a scene in which the rough ferryman, Ivan Westray, throws a posh young woman, Inga Fortin-Bell, on to the deck of his boat and rapes her. The narrator says:

> And I would not have you think either that love is all sweet desire and gratification, and thereafter peace. The essence of love is pain; deep in the heart of love is a terrible wound. Yes, and though a man should grow wise and quiet at last, yet if he hath trafficked in love but once, he shall be borne to his grave with the stigma of suffering on him. His monument shall bleed.

'The essence of love is pain.' There is a stigma of suffering because of one sexual experience. Was there a terrible wound in George, because of sex? And did he take that wound to the grave?

I am sitting in the living room of George Mackay Brown's house in Mayburn Court, Stromness. George is in his familiar rocking chair. He looks a bit grey and worn, though his eyes are sparkling. He has poured me a glass of his homebrew. I have poured him a dram from the bottle of Highland Park I have brought for him – as a peace offering? Well, this conversation might be difficult.

So, what have you been doing with yourself since I last saw you, Ron? he asks with a wan smile.

I've been researching your life, George.

Oh, really? That's not very interesting for you.

On the contrary, it's fascinating.

He drains his glass. I pour him another.

This Highland Park is good. Eighteen years old. Can't be bad.

Did you know that the minister of St Magnus Cathedral used to get a firkin of whisky sent down from the distillery every year?

No, I didn't know that. It's time they restored it, Ron. He smiles.

Too late for me, George. I'm no longer at the cathedral.

You're not? What are you doing now?

I'm a full-time writer.

Oh, what are you writing now?

I'm writing about your work and your life. I've always loved your writing. I love it even more now. I want to ask you some questions about the meaning of your poetry.

I don't know anything about that. It's a bit beyond me, really. Maybe if you had asked me thirty years ago I might have been able to tell you. I'm not sure about that, mind you.

I've been reading some of your letters, George. I'm troubled by what you write. And I'm troubled by the fact that I'm reading what you write. What do you feel about that?

He stretches out his empty whisky glass. I fill it for him.

He is silent for several minutes.

Oh, well.

He rocks his chair back and forward as he looks out of the window. He starts to hum.

No absolution is asked for. No absolution is offered.

CHAPTER 15

The Trial of George Brown

The handsome, confident, silver-haired woman sitting opposite me at Gartnavel Hospital, Glasgow, first went to Orkney in 1972 as part of a group of seven pupils from a private school in Aberdeen. Kate was 17 years of age and, like the others, had just finished her Higher exams. They had all read *An Orkney Tapestry* and had been impressed by George Mackay Brown's prose. They wanted to meet the author.

The girls had heard that George drank at the Braes Hotel, so they sneaked out of the hostel in Stromness and headed up to the hotel. Unfortunately, George wasn't there. One man who was there was Howie Firth (who would later become the first-ever director of the Edinburgh Science Festival, and is currently founding director of the annual Orkney Science Festival). Howie invited all of the girls for a meal.

'I'm sure we weren't really meant to go into a man's house,' Kate told me. 'He cooked us spaghetti bolognaise and also entertained us with Polish records. We felt very sophisticated being invited to spaghetti bolognaise – and slightly daring, I may say. He told us where George Mackay Brown lived. Next day, we duly turned up clutching our copies of *An Orkney Tapestry* and plucked up courage to ring his doorbell. He answered the doorbell and let us in! He was very sweet. I'm sure we all babbled on. He was very gentle with us. We were thoroughly enchanted. Daft schoolgirls, really.'

That was then. Nowadays, that former GMB 'groupie' is Professor Kate Davidson, a consultant clinical psychologist who is director of the Glasgow Institute of Psycho-social Interventions. Her Ph.D. area of speciality was the relationship between alcohol dependence and depression.

Kate herself married an Orcadian (she has since divorced and remarried) – and another member of the group of Aberdeen pupils married GMB's nephew. 'We all loved Orkney,' she said.

I had asked her to comment on the George and Stella letters.

'I think they are quite tragic,' she replied. 'They're almost teenage angst. Stella is saying: "Did you not find me physically attractive?" and "I've grown too old to claim your notice". She sounds a deeply insecure woman. She's got DTs, and thinks she's going to die. It sounds as if her sense of self was very poor and she allied herself, and got involved romantically, with people to almost fill a gap. I thought her letters were stunningly empty or desperately wanting love and affection. There's a desperateness about her letters.

'It does sound like George needed something, or someone else, to sustain him, to give him something to replace the drink eventually. I'm not convinced that he felt intact. I would trace his vulnerability to his childhood and his insecurities as a child. He was a very anxious, fearful child, and that fearfulness would have been multiplied by being ill. Sometimes that vulnerability may have helped his writing, because he was so sensitive. That would be my hypothesis: that George's fearfulness and insecurity made him much more acutely observant because he *needed* to be, because he may have felt so insecure. His talent was useful there, and he managed to write such wonderful work – so the vulnerability was useful for his work but still left him exposed.'

What about George's drinking?

'I would have thought it was an attempt at self-medication. Consuming alcohol makes people more confident initially, so I would have thought that alcohol helped reduce – initially at any rate – his anxiety. But the level at which he was drinking probably made it much worse in the long run, because it affects your central nervous system and lowers your mood. In the end, it probably made him *more* fearful. The secondary effects of alcohol can make people more suspicious and afraid and paranoid – at least, there's the potential to be more paranoid. That may be why he fell out with people and got into arguments.'

And his agoraphobia?

'People with agoraphobia do experience high anxiety, obviously when they're outside. Their world becomes narrower and narrower. I think he had difficulties with relationships. The fact that he was a poet and an author and wrote such beautiful things would have appealed to younger, sensitive women. They might have felt that George would meet their needs as someone who would understand them. But George's own insecurity probably didn't help to sustain the relationship with Stella. She calls him "Sweet Georgie". That's infantilising, it doesn't sit very well with being madly in love with someone. Looks like a coquettish, babying kind of way.'

The spirituality of individual human beings is best evidenced by the decisions they make, rather than by the things they say. A necessary consequence of George's commitment to his life and vocation was his decision to reduce his dependency on alcohol. It is noticeable that, in his letters to Stella, references to his drinking become much less frequent; his energies are mainly directed to persuading Stella to give up alcohol and thereby save her life. He continued to worry that she might commit suicide.

On 1 December 1968, feeling 'friendless and sad', she wrote: 'Your own friend Stel nearly kicked the bucket good and proper this time, I was shoved out of Chalmers Hospital and stuck in the suicide ward of the Royal Infirmary – where they were all going mad at regular intervals ... maybe we will both be happy again soon.'

George continued to suffer from bronchitis. On 29 March 1969, he wrote to Stella: 'How are you, my dear? I am quite well except for a sore eye and a flute, a piccolo, and an oboe in my chest playing a trio over and over again (the slow movement is lovely) ... and now, dear

Stel, I hope with all my heart that you are well. You've had much to thole in this life, that is well called "a vale of tears". But never forget that you carry about with you, wherever you go, whatever happens, the essential Stella that is rarer and richer than any diamond. God bless you.'

Despite his illnesses, GMB's ceremony of daily writing sustained him. The sinner was finding his salvation, one day at a time. The daily ritual of sweeping away the crumbs of his breakfast toast, placing a lined notebook on the table, and conjuring up a world with his biro pen, helped to calm his terrors and fill his life with meaning.

The knowledge that he had a gift never left him for long. Exercising the gift did not and would not make the wound disappear, but a personal reaffirmation of his vocation as a writer supported a daily discipline through which the wound's pain might be diminished. Indeed, the wound might even feed the gift. Without this regular ceremony, George Mackay Brown was staring into a black hole. If he failed to show up for work every day, ready to put in a shift no matter how bad the theatre of the night had been, the oblivion for which he sometimes longed might well have become a reality.

The fact that, in the late 1960s, his stock as a Scottish writer was rising also helped. He no longer had to justify himself to his community. In 1969, another collection of short stories, *A Time to Keep*, was published.

'He would be pleased to make his own way in the world,' said Kate Davidson. 'Becoming successful allowed him to be more adult and probably less neurotic. It must have been wonderful for his self-esteem.'

In June 1969, Stella entered Crichton Royal Mental Hospital. 'Dearest Stel,' wrote George, 'Poor dear girl, get better soon, for all our sakes, but especially for your own sake. There's a good long life in front of you. Play it cool and sober, then there'll be light and happiness and fulfilment, at last.'

On 6 July 1969, he wrote to her: 'I will always pray for you and think of you with kindness. You were so sweet and gentle and understanding to me at various times when I needed these salves

... My own heart has been knocked and battered this past year. I am thankful that I have my work to turn to – I don't know what I'd do without my writing.'

In 1969, *An Orkney Tapestry* was published – illustrations by Sylvia Wishart.

Unsurprisingly, George had occasional lapses. He wrote to Stella on 27 January 1970: 'Dearest Stel, a lovely serene shining day in Orkney, and here I sit writing a few letters, having got up after noon and had breakfast. I expect you understand my complaint – I was a bad drinking man most of last week. Thank goodness my friends looked after me and fed me and saw that I got home safely. Well, it's all over now, without any court appearances, but of course it leaves a bitter after taste in the mouth.'

Soon, George was back as preacher rather than fellow sufferer. On 17 February 1970, he wrote to her: 'None of us can ever justify ourselves entirely by putting the blame on others. This is to enter deeper into the tunnel. The beginning of the return to the light is to say: "Here I am, in such and such a situation, and I alone am to blame for it, because my will is free. And I have had dealings with other people, and in this and that it seems to me that they let me down and did not act as they should have acted. But in the clear light of eternity I alone am responsible for my actions. And now I wish to drag myself out of this rut where I have fallen." And, my dear Stella, with all your kindness and sweetness and gentleness you can do it – the clue is in your hand – you will stand in the full sun once more.'

This does not sound much like George Mackay Brown. Rather, it resembles a cross between a testimony at an Alcoholics Anonymous meeting and a Calvinist sermon.

As the months went on, George made it clear that he was restricting his intake of alcohol in the interests of his vocation, and that he wished Stella would do likewise. Nevertheless, he still poeticised drink. On 6 October 1970, he wrote to her: 'How is that wicked John Barleycorn behaving? It would have been a lot better for us if we had never been introduced to him, and gone wandering with him down the vistas of Rose St., and come dancing back again after 10pm. I have a new rule now, at any rate – I never touch a drop till after 8pm, and then I have to be careful 'cos I've to be up in the morning and at my desk.'

George's literary output continued. In 1971, *Fisherman with Ploughs* was published. The following year came *Greenvoe*, and in 1974 *Hawkfall*.

The onslaught of depressions continued. George wrote on 22 April 1976: 'Dear Stella, all's quiet here – except that in the narrow black smithy of my skull all sorts of furious hammerings and flamings and munchings are going on; to what avail, alas, I do not know.'

With his drinking increasingly under control, his output of brilliant words increased. In 1976, *Winterfold* and *The Sun's Net* were published.

In Rackwick, in the summer of 1970, George met composer Peter Maxwell Davies for the first time. They struck up an immediate rapport. Thus began the partnership of two men who were destined to become giants in their chosen fields. Entranced by the wild Orkney seascapes, Maxwell Davies decided to move to Orkney. George pointed out an abandoned house, at the top of a cliff at Rackwick, with sixty years of sheep muck inside. Once restored, this was to be the composer's island eyrie for more than twenty-five years. It was in this house, exposed to the tumultuous Hoy storms, that he would compose the symphonies which made his name as one of the greatest composers of his generation.

With co-founders Norman Mitchell, organist and music master at St Magnus Cathedral, and Archie Bevan, Max inspired the St Magnus Festival. It began in 1977 with the production of Maxwell Davies's work, *The Martyrdom of St Magnus*, scripted by George Mackay Brown. Many festivals were to feature Maxwell Davies–Mackay Brown collaborations.

On 29 October 1977, George wrote to Stella: 'I think we have much the same illnesses of mind and body … and I wheeze and wheeze like an old badly patched concertina. And I suffer from chronic weariness & occasional hideous depressions. I only seem to come alive when I'm sitting before a blank sheet of paper with a 5p ball-point pen in my hand.'

On 27 July 1978: 'Dearest Stella, You must not say you won't have another May birthday. I hope to be writing a birthday poem to you when you're a sweet old lady of 90, with a cat on your lap and roses in your cheeks.'

In 1981, *Portrait of Orkney* was published.

On 20 April 1982, George wrote to Stella: 'I get out, walking slowly it's true; but I amn't thankful enough, for the black rook of depression comes and sits on my shoulder – not *all* the time, thank goodness – but when I least expect it, there it is.'

George wrote several acrostic poems for Stella on her birthday. This one, I think, is particularly touching:

STELLA: <u>For Her Birthday</u> (15 May, 1982)

So, once, in the 50s
There was this crazy chap, high among clouds,
Edinburgh-bound.
Laurel-seeking he was, out of Orkney.
Long and salt his throat
Among the stanzas that starred the howffs of Rose Street.

Could he not hide forever in that beautiful city?
A sweet girl, one day,
Rose, a star, to greet him.
To him, she was sweeter than rain among roses in summer,
While poets like columns of salt stood
Round the oak Abbotsford Bar.
I, now
Going among the gray houses and piers of Stromness
Hear that voice made of roses and rain still; and see
Through broken storm clouds, the remembered star.

George to Stella, 'Midsummer 1982': 'Dearest Stella, How pleased I was to get your letter, in the middle of our St Magnus Festival, which has left me drained and exhausted. All that culture, in a few days – a burden scarcely to be borne … A black imp comes and squats on my shoulder, for days and weeks on end – and murmurs black things into my ear – and laughs at my trembling pulses. And goes away at last, but never for long. There he is, back again, sniggering and snarling a few days later. Tranquilisers don't seem to do much good.'

George to Stella, 21 January 1983: 'O what a loud earth-shaking cough I have! And sometimes such a mass of dark clouds pour through my skull, I wish I was dissolved into the 4 elements …'

In the midst of his suffering, GMB continued to produce work of high quality. In 1983, his short-story collection *Andrina* was published.

George to Stella, 5 April 1984: 'My pen goes scurrying across blank page after blank page, most days … I have been very depressed, but I've got tablets that help me.'

In March 1985, the 'voice made of roses and rain' was stilled. Stella Cartwright was only 48 years old when she died, a lonely alcoholic. One can only guess at what George's feelings were when he heard the news. We get most of the information about his inner battles over the previous couple of decades through his letters. He was not the kind of man to confide in even close friends about such a relationship.

'Stella was a sad case,' Allison Dixon said. 'I can't understand why, when she died, he didn't go to her funeral. None of us could understand that.'

He may have decided not to go to the funeral because he feared being emotionally overwhelmed. It might have been down to his agoraphobia, or to the fact that the black rook of depression had once more taken up residence on his shoulder.

I have a hunch about this. It is connected to his own favourite character in his fiction. Mrs Elizabeth McKee is the mother of Rev. Simon McKee, the hapless, alcoholic parish minister in *Greenvoe*. Mrs McKee suffers 'assizes' in her mind, in which accusers come four times a year 'to enquire into certain hidden events of her life'. Whatever the charge, she knows that she will be exposed to the whole world as a wicked woman. No-one else, not even her son, knows of her secret suffering.

GMB had intended that Mrs McKee would be a minor character in the novel; but, as the narrative developed, this reticent Calvinistic woman with her guilty secrets began to assert herself. Here is what he wrote about her in his autobiography:

And so Mrs McKee, whom I grew to love more and more as the novel unfolded, led me gently into her past life; and, wisely, she led me among places I was familiar with: Edinburgh, and chiefly the district of Marchmont where both of us had lived at different times. Also she led me into places of the mind that I knew a little about, those places of guilt, prosecution, judgement, which, while they last, make life bitter and terrible. One endures, somehow – a little light comes in, and grows – and one wakes from the dark dream with a few syllables of thankfulness. But one knows that the evil time will return, sooner or later.

I think Elizabeth McKee and I have had more joy and understanding of each other than any other character I have imagined. When I say 'imagined', I mean a richness and resonance. Existence is still mysterious, especially for an artist, that the shapes of his imagination can be more real than most of the living shadows he nods to in passing on the street every day.

Referring to the novel itself, GMB adds: *As for me, I do not care to turn its pages anymore. I quickly grow cold to what I have written. Occasionally, over a glass of whisky, I take* Greenvoe *off the bookshelf and commune for half an hour with my friend Mrs McKee. She is a consolation. We have things we can say to one another.*

Mrs McKee felt guilty about everything, from the failure to return a teapot to the looming destruction of Greenvoe. When black depression visited GMB, he also felt that he was to blame for everything bad that was happening.

If George had thought that when he became a Roman Catholic the sacrament of confession would relieve him of his guilt, he found that things were not as simple as that. He told Isobel Murray: 'You never really get rid of Calvinism all the same. It's sort of bred in your bone, you know, and you're born into it; no amount of other religions will shift that, I know quite well. It's very difficult.' As George wrote in his autobiography: *Textures of Calvinism, generations old, are still part of me and I think I will never be rid of them: ancient guilts, rebukes in the silence of thought, or when I am reading or writing, weigh on the heart, as if some Presbyterian ancestor from the seventeenth century was murmuring to me, and not mildly.*

George rebuked himself, in the silence of thought, about Stella Cartwright. The news of her death, although not entirely unexpected, must have been a terrible blow to him. Given his fears, it would not have been surprising if he himself had been pushed into the kind of terrible assize with which he was not unfamiliar. Of Mrs McKee's trials, he wrote: *For a few days, sometimes for as long as a week, the manse was an abode of secret suffering.*

Whatever the reason or reasons, George just could not face the trip to Edinburgh for Stella's cremation. My guess is that, as he sat, alone, at the sombre funeral hour, his home in Mayburn Court was an abode of secret suffering. The trial of George Brown, the man, would have been a hard assize to thole.

What was the relationship between George Mackay Brown's times of intense suffering and his art? Did the suffering produce the art? If George had not had life-threatening tuberculosis and sanity-threatening depressions, would he have produced such high-quality writing?

It is, of course, impossible to provide definitive answers to these questions. What I can say is that there seems to be no direct correlation between specific depressions mentioned in letters to Stella and a particular quality of work produced at these times. As a rule, GMB does not bring his personal struggles overtly into his writing.

I asked Rowena Murray, co-author of *Interrogation of Silence*, what she thought the relationship between his religion and his depressions might be.

'Religion wasn't the antidote, but the safety net maybe,' she told me. 'It was a way of talking about other things. His religion doesn't solve the problem of depression, it doesn't heal the condition. It's writing which stops him from going over the edge. This is where we come to your "wound and the gift". I think he would have nodded and said yes to that! He deserves credit for not sinking into the mire.

There were so many points at which he could have gone downhill and chosen the wrong path or the wrong person.'

Some commentators in the past have come close to saying that intense suffering is necessary for great art to appear. Certainly, several great writers or painters or composers have experienced much suffering in their lives. One needs only think of van Gogh, Beethoven and Dostoyevsky.

Many successful writers have had times of illness in childhood or adolescence. Whether it was the particular suffering, or simply the enforced isolation – being cast upon their own imaginative resources or opened up to the world of books – that produced the necessary alchemy, is hard to say. The opening-up of the world of literature created by serious illness was certainly formative for GMB.

Writing is a solitary occupation. There are no work colleagues with whom to interact on a daily basis. Writers can be insecure, anxious, obsessional and sometimes even paranoid. Unfavourable reviews may provoke a crisis. All of these factors can lead to abuse of alcohol, or other drugs, in turn reinforcing the stereotype – particularly strong in America – of the crazed writer with a wine or whisky bottle on the desk. The alcoholic route has been much traversed by some prominent writers: Raymond Carver, Dylan Thomas, Truman Capote, Edgar Allen Poe, Theodore Roethke, Herman Melville, Scott Fitzgerald, Eugene O'Neill, William Faulkner, Ernest Hemingway, John Steinbeck. The list goes on and on.

Some gloried in it, insisting that their creativity depended on alcohol or drugs; others, playing up to the romantic image of the writer as a tormented genius, became self-indulgent narcissists, whose talents ran into the sands of their own self-absorption. There were those who became mad, or committed suicide – either instantly or slowly, bottle by bottle, drop by drop. Some writers bought into the myth of the permanently inebriated artist whose sufferings bring redemption to a community or nation.

Graham Greene, one of GMB's favourite novelists, said that writing was a form of therapy. He wondered aloud as to how people who did not write, compose or paint could escape the madness, the melancholia, the panic and the fear inherent in the human situation.

I have neither the capacity nor the desire to create some grand theory about the relationship between art and suffering. But I do want to reflect further on the relationship between George Mackay Brown the writer and George Brown the secretly suffering man.

To help me with this, I turned to Angus Peter Campbell, Joyce Gunn Cairns and A. L. Kennedy, partly because they are creative artists whose work I particularly admire – there are many others I could have chosen – and also because, like George Mackay Brown, they have had to deal with depressive crises in their own lives.

Angus Peter Campbell is an accomplished poet, short-story writer, novelist and actor. He does most of his work now in Gaelic. Sorley MacLean said of him: 'I have no doubts that Angus Peter Campbell is one of the few really significant living poets in Scotland, writing in any language'.

He was brought up on the island of South Uist in the Western Isles of Scotland. After university studies, he worked in television. He had a serious struggle with alcoholism before returning to the islands. He now lives in Kyle of Lochalsh with his wife and six children, and works as a freelance writer, journalist, broadcaster and actor.

He first encountered GMB's work when he was a pupil at Oban High School. He was taught by Iain Crichton Smith, another fine island poet and novelist whose life was blighted by depression. Angus Peter Campbell read *Loaves and Fishes*, then read some more of GMB's work at university. I asked him how the Orcadian writer's work struck him at that time.

'When you're that age and you're under the influence of American black beat poetry or Allen Ginsberg or the East Europeans or the Russians,' he told me, 'George Mackay Brown maybe seemed a bit light; but I now realise he's tremendously limpid and clear and lucid and wafer-like. It's a simplicity I would die for. It's so difficult to achieve. When I read his work, I'm just amazed by its clarity – the clarity of language and the vision that lies behind it, which is mostly unsaid.'

As an island poet, he must appreciate some of the things GMB was saying?

'I recently went on a journey through the Western Isles and went back to South Uist. I still call it home. You know, if you were conscious at all of an Eden, and you're going to be a poet, you're going to be a grieving poet. I think once you've experienced – the word in Gaelic would be *blas*, tasted; the Psalmist says "O taste and see that the Lord is good" – once you've tasted the possibility of love and grace and of community, you taste inwardly a sense of possible glory and of achievement and of greatness for the human race and for yourself. And you think: "I could reach the skies, I could reach the stars, and my people and my island and my language and my culture could reach to the Milky Way in terms of what they could achieve". And when that becomes a kind of seedbed possibility in your heart, inwardly, and in your head, then you also realise you're in a fallen world. You realise how chaotic you are yourself, and how disappointed you are in yourself, how little you really achieve and how petty you are in your ambitions and in your drive, and how petty those around you are, how fallen the world is, and how broken and how mischievous and how cruel and how vindictive and how hateful it really is.

'These two are huge giants clashing psychologically within you – you say: "Well, we have such possibility of greatness, and simultaneously we have such a depth of hatred". Of course, clash and tumult and chaos and possible greatness come out of that contest, out of that rage between these two things. I've sensed that and I've experienced that, and I've no doubt whatsoever that Iain Crichton Smith, who went into the middle of the wood, knew it and sensed it, and certainly when I read George Mackay Brown I have no doubt whatsoever that he would know both of these – the contest that is going on there, between good and evil, you could call it.'

Didn't Angus Peter once call himself a Calvinist Catholic? What was all that about?

'I don't know where to start or finish!' he said. 'My recollection is that our schooling and my childhood was a collective, as opposed to an individual, experience. So, at the church we genuflected together, we rose together, we prayed together, we recited the liturgy together. The whole notion of individual salvation and being separated from that collective salvation was absolutely alien. Then I came to a point in my own life post-university, through my own chaos in terms of my drinking and in terms of what my life was about. I came to a crossroads at which I said to myself: "Beyond your poetry and beyond your knowledge of Sartre and Hegel and Marx and politics and all the rest of it, where are you? Where do you stand in terms of this?" It's a fairly lonely and a fairly stark and a pretty challenging individual place to be at, and I give thanks that I've been there, and that I would then say to my Lord and my Christ: "I am yours and You are mine. I follow you."'

So, it becomes an individual relationship with Christ in that classic Protestant fashion.

'But, having gone through that – the circle is almost complete – I desired increasingly the quiet collective consciousness of Catholicism; we're all fragile, and, as we kneel together and as we take this thin wafer together, it's a kind of fragility that says, right, we're all in this level place together.'

What Angus Peter is saying makes a lot of sense to me. He is bringing together the values both of the corporate Catholic community's rituals and of the Protestant stress on individual decision and commitment, particularly at a time of crisis.

After reading this part of the conversation, novelist Alison Miller e-mailed me: 'It's almost as if his Catholicism is his mother tongue or family, and to achieve separation/individuation he recognises Protestantism as offering more help. Once he's achieved separation, it's safe to come back to the fold.'

Angus Peter finds grace in unexpected places. 'I am increasingly drawn to grace. Grace could be expressed, for instance, by the most orthodox wing of the Free Presbyterian Church, unexpectedly, and not expressed in a liberal Catholic church! Or vice versa. You never know!'

What, I asked him, did he feel about GMB's description of Scotland, the 'Knox-ruined nation'?

'I don't know anything about that. In my childhood, Knox had not come aboard at Lochboisdale! He had never landed in South Uist. He was absent from Oban as well. In Edinburgh, when I was a student, he was a statue on the Mound, but I was reading Marx then. Knox was just a figure. But, of course, I understand what George was saying.'

The very act of writing, I said, kept GMB sane in the face of suffering. How did APC deal with this kind of struggle in his own life?

He told me that one part of his response stemmed from the Protestant work ethic and individual responsibility. It was about sacrifice and effort and taking your gift and your work 'completely seriously, bowing down before that yoke and delivering it. The great Italian writer Italo Calvino described it as the Calvin within his Roman name! There's that one side which I had – I needed to prove myself. It can be hugely and richly rewarding. Of course, drink destroys that. At first, you believe the mythology that you need to be Dylan Thomas or Faulkner – which is a whole load of nonsense … When you glimpse greatness and simultaneously the miry clay of living, it's despairing, and it's sometimes easier just to give in to despair than not.'

Campbell talked about a Lowland piper he knew who, even when he was drunk, was able to produce, 'from some well deep within him', exquisite music. 'But that can't go on. The fact that he can do this can be a justification for continuing to do this, but you can't. It's unsustainable.'

So, how about the relationship between the wound and the gift, between mental illness and art?

Angus Peter points me in the direction of W. H. Auden's poem about suffering, 'Musée des Beaux Arts'. It talks about how ordinary life goes on while people suffer. That is one attitude to take to suffering: it happens, life goes on. I am reminded of Robert Frost's observation that he could sum up everything he'd learned in life in three words: it goes on.

'If you're sensitive and aware of your own frailties and the world's frailties,' said Angus Peter, 'at any moment there's a thin line between genius and the pit.'

There is another attitude for the writer to take, and it has to do with the magic of language. 'If you take the fragments of your ruin – as T. S. Eliot said – you will hear the art. I think you can make, or remake, an amazing world out of them, through the power of words. There's a wonderful phrase from Italo Calvino: "Literature is the promised land of language". When you glimpse that promised land of language and literature, as George Mackay Brown did, each, day, each moment, you think: "Well, there is a promised land, and it can be achieved and made and created through words and the joie de vivre of words".

'There's another wonderful quote from Milan Kundera, who talked about "the tyranny of the narrative". Mostly through nine-teenth-century serialisations, the storyline became all-important. Diversion and jokes and meditations and this, that and the other became less important; whereas traditionally, as in great Gaelic storytelling, there's sometimes a huge run of words which serve no narrative function whatsoever – but it's a pure delight in just being alive. That's what keeps me going: language somehow magically creates a world around you. Like George Mackay Brown, I prefer to stay there; but, as Rev. Andy Scarcliffe, a Baptist minister friend who was a mentor to me at the time of my crisis, said: "It's great to be redeemed and brought back from Egypt, but it's maybe better not to have had to go there in the first place!" That's what I say to my children: "Just stay on Mount Zion, just stay in the Cuillin [the rocky mountain range in Skye]!"'

Alison Miller commented: 'This sounds a bit like another Protestant/Catholic split – the narrative engine of Protestantism and the sitting-about attending to the beauty of words of Catholicism'.

For the writer, then, one possible response to despair and suffering is, through the magic of language, to create new worlds. In George Mackay Brown's case, he chose to re-create traditional worlds in new and brilliant language. He ransacked the jewellery boxes of Christian spirituality and re-presented some of the contents in ways which, while not doing away with personal anguish, might make it more bearable.

After our conversation, I received an e-mail from Angus Peter Campbell.

Hi Ron:

Thanks for the conversation journey this evening.

I've been thinking of fragments/broken things since, and those two great portions of scripture – the great recognition at the breaking of the bread after the Emmaus road walk, of course, and that other wonderful text from Acts where everyone finally reaches safety, some on tiny broken bits of wood, after Paul's shipwreck on Malta.

George's gift, I think, was to make an altar of the fragments of wood, and a harvest meal of the crumbs of love and grace.

with my best wishes

angus peter

Making an altar of the fragments of wood, and a harvest meal of the crumbs of love and grace: I like that. It takes me in my imagination to Orkney's Italian Chapel, where the prisoners-of-war gratefully received the fragments and the wreckage from the seas and made them into something beautiful for God. In creating a place of worship where the simple ceremonies of faith, including the Eucharist, would be enacted, they did not solve the problem of human suffering, but they made the terrors and the fears of their exiled life more bearable.

Joyce Gunn Cairns MBE is one of Scotland's finest artists. She exhibits on a regular basis at home and abroad. She has drawings in the permanent collections of the Scottish National Portrait Gallery and at the universities of Oxford, Cambridge and Edinburgh.

Her uncompromising integrity as an artist has meant that she has not made a lot of money. She lives in a council house in the Edinburgh housing estate of West Pilton. Over the years, she has suffered from depression, sometimes suicidal. She is a living embodiment of the French poet and playwright Antonin Artaud's observation that no-one has ever written, painted, sculpted, modelled, built or invented except to get out of hell.

I have known Joyce for a long time. George Mackay Brown would have agreed with her statement about art on her website: 'I am now of the conviction that there is no such thing as a talented elite. Robert

Louis Stevenson said of himself that his talent was for hard work. For me too, any facility with line and paint I have developed and go on developing, and any acclaim I have enjoyed, is as a result of grit and determination and a willingness to risk my significance and bear the pain of rejection, again and again and again. It is trite, but absolutely true, to say that any accomplishment is 1 per cent inspiration and 99 per cent perspiration. I remind anyone of this when they tell me they wish they had my talent. I ask them if they are willing to make the sacrifices required to maximise their potential, whatever it might be.'

I met Joyce at Henderson's Restaurant in Edinburgh, where some of her portraits formed part of an exhibition. Hers is a very striking presence: blonde-white hair, ruby lips, broad Scots accent, formidable articulacy, tears and flashes of sunshine. I asked Joyce about her current state of mind.

'I'm not consumed by suicidal depression as often as I was when I was younger, but that's probably because I've increasingly honoured my God-given vocation, however it expresses itself. I remember struggling with melancholy, even as a child. Then there were depressions in my twenties and thirties, and a profound sense of ugliness. And yet at the same time there was always something that was driving me, impelling me – some core of belief, I suppose.

'There was one moment, I suppose an epiphany – is that the right word? – where I remember being in the depths of despair, and praying. Now, I didn't believe in getting literal answers to prayer, but I did pray – and that was at a time when I felt that all my work was rubbish, that it wasn't going anywhere. I prayed: "Please God, if there's a purpose in what I'm struggling to say, however I might say it, show me a way. Otherwise, free me from it. Because it would be nice to just have an ordinary job and make a living without going through all this agony." Something was always there that was driving me. So, I can only say I'm grateful for that. By struggling to honour it, somehow that has brought about a level of liberation. I still suffer, but perhaps it's not with quite the same level of bleakness, not always, anyway. I do find I'm getting more likely to speak my mind, and alienate people, but maybe with that comes a certain serenity I suppose, and greater self-acceptance. One is never going to find the answers, but you are always approximating towards something, and maybe it's acceptance of that as well.

'When George Mackay Brown says that the task of the artist is to keep and repair the sacred web of creation, it speaks to me. So does the fact that he felt that the old women of Stromness looked down on him because he didn't do any proper work. That's been part of my depression as well, the sense of "What are you doing?" and the underlying "Why don't you get out and get a proper job?" Like George, fear is a big thing for me. I wake up every morning with these dark visions of things that I maybe read years ago, and they still go round in my mind. It's always there, and I have a lot of – I wouldn't call them nightmares, but some of them are quite nightmarish.'

In the midst of her troubles, how did she understand God?

'I would find it hard to put words round it. I can only say that I have experiences which confirm for me a sense of being held, through all the pain, all the confusion. There is some sense of being directed, a sense of guidance, angels – but I struggle with that. Because I think, how can I arrogate to myself that sense of being singled out, when I'm living alongside children who are fucked up from the minute they are born? How do you reconcile that? I don't know, Ron. That's where I struggle with my faith. I think: how can there be any benign presence? And yet, I do feel that I benefit from a benign presence.

'It's the spirit thing. I suppose I have gleaned some comfort from the knowledge that, however many millions of people are out there calling themselves artists or writers, the miraculous thing is that nobody has ever drawn like me or written like you. For me, that's bound up with a greater serenity, it's knowing that there are no answers and no solutions, and yet somehow there's something that's holding and binding.'

Joyce found herself able to sympathise with GMB in his self-loathing. She also echoed some of the things that Angus Peter Campbell said, when she went on: 'Would you say that the Church – Catholic or Protestant – helps people to engage with their capacity for unsavoury emotion and behaviour? By that I mean: it's one thing to say "I'm a sinner, forgive me God", it's quite another thing – in my experience – to live with that raw awareness of just how unpleasant a person I am. That resentment, or jealousy or pride. Pride is a terrible thing. I hate it in myself. I hate that lack of humility and always trying to get my oar in and reminding people how important I am; and of course it's really because I feel unimportant. It's difficult to bear these things, to bear that reality of how unsavoury we are capable of being, or how cruel. You don't know what you are capable of doing, that's what's scary. I'm no angel myself, but some of the things I've produced have a touch of the angelic about them.'

A. L. Kennedy's short stories and novels, such as *What Becomes*, *Day* and *Original Bliss*, have won many awards. Her book *Everything You Need* is one of the finest novels I have read. She also does stand-up comedy; it is both dark and hilarious stuff. She is a Quaker, and a Unitarian Universalist minister, though I can't imagine that she is a great signer-up to creeds of any kind.

I had met her before, at the Edinburgh International Book Festival; and I arranged to meet her in the Royal Hotel, Stromness, where she had been reading from her short-story collection, *What Becomes*. We were in touch thereafter by e-mail.

ALK is often portrayed as something of a misanthrope. I think this image results from a confusion between the work and the author; her themes are sometimes dark to the point of bleakness. I find her to be good company and a stimulating conversationalist. She has some very funny, deadpan, mordant one-liners.

She has known pain in her life, both physical and mental. In the past, she has made mention of a suicidal impulse. Yet she resists the notion that creativity is necessarily linked to suffering. As Professor Robert Crawford – who heads the department at St Andrews University in which ALK teaches creative writing – says in his comprehensive work *Scotland's Books: The Penguin History of Scottish Literature*:

> She has also called attention to dangers in the Romantic assumption that 'creativity stems directly or almost solely from present mental

anguish', since 'When do I feel like making the huge emotional commitment, the massive leap of faith that writing involves? When my mind is at its fittest. When I am happy and well.'

I wanted to know more about the relationship between the dark times in her life and her writing. Did she feel that her writing 'saved' her, like it seemed to have done for George? Did she reckon that, without the dark times, she would have been a better or worse writer? And where did her own religious outlook fit into all of this? She responded with a remarkable e-mail:

'I do get slightly suspicious of the whole "tortured artist" thing. I don't think that pain is necessary for creation, or that it's desirable. The fact is that anyone creative who keeps at it for any length of time will have the ups and downs that anyone else has ... that's just life. If you've trained yourself to pay attention and be, in that sense, open-minded, then you may well be more aware of your pain, or the pain of a loved one, or the pain of a situation. That's not great, but then again being a creative person, you can make something positive out of the negative. You can create a response to the pain and the dark – and creating that response involves (certainly for writing) an absence from self, a kind of meditative state, which is entirely pleasant and therapeutic – so, really, you're in a very positive position. It can be tiring and the feelings can be overwhelming – especially if you can't get distance from them, or they're very large – and the writer's life involves long periods of solitude, which may lead to other periods of unwelcome solitude – people get tired of your withdrawal, you don't need people most of the time and it's awkward to have their attention when you need it because you have an odd timetable, etc. ... And isolation isn't fun, unless you want it – it can magnify unhappiness. But the situation is largely positive – you make something out of nothing – which is a huge, impossible pleasure – and that pleasure is self-contained – because you are who you are, you can do it – all you need is pen and paper.

'Adding an isolated and relatively small community with quite grim weather and alcohol into that mix makes it much darker. Fewer people to talk to, a greater sense perhaps of no-one listening, of creating things no-one really wants, of being useless. A sense of limitation, lack of sunlight, perhaps certain types of cultural poverty – and the alcohol magnifying emotions and damaging your capacity to think clearly. I can only imagine that would be a nightmare – although, if GMB could get into a piece and be writing, I would think that would provide relief – absence of self, sense of usefulness, sense of reaching out to others, of achievement, of beauty, clarity of vision.

'It's an arduous life, but a very rich one – the big thing to avoid would be psychoactive chemicals – because you live in your head. The religious side of it, I'm not sure about – I think being a creator and thinking of a creator can be very enriching, and I think living in an Eden where you have to be Adam, Eve, God and the snake can be wearying, undermining and confusing.'

I wish I had been able to introduce George Mackay Brown to Angus Peter Campbell, and then to bring Edwin Muir into the conversation. I found Angus Peter's evocation of his island background and of the place of an island poet to be compelling. GMB and Angus Peter both make poetry out of Eden and the Fall. Neither Orkney nor South Uist equates to Eden; Eden stands for a time of innocence and wonder, almost certainly in childhood. When I see children playing in rural Orkney, with its rolling, rich landscapes and its often turbulent seascapes, the word 'enchantment' comes to mind. That is not simply a romantic view. Island life has its own disadvantages, but to grow up in that kind of elemental physical and social environment is to occupy a privileged space.

The Fall is disenchantment. It is about other people, as Sartre might have said. It is also about oneself. Disenchantment comes with the realisation that, while we might come into the world 'trailing clouds of glory', it is not long before we encounter trouble, both personal and corporate.

Angus Peter Campbell and George Mackay Brown are both Calvinist Catholics. (That is a double whammy. Calvinism, as GMB has pointed out, brings its own dark ancestral mutterings; and, as comedian Billy Connolly has observed, 'I'm a Catholic. That means I have A-Level guilt.') They see the glorious possibilities around them, but they are unsparing and even savage in their descriptions of the chaos and self-wounding of their lives. Joyce Gunn Cairns is the same.

None of those interviewed makes the claim that personal suffering is essential for the production of great literature. I think Professor Kate Davidson and A. L. Kennedy are right to suggest that the practised sensitivity of poets and artists, as they pay attention to what is happening around them, may make them more vulnerable. Yet they are also right to say that artists' sensitivity and skills enable them to create something new from the raw material of their own and other people's lives. The magic of language makes its own spell, creates its own power. The wound can at times be seriously disabling, but it can be assuaged, to some degree, by the gift. Psychiatrist Anthony Storr was of the opinion that the creative act is one way of overcoming helplessness, which is a key component of the depressive state.

Alcohol and drugs may at first help to free the imagination and engender confidence; but, once they get beyond a critical point on the curve, they will consume the gift and destroy the vocation. A. L. Kennedy reinforces this point. Looking at GMB in Orkney, she throws the limitations of a small community and the lack of sunlight into the mix with alcohol; but then she draws attention to something else – that GMB, in the process of writing, might find relief through 'absence of self, sense of usefulness, sense of reaching out to others, of achievement, of beauty, clarity of vision'.

Commenting on the link between suffering and art, Alison Miller told me: 'I imagine there are no definitive answers. I wonder if suffering sometimes drives certain people to take refuge in art; that art necessitates a stepping out of the stream of life in order to look at it and articulate it in ways that make it bearable. In that respect, the artist is also doing something on behalf of the rest of us – turning human suffering into a form that we can engage with, without necessarily having to experience it fully ourselves.

311

'Suffering, of course, doesn't automatically lead to art – but, as we know, a disproportionate number of artists and writers suffer from depression or other mental-health difficulty, or have some kind of chronic physical illness that takes them out of the "normal" flow of life. In artists such as these, it must seem that the "wound and the gift" are inextricable, that "the gift" might lie dormant under the dailiness of ordinary life, without "the wound" to take those distractions away. Which is not to say that artists thus afflicted will be saying "Whoopee, I've got a chronic incurable illness, I'll never have to work, I can get on with my art instead". Part of the pain of existence often stems from an acute awareness that a "normal" life is denied them. It seems as if George Mackay Brown took a long time to come to terms with that.'

Truman Capote said that when God hands someone a gift, he also gives them a whip. The relationship between wound and gift in any one particular creative artist is bound to be a complicated one. I believe that George Mackay Brown managed to live with – rather than heal – his debilitating wound by the disciplined exercise of his formidable gift. This was achieved by his commitment to what he understood as his vocation, the ceremony of daily writing, the choosing of life over death at critical junctures, and the rich resources of his Catholic faith.

The losing of himself in his writing also helped him cope with his personal turmoil. Through his daily ceremony of writing, even in times of depression, he did, as Alison Miller says, do something for the rest of us: step out of the stream of life in order to look at it and articulate it in ways that make it bearable.

As a self-conscious sinner who also knew his own giftedness, George would have said 'amen' to Joyce Gunn Cairns's verdict: 'I'm no angel myself, but some of the things I've produced have a touch of the angelic about them'.

CHAPTER 16

Poetic Dwelling on the Earth as a Mortal

This chapter moves in a different direction altogether. It takes a more personal and existential tack.

I want to think aloud about the extent to which George Mackay Brown's life and work can serve as a spiritual resource for individuals and faith communities, at a time when the credibility of institutional religion is under close scrutiny.

For whom might GMB be useful?

The man himself would have been astounded by questions about his 'usefulness'; he did not write in order to be of use to people, nor did he regard himself as an evangelist or a guru. As I write, I can see his smile of incredulity.

Nevertheless, I know lots of people who turn to GMB's writing not only because they appreciate his style and his craftsmanship, but also because they find spiritual inspiration for their lives, whether they are members of religious institutions or not. So I will persist with my question.

To help me explore this territory, I will talk to a number of people from Roman Catholic and Protestant traditions, and also to some who would describe themselves as agnostics or atheists.

A useful starting point might be this simple question: is GMB's work a helpful spiritual resource only for Roman Catholics?

Many Catholics will not even have heard of George Mackay Brown. They manage to live out their faith on a day-to-day basis without ever invoking his name. Yet, in the United Kingdom, a sizeable minority of Catholics will turn to GMB's writings for spiritual nourishment. For some, indeed, George Mackay Brown is a Catholic icon.

Many of those who, as soon as they arrive in Orkney, ask for directions to the house where GMB used to live are pilgrims whose faith has been enriched – or even prompted – by the Orcadian bard. The day may even come when there will be a move to have George Mackay Brown canonised. (By now, George is laughing aloud with disbelief and embarrassment.) Certainly, Orkney's tourist officials would not object.

Father Jock Dalrymple has already testified in these pages to the impact that GMB's work has made on his own faith and understanding. I asked his cousin, Maggie Fergusson, GMB's biographer, to tell me about what George has meant to her own Catholic faith.

'When I first flew to Orkney in late May 1994, to interview George Mackay Brown for *The Times*,' she responded, 'I knew little about either the man or the islands I was visiting. So it was strange, as I trundled by Peace's bus from Kirkwall to Stromness, to find myself overcome by a sense of familiarity, almost of homecoming. I felt I had arrived in a place I had known all my life, though never seen, and I was amazed when George seemed to confirm this in a letter he sent a week or so after that first visit. In among comments about the weather, and the progress of the St Magnus Festival, he wrote: "I hope you will come back often, Maggie, and enjoy a walk to the kirkyard and Warbeth. I feel you belong here in Orkney."'

This made me smile. Only George Mackay Brown would issue an invitation to go for a walk in a cemetery.

Maggie continued: 'This may seem an odd way to begin to reflect on the effects that George, over time, came to have on my faith, but there are parallels. As I got to know George better, and to have some understanding of his beliefs and the way he lived them, I had this same sense of homecoming. It was not that he planted something new in me, but that he helped to bring alive something that had always been there, though only dimly recognised.

'I don't think that, back in 1994, I'd ever heard of Keats's famous words "beauty is truth, truth beauty"– but they express perfectly what I, and many others, found in George's writing: a beauty so powerful and uncontrived that it could only have come from a man deeply in touch with what was real and true.'

Maggie revealed how GMB had changed her spiritual under-standing. 'I had grown up with the sort of catechism-heavy Catholicism in which the institution of the Church, with all its rules and hierarchy, loomed so large as to block the person of Jesus almost completely from view. The life and promises of Christ seemed, often, too good to be true. But getting to know George was an invitation to consider the opposite possibility: that they were too good – too beautiful – *not* to be true. An invitation, but never anything more coercive than that. Almost everybody who knew George was struck by his humility. He forced his beliefs on nobody; he judged nobody. And yet he was completely true to himself.'

This was part of George's gift. What of his wound?

'It was harrowing, as I worked on George's biography, to discover just how crippling his depressions had been. Yet his response to them remains a source of inspiration, helping me to believe in the unity of creation, and in our responsibilities to one another. We are, as George once wrote to Stella Cartwright, "not alone", but "involved with mankind" – "and that means, as I understand it, that whenever you are brave, enduring, uncomplaining, then the whole world of suffering is helped and soothed somehow. This is sacrifice, and fulfilment and renewal: an incalculable leavening."'

Michael McGrath, Director of the Scottish Catholic Education Service, is one of Scotland's most senior Catholic educators. He responded to my invitation to reflect on GMB's influence on his faith: 'I first met George in Stromness in early June 1973 when I was one of a group of student actors touring with Strathclyde Theatre Group in a production of "Witch", a dramatised version of one of George's short stories. We performed it at a local community arts festival in Stromness – an early forerunner, I suppose, of the St Magnus Festival.

'In anticipation of visiting Orkney, I had been reading *An Orkney Tapestry* and some of George's short stories as we travelled north – and, as we sailed into Stromness harbour, I instantly fell in love with the place. All the images which George had portrayed of a timeless landscape, the long summer daylight, the omnipresence of prehistoric ruins – the whole Orkney experience just made sense at an intellectual, emotional and spiritual level.'

Michael explained how George brought a new dimension to his faith.

'As a "cradle Catholic", of course, I already felt comfortable with the religious dimension in George's writing – the ritual, the saints, the Christian optimism. What was strange to me, as a city boy, was the "paganism", George's sense of pre-Christian ritual in the agricultural cycle and the rhythms of the sea. In time, I came to understand how the "harvest passion", as I came to describe it, conveyed George's sense of the mythical significance of suffering and redemption, of sacrifice and resurrection being at the heart of the universe.'

What of George at a personal level?

'George made a personal impact on our first meeting at Stromness pier as we disembarked from the old St Ola ferry (before the days of ro-ro ferries). He was immediately welcoming, friendly, smiling that sweet smile which I'll always remember. In the coming days, he was a regular visitor to our rehearsals and performances, and he was always positive and encouraging to this ragamuffin group of students.

'By the end of a week, I had decided that I wanted to spend some more time in Orkney, as had a few others in the group. Queenie Campbell, a local teacher who had helped to organise our visit to Orkney, without hesitation and with great generosity, offered us the use of her house for three weeks as she visited a relative in the south. In those weeks, we saw a great deal of George over dinner or in the bar of the Braes Hotel. He and I spoke at some length about the Honours dissertation which I was writing on "Modern Love", an obscure sequence of fifty sonnets by the Victorian novelist George Meredith. His knowledge of literature from all ages and all traditions was staggering. We shared not only our faith, but also a love of literature and a passion for Celtic Football Club.

'Thus began a long friendship over many years when, as a young teacher, I visited Stromness as often as I could, sometimes staying with George or renting local houses. It was a great joy to introduce my future wife Maureen to him and his many friends. He was invited to our wedding in Glasgow in July 1977, but, unsurprisingly, he was reluctant to travel. He did, however, send us the unique wedding gift of a copy of *Selected Poems* (1977), in which he had handwritten on the cover plate a short poem entitled "Wedding" – a form of blessing which we treasure still. Some years later, during Orkney holidays, three of our children loved to visit George and sit in his rocking chair and listen to his stories (often with funny voices).'

In the meantime, Michael had written a dissertation on George's work and was awarded the degree of M.Litt. by Strathclyde University in 1981.

'I regard it as a great blessing on my life to have met and known George. His writing absolutely affirmed my personal faith in Jesus Christ; indeed, it expanded it because it added various perspectives – a sense of the timelessness of God, an appreciation of the effects of the land and sea on the rhythms of people's lives, a respect for the pagan traditions as well as the rationality of our prehistoric ancestors – and, above all, the central importance of the redeeming power of Christ's death and resurrection for humanity, guaranteeing the promise of life in eternity.

'That promise became all the more important for Maureen and me on 9 November 1995 when our youngest daughter Ciara died suddenly at the age of 13 months. George never met her, but we are certain that she has sat on his heavenly rocking chair, laughing at his funny voices. I look forward, in a time to come, to being able to resume happy conversations with both of them.'

Father Jock Dalrymple, Maggie Fergusson and Michael McGrath are representative of a number of Roman Catholics whose faith was both confirmed and reinvigorated by GMB's poetry and prose, and also by his life despite – perhaps even because of – his personal struggles. But could he be a help for non-Catholics of a new generation who are seeking a spiritual path and want to examine Catholicism as part of their exploration?

I was put in touch with Linden Bicket, a young woman whose conversion to Roman Catholicism was aided by reading GMB's work. We met for coffee near Glasgow University, where she was researching for a Ph.D. on the subject of Catholicism and GMB's creative process.

'Yes, I'm sure my conversion was partly to do with reading George's work,' she told me. 'My background was fairly secular, vaguely Church of Scotland, through primary school. My grandparents attended Church of Scotland services, but my mother and father had no interest in that, really. I started thinking about Catholicism in my teens and felt quite attracted to it. I couldn't really say why. I didn't think about it in any particular way, and then when I came to university, that's when I really became interested in Catholicism. And that's partly because of George, I think.'

What impact did he make? 'I remember reading "Andrina", his short story. I read that text in my first year of university, and it had such a big impact on me. I found the writing really irresistible – it was the combination of it being a story of grace and forgiveness, with beautiful, well-crafted descriptions, and a very touching relationship at its centre. And I thought the story just glowed. It was really about the sacramental imagination, and that's what appealed to me most: that perception – seeing God in everything, in ordinary things and everyday things, which is something that I already felt in a vague way – and then, when I read stories like that, my imagination was fired.

'I think George found Catholicism attractive because it made provision for fallen people. I think that people who are outside, people who are broken, were of interest to him, and I think that wounds, literal ones as well as metaphorical ones in communities and people's lives, interested him as well.'

318

So, how did she follow her interest in Catholicism through?

'I bought other short-story collections by George, as well as works by other Catholic writers and poets. And I think as well, being an imaginative 17-year-old, purgatorial stories and ghost stories really appealed to me; but what interested me most was the pre-Reformation setting that George explores in his stories. The harmonious relationship with the land that people have in his work appealed to me, and I felt it connected with other writers I was reading at the time, like Muriel Spark, who discusses the relationship between imagination and belief. Also, I was interested in the medieval Makars for the same reason. I felt the medieval aspect of Catholicism was so appealing. I remember reading Dunbar's lyrics – I think one was "Ane Ballat of Our Lady" – and I really loved that. It was aesthetic and ornamental and devotional, but truly profound, and also Scottish. Then I read *Greenvoe*, and I became interested in George because he converted to Catholicism. And I thought: this can't really be! Do people actually do this kind of thing? It didn't occur to me that they might do!'

Did she then take instruction? 'I did. I hesitated for a long time, because I felt shy, and I felt that it might be slightly intrusive, or awkward, were I to go to Mass. I had no idea that people went to see priests to talk about their feelings about conversion. Eventually I worked up the courage, and I decided that I would go and find out some more. I turned up and met a really kind, encouraging priest at the university chaplaincy, who was interested in the same kind of things I was. Maybe I forced my reading on him, and we talked about George, as well as other writers, a lot. By this stage I was a postgraduate student, and it all went from there. George was partly the catalyst at the beginning, and then it led on to something much bigger.'

George Mackay Brown's writings are a spiritual store for practising Roman Catholics, and also for some non-Catholics who want to explore traditional religious faith. But what about the Protestant community, or, more correctly, Protestant communities? I know many people in the Church of Scotland and in other Protestant traditions who find GMB's writings to be of great help in nourishing and sustaining their own religious life.

Rev. Kathy Galloway, a Church of Scotland minister who is head of Christian Aid in Scotland, is one of the most able theologians in the Church today. Dr Rowan Williams, Archbishop of Canterbury, said of her: 'If there is such a thing as theological perfect pitch, Kathy Galloway has got it'.

Before she became Leader of the ecumenical Iona Community, Kathy lived in a stair community in Edinburgh's West Pilton housing scheme – the same area in which artist Joyce Gunn Cairns lives and works. I interviewed Kathy at her home in Glasgow, and asked her about the influence of George Mackay Brown on her thinking.

'George's work really spoke to something in me. I read the poems over and over again. My own theological understanding is fairly non-ideological and non-propositional. A great deal of what is taught by the Christian Church is wordy. It seems to miss the essence of what speaks to me in Christianity. For me, GMB was a real expression of that which was both Scottish – although Orcadian, but still close enough to being Scottish – and contemporary and poetic, with a sense of history and a real sense of the "communion of saints" – that sense that you're part of an ongoing generation. It makes you realise how close you are to people and how short our lives are. It places you within a bigger framework.

'When I went to Orkney, there was a tremendous consciousness of GMB, because Orkney had always been mediated for me through his writing. I remember going to Rackwick Bay and thinking I had never been anywhere more mysterious in my life. All of the time, I was expecting people from his books to appear – it's like reading Ian Rankin when you've grown up in Edinburgh!'

Kathy said that there were bits in GMB's story, 'The Tarn and the Rosary', that for her, as a theologian and liturgist, said exactly what she thought she was doing.

Did she mean George's emphasis on the importance of ceremony?

'Yes. The idea of doing the rituals is so far beyond someone like Richard Dawkins, who just wouldn't begin to understand. His life seems so two-dimensional – at least, his writing certainly is. How could you explain this to someone living in north Oxford in an academic environment, when you've lived all these years in West Pilton and Glasgow, and having actually seen that, for so many people, it's the ceremonies that get them by? For me, that led on to an interest in and appreciation of the writing of poet Kenneth White. I love his sense of place, and of the numinous and the eternal and the temporal. I would say that George Mackay Brown and Kenneth White are probably among my main theological influences. For me, theology is poetry. It's a question of leaving enough *space,* because what so much propositional theology wants to do is tie down and reduce the space in which people might be themselves. It's oppressive, boxing people in. In my view, it leaves out the work of the Holy Spirit.'

Anything surprising about GMB?

'Yes, in some ways GMB is quite pagan! Pagan for me is not pejorative: I mean it in a precise sense of being earthy or earthed, and I think a lot of women understand that sense of embodiment. Men aren't really more cerebral: they still have bodies, but they can pretend that they don't. It's harder for women to distance themselves from their bodies. I'm not anti-intellectual at all – I would in some ways consider myself to be an intellectual – but so much theology has been about belief and it's been about *power,* and the abuse of power.

'Protestant theology would not "wear" this pagan aspect, whereas the Catholic Church seems to make space for it. Most educated Catholics I know disagree with official Catholic teaching on all sorts of things, but they're not going to argue about it, because what's important to them is not really so much the theology but the liturgy, the community, the practice and the spiritual formation that they have. In a way it's unfortunate, because they just leave the hierarchy to get on with some very dubious business. It leads to corruption because it becomes a matter of "You just get on with this, and we'll just get on with living our lives. We'll use contraception, we'll welcome our gay members, and you just have this separate thing" – but under the "separate thing", terrible things can happen.

'It does seem to me that what being a Catholic did for George was to give him space to be a pagan. Protestantism in the early part of the twentieth century was so associated with intellectualism, and with a killjoy attitude to all sorts of things. I think Jesus was quite pagan in that regard – non-ideological, concerned much more about *behaving* than believing. George Mackay Brown has a religious sensibility in the sense of "the mystery", which is what religious really means. For him, it's about the sacred and the mysterious, the numinous in the midst of life.'

And that's what he didn't find in the Presbyterianism of his day?

'It's a shame, really, because there are a lot of good things about the Reformed tradition in Scotland. There's this idea that the Reformation was a cultural devastation; certainly, artistically this is not the case. It is very contextual, isn't it? In the Western Isles, Presbyterianism has been hard, it has been extreme, it has been austere, but Presbyterianism in Edinburgh or Glasgow produced some of the leaders of the Enlightenment, some of the leaders of artistic development. John Knox got tied up with power, and he was a misogynist; on the other hand, he was no more misogynist than many of the popes!'

It is certainly not unusual to hear GMB quoted from Protestant pulpits. His inclusive Catholicism is neither ideological nor proselytising, and has an appeal across the Christian spectrum.

In his sixties and seventies, George's view of Protestantism mellowed. He wrote appreciatively of some Church of Scotland minister-scholars in Orkney since Reformation times. His friendships with Presbyterian ministers such as Dr James Maitland, Rev. Harold Mooney (minister of an Orkney parish for more than fifty years) and myself were warm and open.

GMB was much interested in the ecumenical work of the Iona Community, and in the fact that it had Protestants and Roman Catholics in its membership. He often expressed admiration for Dr George MacLeod, the Community's founder. He was also interested in James Maitland's pioneering ecumenical work in one of Scotland's new towns, Livingston. When Dr Maitland wrote a book describing the ecumenical experiment, in which congregations of different Christian traditions shared places of worship, George was glad to write a foreword. Here is what he wrote: *When I was a small boy in Stromness, Orkney, there were three Presbyterian kirks serving about 1,700 people. I often used to pause and wonder about that, in the intervals of playing football and reading 'The Wizard'.*

There was also a small 'piskey' church.

There were only two Catholics among us – an Irish barber called Paddy Mee and an Italian ice-cream man called Giulio Faggacia.

There was never the slightest religious intolerance, that I remember. There was just the slightest unease, among certain townsfolk, at the fact that there were three Presbyterian congregations: the Old Kirk, the UP Kirk and the Free Kirk. Despite the unions of 1900 and 1929, there was a certain stubborn pride in the sacrifice and labour that had gone into the buildings, and the bells and the organs, and all the history connected with kirks and manses and pastors.

Now all three congregations are gathered under one roof, and all resentments are forgotten.

Never, in my childhood, would the Catholic priest from Kirkwall have been invited to speak at a Kirk gathering. But such comings together are fairly frequent nowadays ... It is a scandal that the seamless garment should be rent. But the work of invisible mending is now far advanced – as Jim Maitland shows in his valuable book – and the thread that makes whole what has been sundered will be very precious in the finished garment.

George's ecumenical sympathies were not restricted to Christian traditions. When James Maitland told him about a multi-faith service he was involved with, George replied: 'The multi-faith service is just what the world needs among so much hatred and violence'.

Sir Peter Maxwell Davies, Master of the Queen's Music, who set several of GMB's poems to music, sensed something special about George on their first meeting in Rackwick in 1970. I asked him about that encounter.

'George was completely modest – he just talked about the beer and the whisky, but he radiated this extraordinary sense of what I can only call "spirituality". I was very, very impressed, although I couldn't really get to know him very well on that kind of occasion – it was very much suffused with a lot of drink and nice food!

'We became very good friends. I think a lot of my work rather baffled him! But he was very tolerant when I set his poetry to music. When I turned the martyrdom of St Magnus into an opera, I reduced the novel to a certain number of scenes, and even invented some dialogue – which he didn't seem to mind terribly much! It was the very first thing in the very first St Magnus Festival in 1977. That was one of the intensest experiences I've ever had, writing it and bringing it to performance there.'

What were the qualities of GMB's poems that drew him?

'He makes words work hard. They're ordinary words, most of them, and they have huge resonance, what I think of as a musical resonance – that really is appealing. It's a musical resonance that doesn't exclude the possibility of adding music.

'It's the transparency of the poems which is so appealing. They're not at all cluttered, and I immediately respected that. People who are not particularly interested in contemporary poetry can get a great deal out of it, and it's full of meaning for their lives. For me, it is this welding together, this marriage of the agricultural and the fishing year with the Christian year, and the way that the simplest action – feeding cattle, or going out to set creels – becomes a ritual, that has got an enormous significance. It's the way in which, through his poetry, even the simplest gesture can have a very profound meaning that I found so enriching.'

I was interested in the fruitfulness of the coming together of the two different spiritualities of these two highly creative men. I asked Max how he would characterise his own position *vis à vis* religion.

'As I get older,' he said, 'my position becomes more and more atheist. That is an admission that I can't identify the creative power that is there, and I can't circumscribe it. For me, to say that it's made in the image of man or man is made in its image is terribly restrictive.

As we learn more and more about not really having access to other dimensions, and we realise more and more how much we are restricted by our animal perceptions, I think that the fullness of nature has got so much that we don't understand.

'I can understand anybody being very happy with God the Father, God the Son and God the Holy Ghost, but I don't really understand it – I've never met anybody who did! I've studied Aquinas in Latin, and I still don't understand it! I've got some sympathy with Isaac Newton on that one. I am completely knocked out by the strangeness and wonder of it all.

'I find religion historically of enormous significance. I find huge inspiration from the Bible and from the wonderful poetry of the Mass and of the wonderful Motets. These things I still find tremendously inspiring, but I think that the idea of "theos", God, is very strange now.'

How did Max find that the combination of the different spiritualities of George and himself worked in practice?

'I think it worked very well. It's to George's enormous credit that he's never preaching. If within yourself you are absolutely certain, and you have one kind of spirituality which goes in one direction without any conflicts, I don't think you know yourself! I think an awareness of different kinds of spirituality and an awareness of conflict in spirituality – What is truth? What is symbolic truth? What is physical truth? What is psychological truth, in any statement or point of view or dogma? – is important. I think these things are warring in George. He is so aware of paganism and he is so aware of the Roman Catholic point of view, which he made entirely his own. He's also sometimes, strangely, almost anti-religious!

'Archie Bevan told me that George became more circumspect later on. There's a strange parallel with Hindemith the composer – he made revisions of some of his early work, toned it down a lot, and everybody plays the original ones!'

Ben Myers wrote in the *Guardian*: 'As a converted Catholic, Brown wrote of his subjects – Orkney and the characters who inhabited it, mainly – with the reverence of a man who finds God in the crashing waves, the coastal reaches as prominent as his own jawline and the treeless hills of the islands. His is religious writing that is all-inclusive and non-dogmatic, perfect for atheists such as myself.'

Novelist John McGill is a robust atheist. As a reader of the developing manuscript of this book, the former English teacher at Stromness Academy was trenchant and observant and funny. He first met GMB in 1968, between *A Calendar of Love* and *A Time to Keep*, the collections which established the Orcadian poet as a significant writer of prose fiction. In the process of reading this manuscript, John's view of George Mackay Brown's religion changed. I wondered what he now made of George as a religious figure.

'George never made a display of his religion,' he said, 'even in the most unthreatening of situations. Sometime around 1970, I drove him through to Kirkwall for a showing of *Shane* at the Phoenix cinema. It was (and remains) my favourite film, and I was delighted to discover that he was about as excited by it, and as caught up in the action, as I was myself. At the thrilling transfiguration scene, when the music explodes and Shane appears in his buckskin with his gunbelt all sparkling in the moonlight, he not only shared in the general intake of breath, but whispered to me: "That's the stuff – that's what we've been waiting for".

'On the way back to Stromness, I tried to sell him the idea – admittedly a bit trite – of *Shane* as the quintessential Jesus-movie, packed with quasi-religious imagery from the opening scene, when the redeemer-hero descends from on high to mingle with the suffering plainsfolk, to the closing one, when – mission accomplished – he rides off, clutching the wound in his side, back to the faraway hills, ever upwards. He listened with his usual patience, then said: "That was a lovely horse he was riding, at the end there".

'Most of my encounters with him were at social gatherings in Stromness, usually at the MacInneses'. Given that the host was something of a crusading atheist, there were no polite embargoes on the topics of conversation, and George sometimes found himself caught in the middle of a heated political or religious ding-dong. There was never any awkwardness or embarrassment: he had the remarkable knack of *appearing* to participate, and it wasn't until afterwards that you realised his contributions were limited to small gnomic utterances – sometimes witty, sometimes banal, always totally benign and unexceptionable.'

So, what had now changed in his perception of GMB's spiritual journey?

'I used to assume that his conversion to Roman Catholicism was primarily a modish gesture, an attempt to align himself with Waugh, Greene, Spark, the high-Anglican Eliot and so on. In this I was clearly, stupidly, wrong: quirky it may have been, but his religion was central to both his everyday life and his writing. Alongside the Icelandic sagas, the history of Orkney, the treasure-trove of Orcadian–Scottish–European folklore and, I'm sure, many other things, the rhythms and rituals of the Catholic calendar provided him with a rich source of theme and image.

'I find little value, however, in pigeon-holing him as a "Catholic writer", and still less in beatifying him as the Holy Innocent of Mayburn Court. I'm sure he would have been perfectly in sympathy with Keats's assertion that "We hate poetry that has a palpable design upon us". There may be a tendency for the liturgical and overtly Scriptural aspects of his poetry to become more evident as he grows older – though I haven't made the detailed study that would allow me to say this with any authority at all – but I can think of few instances where it obtrudes, or where it obscures. Always, it remains part of the drama. At its best, George's work speaks to and for everybody, and no particular kind of religious sensibility is required for us to enjoy and appreciate it, to feel that it has enlarged our sense of what a sad and joyful and wondrous business it is, this being alive.

'Mind you, I do have a feeling that, insofar as it reinforced an already quite strong strain of prudery in George's personality, his fear of the Great Judgement had a mildly detrimental effect on his fiction. Was there ever such an etiolated, sexless, unrandy bunch of Vikings as the ones who feast their way through *Vinland*? I'm fairly sure that the author's timidity about matters carnal leads to overcompensation in the form of an excessive emphasis on eating and drinking: all that quaffing of ale, breaking of bread, spreading of honey on bannocks, licking of grease, belching! In one rapid skim, I counted over forty food-references. I'm as partial to a mug of fine homebrew as the next man, but you can get too much of a good thing.'

How will George Mackay Brown play out in what promises to be increasingly robust cultural and philosophical debates in the second decade of the twenty-first century? Is he past his theological sell-by date, an interesting but essentially quaint throwback to more secure religious times? Before attempting to sketch out an answer to that question, some context is necessary.

Religion, in some form or another, has been around for a long, long time, for good or for ill. For good *and* for ill. Given the widespread sweep of religion over aeons, the desire/need to worship has been pretty constant for countless human beings. The instinct for worship may have arisen out of insecurity, wonder or profound religious experience. GMB, living in an Orkney in which archaeological remains pre-date the Pyramid tombs of Egypt, understood this.

Going with mildly inebriated companions from Mass in Kirkwall to the Ring of Brodgar in Attie Campbell's car, before going back home to the domestic routine – alcohol, Catholicism, technology and paganism – has a nice, if idiosyncratic, coherence about it.

Nobody is entirely sure what purposes the stone circles fulfilled, but the front-running theory is that the Ring, which is set dramatically against the wide Orkney skyline, was a temple for Druidic rituals, possibly including human sacrifice. It may have been a combination of cathedral, community hall, memorial for ancestors, observatory and slaughter-house for the gods.

In 2009, the site of a huge Neolithic cathedral, unlike anything else that can be seen in Britain, was discovered in Orkney. The leader of the dig, Nick Card, said that the cathedral would have been constructed to 'amaze' and 'create a sense of awe' among those who saw it.

It may be that, in the third century BC, a wild-eyed Druid priest offered up a human sacrifice at the awesome Ring of Brodgar, with the moon glinting on the big stones. It was felt to be a good idea to keep in with the gods, especially if sacrifice might get them 'on side'.

As humans developed their mental powers, the dread knowledge of personal mortality dawned. What happened to humans after they died? How could humans control fertility and the environment? Out of such reflections, religious traditions may have slowly evolved, bringing priesthoods, sacred places, belief systems, rituals, moral codes. Special prophets spoke in ecstatic terms, delivering what had been experienced by the community as a revelation from a particular god. Religious communities passed transformational stories down the generations by oral transmission, then by words on papyrus. Beliefs and moral rules were codified into creeds and law codes. Orthodoxies were formulated and even enforced.

Fast-forward four millennia to St Magnus Cathedral in Kirkwall. The wildness has gone. There is no human sacrifice: at least, I don't remember conducting such a service in my time there. Yet sacrifice is in the air. The minister holds up the fractured bread and the red cup: 'This is my body, this is my blood; do this to remember me'. In hymn, stone, prayer, Scripture, sermon, music and stained glass, things beyond words are mediated. There is continuity with the ancient times in that human creatures are still trying to make sense of the world and their place in it, still negotiating with the divine, perhaps pleading that their loved one's cancer might be taken away.

Terry Eagleton, former Professor of English Literature at Oxford University, is right to describe religion as 'the richest, most enduring form of popular culture in human history'.

But, like religion, scepticism about God, or the gods, has also been around for aeons. It has an honourable pedigree, dating back to before the Greek philosophers. Christianity was dominant in the Western world for centuries, but – particularly after the wars of religion in Europe in the seventeenth century, and the Enlightenment in the eighteenth century, with its rational and scientific emphases – scepticism gained ground.

In 1882, Friedrich Nietzsche, the brilliant Prussian-born philosopher, who had many clerics in his ancestry, told of a madman who lit a lantern early in the morning and ran into the market place shouting: 'I am looking for God! I am looking for God!' When he was mocked by the bystanders, the madman cried: 'Where has God gone? I shall tell you. We are his murderers ... How shall we, murderers of all murderers, console ourselves?' Then he went on: 'I have come too early, my time has not come yet. The tremendous event is still on its way, still travelling – it has not yet reached the ears of men.'

Little more than four decades or so ago, the philosophical last rites were being pronounced over the religious corpse in parts of the Western world. Leading sociologist Peter Berger famously declared in 1967 that, by the twenty-first century, religious believers would exist only in 'small sects, huddled against a world-wide secular culture'.

What gave most impetus to the rise of a more robust and passionate atheism (the belief that there is no God) as opposed to a quieter live-and-let-live agnosticism (the position that nothing is known or can be known about the existence or nature of a deity) was the devastating attack by extreme Islamists on the twin towers of the World Trade Center in New York on 11 September 2001. The fact that the hijackers died with shouts of praise to Allah on their lips as they drove the planes into the totemic buildings added to the fury about religion. No wonder many people will agree with TV playwright Dennis Potter's assertion that religion is the wound, not the bandage.

Yet, for a religion that is supposed to have died with its deity, Christianity seems to be enjoying a remarkably vital post-mortem existence. In many parts of the world, religion is flourishing and gaining many new adherents. Far from expiring, Christianity is the fastest-growing religion in the world. Peter Berger was forced to concede that his declaration was 'absurd'.

What died in 1882 was an image of God. Today, God seems to be hauntingly present, even in his absence. Religion has endured because it offers a space for the asking of fundamental questions. Why is there something rather than nothing? Is all that we see all that there is? Does life have a transcendent meaning? Is there life after death? Whether the answers provided – and they will vary from religion to religion – even approach adequacy is a matter for heated debate. What distorts the twenty-first-century disputations is the lust for certainty.

Questions about meaning never really go away. The cult of celebrity shows that there is still a need for icons. Consumerism has also moved into the gap left by religion in several areas of the world. Its seductive images are all around us. Wordsworth appears to have foreseen this development. Words from his sonnet, 'The World is Too Much With Us', were often quoted by GMB:

> The world is too much with us; late and soon,
> Getting and spending we lay waste our powers:
> Little we see in Nature that is ours:
> We have given our hearts away, a sordid boon!

Where can one find spiritual resources with which to combat the nihilism that Nietzsche warned about? This is not simply a question for religious believers. Martin Heidegger presents an alternative to nihilism and organised religion that he calls 'poetic dwelling on the earth as a mortal' (words taken from a poem by Hölderlin).

He points towards a simple way of living which respects rather than exploits nature, and which is always aware of human contingency. He believes that a world dominated by technology seeks to conceal the brute facts of human mortality. An authentic spirituality, he argues, has to be lived with the awareness of the death of all living things and the dependence that lies at the heart of human existence, tempered by the hope of a transcendent healing presence.

Heidegger uses religious language, but in unusual ways. He talks about 'divinities' and 'the godhead', but he does not present these concepts in traditional religious ways. His divinities seem to be art, poetry, philosophy and spiritual practices which bring human awareness closer to Nature and to the sense of human contingency. He sees the old Black Forest farmhouse in which he lives as a symbol of the wholeness he is looking for. The traditional farmhouse had an altar corner, a community table, a childbed and a coffin.

This emphasis on an ordered, simple, hallowed house also comes through in the work of George Mackay Brown. While I was thinking about Heidegger's ideas, I came across a GMB poem which was unfamiliar to me. It links community, the gifts of the earth, music, ceremony and blessing. It is called 'The Finished House':

In the finished house a flame is brought to the hearth.
Then a table, between door and window
Where a stranger will eat before the men of the house.
A bed is laid in a secret corner
For the three agonies – love, birth, death –
That are made beautiful with ceremony.
The neighbours come with gifts –
A set of cups, a calendar, some chairs.
A fiddle is hung at the wall.
A girl puts lucky salt in a dish.
The cupboard will have its loaf and bottle, come winter.
On the seventh morning
One spills water of blessing over the threshold.

At his best, Heidegger is seeking a spirituality that respects the elemental, resists technological fixes for every problem, affirms the transforming power of the arts, and lives with profound hope in an ultimate acceptance and consummation which cannot be described in human language. His view is much richer and more complex than the simplified, truncated account I have given; nevertheless, one can trace the outline of a spiritual way of living that depends on neither orthodox religion nor the technological mindset and ethical relativism of the modern world.

Refusing nihilism, Heidegger wants to embrace a spirituality that is both accepting of human mortality and hopeful that, in the end, in the words of the mystic, Julian of Norwich: 'All shall be well and all manner of thing shall be well'. The practices that emerge from this way of life are central to what Heidegger calls 'poetic dwelling'.

I will make no attempt to assess Heidegger's proposals; I am neither familiar enough with his philosophical corpus nor fluent enough in highly convoluted German. I simply want to point to what looks like an interesting alternative both to heavily structured, authoritarian forms of Christianity (Roman Catholic and Protestant) and to nihilism. It can stand as a pointer towards attempts to explore the riches of faith traditions without being trapped in history's prisons.

Caution: at his worst, Heidegger, at one stage in his life, allowed himself to be seduced by Nazism – which shows how even very clever people can be fools.

Comparatively few people come to faith simply by way of intellectual argument. Most do so as a result of being brought up in a particular religious tradition.

Religions are sets of practices as much as – or even more than – they are sets of beliefs. Western Christianity, unlike Eastern Christianity, has tended to emphasise giving assent to belief in propositions. But 'belief' comes from the Anglo-Saxon root *lief*, which means 'love'. Christianity, at its heart, is more about loving God and growing in that love than it is about signing up to propositions. Christianity is not at its best when it is purveying explanations; experiences, Scriptures and stories are all that human beings have.

Some things are beyond human explanation. Poet and novelist John Burnside observes:

> As Wittgenstein says, in the concluding pages of the *Tractatus Logico-Philosophicus*: 'There are, indeed, things that cannot be put into words. They make themselves manifest. They are what is mystical.' At this point, poetry, art and the imagination go to work where logic left off.

Here is the paradox of faith: words are employed to describe that which is literally beyond speech. Something within us makes us want to keep on trying to find and express meaning. I would agree with the verdict of Professor Denys Turner:

> I continue to find theology to be the means most apt to unsettle, to rattle, to haunt the mind with glimpses of something which, as Augustine thought, are very like long-lost memories, memories of the mystery of love from which we have come, sustaining a hope of the mystery of love we are destined for.

Nietzsche seemed to know that this would be the case. 'God is dead,' he wrote, 'but given the way of men, there may still be caves for thousands of years in which his shadow will be shown.'

Novelist Julian Barnes would understand this. He says he doesn't believe in God, but he misses him.

Despite their well-documented flaws – some of them truly terrible – the churches keep alive the rumour of God, tell the stories of faith, nourish the practices and perform the ceremonies. Within this shifting context, what has George Mackay Brown to say to those of us who are religious believers and to those of us who are attempting to find, or shape, a spirituality for post-Christian times in the European West? If he is only a purveyor of nostalgia, then the answer is 'not a lot'. But, while he does lament the dislocations and uprootings created by the Reformation, the naming of some of the cultural and spiritual losses sustained over the centuries does not automatically make him a reactionary. GMB is right to point to the erosion of community and to the wreckage created by unfettered individualism. He directs us to the richness of older wisdoms, and invites us to learn from them as we seek to shape spiritualities – whether formally religious or not – for our times.

I find myself turning to GMB repeatedly for refreshment of the spirit. Time and again, he directs this Presbyterian minister to his Catholic heritage.

Yet, having immersed myself in his poetry and prose, there is, for me, still something missing. At this stage in my journey with GMB, I can identify it more clearly: nowhere in his writings and interviews do I find evidence of an intellectual struggle over faith. Agonising about the very existence of God is not to be found. Nor is there any serious engagement with that terrible wound at the heart of Christianity: the presence of evil in a world said to be run by an omniscient and all-powerful Creator. GMB was able to accept the Catholic 'package' without too many dark nights of the soul – at least over theological matters.

Many Catholic and Protestant seekers, and indeed believers, find it much more of a struggle. I include myself in that number. I need to set a more troubled, questioning voice alongside GMB's uncritical view of the Christian tradition. I must go on pilgrimage to Wales.

Ronald Stuart Thomas is regarded by many as the finest twentieth-century religious poet in the English language. A curmudgeonly Anglican clergyman, he was a fiery Welsh nationalist who campaigned robustly against the Anglicising of his country's culture, yet his most withering criticisms were directed against his own people. He was an uncompromising radical who refused to curry favour with anyone, or to go along with current fashions. He reminds me of Hugh MacDiarmid, who could start a fight in an empty croft. Like Thomas, the contentious, nationalistic Scot also wrote exquisite verse. While Thomas and MacDiarmid were astringent prophets who are great to read in the spirit, they were seriously uncomfortable to know in the flesh.

Thomas's poetic range is exceptional, as is his technical brilliance. It was no surprise when he was nominated for the 1995 Nobel Prize for Literature, which was won by his friend, Seamus Heaney. His religious poems have an austere, subversive quality with the capacity to haunt the modern mind. Here is his 'Jesus':

> He wore no hat, but he produced, say
> from up his sleeve, an answer
> to their questions about
> the next life. It is here,
> he said, tapping his forehead
> as one would to indicate an idiot. The crowd frowned
>
> and took up stones
> to punish his adultery
> with the truth. But he, stooping
> to write on the ground, looked
> sideways at them, as they withdrew
> each to the glass-house of his own mind.

There are many similarities between RST and GMB. Both were poets with deep roots in rural communities. Both warned of the dehumanising consequences of unfettered technology. Both lamented what they saw as the decline of their own culture. Both were Nature poets. Both employed a bare, pared-down style. Both preferred silence to Christian wordiness. Both suffered from depression. Both had a morning ritual of writing that kept them sane.

There is one major difference, though. Thomas's work is much more bleak and edgy than GMB's. It is painfully honest. For Thomas, God is an elusive presence/absence. He is a hidden God, who will show up when he chooses to, and who cannot be domesticated or managed or manipulated. The poet echoes themes from the great Christian mystics who walk the way of the *Via Negativa*, talking in chaste language mainly about what God is not. He also echoes his mentor, the Danish philosopher Søren Kierkegaard, who refused to accept cheap answers to searching questions about ultimate reality. Nothing could be further away from the chirpy certainties of the TV evangelists with their welded-on smiles.

One of Thomas's finest poems, 'Via Negativa', emphasises the elusiveness of the divine:

> Why no! I never thought other than
> That God is that great absence
> In our lives, the empty silence
> Within, the place where we go
> Seeking, not in hope to
> Arrive or find. He keeps the interstices
> In our knowledge, the darkness
> Between stars. His are the echoes
> We follow, the footprints he has just
> Left. We put our hands in
> His side hoping to find
> It warm. We look at people
> And places as though he had looked
> At them, too; but miss the reflection.

In another poem, 'In Church', Thomas talks about praying after the people have gone. He asks: 'Is this where God hides from my searching?' The poem concludes:

There is no other sound
In the darkness but the sound of a man
Breathing, testing his faith
On emptiness, nailing his questions
One by one to an untenanted cross.

R. S. Thomas is the more intellectually rigorous of the two poets. He is a traditional yet modern man who pushes his questions, preferring silence – 'waiting for the god to speak' – to cheap answers. Like GMB, he ransacks the orthodoxies of the past, but he wants to interrogate them rather than simply receive them. He is a troubled and a troubling Kierkegaardian presence at the Christian feast.

Which poet do I choose? I want and need both of these strange, sometimes dysfunctional travellers.

Spiritual nourishment is required for spiritual journeys. Those who lodge in the inns of institutional religion will perhaps prefer more orthodox religious fare, though they might find their life journeys enriched by the wisdom and practices of other faith traditions and by sources that eschew religious language. Those who prefer to follow secular paths will find their main refreshment at non-religious inns; yet they may benefit also from time-tested religious traditions that prefer silence to anxious chatter.

There are vast treasures around, from which to create a spiritual discipline to live by. The Hebrew and Greek Scriptures of the Old and New Testaments are full of words that sing off the page. The writings of the Catholic mystics and the mainly Anglican Metaphysical Poets can also help anyone to hang on to faith by their fingernails, or to attempt to 'dwell poetically upon the earth as a mortal'. And that is without even touching upon the inspiration of figures such as Simone Weil, Dietrich Bonhoeffer, Mother Julian of Norwich, Martin Luther King or Jean Vanier.

Poetry is a well of continual refreshment. R. S. Thomas said in a television interview that his work as a poet had to do with the presentation of imaginative truth, and that in presenting the Bible to his congregation he was presenting an imaginative interpretation of reality. 'By imagination I mean the highest means known to the human psyche of getting into contact with ultimate reality; imaginative truth is the most immediate way of presenting ultimate reality to a human being, and we call it God.' I also like RST's observation: 'With science and technology so enormously influential, spawning as they do new words every day, and with the decay of traditional beliefs in God, soul and the afterlife, surely what we should be waiting for is a poet who can deploy the new vocabulary and open up new avenues, or should I say airways of the spirit, in the twenty-first century'.

As I approach the end of this quest, George Mackay Brown's Christian humanism, his inclusiveness, and his quiet insistence that Christianity is, at its heart, a religion of grace are integral parts of my own spiritual understanding – though I want to marry that to R. S. Thomas's uncompromising wrestling with the now-you-see-Him-now-you-don't God. There are reserves to be found in other religious traditions; as I attempt to maintain a regular spiritual discipline, I find that Buddhist Mindfulness meditations are helpful.

I believe that GMB's imaginative treatment of time-honoured themes has a great deal to offer to twenty-first-century seekers after relevant forms of spirituality. It is important to attend to ancestral as well as contemporary voices. I also believe that Scotland and England are selling out their historic religious traditions far too cheaply. There is a need for critical and informed dialogue with the mothers and fathers of the faith. GMB is right to say: 'We cannot live fully without the treasury our ancestors have left to us'.

There is also a need for critical and informed dialogue between the Christian Churches. The Reformation was initially intended as a reform movement rather than a breakaway. At what point in ecumenical discussions might it be appropriate to say that the Reformation is over? To get to that place, the Catholic and Protestant Churches would need to release each other from the prisons of history.

George's pilgrimage, encompassing struggles with fearful depressions and near-alcoholism, can itself be a resource for modern pilgrims, religious or secular. Like Jacob, who was wounded in his struggle with an angel of the Lord, the non-saintly George Mackay Brown walks towards the kingdom of God with a limp.

Archbishop William Temple said that Christianity is not an attitude of mind but a type of life, and that a person's spirit is known not by their opinion but by their actions and general conduct. In any new spiritual discipline, there are things that cry out to be learned or relearned by heart, as Simone Weil did with George Herbert's poem, 'Love'. She reported that, when she was under pressure, she would make herself say it over and over, concentrating all her attention upon it. She said that she used to think she was merely reciting it as a beautiful poem; but, without her knowing it, the recitation had become a form of prayer.

That may be what it means to be a practising Christian today: engaging in the practices until the substance becomes a matter of the heart.

PART 4

Finished Fragrance

CHAPTER 17

April is the Cruellest Month

It is 12 April 1996. George Mackay Brown is in the Balfour Hospital in Kirkwall. He has been unwell for a few days, and his condition is gradually worsening. He is the Horizontal Bard once more, for the last time. There is something serene about him. He knows that this time he will not recover from his physical wounds.

He remembers the spells he spent in hospital and sanatorium, sometimes because he needed respite from a threatening world. He thinks back to the time when he believed he would not live beyond the age of 23. He has missed that date with destiny by a mere half-century.

He thinks of the times in his life when he had longed for oblivion. He is ready to go now, to become Warbeth's dust, to move beyond pain and grief.

April has long been his favourite month, giving the lie to T. S. Eliot's line, much repeated by his dear mother and his sister Ruby, mimicking Eliot's 'April is the cruellest month' from the gramophone.

A few days before his admission to hospital, he had written a column for the *Orcadian*, celebrating April. Titled 'The First Wash of Spring', it is the last thing he wrote for publication:

This morning – as I write – is April 3, and the first wash of Spring has gone over the earth.

It is such a beautiful word – April – that even to utter it lightens the heart. It is a little poem in itself. It is full of delightful images. It has its own music – little trembling lamb-cries at the end of a field. The first daring lark lost in light.

You feel, in April, that you have come through another winter, a little bruised maybe, but unbowed.

Those chalices of light, the daffodils, having been sorely battered by the March storms, are shedding, one by one, their green covers and opening their vernal tapers.

Soon all of Orkney will be stitched by golden threads of daffodils, a lovely spread garment for Primavera.

(Goodness, I seem to have got my images all confused there – chalices, tapers, coats – but one may be allowed a little exuberance, tasting now the first wine of Spring. Wine! There's another image to add to the heap!)

So we ought to relish each one of the thirty days of April, the month that tastes of childhood. Easter, too, often falls in April, and April the sixteenth is that wonderful day in the Orkney calendar, the martyrdom of St Magnus in Egilsay.

Most of the months in the calendar have their own beautiful names. May is when the cuithes [young coalfish] have their first drink of the floods, and come swarming in to keep their ancient tryst with men (and of course with women, too, I hasten to add, for you can't be too careful nowadays, with all those militant ladies around; and what about the children? – they have their own rites and secrets that are lost to us adults). But still with a word like mankind – who in their senses would want to use 'personkind'?

I have digressed a long way.

The word 'June' is beautiful too, of course, but like May it has a curtness that lacks the lyricism of 'April'. In midsummer there is perhaps too much – what month-name devised by man could hope to contain the light and multitudinous beauties of the season? Best to be simple and brief, to hold the word to the nostrils like a plucked wild clover ... Such enchantment, under the light that never leaves the sky – not at midnight even. But, of course, in the name of progress and 'enlightenment' we have sacrificed the ancient ceremonies of midsummer, the fires on every hilltop in every parish and island. (There is a price to be paid for Progress; already the 'tabs' are being shown us, one after the other. But let that be, meantime.)

I had hoped to cut a swathe through all the month-names in the year. But alas I have run out of space – and besides, I'm sure we have been that way before; and if there is one thing a writer must beware of it is to offer second-hand goods to his readers.

What a beautiful piece of writing. What a farewell! (Though the 'militant ladies' might have had things to say, some searching questions to ask.)

He is more than 'a little bruised' this time, though. April is about to be the cruellest month for George's friends and admirers. But not for George.

The writer has run out of space, run out of time – and he is not sorry.

His bags are packed.

George Mackay Brown must surely be the only writer to need anti-depressants because he had been nominated for the Booker Prize. His novel, *Beside the Ocean of Time*, was shortlisted for the £20,000 prize in September 1994. He took the pills because he could not cope with the attention.

Looking through his unpublished letters to James Maitland, which his family had passed on to me, I came across George's account: 'I've been swamped by journalists, video people, TV people: so I can't get my real work done: consequently last week I felt deep in the dumps. However medical science has answers to that depression too – thank God – so now I feel a lot better mentally; though there are more media folk on the way next week.'

Interviewers were once more in despair as they tried to coax words from their reluctant subject. At a time when writers were supposed to promote themselves and project their personalities, GMB retreated further into himself. Despite orchestrated rumours to the contrary, there was never any chance that he would go to London for the awards ceremony. Agoraphobia, shyness, distrust of publicity, and a feeling that the whole thing had more to do with commerce than with literature, combined to keep him safe in his island fastness.

'Regarding the Booker: everyone is much more excited about it than me,' he wrote to James Maitland. 'I think of all the prizewinners and also-rans: where are they today? The greatest prize is the inner knowledge of our work well done; and even here I flinch from time to time, thinking of the hundreds of times I slipped up. Writing well is sufficient reward.'

The prize was won by Glasgow's James Kelman. George was spared the problem of what to do with £20,000.

In his later years, GMB was extraordinarily prolific. In the 1980s and 1990s, he produced novels, short-story collections, a poetry collection, children's stories and books about Orkney. His *Selected Poems* was published, as were collections of his weekly columns from the *Orcadian*.

He was well looked after. There was a new woman in his life, though not one from the usual mould. Renée Simm, a retired art-seller in Edinburgh, was twenty years older than George. The two had been in correspondence for some years; then, in 1983, she moved to Stromness to be nearer him. She was a formidable lady. Not only did she feed George twice a week, she also became a self-appointed gatekeeper for him. This was not always appreciated by George's friends.

Renée Simm was not fond of Nora Kennedy. In fact, she thought the rather glamorous and much younger Nora was up to no good. There was a certain *froideur* when the two collided at Mayburn Court. Then another younger, attractive woman entered the scene.

Joanna Ramsey first met GMB in 1988 when she moved from London to be the librarian at Stromness Academy. She came into work one morning and found a couple of big black bin-liners dumped in the middle of the library floor. They were full of old books. She asked Archie Bevan – then depute rector at the Academy – where they had come from. He said that George Mackay Brown was putting out some books and he thought the school library might like them.

'At the time I was living at Faravel, behind Mayburn Court,' Jo told me, 'so I wrote George a letter from the school to thank him for the books, and I mentioned that I'd moved to Faravel. He rang me up and said: "Come and have a cup of tea". And that was the beginning of a friendship. We developed a routine; I would go round two and sometimes three evenings a week. We would just sit and chat, and sometimes watch TV together. Occasionally he would come up and have supper with me.

'I was a divorcée – but George didn't make any judgements about that. He wouldn't, he wasn't that kind of person. Also, because he didn't drive I would take him out, and occasionally he would ask me to drive him to things. Sometimes we would just drive up to the Ring of Brodgar or Birsay, because he loved that. I used to get invited out with George quite a lot. I felt very privileged to be part of it.'

The life of GMB was still – to use a Scotticism – hotching with ministering angels, some of them rather good-looking, and all of them glad to help him.

Sometimes Jo would drive him to Mass, and she occasionally went to the service with him. 'We didn't often discuss religion. He always had a copy of *The Tablet* [the liberal Catholic journal], and when he went off to make a cup of tea he would leave *The Tablet* next to me on the sofa, and I would read it. While he was making the tea, he would always sing "Bread of Heaven" [the Protestant hymn, "Guide me O Thou Great Jehovah"] in his very wavery voice.'

How did George relate to her?

'He was so courteous. When I hear or read about George's earlier life and some of the things he did or said, I sometimes have difficulty reconciling it with the man I knew at the end of his life. It was a shock reading the early parts of Maggie Fergusson's biography, because I didn't recognise the person I was reading about. I knew him as an altogether gentler person.'

Did he reveal much of himself, and was she aware of his depressions?

'Although we did spend a lot of time together, I was always very aware that George was holding a lot in reserve. He was occasionally down, but so was I, and there was a kind of empathy. In general, when we were together, he seemed happy. When I read some of the obituaries, I didn't actually recognise this melancholy, depressed person. I was shocked and distressed to learn that he even thought of taking his own life. He was quite happy in my company, so I maybe just didn't see the dark side, he maybe hid it. Undoubtedly it was there, in the earlier years. Depression can be something that comes and goes in your life, so it may be that George hid it in later years, or it may be that he had passed through it, which people do. The times that I saw him down, he would get worried about one particular thing. One time, he had rats in the house – he became completely tormented and distressed by it.'

How about Nora?

'She was lovely to me, couldn't have been nicer, always friendly. Although Nora irritated George sometimes and they would have little niggly arguments – a bit like an old married couple niggling at each other – he always spoke of Nora in very affectionate terms. I always remember he said early on: "You must meet my dear friend Nora". Gradually I learned more about her. They had a lovely friendship. He worried about her, because she was always in financial difficulty. She lived in Deerness and couldn't drive, and then she became ill, so he worried a lot about her. He had a nice friendship with her at the end.

'One time, George said to me on the telephone: "Nora is here, do you want to come down later?" When I went in, they had been watching TV together and were just sitting side by side on the sofa, holding hands. There were flowers on the table, brought by Nora. Every time she went to see him, she brought a lovely mixed bunch of flowers from her garden. There was a gentleness about their relationship – there had obviously been difficulties in the past, but it had all settled down, in the way that things sometimes do.'

How did Jo fare with Renée Simm?

'Renée was very protective of George. She was motherly, but more than that, she clearly adored him. She didn't like me at all. I imagine she felt Nora and I were hussies! George would invite me round on a particular day, and I would see Renée's car outside. Sometimes I would just go back home and ring him and say: "Sorry George, I'm not coming". Other times I'd be there first, then Renée would arrive and realise I was already there, and not be happy. I think sometimes George just did it out of sheer mischievousness!'

George occasionally let his mask slip, revealing an element of cunning. He was not beyond orchestrating situations in which others acted out the kind of spitefulness and jealousies that he could not exhibit himself without risking confrontation (and damage to his public persona?). On one occasion, he invited both Renée and Joanna to his house to watch a film of D. H. Lawrence's sexually explicit novel, *The Rainbow*.

'Of course, there was quite a bit of sex and nudity,' said Jo. 'It was a completely excruciating hour-and-a-half – sitting there with Renée staring disapprovingly at the TV, and George enjoying it, but also enjoying the discomfort of Renée and myself!

'I think that, although George was obviously very fond of Renée, he did find her overpowering. There were tensions and jealousies among George's friends about this. There was a feeling that Renée had ousted some of George's old friends. Allison Dixon often invited George for Christmas lunch, and Renée and Nora had to come as well. I think it could be very tricky, but they all had to be invited!'

Allison Dixon laughed as she confirmed this account. 'Yes, George always came here on Christmas Day, and he brought an entourage,' she told me. 'It started off with Nora, and then it was Nora and Renée, who didn't get on. We had to make sure they didn't sit near each other. They were both vying with each other – the clothes they were wearing, who looked at whom, and so on.'

George managed to be both above the fray and the director of a soap opera that was not entirely free of mischievousness.

The enigmatic, complicated nature of the relationships between George and the women close to him became increasingly evident as I reflected on his life. He was skilled in ways of making himself emotionally unavailable when things got too hot for him; he knew how to remain in control from a passive position. This caused some distress in women who were confused and hurt by the sudden movement from ardour to withdrawal. But his mother was allowed to look after him until she was too ill to do so, and other female relatives were drafted in to clear up after him – Allison Dixon when he was 'flitted' while her baby played on the floor, and Allison's mother when she was summoned to bail him out of jail.

Alison Miller read the manuscript of this book. As a writer who knows Orkney and knew GMB, she has provided perceptive observations. I asked her to reflect on George's attitude to women.

'Whenever I met George in person, he was quiet, gentle, courteous and friendly, if somewhat shy. He didn't patronise or try to dominate me, and I never saw him do that with any other woman either, nor, come to that, with any man. I found his melancholy and wistfulness appealing and endearing, his face lit, as it sometimes was, by a sudden boyish smile.

'But I can't say I like the views he stated publicly on the question of gender, from the beginning to the end of his career in journalism. In that early piece quoted from the *Orkney Herald*, he inveighed against "the ridiculous pampering of women". Given that his mother looked after his every physical need until she was too frail to work, he must be referring to some other kind of woman. Those around him continued to take care of him on a daily basis, as did some men. If anyone was "pampered", GMB was.

'Then there's that very last piece of journalism he wrote for the *Orcadian*, a lovely piece of writing, except for the silly diatribe on "political correctness" ("personkind", George? What's wrong with "humankind"?) and the jibe at the "militant ladies" who drew attention to the way language reflects prevailing power structures.

'As I've got older, I've become increasingly attracted to many strands of GMB's writing, the utterly stunning ways he can evoke nature, light and dark, the weather, the seasons, the land, the sea, his consummate skill with language – that little poem-in-a-single-word, April, in which you *can* hear the lamb's cry shaken out on the hill. But I don't suppose his religion ever did much to challenge his views on women. In the poem "Runes from a Holy Island", he wrote:

Hierarchy
A claret laird,
Seven fishermen with ploughs,
Women, beasts, corn, fish, stones.

'Now, of course it's not entirely possible to know GMB's attitude to this ordering of creatures, but I suspect that "women" appearing not in the first two lines with "mankind", but in the third line, only just preceding "beasts, corn, fish, stones", does represent George's view of the natural order of things. In my book, that's a rent in the "seamless garment" of humanity that Catholicism has yet to mend.'

The dynamics of the relationships between George and those around him changed further in 1991 when Surinder Punjya came to Stromness to live. Surinder, whose parents had come to England from the Punjab, studied philosophy at Warwick University and also lectured there.

'He became a very important friend to George,' Jo Ramsey said, 'and the good thing was that Renée liked him very much and approved of him. Surinder was incredibly self-effacing. He was very like George in that he had so few material needs. He was a sweet person.'

I was interested to read this reference to Surinder in the Maitland correspondence: 'My other friend Surinder Punjya who does all my shopping and cuts my toe-nails and polishes my shoes – when he isn't studying Latin and Sanskrit scripts – has been in Coventry all summer, ministering to his sick father, and he returns at September's end. I wish you could meet him: he's the nearest to a saint I've met so far. So, then I'll have a full roll-call of servants in my domain.'

Indeed. Here is the full roll-call of servants: Brian Murray, retired education adviser for Ayrshire, lit George's fire in the morning; Surinder Punjya was in charge of shopping, banking, cutting of toenails and polishing of shoes; Renée Simm fed George twice a week and acted as his minder; Archie and Elizabeth Bevan had him to lunch every Friday; Allison and Fraser Dixon entertained him on numerous occasions; Joanna Ramsey was his driver and friend.

I wanted to track down Surinder. He was no longer in Orkney, nor even in Britain. It turned out that he was in Hong Kong, where he runs a school for children with additional learning needs. In a telephone conversation, he told me that he first learned about George in 1991. At that time, he was on the staff of the classics department at Warwick University.

'I'd heard of Orkney as a young child, in particular a little island called Eynhallow,' he said. 'I read about it in the *Encyclopedia Britannica*, and I always wanted to go there. A friend of mine in the French department at Warwick said: "Surinder, I hear you are going to Orkney. There is an amazing writer there called George Mackay Brown." My friend gave me George's poetry collection called *Winterfold*. I took the book but didn't read it.'

Surinder, who was 30 years old when he moved to Orkney, got a job at the Stromness bookshop, through which he met GMB. 'I hadn't read George's poetry by then,' he said, 'but what I was impressed about most was the man himself – his gentle nature and his attitude to life.'

Surinder told me he was brought up as a Hindu. 'My mother is religious,' he said. 'She prays twice a day, and lights a candle, like most Indian families. The way in which George practised his faith inspired me a lot – it was part of his daily life. He was very careful that no-one noticed that he was practising his faith. I would sometimes inadvertently see him, just before eating, making the sign of the Cross under the table – he never did it openly, and he never said grace.'

On the feast-days of particular saints – Peter and Paul, Cecilia, Lucy, Magnus – George would light a candle as he sat in his rocking chair after finishing his morning's work. 'I never thought of George as being a Catholic or an Anglican or a Presbyterian or Church of England – it was just that he practised his faith,' Surinder said. 'He never made a thing about being a Catholic. As far as I could see, he never made a distinction between the denominations of Christianity.

'During my time in Orkney with George, I was very inspired by him. When you are inspired by someone, you want to do similar things to them. George had converted to Catholicism, and I thought, hey, I would like to do that too! I spoke to George, and he didn't urge me, he didn't say "go ahead". He said: "If it happens, it will happen in its time".

'I think if I'd been wanting to be a friend of George just because he was a poet, he would soon have realised that, and he would not have been happy about it. He felt that artists, including poets, were over-rated. He always said that the thing that made him most uncomfortable was going to a poetry evening to hear poets read.

'When Scotland were in the World Cup, in 1994, the *Scotsman* asked George to write a poem celebrating it. He started it at the weekend, and the fifty-line poem was ready for posting on Monday. I said: "George, how did you do this?" He looked at me and said: "Being a poet is no different from being a carpenter. If you went to a carpenter and said: 'Would you make me a table?' and the carpenter said: 'I don't feel inspired today', what a lousy carpenter he would be!"'

Was he aware of George's depressions?

'He had some dark days, when he was very low. I always felt that those low moments were also something very special. In those moments, he was never negative – or at least, he was only negative about his own self-worth, his own life. He often felt that his life and his work were not of much worth. But that was also part of his humility.'

George still managed to conceal his depressions from many people. Even on dark days, his disarming smile would soften his features and chase away the melancholy look. In his later years, he seemed more benign and contented; this may have been related to the fact that he drank very little alcohol. People who met George for the first time in his late sixties and seventies were, like Jo Ramsey, astonished when they learned of his travails.

George had a special affection for his nephew, David Dixon, who had cerebral palsy. David was very bright. He got a First in English at Edinburgh University, and then did research on the American poet Emily Dickinson. George was thrilled when he got news of David's achievements.

'Over the years of my friendship with George,' Surinder said, 'one of the privileges was that at Christmas I used to go with him to Allison's place for Christmas dinner, and David would be there. I must confess that, the first time I met him, I could not understand him at all. But George spoke to him as if he were speaking a completely different language that I couldn't understand. They were completely at ease with each other. David had a great affection for George.'

This was confirmed to me by Allison Dixon. 'George was like a grandfather to my children, because my father died young and they didn't know him. George had a great rapport with children, and could tell many a long story. He pretended he had a family in his attic, and he would recount the tales of the children, and what they were doing and what they'd been up to, often mirroring things that our children had done or said or were interested in. At birthdays and Christmas time, he invariably bought a book for the children, and he would write his own story inside the front cover usually. My family regard these as very precious now.

'George was kind to David, without being patronising in any way. He didn't make him any different from the other two. He didn't make a thing of it. He could see that Dave was a clever boy, and that he would probably go far. When Dave came home on holiday from university, he had so much to talk to George about. There are a lot of photos of George taking Dave's hand as a young boy because he was a bit unsteady on his feet, and George would always remember to take his hand as he walked along. You never ever got the feeling that George was sorry for Dave, which was a great comfort to us, because he realised that he was a worthwhile human being. And of course Dave's head was just full of everything that George pumped into it. He just loved George.'

In his later years, George started tinkering with his own poems in the interests of prudery. Sexual imagery, or hints of sexual waywardness, were the particular targets in his troubled bouts of self-censorship. Even his most-anthologised poem, 'Hamnavoe', did not escape attention. The lines 'A stallion at the sweet fountain / Dredged water, and touched / fire from steel-kissed cobbles' were deemed to be too full of sexual energy; in the amended version, the stallion became a carthorse. In the same poem, the lines 'And lovers / Unblessed by steeples, lay under / The buttered bannock of the moon' became 'Ploughboy / And milklass tarried under / The buttered bannock of the moon'. George omitted one of his finest poems, 'The Funeral of Ally Flett', from his *Selected Poems, 1954–1992*, presumably because of the improprieties of the young Mr Flett. He even changed the line 'Sit on my bum' in his poem 'Beachcomber'.

Why did he make these changes so late in his life? Some of George's friends blamed Renée Simm's influence. It may simply have been an old man, coming nearer to death and judgement, fearing that he would be called to account for failing to buttress family values in everything that he wrote. It may represent an untypical narrowing of his Roman Catholic faith. Surely not a Mrs McKee-type assize for such trivial matters?

I like poet Don Paterson's aphorism: 'A correction made to work over five years old is less a revision than the cancellation of the opinion of another man'.

The changes drained energy from the originals. When compiling George's *Collected Poems*, Archie Bevan and Brian Murray rightly selected the more robust versions. Their judgements were backed by Christopher Rush, who told me: 'You can live too long and you can become too conservative. Perhaps there should be a law that poets are not allowed to touch their own poems after a certain length of time.'

Chris told me that he saw a lot of Calvinism in GMB. 'Calvinism, Catholicism and paganism – it's a blend, it's just George. It's the old "Give me a child until he is seven" business. George has the Calvinist thing, and I don't think he ever lost that. How much was part of his nature is very hard to disentangle. Or to what extent it was a sexually repressed thing, deeply submerged. We are in deep waters and boxing shadows there. The Puritan in him didn't like a lot of things that were happening in the literary world. I remember there was a huge outpouring of adulation when Alasdair Gray wrote *Lanark*. George said to me he was disgusted by the book – it was sickening, it was obscene, it was all sorts of things, and he was sickened not only by that but also by the parties which the Arts Council were throwing for this "sham writer".'

George was offended by the strong language in a novel by Orkney-based writer Duncan McLean. McLean is a fine writer with a deserved reputation; he would be entitled to a sardonic smile when he reads GMB's condemnation of the allegedly Presbyterian, moralistic chorus of women.

Christopher Rush remembers how a novel of his upset George. 'I never fell out with him,' he told me, 'but I wrote a novel called *Last Lesson of the Afternoon*, which used sex as a fairly blunt instrument to talk about the sterility of the educational system. I suppose there was a lot of strong language and there were colourful scenes, intended symbolically. I know he never liked it. He just never mentioned it. It was as if I had never written it – which was an act of friendship, I think. He just pretended that it hadn't happened. There was just silence. He shut the door on things he didn't like. It was in another room.'

One doesn't have to be a Freudian analyst to spot the denial and projection going on.

Alison Miller's take on the situation is interesting. 'I think of George as someone afflicted by shame in some way,' she told me. 'There is something there about being scared to integrate the darker aspects of human life and behaviour, in case it tips you into the abyss. I've sometimes thought that GMB's late bowdlerising of his own work has to do with that. He had problems all his life with sexuality and eventually wanted to deny it completely, along with "bad" language. His way of dealing with the dark side in his writing was to distil it down to something like its essence – the bones of it, with no messy flesh or blood or viscera – and imbue it with magic and myth. Which is not to say there is no emotion in his writing – it often evokes an emotional response in the reader – but it gives a sense of emotion, of life held somewhat at bay.'

How did it feel to be an Orkney writer 'after George', especially given his discomfort with the dark side?

'As a writer born and brought up in Orkney, I've found myself sometimes inhibited in my writing about the place in the years since George died,' Alison said. 'He "wrote" his Orkney so beautifully, created such a powerfully numinous vision of it, that to contemplate capturing a different reality seems almost a desecration. The exploration of the nuances of human relations most novelists work with he shied away from. I remember, when I read Maggie Fergusson's biography, the pang I felt to learn of George's rejection of Duncan McLean because of the "bad"language in his book. He wouldn't have liked mine either, for the same reason, and that makes me sad.'

In letters to James Maitland, George was reflective. 'I have written quite a lot in the past year but am uncertain as to the quality of most of it. Time sifts and proves all ... Publishing – seeing one's name in print – has lost most of its glamour. To think how I hungered and thirsted for it 30 years ago ... I delve like a miner in the darkness of the year, hoping every day that my pen will turn up something good. All one can be sure of, after a long apprenticeship, is one can do a fair day's work – whether good, bad, or halfway between, "heaven pronounces lastly", as Milton said.'

He complained to James Maitland about the Thatcherite political and cultural climate, which he described as 'ominous' and 'sinister' – 'all that worship of money, and the shameless flaunting of greed as if it was really for the general good'. He felt that the pursuit of money and technology could not go on indefinitely. 'It may be, we are going to discover soon what comes of worship to Goddess of Progress-without-End. Maybe a sharp taste of poverty would "stab our spirits broad awake", as R. L. Stevenson said.'

When he was diagnosed with bowel cancer in 1989, he wrote to me from his ward in Foresterhill Hospital, Aberdeen: 'My stay in hospital is almost over and though they are kind and considerate always – in addition to the skill and efficiency of doctors and radiotherapists – I'll be glad to be home again. Wind and rain of Orkney – but not too much! – will be welcome after the central heating.' Thus speaks an islander. He added: 'Most of all I'll be glad to be free of TV intrusions. I think TV must be one of man's worse inventions.'

In 1990, he had to go to Aberdeen again for surgery for bowel cancer. 'I came home from Foresterhill last Friday,' he told Jim Maitland, 'having been a patient for 3 weeks. This time it was a deep black depression, consequent on some kind of virus I contracted.'

He returned to Orkney thinner and greyer. James Maitland had been having treatment for cancer as well. 'I hope you have good news of your health, Jim, and Elizabeth too. Even the strongest are so fragile, and in our days of hardihood we don't realise it. However, I won't launch into any Job-like lamentations.'

In June 1993, George came for dinner at the St Magnus Cathedral manse. I had written a one-man play, *Every Blessed Thing*, based on the life of Lord George MacLeod, and it was premiered at the St Magnus Festival by Scottish actor and director, Tom Fleming. At the pre-theatre meal in the manse, George was seated next to writer and journalist Maxwell MacLeod, son of George MacLeod. Knowledge of GMB's cancer was in the public domain, and his frailty was evident. Maxwell asked him how he was coping with the illness. 'Well, Maxwell, we're all dying,' said George with a shy smile, 'but some of us are dying faster than the rest of you.'

Despite bouts of ill-health, physical and mental – he described himself as 'trenched by wounds' – the morning ceremony of writing was maintained. 'I try to do a little writing every day,' he told James Maitland. 'But sometimes one thinks: "What's the point of it all?" ... Then, after a while the sun comes out in the mind and spirit again, and life is full of light and colour. I have been going through a dark period this past fortnight. It will pass, as it has always done up to now, since childhood.'

The awards continued. 'I am fairly well – a wonder that I've passed the 71st milestone,' he had written to James Maitland in 1992. 'And still, of a morning, I'm eager to get down to the work of words. The Arts Council has given me £1,000 for *Vinland* – there's not all that much I can spend it on: travel is out – I drink only moderately – don't bother with new clothes – eat mostly in friends' houses – have no children to leave it to ... ah well ... now it's time for the weekly bath.'

In 1994, he received the Scottish Saltire Book of the Year Award for *Beside the Ocean of Time*. 'I was pleasantly surprised by the Saltire prize, and sent my publishing editor to collect it while I hid away at home.'

He was often invited to speak at public events. 'They actually asked me to preach or read poems at St Andrews chaplaincy, but I've had to refuse,' he wrote to James Maitland. 'And I've just refused to read at the Colchester Festival and the Galway Festival. I think poets are best in their little monastic cells. The honey of praise isn't all that good for them.' In 1994, he was asked if he would be willing to be filmed in Orkney with Scottish comedian Billy Connolly, 'but I turned it down'.

In 1995, George collaborated with Swedish photographer Gunnie Moberg. Gunnie had come to Orkney in 1976 with her husband Tam McPhail and their family. A brilliant photographer with a vivacious personality, Gunnie asked George if he would compose captions for forty-seven of her stunning photographs of Orkney. George produced not only captions but also individual poems for each photograph. Stewart Conn reckons that the poems in the book, *Orkney Pictures and Poems*, are among George's best.

Such was George's respect and affection for Gunnie that he agreed to travel to Nairn for her son's wedding. Tam McPhail – whose crammed Aladdin's Cave of a bookshop in Stromness must be one of the finest independent bookshops anywhere – told me that, on the car journey south, George mimicked the accent of the residents of each town on the journey.

The advent of spring always cheered George up. 'I think Spring may have arrived at last,' he told Jim Maitland. 'March was a cruel kind of month. Now the daffodils are rising in all their glory. I noticed this morning at breakfast the butter was not a yellow stone any more, but malleable. How age begins to work its erosions! Now I walk outside with a stick, the few times I am out. And I don't feel comfortable any more in my old friend the rocker. But enough of grouses. I can eat and sleep and write and enjoy my friends. (But another erosion: beer – mild delightful beer, good friend and comforter – leaves a hangover, even taken in small quantities.)'

In his final letter to Jim Maitland, he wrote: 'It has been a cold Spring but the light is lovely and Orkney seems to be invaded by daffodils – they have even invaded my house and shout their silent "glorias" in three vases. I think I'll be going to Kirkwall today for Stations of the

Cross. A few Easter/Spring/St Magnus poems have come: none, I fear, masterpieces – but the urge to rejoice is (almost) all.'

In an article for the *Scotsman*, George reflected on ageing and on the question of life after death. He said that the best a writer could do, in the way of summing up, was to note down a few images. Here are some of them:

The old man asks himself: 'What have I come all this way for? Is there an inn at the end of the road? Or is there silence and nothingness? Or are we mingled at last with the four elements out of which we came?'

Time is there always, hurrying you on to your destination, whatever it may be: inn, or tombstone, or the four elements that weave and unweave for ever ...

Religious people say, 'after death' ... but more and more people, in this age of new gods – materialism and technology and property – say that the only voyage we can be sure of is birth-to-death ... beyond, the silence and the darkness.

I feel sure, though, that we all bear the freight of our experience somewhere, for unloading and proper valuing.

What if the ship, full freighted, ends on a rock, or in a whirlpool, or among Arctic floes? ... There are mysteries of suffering and loss that we don't like to contemplate, but I think we are here not only to accept them but to offer them.

Living in the kind of place I have known since childhood, it ought to have been the image of a sea voyage (as, willy-nilly, it has turned out to be).

Think of an old man standing on a pier among the tall masts and salt smells and seagulls, just as the evening star appears in the west.

Just over two weeks before he died, GMB wrote an article about the arts. It was never published, but was found at his house. He said he wanted to think about the use of the arts; what impulse made people indulge in poetry and music and sculpture and pottery and weaving and the dance.

The necessity to make things is part of our make-up. But not only of 'artists' in the various kinds of art, but of all crafts people, and 'all trades, their gear and tackle and trim'. Even the pavement sweeper moves in a rhythm that approximates to dancing.

The most backward peasant in history, digging with a mattock and cutting his few ears of corn with a sickle or scythe, is vividly aware of the changing seasons and the great rhythms he is part of. He knew nothing of the music and tapestries and architecture in the castle of the lord to which he was thirled; but from his sweat and toil all that beauty issued.

He glimpsed it at Mass on Sunday and holy days, on the walls of the village church, and in the chants, and in the slow grave dance at the altar. He was almost certainly illiterate, but he gleaned some of the great Old Testament stories from the painted wall of the church, and the gospel stories.

Our 20th-century imaginations are atrophied by bad or indifferent books, or films, or TV programmes – though not all of them are bad, by any means, and the best can bring out positive and joyous responses in us. But creatively, I feel that the dice are loaded against us. The tabloid press, read by so many millions, is a stain on any society ...

He said that the pure primitive urge to be at home with all of creation was absent from most of the celebrated works of art in the late twentieth century.

What is the significance of a dead sheep or cow in a frame? Or a pile of bricks in a famous gallery? T. S. Eliot said: The cycles of Heaven in twenty centuries / Bring us farther from God and nearer to the Dust.

The hunter and the herdsman became the farmer with his ox and plough and his few acres. Perhaps it was the subjugation of beasts to do the will of the farmer that broke 'the social union' of men and animals – we lord it over the animals and in the end think ourselves free to do anything we like with them in the way of experiment (ending in the horror of the 'mad cow disease') – and the ancient treaty/dance is quite forgotten, after having been ridiculed since the time for art's sake; the wisdom and the beauty are gone with the dance.

I can't help thinking that most modern art and literature and music are destined for the dustbin of history ...

Tolstoy in his old age was right. This greatest of all the novelists turned to the simplicity and potency of folk tales and parable, the kind that had been enjoyed from the beginning; and at the heart of the tale was a moral – not in the smug Victorian sense – but a pearl of great price that yet cost nothing, a piece of universal wisdom … He who had watered the fields under snow in winter, and set plough to them in spring, and seeded them, and watched anxiously for the ripening under rain and sun and wind, and reaped and threshed and winnowed, and seen the loaves brought out of the oven by his wife – he knew well what Mass was on Sunday morning in the village church. He needed nobody really, to interpret to him what was the meaning of 'I am the Bread of Life'. He had no need of the theologians to expound transubstantiation to him. He knew that he was made out of dust, like Adam, and to dust he would return. In between were the seventy marvellous and anxious years, in which he hungered, in the body and in the mind and in the soul.

It seems to me that there can never be art without religion. I don't mean that every musician and dancer and writer and weaver and potter has to be Christian or Buddhist or Muslim, but unless there is some awe and wonderment at the things that occur under the sun, little of value will be done, however much it is praised in the galleries and the reviews.

For the artist – and for all men and women – to wonder is to praise.

DH Lawrence sat at his writing table and waited for the flame of God to take possession of him.

It takes patience. It requires, sometimes, a little courage; especially at a time when it is not fashionable to mention the divine in connection with art.

The early, bitterly cold weeks of 1996 saw George become weaker. At the beginning of April, Matilda Tumin and Christopher Prendergast, friends who lived on the outskirts of Stromness, invited him to stay in their house for a couple of weeks when they were away. George and Surinder stayed there. They were not practical men, and they could not work the Rayburn cooker. George had a cold and was not very well. He took to his bed.

On 12 April, when his breathing difficulties increased, his GP and friend, Dr Derrick Johnstone, was summoned. George's weakness was such that Dr Johnstone drove him to Kirkwall.

Next morning, Joanna Ramsey was with her 2½-year-old daughter, Emma, at a birthday party for Archie and Elizabeth Bevan's granddaughter. When she heard the news about George, Jo arranged to drive Surinder to the Balfour Hospital in Kirkwall in the afternoon.

'When we got there,' Jo recalled, 'we got out of the car, and the first thing I saw was members of George's family going in to the hospital. I thought: "Something's wrong here," and there clearly was. I'm so glad I saw George, because although he wasn't really conscious, I could speak to him.

'What I remember – you know how you get a lasting image of the day – was standing in the car park of Safeway with Surinder, after leaving the hospital. George was still alive at that time. Surinder and I stood there looking at each other, and we were completely distraught. It was a dreadful day. Surinder felt that if George had just stayed at Mayburn Court it might all have been different, which was nonsense. It was terribly distressing for him, but he was that kind of person, a very humble person.'

George's last words in the hospital were: 'I see hundreds and hundreds of ships sailing out of the harbour'. This was the same imagery that had appeared in the hallucinations of Jimmy Brown, the uncle whose suicide affected young Georgie Brown so much.

The evening star had appeared in the west; the tall masts were leaving the harbour, bearing the legend-maker into legend, on a farther, timeless shore.

The consummate artist, the man who created the modern myth of Orkney and the myth of George Mackay Brown, had contrived to die in perfect time for his burial on the feast day of St Magnus, 16 April 1996.

In the cathedral vestry, as the great bell of St Magnus tolls, the Right Rev. Mario Conti (the then Roman Catholic Bishop of Aberdeen), Father Jock Dalrymple, Father Michael Spencer and I are robing for what will be only the second Requiem Mass in the nave of the cathedral since the Reformation. (When I was asked by Father Spencer if the service could be held in the cathedral rather than in the local Roman Catholic church, I had, without a moment's hesitation, said 'Of course'. What could have been more fitting?)

I notice that Bishop Mario is a little nervous. He speaks to me, almost conspiratorially. I hope you don't mind, he says, that I will be unable to offer you communion during the Mass.

I know that, whatever his own private inclinations might be, his public position necessitates that he represent the Roman Catholic Church's ruling that the consecrated bread and wine of communion should not be knowingly offered to non-Roman Catholics. I have always got on well with Mario; he has broken bread with us at the cathedral manse, and has preached at the Church of Scotland morning service in the cathedral at my invitation. While I had received communion from Catholic priests when I was Leader of the Iona Community, I respect Bishop Mario's adherence to his Church's official position, and have no desire to embarrass him.

Nevertheless, it is hurtful to be excluded from participation in the Eucharist in the cathedral of which I am minister, especially at a service celebrating the life of a friend whose Catholicism was so inclusive.

When I welcome the congregation – which includes Renée Simm, Nora Kennedy, Kenna Crawford, Joanna Ramsey and Surinder Punjya – to the cathedral, I say that all the churches in Orkney honour George's Christian convictions and recognise him as a Catholic in the deepest sense of that word, a man of the widest Christian sympathies. How appropriate, too, that the service should be held in St Magnus Cathedral, when George wrote so much about Magnus and indeed, by his writings, sparked a revival of interest in the Orkney saint.

The cathedral choir sings the Hymn to St Magnus, and also a lovely poem by GMB, 'The Shepherds of Hoy', which Sir Peter Maxwell Davies had set to music. Then a heart-stopping moment: Max himself, as a tribute to his friend and collaborator, sits down at the grand piano in the cathedral and plays his haunting 'Farewell to Stromness'. Tears are shed.

In the Liturgy of the Word, Bishop Conti speaks of the saying of Jesus that was quoted so often by GMB: 'Unless a seed fall into the ground and die, it remains only a seed, but if it dies, it brings forth much fruit'.

'I remember George describing the earth under the farmer's plough as being scourged – or was it the back of Christ he saw being ploughed?' says Bishop Conti. 'If my memory falters, it is because of George's characteristic interchanging of images, which revealed not only the twin sources of his deepest inspiration, namely his native Orkney and his adopted Catholicism, but also his easy integration of what for so many remain separate orders of life and faith. This is why his death at this season seems so right, for this is the season when the life of faith and the life of nature so marvellously correspond; when he who was hung up on the bare wood, and moistened it with his blood, made it to flower as the instrument of salvation; when He who was buried in the dark earth, and shared its apparent sleep, burst forth from it revealing the new life of grace.'

In the silence of St Magnus Cathedral, the circle of bread is broken and the cup of wine lifted high in re-enactment of the mythic salvation story that George Mackay Brown did so much to illuminate.

And yet the sacrament of unity is at the same time the sacrament of division, as the fault line within the Christian community is laid bare. Only those who are Roman Catholics leave their seats to receive the consecrated bread and wine, while those who worship each week in St Magnus Cathedral are onlookers.

The pain at the heart of the fractured Christian community is palpable.

The cathedral bell tolls again as the members of the congregation leave. Then it is out to the windswept Warbeth cemetery on the edge of Stromness: the place where George had wandered as a melancholy adolescent.

The poet of Hamnavoe is laid next to John Brown and Mary Jane Brown. His earthly journey is over.

His spiritual journey is now in uncharted territory.

After the funeral, two people sought out Father Jock Dalrymple and asked him about becoming Catholics – Surinder Punjya and Renée Simm. Surinder told me: 'Jock was very kind to me. I was baptised in 1996 and became a Catholic in 1997, along with Renée, in Glenrothes, where Jock was a priest. If you asked me: "Are you a practising Catholic?", I'd have to be very honest with you and say: "If George is listening, I have disappointed myself in that respect". I haven't been able to adopt the things I should be doing as a Catholic, like going to Mass. When George passed away, I missed his friendship and companionship and wisdom.'

Joanna Ramsey also found it hard to adjust to George's death. 'It was a very emotional time for me,' she told me. 'It was a precious friendship.' She wrote a poem in remembrance of George, called 'Images'. Here is the opening stanza:

> After you died I searched for you
> in the newsprint words.
> You were distant, changed; a stranger
> staring out in monochrome, jaw jutted
> against a skyline carefully composed.
> Once a smile flashed from the page
> but still you evaded capture.
> You used to sing to my daughter.

It is a poem about loss, about looking for George, ending with these words:

> I dip again into the pool of images,
> and catch you: holding my hand
> in a taxi, rain on the window –
> you lie gleaming for a second
> in the net.

Poet Pamela Beasant, who describes herself as a 'lapsed Baptist', told me how strange Stromness feels after George's death. 'It feels sometimes as though he were still here,' she said. 'There's a great ongoing thread now, with various things that keep him very much present, although his absence in the town is something that a lot of people feel, especially when walking past his house. There was a programme about him recently that showed some old film of him walking through the town – and it was such a jolt, it was very poignant. It still seems to me that he's here in an odd sort of way; he's in the stones and the air.

'If I'm trying to find something particular – you know how much he wrote, masses! – and you think you'll never find it, and then I locate it, I find myself saying "Thanks George!" It's as if he's saying "You know where it is, it's here!"

'It's one of the most powerful presences I've ever felt, a continuing presence: and that's odd because I'm not religious, although I grew up a Baptist. I'm very envious of George's Catholicism. I'm envious of faith and wish I had it. It's something I've tussled with all these years. Some of the best poetry has grown out of spirituality, or some sort of tussle with spirituality. And what do we do when we don't have that? It doesn't seem to make any sense without it. What something beyond ourselves are we trying to express?'

It was not only in Stromness that George was missed. More than a decade after his funeral, Alison Miller gave me this account of her response on the day of George's funeral.

'When George Mackay Brown died, I felt bereft. It wasn't that I knew him well, or even – the further I read into the draft of your book – at all. On the day of his funeral, I was at work in Glasgow at the Centre for Women's Health on Sauchiehall Street. It must have been a Tuesday, because the Asian Women's Support Group was in, fifteen or so women in bright salwar kamiz, passing the door of my room between the kitchen and the meeting room, talking and laughing. Usually I'd leave my door open. That day, I closed it and let the voices outside drift away.

'My mother in Orkney had told me the time of the funeral. I couldn't get away from work to travel north to join her, so I had planned a little ceremony of my own. In the morning, I opened a book of George's at random, and the first words my eye fell on were:

Now the door is opened. Now the bell
peals thrice to summon the people …

367

'That morning I had also taken two Orkney pebbles to work: one of red sandstone to represent the cathedral, the other green for the fields. I sat down at my desk, a pebble in each hand, closed my eyes and teleported myself to the cathedral. It wasn't hard to imagine myself there in "the roseate gloom", not quite sitting among the folk, but definitely in the cathedral. I'd have to say the proceedings at the altar were a bit hazy. But a white jug of daffodils glimmered against one of the red pillars. I thought about some of the people I knew who would likely be there, close friends of George, Archie and Elizabeth Bevan, Ian and Jean MacInnes. It would be hard for them. I thought about my mum, not sure until the last minute if she should go. I wondered how the melding of the Presbyterian and the Catholic bits of the service would be done.

'I don't know how long the reverie lasted, and I'm not sure I can explain what I was doing. When I look at it now, it seems a bit pagan. The stones originated in the beginning of time, or near enough for me; George wrote about stone; my father was a stonemason; his funeral had been three years before. The "ceremony" is about connectedness, I think. It was meant to honour George, acknowledge his place in my imagination, link that in to important connections in my life.

'The following day, I opened a book of George's at random again. This time, the words that leapt out were:

> *What bard now to strike*
> *The rock of elegy*
> *For sea, the lost mother?*

'I've often seen you quote George MacLeod's dictum: "If you think that's a coincidence, I wish you a very dull life". I do think it's a coincidence, but somehow it named the loss I felt. And that isn't dull at all.'

Fourteen years after George's death, his biographer, Maggie Fergusson, still found him to be something of a guide. 'If the day ahead seems daunting,' she told me, 'I think of a sentence from another of George's letters to Stella: "true heroism is to try to live this one day well, whatever the circumstances", or of these lines from his poem "Foresterhill" – "Blessings may break from stone, who knows how?" And in moments of doubt, when faith wavers, I think of the last time I saw George, lying in his coffin ahead of his Requiem Mass in St Magnus Cathedral. He looked, as I scribbled in a note to myself afterwards, "like a child, and a saint". Standing by him, I was aware both of the limits of human understanding, and of an absolute conviction that death was not an end but a beginning. That rich mystery was summed up in an unpublished essay found, some weeks later, in the attic of George's council flat. I find myself returning again and again to its final paragraph, trying to tease out its full meaning: *I have a deep-rooted belief that what has once existed can never die: not even the frailest things, spindrift or clover-scent or glitter of star on a wet stone. All is gathered into the web of creation, that is apparently established and yet perhaps only a dream in the eternal mind; and yet, too, we work at the making of it with every word and thought and action of our lives.'*

In Warbeth, an Orkney stone now bears the legend:

GEORGE MACKAY BROWN

POET

1921–1996

Around the edge of the stone are these words: 'CARVE THE RUNES THEN BE CONTENT WITH SILENCE'. They come from one of George's best-known poems, 'A Work for Poets':

> *To have carved on the days of our vanity*
> *A sun*
> *A ship*
> *A star*
> *A cornstalk*
>
> *Also a few marks*
> *From an ancient forgotten time*
> *A child may read*
> *That not far from the stone*

> *A well*
> *Might open for wayfarers*
>
> *Here is a work for poets –*
> *Carve the runes*
> *Then be content with silence*

The lack of a full stop at the end is, of course, deliberate. It is a silence that has no end point.

There is now a full stop at the end of George Mackay Brown's physical life. So, has the troubled, inspirational, horizontal bard borne the freight of his experience *somewhere*, for unloading and proper valuing? Or has he simply gained the oblivion for which he often longed?

Death, critics say, is a theme that nags through my work: the end, the darkness, the silence. So it must be with every serious artist, but still I think art strikes out in the end for life, quickening, joy. The good things that we enjoy under the sun have no meaning unless they are surrounded by the mysterious fecund sleep.

As I stand at the grave, the words of one of Spain's finest poets, Antonio Machado, come to mind:

> And you, Lord, through whom we all
> have eyes, and who sees souls,
> tell us if we all one
> day will see your face.

Epilogue

I have a tiny miracle in my hand. It is the kind of little jewel for which the phrase 'small, but perfectly formed' might have been coined. It was given to me by my family. It will be perfect for the decking of the house on those lovely summer evenings.

The iPod Nano has music on it – Bach's Mass in B Minor of course, plus James MacMillan's *Seven Last Words from the Cross*, Mahler's Fifth Symphony, the Scottish metrical Psalms, Bruce Springsteen, Orcadian Kris Drever, and – since I'm learning to play the blues harmonica (or blues harp, as us dudes refer to it) – lots of Little Walter and Sonny Boy Williamson. Not only that, I also have R. S. Thomas and George Mackay Brown reading their poems. Just touch the screen, and T. S. Eliot starts reading *The Waste Land*. I start chanting 'April is the cruellest month', accompanied by Mary Jane Brown and her daughter, Ruby.

All this from a beautiful gadget that sits easily on the palm of my hand. I wonder: would George have approved of this brilliant piece of technology? I doubt it … he did not approve of radio and television. Did he?

I don't have the black rook of depression on my shoulder, but I do have George's voice right here, in my brain. He is, as ever, present in his absence.

Back in Edinburgh for a few days, I go into Milne's Bar to drink in the atmosphere once more. As I enter the pub, I notice the change immediately. The place has been tarted up. The fifteen historic portraits have gone. The 'Little Kremlin' sign is nowhere to be seen.

I ask the barman about it. Milne's Bar, I learn, is now part of an English chain called Punch Taverns. The portraits will not be back, he tells me. They are going to be auctioned off for charity. He is sad about it, he says, but he adds: 'I suppose we have to keep up with the times'.

Really? To what end? I particularly miss the irascible MacDiarmid's scowling face, set beside his poem.

Despite its dark side, it is distressing that this famous Scottish watering hole is now indistinguishable from other pubs. The distinctive atmosphere of one of Scotland's literary institutions has been silently traded for a smooth corporate image. 'Scots often undervalue literary or cultural history, occasionally treating it with rancour, and more often with the kind of casual abandon that simply lets it get lost', says Robert Crawford in his fine study, *Scotland's Books*.

The poets have left the building, all in the name of a vacuous trendiness. As another great Scottish contrarian, R. B. Cunninghame Graham, put it with typical clarity: 'So does our progress make commercial travellers of us all'.

George Mackay Brown would have understood. I make my excuses, and leave.

This particular journey is over. Or, at least, this particular part of a journey is over. The manuscript is ready for the publisher – although a manuscript is never ready for a publisher. Leonardo da Vinci's observation that art is never finished, only abandoned, is apposite. George Mackay Brown would certainly have agreed with that.

In this two-and-a-half-year pilgrimage, have I got closer to understanding George Mackay Brown? A bit. I certainly have a much clearer picture of his movement from the Presbyterianism of his upbringing to Roman Catholicism.

The fact that the reasons for this critical decision in his life are more complex than the more popular accounts allow should not be surprising. Studies of the reasons given for a sense of calling to the Presbyterian ministry have revealed discrepancies between the accounts given by candidates at the time of the original testing of their candidature and later versions of the same events. My own decision to leave journalism to study for the ministry of the Kirk came out of a genuine sense of vocation; but, over the years, my understanding of the various forces at work has changed. At the time, I was not aware of the romanticising and idealising that was going on 'under the bonnet', nor of the force of my non-churchgoing mother's sense of my 'specialness' as a survivor of life-threatening lung disease. She told me – in fact, it became part of a litany – that a mirror had to be held up to my mouth to establish whether or not I was still breathing. (Note to self: is this 'really' why I was drawn, tenpenny biro and digital recorder in hand, to track TB-stricken George Mackay Brown's spiritual journey? How hard it is to know oneself, never mind another human being.)

To what extent George was aware of the psychological under-pinnings of his own life choices is hard to say. I believe that his obsession with Calvinism as a catch-all for everything that was bad, following Edwin Muir, made for a distorting explanatory force. It was too easy to blame black Geneva for the depressions, the self-loathing, the abuse of alcohol and the critics in Stromness. At the same time, he had an acute understanding of the masks that human beings hide behind. As George himself said, about overhearing his father's anxious monologues, *Perhaps I was beginning to realise that human beings are much more complex than they seem to be. We put on masks when we go out of our houses into the community. Communal life is complex; we have a different mask for everyone we encounter. When there are four or five people in a group, the communication between them, however seemingly simple, can be very subtle.*

I think back to the questions I had when I was sitting on the house decking on that glorious June evening, reading *An Orkney Tapestry*. When GMB talked about Orkney's flattering mask, he was extending the mask analogy to the community in which he was set. Yet underneath each mask, personal or corporate, was a hidden truth – 'the true face dreams on'. Did he, like Orkney, wear a mask? Yes, he did. This notion lay at the heart of his role as a poet: he puts on a social mask until the revelry is over, before returning to his 'true task – the interrogation of silence'. He was certainly disinclined to remove his own mask publicly, believing that what lay under it was too unattractive to be exposed. (This may go some way to explaining why he could reveal his severe and sometimes suicidal depressions to strangers and friends far away, while concealing the depths of his despair from those closest to him.) The only thing with the power to lift his 'stoical mask' was alcohol; when it did so, it sometimes led to the 'discharge of black hatred', followed by dark despair.

Was GMB mentally and emotionally embedded in a mythical golden age? The jury in my own head is still out on this one. He did sometimes yearn for the pre-Enlightenment and pre-Reformation stable order of an era dominated by the Catholic Church; on the other hand, he recognised the impossibility of recreating that era. He was, as Professor Douglas Dunn observed, 'a modern poet of the pre-modern'.

Was he a provincial writer with a small-town mentality? Only on a superficial reading. For GMB, the local was the theatre of the universal. While his Hamnavoe was a romanticised version of Stromness, there was enough grit in that particular oyster to make his poetry and his stories work. Having said all that, Alison Miller's observation that she has found herself sometimes inhibited when it comes to capturing a different version of Orkney 'after George' – making it seem like a form of desecration – needs to be taken on board. It is time for Orkney writers to step outside of the master's shadow and create their own versions of the Orkney of the twenty-first century.

This does not mean that George Mackay Brown's monk-like vocation is past its philosophically credible sell-by date. His religious world-view may be counter-cultural in today's more secular world, but its integrity and its beauty shines on. The secular world itself is a mythical and romanticised world. The so-called 'real world' is itself a fiction – but that is a story for another day, perhaps for another book.

More questions from the decking. How much of an intellectual struggle did George endure in order to find faith? Did he have times of agnosticism, of dark nights of the soul? Did he observe his religion rigorously at a personal level?

He did not seem to have times of agnosticism, though that cannot be established securely. It would be hard to say for sure that he observed his religion rigorously at a personal level, since he was not demonstrative as far as his personal faith was concerned. Making the sign of the Cross under the meal table is not the action of a man who wants to draw attention to his piety. I am in no doubt that his faith was genuine; I have resisted, and continue to resist, the notion that his Christian faith was a front for something else, even though, like every member of the human race, his conscious knowledge of all of his motivations was less than comprehensive.

In reading the sources and in talking to poets and to people who knew George – or thought they did – I have certainly learned more about GMB, the man and the writer. In the course of this quest, I have revisited some old personal territory and viewed it with new eyes – the Catholic mystics, the Anglican Metaphysical Poets, the theology of the Catholic Church, the Scottish Reformation, the Presbyterian tradition in Scotland, Gerard Manley Hopkins and Edwin Muir – and have learned again how we are all, to varying degrees, prisoners of our times.

Some readers will have been disturbed by what they have learned about George Mackay Brown, particularly those whose only encounters with the man were in his later, more serene years. Even more troubled will be those who have put a halo around GMB. (One astute commentator on the text, who is aware of a growing cult of GMB, said that I can expect 'a few fatwas'!) I suppose that, both as a journalist and as a parish minister, I learned too much about the lives of people behind their social masks to be shocked by defects or moral failures that contradicted the public image.

My understanding of this, and other issues, has been enriched by my conversational fellow travellers on this quest. On reading the whole text, historian Jocelyn Rendall e-mailed me: 'Sometimes when thinking about your book (usually when cooking, or cleaning the byre) I wonder if we try too hard to reconcile what we know about an artist's personal life and spirituality and the religious message and inspiration of their art. I love Verdi's *Requiem*, and I was quite shocked when I was told he was an atheist! You have the problem of reconciling George the drunk, the depressive, the sponger, with the sheer beauty and potency of his religious writing; but perhaps we would be surprised if we knew as much about the lives of the great religious poets of the past as we do about George's. It seems that the ability to communicate profound insights in beautiful words or music or painting is indeed a gift from outside, not something produced by the "goodness" of an artist's life.'

I like the idea of Jocelyn ruminating on these topics while mucking out the byre in Papa Westray.

I end this journey with even more admiration for the flawed, sometimes broken, supremely talented George Mackay Brown than I had at the beginning. For me, knowing about his personal travails in more depth makes his formidable achievements all the greater. Keep him away from the makers of stained-glass windows and the fashioners of idols. Not a saint, not quite a hero, he is perhaps an example of the 'knight of faith' of R. S. Thomas's mentor, Søren Kierkegaard: a self-effacing, wounded but gifted artist, a scarecrow with a faltering gait, a poet with a mask and a guitar whose interrogation of silence yielded up some unspeakably beautiful treasures.

A year before his death, George wrote a poem called 'Ikey, His Will in Winter Written'. Ikey Faa is a tinker who appears in several GMB poems and stories. In this poem, Ikey, knowing that he is dying, and being penniless, bequeaths, in his will, gifts from the natural world to various people. To the child John Sweynson, who gave to Ikey and the birds a bite to eat in the winter snow, he bequeaths 'the birds of the isle, hawk and swan, eider and blackbird and dotterel'; to fisherman Jock Sinclair, who was poorly paid by the laird for his hard and dangerous work, he leaves 'the fish in the tides and rips and races about this isle'.

I have rejoiced greatly in the
elements that are soon to shake me out and away, all but
    earth – 'twixt
Yule and Hogmanay, as near as I can
guess – and I leave what is all mine and all men's and
    God's to them that
will enjoy and use it best.

This last will and testament from a poor, uninhibited and generous tinker is surely George Mackay Brown's last will and testament for all – religious or not, deserving or not.

These musings are fine; but something has to be *done*, not just spoken, to mark the end of this stage of a personal passage.

That is why three of us are standing at a graveside on a winter's day.

My wife Cristine, Maxwell MacLeod (who is writing his own book about journeys and stories, and who knows that, while we are all dying, some are dying faster than others), and I have a ceremony to perform.

The view at Warbeth is, as ever, stunning.

George Mackay Brown is dust now. As we three will be.

We think of the ancestors.

John Brown, postman and tailor, and Mary Jane (Mackay) Brown, Gaelic singer, are dust, right where we stand.

We read together GMB's poem, 'Kirkyard'. As we do so, we look around at the columns of the 'silent conquering army'. George came to this honeycomb often – maybe too often for his own good – to 'sip the finished fragrance of men'.

Cristine reads George's poem, 'The Year of the Whale'. Tammag the bee-man lives again, momentarily. Heddle has lost his limp.

Maxwell declaims 'Hamnavoe', George's great poem about his postman father. All things still wear to a common soiling. John Brown does not stir; but is he somewhere stirred to hear the words of his son: 'In the fire of images / Gladly I put my hand / To save that day for him'?

I read the opening sentences of Chapter 14 above, 'Lost in the Barleycorn Labyrinth'. I imagine that I am George standing, holding flowers, before his mother's grave, while the taxi-driver waits patiently. I think of him, with decisions to make, decisions that will save his life.

We place the flowers, purchased from the Stromness Co-operative store, on the grave.

Cristine reads George's poem, 'The Statue in the Hills'. Our Lady of Cornstalks is invoked once more.

Then we, all three, read together:

Here is a work for poets –
Carve the runes
Then be content with silence

The ceremony is over. It is finished. I feel released: to go home again, probably to carve some more runes. As the man himself put it, with measured eloquence: *There are mysterious marks on the stone circle of Brodgar in Orkney, and on the stones of Skara Brae village, from 5,000 years ago. We will never know what they mean. I am making marks on a paper, that will have no meaning 5,000 years from now. A mystery abides. We move from silence into silence, and there is a brief stir between, every person's attempt to make a meaning of life and time. Death is certain; it may be that the dust of good men and women lies more richly in the earth than that of the unjust; between the silences they may be touched, however briefly, with the music of the spheres.*

Notes

All material written by George Mackay Brown appears in this book by kind permission of the George Mackay Brown Estate, holders of almost all the copyright of all GMB's published works.

ABBREVIATIONS

AA Edwin Muir, *An Autobiography* (Canongate Classics, 1954)

AIS Neil Dickson, *An Island Shore* (Orkney Press, 1990)

BH George Mackay Brown, 'The Broken Heraldry', in Karl Miller (ed.), *Memoirs of a Modern Scotland* (Faber and Faber, 2008)

CP *The Collected Poems of George Mackay Brown*, ed. Archie Bevan and Brian Murray (John Murray (Publishers) Ltd, 2005)

EWMC Ernest Walker Marwick Collection, Orkney Library and Archive

FIS George Mackay Brown, *For the Islands I Sing* (Polygon, 2008)

NL *George Mackay Brown: Northern Lights, a Poet's Sources*, ed. Archie Bevan and Brian Murray (Polygon, an imprint of Birlinn, 2007)

NLS National Library of Scotland

OH *Orkney Herald*

OLA   Orkney Library and Archive

 OT   George Mackay Brown, *An Orkney Tapestry* (Quartet Books, 1973)

Preface

Page

ix   W. B. Yeats, *The Poems* (London: Everyman), p. 394.

Prologue

xx   'This book takes its stand with the poets ...': GMB, *An Orkney Tapestry* (Quartet Books, 1973), p. 1. All quotations from *An Orkney Tapestry* by kind permission of the George Mackay Brown Estate.

xx   'There is the Pentland Firth ...': *OT*, p. 7.

xxi   'History can tell us nothing ...': *OT*, p. 18.

xxii   'There is a new religion ...': *OT*, p. 20.

xxii   'A community like Orkney ...': *OT*, p. 21.

xxiv   'It is a word ...': *OT*, p. 21.

xxvi   'From a pub door ...': 'The Lodging', in *The Collected Poems of George Mackay Brown*, ed. Archie Bevan and Brian Murray, reproduced by permission of John Murray (Publishers) Ltd (2005), p. 28.

xxix   'He was not a person ...': Howard Jacobson, *Kalooki Nights* (Vintage, Random House, 2007), p. 214.

xxxiii 'For the past two centuries ...': 'Sealskin', in *Hawkfall and Other Stories* (Polygon, 2004), p. 131.

Chapter 1: Sweet Georgie Broon

4   'Kirkyard', in *CP*, p. 68.

7   'Probably she was out visiting ...': *George Mackay Brown: Northern Lights, a Poet's Sources*, ed. Archie Bevan and Brian Murray (Polygon, 2007), p. 131.

7   'One symptom …': GMB, *For the Islands I Sing* (Polygon, 2008), p. 39.

9   'Touch the forehead …': *NL*, p. 149.

9   'A quintessence of dust …': *NL*, p. 150.

9   'Hamnavoe', in *CP*, pp. 24–5.

11   'When the medical officer confirmed …': *FIS*, p. 49.

12   'It saved me from the world …': *FIS*, p. 49.

12   'In some strange way …': *FIS*, p. 50.

12   'I knew that the slow smouldering …': *FIS*, p. 51.

13   'There were never any "scenes"…': *NL*, pp. 133–4.

15   'The great outpouring of joy …': *FIS*, p. 53.

16   'There may have been less accurate correspondents …': *Orkney Herald*, 19 April 1960.

17   'I have a peculiar and diverse gift …': 'Island Diary: History of a Column', *OH*, 2 November 1948.

18   'The desert was actually becoming interesting …': *FIS*, p. 55.

19   'True, he knows and deplores …': *OH*, 9 January 1945.

19   'Now there are one or two selections …': *OH*, 9 January 1945.

20   'I still believe that the Orkney people …': *OH*, 2 November 1948.

20   'One day near the end of the war …': *OH*, 19 April 1960.

21   'I am gall, I am heartburn …': *OH*, 8 March 1949.

22   'I was walking down the road …': Sue Prideaux, *Edvard Munch: Behind the Scream* (Yale University Press, New Haven, 2005).

Chapter 2: The View from the Magic Mountain

25   'We who are brought up …': *OH*, 21 August 1945.

31   'sang the hymns and psalms …': *FIS*, p. 12.

32   'Those words should be carved …': *FIS*, p. 32.

32   'It was never openly said …': GMB, *As I Remember* (Robert Hale Ltd, 1979), p. 18.

33   'I think, looking back …': *FIS*, p. 42.

35   'Except that the experience was intense …': *FIS*, p. 72.

35   'One afternoon, in the Stromness bookshop …': *FIS*, p. 57.

Chapter 3: Scarecrow in the Community

39   'The first few glasses of beer ...': *FIS*, p. 59.

40   'Apart from the anodyne of the drink ...': *FIS*, p. 59.

40   'On one occasion the police van picked me up ...': *FIS*, p. 60.

41   'It gave me a kind of insight ...': *FIS*, p. 60.

41   'At least once ...': *FIS*, p. 61.

42   'Another New Year's night ...': *FIS*, p. 62.

43   'The Old Women', in *CP*, p. 16.

44   'It is characteristic of the Tory ...': *OH*, 13 February 1945.

46   'Those that stamped grimly ...': *OH*, 4 January 1955.

47   'The next day was Sunday ...': *OH*, 19 October 1954.

51   'He wakens about 9 a.m. ...': *OH*, 17 January 1950.

52   'That Sunday, the beauty of Rackwick ...': *FIS*, p. 73.

53   Alfred, Lord Tennyson, 'The Passing of Arthur', in *Idylls of the King* (Penguin Classics, 2004).

53   'Soon after I got home ...': *FIS*, p. 73.

54   'We must always be on our guard ...': *FIS*, p. 74.

54   'The symbol is lodged ...': *FIS*, p. 73.

55   'Rackwick', in *CP*, p. 5.

Chapter 4: Ministering Angels

58   'The Storm', in *CP*, pp. 3–4.

60   Robert Rendall, 'Without God', in Neil Dickson, *An Island Shore* (Orkney Press, 1990), p. 208.

61   'One day in a Kirkwall street ...': *OT*, p. 182.

61   Rendall, 'I' the Kirk Laft', in *AIS*, p. 193.

61   'Rendall's faith, though secure ...': *AIS*, p. 42.

62   'I struggled through five pages ...': *OT*, p. 186.

62   'You have projected yourself ...': *AIS*, p. 57.

63   'In strict contrast ...': *FIS*, p. 68.

64   'The tide of the spirit was shrunken ...': *OH*, 15 May 1956.

66   'To pretend that it was a genuine religious conversion ...': Edwin Muir, *An Autobiography* (Canongate Classics, 1954), pp. 77–9.

67   'Edwin Muir was too intelligent ...': GMB, 'The Broken Heraldry', in Karl Miller (ed.), *Memoirs of a Modern Scotland* (Faber and Faber, 2008), p. 143.

67   'After a certain age ...': *AA*, pp. 239ff.

68   'Last night, going to bed alone ...': *AA*, pp. 241–2.

68   'The grass in the courtyard of the Temple ...': *AA*, pp. 273–4.

69   'As I look back on the part ...': *AA*, p. 277.

70   'I was introduced ...': Edwin Muir, *A Brief Memoir* (The Castlelaw Press, West Linton, 1975), p. 7.

Chapter 5: 'Men of Sorrows and Acquainted with Grieve'

71   'A shyness, broken tentatively ...': *FIS*, p. 85.

72   'There is no doubt that the influence ...': *FIS*, p. 84.

72   'The Labyrinth', in *Edwin Muir: Collected Poems* (Faber, 1960), p. 165.

75   'The Death of Peter Esson', in *CP*, p. 18.

76   'Robert Rendall came to see me ...': *OT*, p. 184.

77   'The Stoic', in *Saga*, summer term 1953.

77   'Forgive me for preaching ...': 31 March 1953, Edinburgh University Library.

79   'Saint', in *CP*, pp. 13–14.

80   'Will it give a death-blow ...?': *OH*, 2 February 1954.

80   'After the death of my brother Hughie ...': *FIS*, p. 101.

80   'Here I am perfectly happy ...': 8 May 1956, Ernest Walker Marwick Collection, Orkney Library and Archive.

81   'The two drunk students arrived ...': *FIS*, p. 102.

81   'Studies start in earnest ...': undated letter, EWMC.

82   'In his house ...': *FIS*, pp. 108–9.

82   'I must go to the Abbotsford ...': 8 May 1956, EWMC.

82   'Simply to be there ...': *FIS*, pp. 111–12.

84   'At the interval ...': *FIS*, p. 116.

84   'Some of the happiest hours ...': *Edinburgh Evening News*, 23 April 1983.

85   'Stars', in *CP*, p. 25.

85   'Elegy', in *CP*, p. 32.

86   'In fact, no two kinds of poetry ...': *FIS*, pp. 153–4.

87   'We begin life not by knowing ...': *AA*, p. 15.

87   'Much has been written ...': BH, p. 143.

Chapter 6: The Odd Couple

89   'this girl with the sweet-smelling, honey-coloured skin ...': *FIS*, pp. 125–6.

89   'Even our hosts had gone to bed ...': *FIS*, p. 126.

90   'She suffered, because of her endowments ...': *FIS*, pp. 127.

91   'She at once asked me ...': Stanley Roger Green, *A Clamjamfray of Poets: A Tale of Literary Edinburgh* (Saltire Society, 2007), pp. 28–9.

93   'They were temperamental ...': ibid., p. 30.

101 'My dearest George ...': 21 March 1962, National Library of Scotland.

101 'Dear, dear George ...': 15 March 1960, NLS.

102 'I will write you a long letter ...': 17 March 1960, NLS.

102 'The Italian soldier is a far more spiritual being ...': *OH*, 21 August 1945.

103 'Of the buildings clustering on Lamb Holm ...': *Orkney's Italian Chapel*, PoW Chapel Preservation Committee, p. 7.

104 'Last week I did a short story ...': 8 December 1960, EWMC.

104 'I am quite well again ...': ibid.

104 'My dearest George ...': 20 December 1960, NLS.

Chapter 7: A Knox-ruined Nation?

110 'We knew little about Catholicism ...': *FIS*, p. 41.

112 'The Incarnate One', in *Edwin Muir: Collected Poems*, pp. 228–9.

114 'Scotland in 1941', in ibid., p. 97.

115 'more particularly written ...': *Selected Letters of Edwin Muir*, ed. P. H. Butter (Hogarth Press, 1974), p. 66.

115 'With the historical figure …': Edwin Muir, *John Knox: Portrait of a Calvinist* (Jonathan Cape, 1929), p. x.

116 'For the Islands I Sing', in *CP*, p. ix.

118 'He learned much from Calvin …': Harry Reid, *Reformation: The Dangerous Birth of the Modern World* (Saint Andrew Press, 2009), p. xxvi.

Chapter 8: Home at Last

131 'In the end it was literature …': *FIS*, p. 45.

132 George Herbert, 'Love', in *The Oxford Book of English Verse, 1250–1900*, ed. Arthur Quiller-Couch (1919).

134 'No man is an island …': John Donne, *Devotions on Emergent Occasions*, no. 17 (1624).

134 'Our blessedness to see …': Thomas Traherne, *Centuries* (Mowbray, 1960).

135 'Long time before …': ibid.

135 Wordsworth, 'Ode: Intimations of Immortality', in *The Oxford Book of English Verse, 1250–1900*, ed. Quiller-Couch.

137 Gerard Manley Hopkins, 'Pied Beauty', in *Poems and Prose* (Penguin Classics, 1985).

138 'It was a heroic lonely attempt …': *FIS*, p. 138.

139 Hopkins, 'God's Grandeur', in *God's Grandeur and Other Poems* (Dover Publications, 1995).

139 'Nowhere in all created literature …': *Scotsman*, 12 October 1991.

140 'The mystery and the beauty increased …': *FIS*, pp. 46–7, 48.

141 'The beauty of Christ's parables …': *FIS*, p. 45.

141 'That the toil of the earthworker …': *FIS*, p. 46.

143 'demonstrates gleefully how the dogmas …': *FIS*, p. 43.

146 'Through the violent history …': John McGahern, *Memoir* (Faber and Faber, 2005), p. 271.

150 'Attie Campbell, 1900–1967', in *CP*, p. 374.

Chapter 9: Poet of Silence

155 'Well, when you say that …': 'The Poet Speaks', interview recorded in Edinburgh, 13 October 1964.

157 'The Statue in the Hills', in *CP*, pp. 98ff.

158 'Our Lady of the Waves', in *CP*, p. 44.

159 'The Year of the Whale', in *CP*, p. 47.

159 'The Poet', in *CP*, p. 45.

162 'The first thing we notice …': 'In the Beginning was Sound', Reith Lectures, 2006.

163 'Of course there must be relationships …': Satish Kumar, 'George Mackay Brown: Orkney Oracle', *Resurgence*, 122 (May–June 1987), p. 10.

163 'I think the only perfect poem …': ibid.

164 'Its secret is always …': 'The Poet', *New Statesman*, 17 May 1974.

164 'In the morning I will bring …': 'Poet and Prince: A Fable', in *The Island of the Women and Other Stories* (Polygon, 2006).

164 'The poem was, as never before …': 'Brig-o-Dread', in *The Sun's Net* (Polygon, 2010).

167 'In the making of a story …': *FIS*, p. 157.

167 'Stations of the Cross', in *CP*, p. 179.

167 'Stations of the Cross: The Good Thief', in *CP*, p. 360.

167 'Daffodil Time', in *CP*, p. 352.

169 'The Harrowing of Hell', in *CP*, p. 400.

170 'Shroud', in *CP*, p. 104.

171 'With his conversion to Catholicism …': Stewart Conn, *Distances*, p. 80.

172 'Port of Venus', in *CP*, p. 22.

175 'His sense of the world …': Seamus Heaney, on the cover of GMB's *Selected Poems, 1954–1983* (John Murray, 1991).

175 'The main business of any poet …': GMB, letter to Ernest Marwick, 1 September 1965, EWMC.

176 'Our Lady of Cornstalks', in *CP*, p. 99.

Chapter 10: Tell Me the Old, Old Story

184 'In Scotland, when people congregate ...': *OT*, p. 10.

188 'Well, they're on the edges of society ...': *Scottish Writers Talking 1* (Kennedy & Boyd, 2008), pp. 25–6.

188 'I mention those trivial events ...': *FIS*, p. 19.

189 'Suddenly three words ...': 'Five Green Waves', in *A Calendar of Love* (Polygon, 2006), pp. 39ff.

195 'Local, though not parochial ...': *The Scotsman*, 12 October 2010.

Chapter 11: Making the Terrors Bearable

197 'A hundred Lents from now ...': 'Chinoiseries, Small Songs for the Beginning of Lent', section 6, in *CP*, p. 500.

199 'The stench and corruption ...': www.catholictradition.org

200 'Bird in the Lighted Hall', in *CP*, p. 201.

202 'My kirk, St Peter's ...': extracts from 'Master Halcrow, Priest', in *A Calendar of Love*, pp. 117–28.

204 'Then the probe was put ...': extracts from 'Witch', in *A Calendar of Love*, pp. 97–115.

206 'It's the Pope that decides ...': extracts from 'The Tarn and the Rosary', in *Hawkfall*, pp. 160–92.

214 'It was only when I rose ...': Sally Magnusson, *Glorious Things: A Treasury of Hymns* (Continuum International Publishing Group, 2004), p. 29.

216 'It allows us as individuals ...': Kathy Galloway, *Getting Personal* (SPCK, 1995), p. 71.

216 Seamus Heaney, 'Out of This World', in *District and Circle* (Faber, 2006), p. 47.

218 'If the definition of the divine ...': Robert Carroll, *Wolf in the Sheepfold: The Bible as Problematic for Christianity* (SCM Press, 2nd rev. edn 1997), p. 35.

218 'Everywhere we look ...': Robert Carroll, unpublished Renfield Seminars.

219 'Jock felt in his coat pocket ...': extracts from *Magnus* (Polygon, 2008), pp. 175ff.

Chapter 12: Orkney's Still Centre

222 'You mustn't weep …': *Magnus' Saga*, trans. Hermann Pálsson and Paul Edwards (Kirk Session of St Magnus Cathedral, 1996), pp. 31–2.

223 'These historical events …': *FIS*, p. 3.

223 'Orkney is a small green world …': Preface to *A Calendar of Love*.

224 'Not long after the burial …': *Magnus' Saga*, pp. 33–4.

224 'As a leader …': *Magnus' Saga*, pp. 26–7.

225 'I used to reproach myself …': *FIS*, pp. 166ff.

227 'When the King asked …': *Shorter Magnus Saga*, p. 23.

232 'He comes to us as One unknown …': Albert Schweitzer, *The Quest of the Historical Jesus* (Macmillan, 1956), p. 403.

233 'by interweaving a variety of styles …': Timothy Baker, *George Mackay Brown and the Philosophy of Community* (Edinburgh University Press, 2009), p. 76.

234 'Nor was the pattern …': extracts from *Magnus*, pp. 105–59.

242 'In the novel *Magnus* there is another chapter …': *FIS*, pp. 166ff.

Chapter 13: Heidegger's Biro

246 'Exactly, yes. It has gone far too far …': extracts from Satish Kumar, 'George Mackay Brown: Orkney Oracle', *Resurgence*, 122 (May–June 1987).

247 'He often felt …': 'Sealskin', in *Hawkfall*, p. 127.

248 'He thought of the men …': ibid., p. 131.

250 'Oh, to progress …': *Scottish Writers Talking 1*, pp. 42–3.

251 'Oh, yes, I'm sure there's quite a lot …': *Seven Poets* (Third Eye Centre, 1981), p. 55.

252 'On the first day the horse-coach …': BH, p. 138.

252 'Formerly a people of strongly-marked individuality …': BH, p. 144.

254 'Perhaps this break-down …': BH, pp. 149–50.

255 'Perhaps something we cannot imagine …' BH, pp. 149–50.

256 'it is not the number of sovereign states …': John Gray, *Straw Dogs* (Granta Books, 2003), pp. 12–13.

260 'For a full two minutes …': 'The Wireless Set', in *A Time to Keep and Other Stories* (Polygon, 2006), pp. 100–1.

Chapter 14: Lost in the Barleycorn Labyrinth

265 'For years – but for her protection …': *NL*, p. 140.

266 'Now she was learning …': *NL*, p. 138.

270 'We were, all three, in the miseries …': *FIS*, p. 63.

284 'I used to wonder about this gap …': *FIS*, p. 70.

285 'I said that Runcie had told me …': Humphrey Carpenter, *Robert Runcie* (Hodder & Stoughton, 1996), p. 137.

286 'And I would not have you think either …': *Greenvoe* (Polygon, 2007), p. 199.

Chapter 15: The Trial of George Brown

297 'And so Mrs McKee …': *FIS*, pp. 162ff.

297 'Textures of Calvinism …': *FIS*, p. 109.

308 'She has also called attention …': Robert Crawford, *Scotland's Books: The Penguin History of Scottish Literature* (Penguin, 2007), p. 708. Reproduced with permission of Penguin Books Ltd.

Chapter 16: Poetic Dwelling on the Earth as a Mortal

323 'When I was a small boy in Stromness …': GMB, 'Foreword' to James Maitland, *New Beginnings: Breaking Through to Unity* (Saint Andrew Press, 1998).

323 'The multi-faith service …': James Maitland letters, 25 May 1989.

332 'The Finished House', in *CP*, p. 468.

333 'As Wittgenstein says …': *Sunday Herald*, 6 September 2009.

333 'I continue to find theology …': Denys Turner, *Faith Seeking* (SCM Press, 2002), p. xi.

335 'He wore no hat …': R. S. Thomas, 'Covenanters', in *Collected Poems 1945–1990* (Orion Publishing Group, London, 1995), p. 404.

336 'Via Negativa': ibid., p. 220.

336 'In Church': ibid., p. 180.

Chapter 17: April is the Cruellest Month

344 'This morning – as I write …': 'The First Wash of Spring', in *The First Wash of Spring* (Steve Savage, 2006), p. 254.

351 'Runes from a Holy Island', in *CP*, p. 78.

360 'The old man asks himself …': 'The Old Man and his writing desk', *Scotsman*, 12 October 1991.

369 'A Work for Poets', in *CP*, p. 378.

370 'Death, critics say …': *A Writer in Orkney*, unpublished TV script, August 1970.

370 'And you, Lord …': Antonio Machado, *The Soul is Here for its Own Joy: Sacred Poems from Many Cultures*, trans. Robert Bly (Ecco Books, HarperCollins, 1995), p. 21.

Epilogue

373 'Perhaps I was beginning to realise …': *FIS*, p. 11.

376 'Ikey, His Will in Winter Written', in *CP*, p. 526.

378 'There are mysterious marks …': *FIS*, p. 168.

Index